JACQUES ELLUL: INTERPRETIVE ESSAYS

JACQUES ELLUL

INTERPRETIVE ESSAYS

Edited by Clifford G. Christians and Jay M. Van Hook

UNIVERSITY OF ILLINOIS PRESS
Urbana   Chicago   London

Cop. 2

Library of Congress Cataloging in Publication Data

Main entry under title:

Jacques Ellul: interpretive essays.

Bibliography: p.
Includes index.
1.   Ellul, Jacques—Addresses, essays, lectures.
I.   Christians, Clifford G.   II.   Van Hook, Jay M.,
1939–
BX4827.E5J3   261.8   80–12342
ISBN 0–252–00812–X (cloth)
ISBN 0–252–00890–1 (paper)

Contents

PART III: ETHICS AND THEOLOGY

Foreword

The time is long since past, happily, when the name of Jacques Ellul rings only one bell of response in America, that of his *The Technological Society*. Even that work, although well known by the end of the 1960s, can hardly be said to have been known well. Too many people were content to infer from the title that it was an attack upon technology, which it is not, being rather a profound analysis of the role of what Ellul had described in his own French title as *"la technique,"* a term he made cover the whole vast network of rules, regulations, ordinances, and administrative decrees in modern society, with technology as such scarcely mentioned. If there is a single institution or set of values in the modern world that Ellul concentrates his fire on, it is the political state, not technology.

Ellul is above all, though, a Protestant lay theologian, "the quintessential Protestant of his time," as Martin Marty observes in the Introduction herein. It is the measure of his grasp of Christian theology and also of the age he lives in that he has restored to theology such vital issues and themes as the nature of the social bond, the foundations of personality, the contrast between authority and power, and the roots of liberty. From the very beginning of his studies, just after World War II, Ellul made it clear to his readers that we can understand the evils of this century only in the light of a receding Christianity. It was, I believe, Chesterton who said that the danger of ceasing to believe in God is not that one will then believe in nothing, but that one will believe in anything. Ellul has made us see as no one else has the kinds of belief which exist in the twentieth century as substitutes for belief in God: on the one hand the absolute state and its unique intensity of appeal to the masses and, on the other, the cult of personality with its bizarre, often horrifying, adoration of self. As Ellul has emphasized, most strongly perhaps in his *The New Demons*, we err in describing the twentieth century as transcendingly secular and nonreligious. In truth there is much that has been given sacred, religious significance: politics and the whole political cast of mind, the pleasure principle, sex, narcotics, and a score of other consecrations. All that we are able to say precisely is that large and currently spreading areas of life have been made bare of the Judeo-Christian authority that for so many centuries largely governed family and community and offered restraint to impulses toward state- and self-worship alike. Ellul's "new demons" are not the less religious for all their manifest evil. Man may indeed be ineradicably drawn to religion, but on the evidence of many thousands of years, there is seemingly no barbarism, savagery, and degeneration in which religion has not figured in some degree.

The greatest danger to constituted authority and to liberty proceeds, Ellul repeatedly warns us, from the political state, most especially the military-political state born, intellectually at least, of some dream of utopian perfection on earth. The dream is gone; what remains is the absolute power that had its original justification in the fantasy of human beings brought to ideal proportions on earth, but that now has become its own end, at whatever horrifying cost, as in the Cambodia of Pol Pot.

In his historic Commencement Address at Harvard in June 1978, Solzhenitsyn—to whom Ellul has been appropriately compared in this book—concluded with these words: "If the world has not approached its end, it has reached a major watershed in history, equal in importance to the turn from the Middle Ages to the Renaissance. It will demand from us a spiritual blaze; we shall have to rise to a new height of vision, to a new level of life, where our physical nature will not be cursed, as in the Middle Ages, but even more importantly, our spiritual being will not be trampled upon, as in the Modern Era."

No one, in my judgment, has done quite as much as Jacques Ellul during the past three decades in making us aware of the diverse ways in which "our spiritual being" has been eroded, sapped, and trampled upon: by "the new demons" of narcissistic libertinism and by the forces which have grown so vast and so penetrating of body and of mind under the spell of "the political illusion." And no one has done more to make forever clear to those with eyes to see just how we are to begin our escape from these new demons and from the New Leviathan within which they cavort. Long before Solzhenitsyn gave his memorable address at Harvard, Ellul in his own way, the way of scholar as well as the prophet, wrote of a "new height of vision" and of a "spiritual blaze," both Christian in nature. If, as some have prophesied, a fresh renascence or reformation of Christianity lies ahead, one in which the demons of the twentieth century will be routed, in which the necessary balance between liberty and moral authority will be regained, and in which, above all, the sense of the sacred, the true sacred of Judeo-Christianity, will become again commanding, the writings of Jacques Ellul are bound to be honored as among the central forces leading to this renascence.

Now, in conclusion, a few words on this book. Professors Christians and Van Hook have rendered high service to American thought and scholarship in bringing together these rich essays on Jacques Ellul. Here we find exploration of Ellul's intellectual sources, cogent analysis of his political and social theories and of his theological contributions together with a comprehensive bibliography of his writings. To complete the volume there is a previously unpublished essay by Ellul, "On Dialectic," that stands in the top rank of his thought and writing. Each chapter has been written specially for this book, and such has been the care in organizing the book and in the editing of the individual essays that we have an unusually high combination of logical order and of individual creativity in each of the essays. The result is the first extensive and serious study of Ellul in English and, to my knowledge, the best work on Ellul in any language. The book deserves very wide reading, by theologians and philosophers, by social scientists, and by all others concerned with the dominant moral, social, and spiritual issues of the twentieth century.

Robert Nisbet
Albert Schweitzer Professor Emeritus,
Columbia University

Preface

During the past decade, an impressive number of books from the pen of Jacques Ellul have been translated. As of now, twenty-two of his thirty-five works are available to English readers. A professor of the history and sociology of institutions in the law faculty at the University of Bordeaux, Ellul is noted both for his penetrating analysis of our technological society and for his astute criticism of current religious thought and practice. Like Tillich before him, Ellul stands "on the boundary" between culture and religion. Unlike Tillich, however, he attempts no synthesis of the two but seeks instead to confront his sociological perception with theological insight.

While neither the academic nor the religious community in America has found Ellul's views entirely congenial, both are discovering in him a thinker too significant to be ignored. The sociologist Robert A. Nisbet, for one example, thinks that Ellul "has published some of the finest books to come out of Europe in the sphere of politics and sociology during the last half century." Theologian Martin E. Marty has referred to Ellul as "probably the most Protestant theologian in the world today, and certainly the most notable lay theologian."

In spite of the attention which Ellul is beginning to receive from such disparate fields as sociology, political science, communications, philosophy, and theology, surprisingly little serious analysis, interpretation, and criticism of his work has appeared in print. The only book on Ellul in English is a reprint of articles from *Katallagete*, on the whole a popular rather than a scholarly volume. The dearth of secondary sources stems directly from the complexities of handling thought patterns which cut across the usual academic disciplines. The present book results from our effort to fill—at least partly—the void in Ellul scholarship. We opted for an edited volume because we were convinced that the people we asked to contribute could do a more adequate job with greater range than we together or any single writer could accomplish.

At every stage of this project we have been acutely aware of the frequent criticisms directed against edited anthologies. We have tried to overcome these difficulties by choosing writers known to be seriously engaged with Ellul's thought and by insisting upon original essays. Our aim has been to produce a volume which deals with the major issues in Ellul's thought of current interest to thinkers in the various disciplines which he touches and which will be useful to students of Ellul in the years ahead. We do not presume that this book is the last word. Ellul is still writing and the many issues treated in this volume will undoubtedly generate further discussion. Our goal has not been to establish a cult around Jacques Ellul. We have instead asked our writers to interpret and criticize freely, and to enter into dialogue with him. For this purpose too we have invited Jacques Ellul to respond to these essays. Needless to say, however, the writers vary considerably in their assessment, some being very sympathetic and others considerably less so.

In the opening section, Martin Marty introduces readers to this volume by integrating its major themes. At this point, the book divides into three major components. In Part I, the three significant influences on Ellul's thought are brought together: Menninger comments upon Marx's influence, Bromiley traces Ellul's debt to Karl Barth, and Eller examines the kinship between Ellul and Søren Kierkegaard. Part II takes its inspiration from the major trilogy which has secured Ellul's reputation (*Technological Society*, *Propaganda*, and *Political Illusion*) by focusing on the issues arising from these and related works. Stanley opens this division with an overview which connects Ellul with his contemporaries who treat similar themes. Benello then examines the concept of "technique" for which Ellul is most well known, and Real discusses Ellul's notion of propaganda in the context of contemporary communications theory. Van Hook analyzes the relationship of his politics and political theology. Christians concludes the section with an assessment of Ellul's ideas about solution. In Part III, the essays confront significant aspects of Ellul's ethics and theology. Outka investigates Ellul's ethics in terms of today's larger ethical arena. Holmes then provides a philosophical and theological critique of Ellul's aversion to natural-law theory, while Konyndyk examines Ellul's antipathy to the use of violence. Clark contributes a discussion of mythic meaning in Ellul's theology. After reading the essays, Jacques Ellul wrote his important statement on the dialectic as a response to them.

David Gill meets a long-standing need by providing an accurate and exhaustive bibliography to complete the book. In order to demonstrate Ellul's intellectual development, his writings are listed chronologically, with appropriate references in the chapter notes to the language and date of the first edition.

We wish to thank our writers for their promptness in meeting deadlines and for their patience with our editorial demands. We are grateful to Robert Nisbet, Harvey Cox, and William Stringfellow for the encouragement they have given us along the way. We also acknowledge with gratitude faculty research grants from the University of Illinois and Northwestern College to defray the cost of typing the manuscript. Richard L. Wentworth and Doris J. Dyen of the University of Illinois Press provided expert editorial assistance. And finally, we wish to thank our wives, Priscilla and Mary, for their patience and support during this project.

Clifford G. Christians
Jay M. Van Hook

JACQUES ELLUL: INTERPRETIVE ESSAYS

Creative Misuses of Jacques Ellul

Martin E. Marty

Ellul does not lack readers, but there can no more be an "Ellul Mass Movement" truly faithful to his thought than there can be a "Søren Kierkegaard Club." The American lawyer and lay theologian William Stringfellow has much in common with Ellul, but takes pains to point out that he and his French counterpart tend to be on parallel tracks, that they come to their kindred positions independently of each other, and that after the fact they enjoy a kind of communion by correspondence as they check their notes with each other, both growing from the exchange.[1] Like all strong personalities, Ellul cannot help attracting some devotees, but almost every thoughtful person who engages Ellul also finds it necessary to back away at many strategic points. For Ellul to show any surprise over such a situation would be a sign of naiveté: one cannot speak as a prophet of judgment against a way of life and expect the public to welcome the words. Like the prophet Jeremiah, who considered his calling a burden and who often reflected on the loneliness his apparent misanthropy caused him, Ellul sends out darts and jabs in his writings that reveal a loving and hoping heart in a time of abandonment. Yet, like Jeremiah, who dared not pretend away the coming of the foe from the North, Ellul feels he must speak out.

If Ellul cannot have a large following fully faithful to his thought, he does merit a readership that will confront and argue with him and his vision. I use "confront" advisedly, and am not alone among the writers of these pages who do so. One engages the thought of Ellul; there is no such thing as casual reading followed by mild acceptance or bland rejection. In his writing there is much of the spirit that says, in effect, "Eat, bird, or die."

The "bird" who comes across what Ellul offers cannot choose a crumb of this and a twiglet of that. Despite his fine legal mind, Ellul does not lay out his case with conventional logical reasoning and ask the reader to follow him bit by bit. The historian or social scientist is often dismayed when he looks for the careful documentation by which a writer protects himself and assures balance in his predictions. Ellul instead tends simply to point and then describe what comes into his sweep. With one hand he indicates the empirical situation, and with the other—as if he were John the Baptist in the Isenheim Altarpiece—he points to a divine reference from which one measures the human situation. Even there my language turns to evasion, an attempt to compromise. The phrase "divine reference" is too abstract, so Ellul points to the uncompromising Word that God speaks in the Bible and in Jesus Christ.

In these terms, Ellul is the quintessential Protestant of his time. Paul Tillich may choose to speak dialectically of the way the Protestant principle interacts with the motif of Catholic substance,[2] but such a dialectic is not characteristic of Ellul. Catholic substance celebrates the way the divine or sacral penetrates every aspect of being. On its impulse Christian people affirm the created world and the human acts that devise Christendom or a Christian culture. They build and dedicate cathedrals on its terms, and because of it look for God's work in the secular political order or in the artifacts of a productive society. Against this, the Protestant principle of prophetic protest wars against artifact, particularly because its inevitable distraction from the divine source to human creativity brings with it the spirit of idolatry. Ellul, in the end, sounds judgment always closest to home, against the cause one defends and for which one dies, not against some alien and hostile force far away.

Though Ellul is a Protestant not only in outlook but by churchly commitment, it is not necessary to be a Protestant to share his outlook. Nor need one be a lay person, though the lay stance seems to provide a special point of view. The truly Protestant outlook is always that of a misfit in culture; it is angular, apparently eccentric and idiosyncratic, because it does not compromise. It compels, not necessarily by its attractiveness, but by the clarity of its vision.

In our time, Ellul belongs to the company of such diverse thinkers as Simone Weil, Alexandr Solzhenitsyn, William Stringfellow (mentioned before), and, less seriously, the journalist Malcolm Muggeridge. That Ellul might not recognize this company as his own does not disturb me. Like Ellul, Weil was a superbly trained intellectual from a highly cultured background. Though from a theological viewpoint different from his own, she was a Protestant so pure that she could not even accept baptism or the rites of church membership. She lived before and during World War II, when causes—first of the laboring classes and then of the resistance movements—were compelling to people. Yet she remained a misfit in all of them and recoiled with horror at compromises until the world had no room for her and she starved.

Solzhenitsyn holds to a far more robust and even affirmative vision; he calls Russia back to the virtues of Orthodox Christianity even at the expense of liberal democrat values. Orthodoxy to him signifies a spirituality that transcends the political commitments of any year, while liberal democracy is a partial sham and, as a total human achievement, it can enslave. Malcolm Muggeridge, like many an old rake who "comes to Jesus" radically and frontally, uses his vantage to judge all kinds of liberal thought and ecclesiastical order. Conservative Christianity and right-wing elements in the culture are largely unaware of such a thinker as William Stringfellow, and are unstung by him if they are aware, but those who share Stringfellow's political sense know that he speaks of them and to them.

Is there something distinctively laic about these five critical analysts? Clerics, of course, can be and have been capable of self-hate and denunciation of institutions, but the public takes their role less seriously. If the church is that bad, why do they keep taking paychecks from it? The lay person who could afford vocationally to go elsewhere and usually does commands a different kind of hearing. One can read thousands of pages of Solzhenitsyn and not hear mention of Christianity; it is only when in his essays he turns toward Christianity that the consistency of his cultural outlook in relation to it becomes clear. Ellul spends much of his energy on technique, propaganda, politics; it is only when his counterpart books address Christians in the churches that one hears again how much the churches participate in the order he attacks.

From some points of view, Ellul and the other people mentioned here seem to write themselves entirely out of the circle of humanist concern. On the surface at least one could answer questions about the limited impact of Ellul among the secular intellectuals he wishes to address by saying that he seems to doom all their commitments and enterprises *a priori*. If what he says is true, the "end" is already past, and they live in whited sepulchers. The kitchen has burned and the intellectuals keep writing cookbooks; the boats have sunk and the people on the lifeboats still worry about time schedules. Ellul has no room for humanists, why should they have time for him?

The dismissal of humanism and humanist enterprises is, however, only superficial. One has to read on until the realization comes: Ellul cares. For a parallel to this aspect of his achievement I think of St. Augustine, who wrote several hundred pages of *The City of God* in order to show the futility of the earthly city apart from the heavenly one. On first impression, the effect is to see a complete disvaluing of anything called Rome for the sake of heaven. And then the reader realizes that Augustine is taking great pains to explain to "Rome" why it fell and what positive or negative role Christians played in that fall. He must have cared somehow, to show so much concern to explain and apologize for the Christian part in and the divine impact on the human city.[3]

Ellul writes thousands of pages on the futility of the earthly city and its endeavors and artifacts. Yet he speaks not from a Tibetan monastery, or from an island, but from an area of political participation, in the context of a professional career, and with a distinguished record of involvement in ecclesiastical life. Is he operating here on bad faith, like the American hippies of the 1960s who berated technology while strumming sophisticated amplified guitars, riding jet aircraft to their festivals, and seeking anesthetics and high-speed drills for their toothaches? Presumably Ellul is aware that his books are widely advertised (propaganda) and published on presses that could not exist apart from technique; let us assume he draws some sort of royalty from the publics and libraries that buy them. He is not above the human city. He cares about it, and like Augustine keeps addressing it for a special purpose.

In the pages that follow all the authors insist that Ellul brooks no compromises, that to suggest he can be blended into other thought patterns is to misunderstand or even bastardize him; and they are right. He is a thinker who must be misused in order to be used at all. Each of us pays him the compliment of wrestling with his thought by finding ways to reckon with its absolutist character. I am tempted to say—as one who apprehends the Word to which Ellul points but who does not embrace his style of prophecy—that whereas on first hearing Ellul seemed to be half right about all of culture and Christianity, he now appears to be almost completely right about half of culture and one side of that faith.

To make that claim is to confront and engage him, so that he might repudiate such an approach; this demands that one should say what one thinks is missing and why. In the Christian instance this means one must use the same rules that he does, that is listen to the same whole Bible.

What is in Ellul for secular intellectuals (the humanists whose audience he covets)? What, it may be asked, does he offer that they cannot get more palatably—without obscure references to God and the Bible—from Karl Marx or Franz Kafka or George Orwell? On some levels, nothing: these other writers, too, have discerned a human impulse to convert everything to an order that enslaves, and they have seen the process by which machines generate machines unstoppably. In one set of terms, it hardly matters whether the place for standing to move a world is materialistic as in Marx or spiritual as in Ellul after his Marxian stages—so long as there *is* an eye-clearing vantage point.

In recent American political history the "any vantage" concept helped a minority gain some perspective on the clusters of events called "Watergate" and "Vietnam." In the case of Watergate, it became clear that political ideologies were not primarily at stake. Had the Republican conspirators in the Committee to Reelect the

President feared for the country's future, they would have tried to sabotage the more leftist potential Democratic candidates because from the viewpoint of conservative or moderate Republicans these represented a greater threat. However, they worked to undercut the conservative Democrats and helped to advance George McGovern because he appeared beatable. The conspirators made it clear that they served only administrative technique —an all-embracing way of life—more than any set of ideas. Weil, Kafka, Orwell, and most notably Ellul had been teaching all along that this totalist and rational approach, not one or another set of political ideals, would dominate post-modern life.

In the case of the war in Vietnam, Ellul's thought is more important as a critique of the anti-war movement than of the war itself. Those who listen to Ellul have no difficulty coming to the point of morally condemning the war. The problem, as he put it, is then their idolization of their own movements. If the people who advocated peace and justice really cared for the victimized and poor of the world, they would have devoted energies to the unpopular or useless poor, such as those in the Sudan. Instead they used the peasants and injured children of Vietnam to advance their own political movements against the United States government more than actually working for the care of the Vietnamese. No passage I read during that war stung my conscience—and, I hope, helped alter my outlook—more than did Ellul's on the subject in *Violence*.

What Ellul offers is not a pose but a worldview. Whether through genius, gift, or skills and habits acquired through a lifetime of discipline, Ellul has put himself consistently inside a web of integrated parts informed by the Bible that lets him see what other people overlook. He suggests that one cannot adopt some of these parts and reject others, but instead must either adopt all or reject all.

In the end Ellul shows how all humans are trapped in a cosmos not of their own making. Who shall deliver them? Sometimes he talks as if leaving the world is the only solution, the only proper direction. His pages then evidence the Augustinian and Lutheran-Calvinist concern which some people misread as an interest in individual souls apart from the whole people of God and certainly apart from those who do not measure themselves by reference to Jesus Christ. It is at this point that both Christian and humanistic alternatives to Ellul at least merit a hearing.

Take, as a first example, Ellul's inclusive word for the modern problem, the fundamental motif, *technique.* Essayists in this book reproduce and refine his definitions of technique. Suffice it to say here that he sees it as the root of the modern process, basic to and not the product of modern philosophy and science. For Ellul, in a way, technique and its development are "the Fall" for moderns. Among the many possible criticisms of this viewpoint, two stand out.

First, while it is hard to escape Ellul's realism or pessimism about most dimensions of technique and technology—as one examines weaponry or environmental pollution, for example—he does not do justice to the possibility that technique can also enhance people's lives. Given the choice between short and painful life with drudging and unrewarding labor on one hand, or longer, physically more secure life, with the possibility of more rewarding vocations for many, the people of less developed nations or the people less reached by technique in developed countries will gradually be influenced by the industrial order. Will every aspect of their industrialization necessarily be enslaving, idol-producing? Like Ivan Illich, with whom he shares much, Ellul might point to the evils of modern medicine as a case for his point, but anyone wracked by pain is not likely to give up anesthetics just because at some other point in technological logic there lurks the impersonal, bureaucratized American hospital. Can one not be distracted from the divine as much by necessity as by luxury, by pain as by relief from pain?

Second, for all his efforts to avoid it, Ellul implies a nostalgia for the order that existed before technique. Does this not carry its own kind of temptation to idolize a past? His logic contends that a great quantitative change amounts to a qualitative difference; this has something important to say about the Industrial Revolution. The great expansion in economic growth and industrialization in a certain period changed all our circumstances more than has anything else since the development of agriculture or the village.[4] But agriculture and the village were themselves an aspect of technique. So were the invention of wheels and learning about fire. These made as great a difference in the lives of people in their epoch as the Cornish boiler made for early industrial people. Why are the earlier inventors exempted from such searching criticism? At times Ellul goes behind his tendency to speak well of previous ages and sounds like the Romanian philosopher and aphorist E. M. Cioran, who speaks of "the fall into time," the taint of historical existence itself.[5] On these terms, he comes close to using the Christian doctrine of original sin exclusively as a tool for historical analysis.

Ellul invites the reader into the web of anti-technique thought and despises compromise. A creative misuse of his thought might begin by criticizing its limits and then using it to judge technological order, to seek a more human way within such an order. This can be done by people who share his concept of original sin but who do not believe in the implied fatefulness that goes with his tendencies to see "the fall into time."

Something similar can be said about Ellul's concept of politicization. Here he is the great opponent of the "Christian realism" associated with Reinhold Niebuhr. Niebuhr often talked about the "impossible possibility" of an ethics based on the Sermon on the Mount, and the need for political action informed by Christian faith in the midst of a world of compromise. But how can one believe in Jesus and the Sermon on the Mount and still celebrate the compromising arena of politics? My short course in Ellul and Niebuhr leaves me more on the Niebuhrian side, but here, as so often, were it not for the vehemence and singularity of Ellul, the other side of the biblical message might well go neglected.

Politics, it is often pointed out, is tainted; it does not save souls or make all hearts glad. It does not make one "right with God" in the biblical sense. But it can also be an order of ameliorization where people mitigate sufferings and perhaps fulfill many biblical mandates. When Ellul talks about politicization, he refers to the encompassing of all aspects of life by politics. Here again, one must ask whether there was ever an order that was not political to some degree. Was the primitive tribal condition not politicized? Or was not Christendom? Why must politics in the modern period, the time of technique, be the one that is especially conducive to thinking idolatrously? The record of history does not show that ancient kings and their subjects were in any way exempt from the enslavements and temptations Ellul attributes to moderns.

Ellul offers a witness that stands people in the best stead when they are forced into isolation. In the concentration camp, in the resistance, or in other extreme circumstances, Christian realism would not be as illuminating as resistance to politicization. But for people who muck through decisions in the daily world of union cards and eight-hour days, the ballot box and town forum, politics offers possibilities that Ellul as Christian (not as human actor) partly overlooks. But to use him only as the dropper of a plumb line through history and the great corrector of compromisers is, of course, to compromise his thought, and at best passes as another creative misuse.

One could illustrate the point with a third area of Ellul's concern, *propaganda.* Again technique links up with a sphere of human action to enslave and doom. Little more need be said in criticism of the searching attitude with which Ellul and the Marxist analysts of media go about their work. Still, do they do justice to the healing and therapeutic aspects of communication? I may denounce the way the telephone distracts and enslaves me, but I know that to my aunt whose home is remote from others it is the only point of vivid contact with people she loves. Without technique she would be isolated from expressions of love. Cannot aspects of Ellul be sorted out from his totalism by those who see positives in the kind of communities generated by media?

Throughout these remarks I have implied that Ellul undervalues certain themes in Christian theology by which Christians connect with others, among them common grace and *justitia civilis* (civil righteousness), as formulated by Augustine, Calvin, and Luther. I have suggested further that his analysis of technique and modernity might lead people to idolize a romanticized pre-technical past or to see all human existence as a "fall into time," an idea which verges on Christian heresy. Yet my overall view of Ellul, like that of most contributors herein, is largely positive.

Ellul does help his secular colleagues see gaps between the conventional modern mindset and biblical thinking. Such colleagues will not achieve this insight from either the obscurantist fundamentalist who simply has not thought about the subject or the concessionist liberal who disguises the scandal of the Christian faith. During the years of "secular theology" in the 1960s it was interesting to see how little response its adaptations evoked from humanists in the academy, who seemed to think that an approach that minimized Christian myth and symbol must be a disguised form of apology and evangelism; sooner or later, they assumed, the evangelist would lay it on the table. Why not save time and go directly to the person who hides nothing? Ellul does not hide the character of the Christian claim or its distance from ordinary thought.

Further, the gulf he describes serves to remind us how Christianity has lost its privileged position in the soil of post-Christendom. In no age would an Ellul have had the field to himself. But today the Christian's faith—that is, his eccentricity or quaintness in the eyes of many among those he would like to reach—is at a particular disadvantage. Such faith is seen as a strange kind of pseudo-science, a mark of cultural lag, mere pious mouthings from the edge of a culture. One has the impression that Tibetan Buddhism, Hasidic Judaism, unidentified flying objects, or extrasensory perception would get a better hearing among American humanists than does a frontal articulation of a faith professedly held by a majority of citizens. The uneasiness created by contact with Ellulian Christian thought is a creative misuse of it, and one acquires through this contact a better sense of how things are than one would through contact with accommodationist thought which glosses over differences. Is the "myth" out of which Ellul works inherently less plausible than the framework of B. F. Skinner and behaviorism, or that of Marxian messianism (which also deals with an as-yet-unseen and unrealized future), or the anthropology of Lévi-Strauss—and do not each of these create a web, a "plausibility structure"?

The character of Ellul's biblical thinking is the third great boon in his work that motivates heretics to misuse it creatively. Fundamentalists will not be satisfied by his apparent lack of interest in doctrines of biblical inerrancy. Beneficiaries of two centuries of critical analysis of Scripture disdain his lack of excitement over their findings. Although he appears unsophisticated, he has a well-developed holistic approach to the Bible. Ellul seems to believe the Bible to be sufficiently inspired for all practical purposes: the Bible is shaped by a community that oversees the engendering of faith, and, he is saying, this book helps shape such a community. Ellul urges us to listen to the Bible as a whole, to let its impact and impulse hit us (the way a critically dissected Bible or one protected by an idolized doctrine does not).

Once one evokes a transcendent point of view, all the words, thoughts, and intentions that one employs are compromising. In the end, the best creative misuse of Ellul, then, is to say that he does not go far enough, is not searching enough. Ellul is a substantive philosopher of history, thanks to his faith in God and Jesus Christ. But would not a consistent Ellulian go further and call that kind of knowledge into question, lest its claims also generate self-assurance and idolatry? If so, one might do well to be skeptical about the outcomes that Ellul considers inevitable, to be ready for surprises in God's purpose and in human artifice. In its own way this is a waiting for God in our time, a listening to him. No doubt those who adopt such a stance will find that, perhaps in spite of himself, Ellul will have the genius or grace to be there waiting and listening already.

NOTES

1. For a typical example, see William F. Stringfellow, "Kindred Mind and Brother," *Sojourners*, 6 (June 1977), 13.
2. Paul Tillich, *Systematic Theology* (Chicago: University of Chicago Press, 1967), chap. 3, p. 245: "The Protestant principle is an expression of the conquest of religion by the Spiritual Presence and consequently an expression of the victory over the ambiguities of religion, its profanization, and its demonization. . . . It alone is not enough; it needs the 'Catholic substance,' the concrete embodiment of the Spiritual Presence; but it is the criterion of the demonization (and profanization) of such embodiment."
3. This argument is developed in John O'Meara, *Charter of Christendom: The Significance of the City of God* (New York: Macmillan, 1961).
4. See E. J. Hobsbawm, *The Age of Revolution* (Cleveland: World, 1962), chap. 2, p. 27ff.
5. E. M. Cioran, *The Fall into Time* (Chicago: Quadrangle, 1970).

Part I

ELLUL'S INTELLECTUAL ROOTS

Chapter 1

Marx in the Social Thought of Jacques Ellul

David C. Menninger

It is Karl Marx more than any other social theorist to whom Jacques Ellul acknowledges a deep intellectual debt. Though the other two chapters in this section of the book take issue with this assertion, at least in a minor sense, there are personal and abstract reasons for making Marx central. In the early 1930s, Ellul was himself a committed Marxist, along with many other young French intellectuals. He had read Marx's *Das Kapital*, and, he has written, "it answered all the questions I had been asking myself."[1] Ellul's attraction to Marxism, however, does not extend to political activism; he resisted joining the French Communist Party, whose interpretation of Marx did not coincide with his own. Even today, he remains a strong critic of Marxist political regimes and movements since he finds them as much entrapped in the political illusion of technological society as is any other major political group. Any attempt to extract from Ellul's social thought some strand of Marxist revolutionary recommendations for action is bound to be fruitless. Ellul simply does not situate himself in a closed Marxist paradigm. Or, as he might put it himself, he did not gain an intellectual liberation through Marx's thought only to lose it in the straightjacket of Marxist "programs."[2] Thus Ellul's personal history as a Marxist is short. His avocation as Marx's student has endured and that requires our attention here.

Marx as Personal Model

At its core, Ellul's appreciation of Marx retains a very personal tone. That is, Marx represents for Ellul a model of the social theorist's personal resistance to impersonal social forces. There is a concrete and fundamental similarity between the image of Marx as a pioneering, solitary critic of the entire western economic system, and that of Ellul as critic of the whole culture of western technology. Both images can be fairly interpreted as depicting the drama of struggle between man and the dumb weight of the universe, a struggle which has been transferred in the modern era from the natural environment to the social realm.

As regards Marx, for example, it would be a mistake—one that many neo-Marxists have made—to assume that his theory's realization depends only on historical material forces playing themselves out. It is true that Marx insisted on the revolution against capitalism having the same material basis which has characterized all economic revolutions. But he also described this material basis as "a passive element," a component of history that needs to be acted upon by another agent (human energy and will). "Theory is only realized in a people so far as it fulfills the needs of the people."[3]

What Marx attempted in addition to outlining history's material basis was to make people fully aware of their needs, so they might act upon history. He did this by acting upon history himself, assuming the role of spokesman for the proletariat, constantly sounding the defiant cry which he believed must be instilled in the proletarian consciousness: "I am nothing, and I should be everything."[4] This personal energy and will of Marx himself, which incites the involvement of others, holds a special attraction for Ellul:

> I would say, along with Marx, that as long as men believe things will resolve themselves, men will do nothing on their own. But when the situation appears to be absolutely deadlocked and tragic, then men will try and do something. That's how Marx described the capitalist revolution and the situation of the proletariat—as something absolutely tragic, without resolution. But he wrote this knowing as soon as the proletarian sees his situation as without resolution, he'll

start to look for one. And he'll find it. Thus it is that I have written to describe things as they are and as they will continue to develop as long as man does nothing, as long as he does not intervene. In other words, if man rests passive in the face of technique, of the state, then these things will exist as I have described them. If man does decide to act, he doesn't have many possibilities for intervention, but some do continue to exist. And he can change the course of social evolution.[5]

Technique's Importance in Marx and Ellul

Marx has provided Ellul with a sensitivity to the special significance of technique and technology as problems in contemporary social development. Given that we most commonly highlight Marx's emphasis on economic factors as holding the key to history, it might seem that Ellul's debt on this point is due to some misinterpretation of Marx more than anything else. But this again would be a criticism reflecting the perspective of Marxist ideology and not a concern for the full range of Marx's social analysis. Moreover, Marx had a keen appreciation for the impact of technical development on both economic relations specifically and historical change generally. M. M. Bober has suggested, for example, that Marx's concept of "modes of production" might best be understood as centering on technical forces in an active sense: "Marx says that the windmill 'gives you' a feudal society and the steam-mill a capitalist society. The implication is not that society using a windmill is at a stage corresponding to feudalism and similarly with the steam-mill and capitalism. 'Gives you' implies that the windmill brings about, fosters, induces. . . . In other words, technique is a productive force, and a change in technique entails a change in the social order and its institutions."[6] Also, one should not forget Friedrich Engels's blunt observation that "all past history can be characterized as the history of the epoch from the practical discovery of the transformation of mechanical motion into heat (that is, fire) up to that of the transformation of heat into mechanical motion."[7] Such a view surely reflects a basic fascination with technique that Engels shared with Marx.

But there are still stronger indications of a certain Marxian attitude toward technique and technology, an attitude which shows Ellul the importance of technical development in contemporary society. Ellul's own attitude toward technique, as he presents it in *The Technological Society*, is a moral one. This fact becomes clear if one reads Ellul's more explicitly moral works— *The Presence of the Kingdom*, for example—where the idea of technique as "sin" is quite apparent.

Now Marx, unlike Ellul, never prepared a piece of work that has come to be recognized as the major statement of his moral philosophy. Indeed, he claimed to produce purely scientific theory. On the other hand, we cannot fail to recognize Marx as a strong moralist. He often does not even try to conceal his scorn for oppressors and his romanticization of the oppressed. This undercurrent of sharp moral criticism could also be extended by Marx to the human condition as a whole. On appropriate occasions, he was not averse to summarizing his vision of the modernization within which he lived. And here can be found prose which is truly striking in its similarity to much of Ellul's work today. The following is from a speech by Marx on the occasion of the fourth anniversary of the Chartist *People's Paper* to which he had sometimes contributed articles:

> There is one great fact, characteristic of this our nineteenth century, a fact which no party dares deny. On the one hand, there have started into life industrial and scientific forces which no epoch of the former human history had ever suspected. On the other hand, there exist symptoms of decay far surpassing the horrors recorded of the latter times of the Roman empire. In our days, everything seems pregnant with its contrary. Machinery, gifted with the wonderful power of shortening and fructifying human labor, we behold starving and overworking it. The new-fangled sources of wealth, by some strange weird spell, are turned into sources of want. The victories of art seem bought by the loss of character. At the same pace that mankind masters nature, man seems to become enslaved to other men or to his own infamy. Even the pure light of science seems unable to shine but on the dark background of ignorance. All our inventions and progress seem to result in endowing material forces with intellectual life, and in stultifying human life into material force.[8]

In comparison, consider this excerpt from Ellul's *Presence of the Kingdom:*

> The first great fact which emerges from our civilization is that today everything has become means. There is no longer an end; we do not know whither we are going. We have forgotten our collective ends, and we possess great means: we set huge machines in motion in order to arrive nowhere. The end (by this I mean the collective end of civilization, for individuals still have their own ends, for instance, to succeed in a competition, or to get a higher salary, and the like) has been effaced by the means. Thus *man*, who used to be the end of the whole humanist system of means, *man*, who is still proclaimed as an end in political speeches, has in reality himself become the means of the very means which ought to serve him, as, for instance, in economics or the State. In order that economics should be in a good condition, man submits to the demands of an economic mechanism, becomes a total producer, and puts all his powers at the disposal of production. He becomes an obedient consumer, and with his eyes shut he swallows everything that economics puts into his mouth. Thus, fully persuaded that we are procuring the happiness of man, we are turning him into an instrument of those modern gods, which are our means.[9]

Marx's Dialecticism

The most enduring connection between Marx and Ellul is a third matter—the exact nature of the dialectic as it applies to social analysis and criticism. "In our days, everything seems pregnant with its contrary"; thus Marx summarized not just the working of the dialectical mind, but the visible process of history itself. Herein lies the crucial difference between Hegelian and Marxist conceptions of dialectic. The convenient aphorism often applied to the relation between these two great thinkers is that "Marx stood Hegel on his head," by taking the dynamic basis of dialectic out of the vague sphere of spirit and grounding it in economic process. Actually, according to Marx, Hegel had dialectic standing on its head: "It must be turned right side up again, if you would discover the rational kernel within the mystical shell."[10]

Marx continued his critique of Hegel in a manner that indicates it was not just the anchoring in economics that he sought to accomplish for dialectic. For Marx, the significance of departing from Hegelian dialectic lay in the fact that one could then more fully realize what Marx felt Hegel had missed—the revolutionary coincidence of thinking, seeing, and acting that *is* the rational kernel within the mystical shell.

> In its mystified form, dialectic became the fashion in Germany, because it seemed to transfigure and to glorify the existing state of things. In its rational form it is a scandal and abomination to bourgeoisdom and its doctrinaire professors, because it includes in its comprehension an affirmative recognition of the existing state of things, at the same time also, the recognition of the negation of that state, of its inevitable breaking up; because it regards every historically developed social form as in fluid movement, and therefore takes into account its transient nature not less than its momentary existence; because it lets nothing impose upon it and is in its essence critical and revolutionary.[11]

Marx's differences with Hegel are very precise, then. One cannot simply acquire an abstract conception of dialectic and expect to gain any real liberation as a consequence or to have any real effect on the world as it happens to exist. Solely as an idea, dialectic for Marx is nothing but a plaything of the intellect, and will soon find itself losing even its intellectual integrity by entering its "mystified form." Thus the revolutionary potential of the idea can be aborted, that is, trapped in the realm of mystification. At that point, its only possible connection to reality is subordinately symbolic. It "transfigures and glorifies," but changes nothing.

Marx's insistence on ideas having their root in material reality is certainly understandable in light of this problem of mystification. His attempt to locate the dialectic in history itself was anything but intellectual gymnastics; he felt it was his only option for safeguarding the idea as a tool for the mind's true understanding. This was his stepping-stone to the creation of a science, and, beyond that, to "critical and revolutionary" action.

Ellul has explicitly taken to heart what might be called Marx's practicalization of dialectic. His own summary of his intent gives first evidence of this: "I have sought to confront theological and biblical knowledge and sociological analysis without trying to come to any artificial or philosophical synthesis; instead, I try and place the two face to face, in order to shed some light on what is real socially and what is real spiritually."[12] That is, religiously devoted as he may be, Ellul retains his own healthy disrespect for the mystification of ideas. He does not ever propose to divorce his theology from what is happening in the world. If that were to occur, he would, by his own admission, be constructing a moral position as ineffectual as Hegel's was in the eyes of Marx. The impact of Marx's thinking on Ellul in connection with this point is so intense that Ellul's complete acknowledgment should be cited. Even after his conversion to Christianity, he notes, he could not forget that

> Marx had brought to me . . . a certain way of "seeing" the political, economic, and social problems—a method of interpretation, a sociology. So it did not seem impossible to utilize this, starting with the Christian faith. I could not accept the view that there should be a Christian faith without social and political consequences. On the other hand, however, I saw clearly that one could not deduce directly from the Biblical texts political or social consequences valid for our epoch. It seemed to me that the method of Karl Marx was superior to all that I had encountered elsewhere.[13]

It may be prudent to indicate here that all this does not lead Ellul to Christian Marxism or vice versa. True to his word, he does not achieve any philosophical synthesis nor construct any grand sociological schema. He criticizes Marx where he feels Marx becomes too dogmatic and systematic in his own theorizing. Ellul even suggests that Marx contributed to the problem of society's obsession with technique by reducing social life to the problem of economics, and then economics to the problem of scientific materialism. "On the plane of human and spiritual life, Marx was—in a deep and not merely formal sense—a faithful representative of bourgeois thought."[14] This rather harsh accusation (which I do not believe is either accurate or sincere) points out where the line must finally be drawn. For Marx, dialectic was an instrument he directed against a specific historical situation of economic injustice with a view toward replacing it with a just order instead. This system had its conditions defined separately from human whims according to objective, material laws.

For Ellul, though, dialectic remains most valuable at the point that only provided a beginning for Marx—as a catalyst for an independent human consciousness which may resist the weight of social constraints, as the organizer of a vision preserving human freedom. More than anything else that Ellul has noted regarding technological society, he is concerned about the dire threat posed to the survival of human consciousness. He worries greatly over the "refusal to become aware of reality" which he sees spreading everywhere. Thus, from his point of view, it must be the human (that is, not "scientific") dynamic of dialectic on which we should become dependent.

Marx envisioned an end to this dialectic in the objective harmony of communist utopia, where there would be human freedom within the apolitical administration of things. It was his subtle capitulation to the material accomplishments of capitalism albeit a capitulation allowable in the logical context of dialectical materialism. But Ellul can envision no end to his dialectic as a desirable outcome for the human condition. On the plane of human freedom, dialectic is the *alternative* to the harmonious adjustment of the world of things. Dialectic is the enduring condition of freedom; it is the guarantor of a tension in life that Ellul believes necessary to avoid the state of death in life actually produced by a total adjustment of everything. In *The Political Illusion* Ellul explicitly makes this point. The continuation of a vibrant form of social and political life, not smothered by the blanket of consensus, depends for him on the provision of tension. "To return true reality to the conflict of private life versus public life, to dissipate the political illusion, is to develop and multiply tension. . . . Tension between groups composing the entire society is a condition for life itself, or life susceptible to creation and adaptation in that society. It is the point of departure for all culture."[15] And as for the direction society might take toward the complete synchronization of social life, the loss of dialectic and its consequences are unmistakable in Ellul's estimation: "In a group in the state of human equilibrium, of human homogeneity, there is entropy. But entropy is exactly the equilibrium of death. We must be cautious when accepting the generalizations made by others and understand that complete adjustment by all to all in a group in reality means that the group is no longer alive: It has been mechanized. Unity attained in a political movement means that life in a given system has disappeared."[16]

ELLUL'S CONTRIBUTION TO DIALECTICISM

I have argued so far that Ellul connects with Marx in three ways. Marx models the best social theorizing, he nudges Ellul toward a focus on technique, and he provides a workable dialecticism.

This third matter needs more development. As I have just noted, in gaining an appreciation for the dialectical method from Marx, Ellul takes the method beyond strict Marxist concerns. Of all social analysts who have subscribed to dialectic, Marx is typically taken today as the most significant. Yet precisely in this area, Ellul demonstrates the greatest independence. He has established some distinctive scholarship by insisting that dialecticism is a means for seeing the reality of life in technological societies. The background for Ellul's contribution lies in his clarification of "technical intention." Once that concept is introduced, we can grasp why Ellul insists that he is "a dialectician above all," that "nothing can be understood without dialectical analysis."[17]

Ellul begins by acknowledging that the unprecedented development of technological means in our century has profoundly affected our ways of action and patterns of thought. Yet he insists that this standard observation is weak without some perspective on the essential relationship between thought and action. It strains the limit of reason, Ellul would contend, to think that this era of gleaming chrome and explosive energy only results from a limitless pursuit of profits or a spreading Yankee ingenuity. He suggests that it could not have been accomplished without a special worldview on man's relation to nature and the possibilities of altering that relation. The universal practice of technological development, in other words, points to a universal state of mind.

Ellul recognizes the existence of a mode of thought specifically supporting technical activity; this mode of thought is at the core of *The Technological Society*. Commenting on what distinguishes the modern technical operation from that of the past, he notes "two factors [which] enter into the extensive field of technical operation: consciousness and judgment."[18] This is not, in Ellul's estimation, an ideological development or even a peculiar scientific attitude. It is a general societal phenomenon, a dominant way of thinking which he labels technical intention—"a precise view of technical possibilities, the will to attain certain ends, application in all areas, and adherence of the whole of society to a conspicuous technical objective."[19] Technical intention has been the mind's visionary catalyst without which the expanding development of technical action in western society from the sixteenth century onwards could not have taken place. In the scientific revolution, in the industrial revolution, and in the technological revolution still going on, there can always be identified in some form or another "a clear technical consciousness [that] shows clearly and to everybody the advantages of technique and what it can accomplish."[20]

But not only action has been affected by technical intention. As a developing style of thought, technical intention has inevitably competed with other modes, some seeking to catalyze people into social action and *some seeking merely to have people reflect on the meaning or purpose of social action.* It may seem strange to put the emphasis on the latter case. If the major goal of technical intention is the promotion of technical activity, what problem could be posed by thought having no specific designs on action? Furthermore, it could rightly be pointed out that technical intention itself has no critical concern with the *ratio essendi* of action.[21] How, then, could reflective modes of thought even find themselves in competition with technical intention? And yet the fact is that technical intention poses a serious challenge to reflective thought. In saturating the consciousness of modern man, technical intention seems to demand as complete a degree of control over thought as it does over action. The fully developed technical consciousness is an obsessed consciousness. It can abide *no* alternatives, and thus attacks even the mind's most distinctive means to alternatives, reflective thought.

Contrary to what many social analysts in the past believed—that the spread of technology and technique throughout society would generate greater efficiency in social administration and governance—Ellul declares that the problems faced by technological society make it appear more vulnerable than ever before. The shortage of oil, coal, and other resources, pollution, and economic fluctuations are all internal dilemmas which suddenly hold a more immediate threat to social well-being than do traditional external challenges such as war. The focus of collective energy is less upon international competition and more upon intranational synchronization. The simple fact is that the scope of free action is greatly reduced in a society composed of interlocking units; the consequences of individual choices need to be carefully calculated and controlled. In these circumstances, social and political supervision require at least matching technical skills, and, more ominously, the cost of error can reach appalling proportions.

This general predicament points to the enormous value of one collective resource always difficult to develop, but now exceedingly useful: consensus. If the costs of error in politics are high in a technological society, no less so are those of serious conflict or sustained dissent. In fact, they may be considerably greater when conflict or dissent become truly widespread. This is true for all western states today. Underlying the momentary appearance of issues of principle or rhetoric are the real internal dilemmas which cannot withstand serious questioning and debate. They relate to the very meaning of western social structure, to the choice for technical development that has already been made. They demand cooperation and the forsaking of debate, and the maximum efficiency that only consensus can provide.[22]

The foundation of consensus in social action lies in thought. For a collective to attain unity in action, some degree of agreement in thought is clearly necessary. Indeed, it is not unknown to have situations where unity of action requires the obviation of thought—in war, for example, or in a national revolution that involves the inculcation of ideological orthodoxy. This is the case with technical intention, a national revolution in its own right. It may begin only as a catalyst for new, exploratory levels of technical development. But as technical advance becomes the very core of social development—forcing an integration of society which complements the integration of technology itself—then technical intention becomes the catalyst for consensus. It becomes, as Ellul describes it, the social consciousness of techno-logical society, the phenomenal as well as practical standard for social life. The role of technical intention, in other words, is the promotion of consensus by the welding of thought to action. *One thinks only for the sake of doing.*

But, Ellul laments, what is ultimately lost in this "necessary" consensus is the role of thought as a willful negation of the imper-atives of action. It is the potential for negating action by thought —the conscious mental ability to assess independently the mean-ing of action, to pass judgment on its desirability, and, if neces-sary, to refuse the dictates of action—which can assure us of the unobstructed awareness of reality by the intellect. However, with technical intention, negation becomes an impossibility. Any truth other than what exists for technique is removed from the mind's field of vision. For thought that is welded to action so in-tensely, the responsibility of making independent moral judg-ments or assessments for choices in action ceases to have any meaning. In politics, in economics, in social relations generally, the technical mode automatically provides not just the answer to any problem, but the meaning of problem in the first place. The dissolution of the distinction between thought and action leads to the elimination of distinctions between means and ends, present and future, principle and practice. "All-embracing technique," in Ellul's words, "the consciousness of the mechanized world," is all that is left.[23]

In this situation of numbing consensus accompanying techni-cal development, the problem for social thought—as Ellul struc-tures it—is to rescue itself from the welding of thought and action. What becomes valuable is a mode of thinking that in-itially assumes a posture of struggle with the circumstances of social reality, and posits a tension between mind and facts.

Ellul's concern for, and claim to, an intellectual method such as dialectic must be understood in the context of this problem of consciousness. In technological societies, the "refusal to become aware of reality" has become an especially pressing problem, pri-marily because technological development requires a specific kind of thought which Ellul calls technical intention. We must insist, he suggests, on this obsessed consciousness shaping man's relation to social reality throughout our discussion of dialecticism. Only in this way can we achieve a sense of urgency behind Ellul's impassioned concern for what he believes is our growing collective blindness to reality.

When considering Ellul as a critic of modern society, one is apt to focus on more obvious themes such as anti-technology and religious motivation. But this essay argues that Ellul is equally concerned with cultivating a particular mode of thought. That places him within an important line of modern social analysis indebted to Marx. By developing dialecticism situationally within the context of technical intention, Ellul uniquely encourages a passionate refusal of the inhuman in social reality.

Conclusion

Ellul's attachment to dialectic, inherited in kernel form from Marx, lies at the heart of his work's purpose. In one sense, dialecticism in Ellul appears as a fundamental confrontation between sociological analysis and spiritual knowledge. The basic situation of the Christian life—to be in the world but not óf it—represents for Ellul as pristine a dialectical condition as could be imagined. On the one hand, to commit oneself to faith is to decide that one's thought, life, and heart "are not controlled by the world and do not depend on the world, for they belong to another Master." On the other hand, there is no escaping sociological reality, especially in the present situation, which is "more penetrating, more crushing, more exacting than it has ever been before."

This conflict is made even more poignant by Ellul's assertion that no synthesis or resolution is really ever possible. Faith will not conquer and vanquish the ways of the world; it will not work to adjust the state of sin inherent in the world. This is true in spite of the fact that faith exists to resist the "disintegrating tendency of the world," and that to lose faith is to be faced with the experience of death that is our modern tragedy. "Thus we seem caught between two necessities, which nothing can alter: On the one hand, it is impossible for us to make the world less sinful; on the other hand, it is impossible for us to accept it as it is."[24]

But it is precisely in these hard issues that the purpose of life becomes clear, that the dialectic continues between the two impossiblities. To recognize this tension between reality and faith is, as Ellul would have it, to gain freedom, a vision that finally permits an evaluation of what must be done *even when nothing seems possible*. Men and women are liberated from the most pressing circumstances, and, in fact, become superior to them by virtue of their understanding. "For nothing is secret that shall not be made manifest; neither anything hid that shall not be known," Jesus assured his apostles.[25] Thus it was that Marx set out to free the proletariat.

NOTES

1. *Introducing Jacques Ellul*, ed. James Y. Holloway, p. 6.
2. See especially Ellul's criticism of contemporary Marxist politics in *A Critique of the New Commonplaces;* French ed. 1966.
3. *The Marx-Engels Reader*, ed. Robert C. Tucker (New York: W. W. Norton, 1965), p. 19.
4. *Ibid.*, p. 21.
5. Interview with Ellul in Bordeaux, 24 Oct. 1973.
6. M. M. Bober, *Karl Marx's Interpretation of History* (New York: W. W. Norton, 1965), pp. 8–9.
7. *Ibid.*, p. 11.
8. *Marx-Engels Reader*, pp. 427–28.
9. *Presence of the Kingdom*, p. 63; French ed. 1948.
10. *Marx-Engels Reader*, p. 198.
11. *Ibid.*, p. 198.
12. *Introducing Jacques Ellul*, p. 6.
13. *Ibid.*, p. 5.
14. *Technological Society*, p. 222; French ed. 1954.
15. *Political Illusion*, pp. 210, 217; French ed. 1965.
16. *Ibid.*, p. 209.
17. Interview with Ellul in Bordeaux, 24 Oct. 1973.
18. *Technological Society*, p. 20.
19. *Ibid.*, p. 52.
20. *Ibid.*, p. 31.
21. As Max Weber noted: "The term 'technology' (*technik*) applied to an action refers to the totality of means employed as opposed to the meaning or end to which the action is, in the last analysis, oriented." See *The Theory of Social and Economic Organization* (New York: Free Press, 1964), pp. 160–61.
22. This is the theme of *Political Illusion*.

23. *Technological Society*, p. 6.
24. *Presence of the Kingdom*, pp. 9–17.
25. Luke 8:17.

Chapter 2

Barth's Influence on Jacques Ellul

Geoffrey W. Bromiley

Ellul has been greatly influenced by Karl Barth and owes many decisive insights to him. Ellul himself recognizes this as clearly as anybody, and pays open tribute to Barth in many of his writings. He does so in different ways, sometimes acknowledging his indebtedness, sometimes championing the significance of Barth's work against those who disparage it, and often expressing regret that on various points he cannot copy the "master."

Ellul's most glowing recognition of Barth appears in the preface to *The Ethics of Freedom,* in which he says that his own work "has to some extent been inspired by the theology of Karl Barth." While not viewing himself as an unconditional Barthian, he suggests that "most of the questions put by the new theology are implied, outlined, and even at times discussed in the *Church Dogmatics.*" He circumspectly follows Barth's version of revelation, for instance, constantly trying "to clarify and criticize his own presuppositions in the light of [that] revelation."[1]

In the same passage Ellul deplores the failure of many contemporary theologians to appreciate Barth's significance. He describes as "very odd" the way in which commentators continually ignore the *Church Dogmatics.* In the body of *The Ethics of Freedom* he makes the interesting observation that faddism in modern theology rests on a psychological and sociological wish to escape "the pressure of Barth's theology." When this pressure became intolerable, "there was a rush in other directions," he complains, which produced the various fashions of Bultmann, Moltmann, and structuralism.[2]

Once again, Ellul is no unqualified Barthian; in fact, he disagrees with him at many points. Thus he contends that "Karl Barth himself confuses the state and politics."[3] And criticizing Barth's practical social teaching, he goes even further: "It pains me to have to say that his deliberations here are no more than academic hypotheses."[4] Ellul apparently respects Barth so much that he parts company reluctantly; indeed his criticisms are delicate enough to be an inverse compliment.[5]

Certainly it would be tedious and unprofitable to list every reference to Barth in Ellul's work. Readers may easily get an impression for themselves by glancing at the respective indexes when these are available. They will note that in many books Barth is not mentioned at all. But *The Ethics of Freedom* has forty-one references and Barth runs second only to Karl Marx, whose view of alienation is analyzed in detail in the first part of the work. In contrast, an important work like *The Meaning of the City* gives short shrift to Barth, as to all other authors. If the book shows a general influence of Barth's hermeneutics, it is an original study and it carries only two or three Barthain references —in one of which Ellul takes issue with him over the question of scriptural myth.

Statistics, of course, can be misleading. Like *The Meaning of the City*, expository studies such as *The Judgment of Jonah* and *The Politics of God and the Politics of Man* carry an implicit reference to Barth. Few names appear in the text, apart from biblical characters, yet those who know Barth at all can detect his presence in the hermeneutical methods themselves.

Explicit references can be deceiving as well. Sometimes listings will include pages on which there is only incidental mention. Furthermore, even when Barth can be more strongly indexed, he is only one of many entries. Ellul has drawn on several other sources besides Barth, the important ones described in this book. Moreover, Ellul is a highly original thinker who can go his own way without obvious dependence on anyone else. Above all, Ellul has also studied the biblical text and drawn conclusions for himself.

These literary connections indicate a close relation between

Ellul and Barth; nevertheless, they must be set in perspective. We cannot use them to establish the general thesis that Barth had an exclusive or even a predominant impact on Ellul. In some areas Barth influenced him greatly, but in many others he did not. Such complexities must be kept in mind as we develop their arenas of special contact.

THE WORD OF GOD

Ellul, of course, is not a technical theologian. Hence he does not develop specific dogmas in a systematic way. To the extent, however, that he manifests a doctrine of the Word of God, he follows Barth closely in at least one element of his presentation: he holds the dynamic concept whereby Scripture or preaching is God's Word only as God himself speaks through it in living power.

Ellul makes this point when introducing *The Politics of God and the Politics of Man*. The Second Book of Kings deals with the theme of divine and human decision. Yet we must not make of this either "a doctrine of God" or "the object of external exegesis and dull science." As he sees it, "we are in the presence of life." God does not theorize. "He acts, and it is his action itself which is the Word of God." When we read the accounts of these primary acts, we attempt to discover "through the text . . . what is the Word of God and the meaning of our own lives in the presence of this text."[6]

Ellul's view of inspiration—which is closely related to his general understanding of the Bible—also parallels Barth's. In *The Judgment of Jonah*, for example, he ties inspiration to canonicity;[7] Jonah is a highly unusual prophetic writing and only its inspiration by the Holy Spirit can account for its acceptance into the prophetic canon. Moreover, inspiration implies an ultimate unity of authorship. This has various ramifications, but for Ellul, as for Barth, one principle is important: no matter how much scriptural books become divided into sources, our present text is the inspired or God-given one. As Ellul says in *The Meaning of the City*, he "takes the biblical text . . . in its entirety"; the compiler is "just as important as the first author." This applies to the whole Bible as well as to individual books. Since the divine author is one, Scripture is "an identical, continuous, and coherent revelation."[8] Ellul worries little about the nature of inspiration as such; he is more concerned about its effect and implication.

In another biblical area, Ellul's understanding of scriptural authority reflects very plainly the great discussion in *Church Dogmatics*, volume I, part 2. For him biblical authority is not so much a theological principle as an accepted reality.[9] This authority does not mean that we are to bring our queries to the Bible as though it were a manual of answers. Nor are we simply to ask questions about the Bible; rather, we begin by listening to the Bible's own questions. It must be a point of departure for our research, not the subject of it. Ellul gives a working example of his thinking about scriptural authority in *The Meaning of the City*. He states plainly that even if, in relation to the story of Cain, all the findings of source criticism are true, Scripture as revelation tells us "what God thinks of the affair." It is to this appraisal, which is truer than any scientific knowledge, that we must orient our own understanding.[10]

But an even more explicit reliance on Barth appears in the discussion of the Word's freedom in *The Ethics of Freedom*. Barth, of course, devoted a whole section of his *Church Dogmatics* to this aspect of Scripture. He put it immediately after the section on the Word's authority, and dealt with it in two subsections, "Freedom of the Word" and "Freedom under the Word."[11] The first subsection is the important one for Ellul.

Ellul introduces the theme at the end of a discussion about the freedom of Jesus, especially in relation to the temptations. Jesus, he says, bears witness to his liberation by fulfilling Scripture as the Word of God. "Being free means discerning God's will in Scripture and obeying it." If we ourselves can live as free men in Christ, it is because of the Word. "The only true, complete, absolute, and intrinsic freedom is that of the Word of God" which is "the basis and ground of our freedom." Expounding this freedom of the Word, Ellul expressly follows "the remarkable analysis" of Barth. He devotes several paragraphs of commentary to Barth's theses about the Bible's freedom.[12] From this discussion Ellul derives a decisive conclusion for his own work: "Whenever the witness of holy scripture is received and accepted, man has a freedom and power which . . . correspond to the freedom and power of the Word of God itself."[13]

INTERPRETATION OF THE BIBLE

Like Barth, but even more so, Ellul denounces historico-literary criticism, even though he pays lip service to it. He acknowledges that researches conducted by it "are of value."[14] He grants that it is "useful to be acquainted with . . . its analyses."[15] And sometimes he can even work up a little more enthusiasm: We are not to be tied to the texts as to "taboos or magical recipes"; we are to wrestle with them in "exegesis, criticism, analysis."[16] Nevertheless any value he detects is qualified by the judgment that critical work is "definitely restricted in scope."[17] Indeed, he sarcastically remarks that the work of biblical scholars reminds us "of exegetes and historians in other fields except that they have now abandoned it."[18] Criticism does its proper hermeneutical work, for Ellul, not when used as a weapon against God nor as "an apologetic machine," but only when it leads us "to a better exposition of God's revelation." Scientific work can be no more than a tool. Its value depends on those who use it. Critical study counts only when it is concerned for God's glory and love of others; then it will engender "a better comprehension and adoration of revelation and a positive ministry which builds up others." His contributions in this field should not be underrated; however, they fall far short of Barth's, who more conscientiously practices the scholarly investigation of Scripture in the service of correct reflection and application.[19] Ellul, of course, never claims to be an expert in lexicography. He believes finally that the Spirit's illumination comes only to the free man not in bondage to the text.[20]

His impatience with academic work on Scripture clearly relates to the theological interpretation which he has learned from Barth. As Ellul sees it, such work must be the sphere of true objectivity. Other things may, of course, be found in the Bible, but "every book should be taken for what it purports to be," for "what it says it is and seeks to be." Nor should one apply this rule merely to the books as individual writings, for "they cannot be rigorously separated from one another."[21] Thus the biblical text constitutes a totality and is to be expounded and understood as such. The biblical texts have "come together" for Ellul and "adapted to each other in order to bear a wider and deeper meaning." "This is why an inclusive reading of the text appears indispensable."[22]

Ellul complains that little biblical research ever reaches the theological meaning either of individual passages or of Scripture as a whole. Non-theological investigations may correct some errors but "bring with them others that are even worse. . . . The sense is reduced to a few grains of dust or to nothing at all." What is needed is "recovery of the Bible" as a whole in which God's own Word is heard, not human intellectualization.[23]

On this basis Ellul, like Barth, resists vigorously the cultural relativizing of Scripture. This resistance works out in different ways. He does not believe, for one thing, that "taking a text back to its date, it primitive identity, gives it its true meaning, or the meaning it was at least meant to have when it was made a part of the whole." If we must seriously confront the revelation of God in history, surely we cannot "fix a word of this revelation to one moment in history, like a butterfly tacked to the wall, so that, completely framed by cultural data, it can no longer be moved from there to mean something else."[24] Again, understanding the meaning of texts from another time or culture does not prove as difficult as many scholars imagine.[25] After all, many westerners easily enter into the thought of Mao Tse-Tung. Hence Ellul cannot agree that it is virtually impossible to make the transition from one language or culture to another. He does not think that knowledge of the cultural background is essential except for giving a better grasp of what is said. In fact, more straightforward reading would mean fewer "hermeneutical crises."[26]

In developing his hermeneutical principles, Ellul makes three additional points regarding the cultural issue. First, much of the transcultural problem arises out of a poor hermeneutic whereby we foolishly explain biblical phenomena in terms of our modern insights instead of letting Scripture speak plainly for itself. The psychological assessment of apocalyptic offers a good example— Ellul labeling it "pure hypothesis, even pure imagination," without any bearing on whether the new Jerusalem is "the revelation of objective truth."[27] Second, Ellul points out that "the idea of total relativity, . . . of entrapment in language and culture, is itself a cultural notion peculiar to our own age and setting." It goes hand in hand, he writes, "with the impact of technical society . . . and expresses our fear of reality; it is a nominalistic refuge." Hence it cannot contribute to solid interpretation, but will simply lead to evasions and unnecessary complications.

Third, God speaks his Word through the scriptural text no matter what may be its cultural or linguistic setting. The overruling factor, which sets a limit to research, is that of revelation. For the Christian revealed truth is the basic issue, not a human aspect ("for example, Scripture as a historical text"). What counts is the meaning, content, and message, and "whether one receives it as revelation or not." To dismiss revelation from biblical study is identical with expelling it from politics, business, or social life. It is attempting to be non-Christian in a given area. It thus leads to the nonsensical situation in which, as Ellul graphically puts it, Christian exegetes act like a surgeon who forgets that his patient is alive and operates "as though he were dissecting a corpse or conducting an autopsy."[28]

But Ellul insists on one more significant element in exegesis. For him, as for Barth, biblical interpretation must be primarily christological. This emphasis appears in all his expository works. In the case of Jonah, for example, the christological understanding rests on Jesus' own reference to Jonah as a sign of himself. This is so important for Ellul that he thinks, as noted above, the canonical status of the work rests ultimately on its intimation of Christ.[29] Note also that Ellul asks at one point whether the Jonah-Nineveh connection is only a fortuitous one. He questions rhetorically. This link displays for him "the connection between the life, death, and resurrection of Jesus Christ and the life, death, and resurrection of all the men he came to save." Jonah's involvement with Nineveh "draws its truth" from Christ's bond with the world. Hence Ellul sees in this and other parts of the Bible a great edifice which "makes no sense except in its crown and head, and which denotes from every angle the unique one who is attended by many generations of those who perform their tasks without knowing they are prophetic, he who is both Savior and Lord, and who reveals to each, and concerning each, what he was in reality."[30]

Similarly, in *The Politics of God and the Politics of Man*, Ellul follows the work of W. Vischer, who so greatly influenced Barth also. Like Vischer, Ellul finds in the prophet Elisha a figure of Christ, so that "Jesus Christ is not absent from the somber adventure of the Second Book of Kings." If Elisha represents only "a second and relative aspect of what Christ will be and do," this aspect must be explored as one element of the total revelation given in Jesus Christ.[31] Thus, at the political level, Jesus Christ stands out as the miraculous goal of history which can be attained by the deliberate act of many in response to God's love demonstrated in the cross.[32]

Ellul even sees the city christologically. From the biblical standpoint the city—the holy city also—constitutes the place of revolt and wickedness standing under the judgment of God. Nevertheless, the story has another, completely different side, for the city leads us constantly to Jesus Christ.[33] In Jesus Christ it finds salvation and fulfillment as represented by the river and the tree at the heart of the new Jerusalem: "The awful mixture made by man is rearranged by grace and benevolence and by the Lord's act of accepting and gracing the chosen city with his presence."[34]

Christological interpretation also includes many less significant details. Thus Ellul describes the four lepers of the Second Book of Kings, chapter 6, as "the four evangelists carrying the good news of deliverance and salvation."[35] Elisha's superabundant miracles prefigure the unbounded presence of the Spirit in Jesus.[36] The judgment on Joram and his officer in this sixth chapter displays Christ's vicarious work by symbolizing the one who is offered up as an expiatory victim, "God taking man's place under the judgment of God."[37] The same theme recurs again and again in *The Judgment of Jonah*. In each of Jonah's three prophetic utterances we are pointed to him who "had to go down to death in order that those who are there should not be hopelessly delivered up to Satan."[38] The centrality of Christ may be seen in *The Meaning of the City*, too. The tree in the city of God, for example, reminds us of the wood from which the crucified Lord hung. It is thus "a living sign, in the center of the city, of the healing and the nourishment which men have reached from Christ in his death."[39] In Ellul then, as in Barth, Christ is the hermeneutical key to Scripture.

THEOLOGY

Turning to some theological themes in Ellul, we note at once that, like Barth, he underscores Christ's reconciling death and resurrection. Jesus' substitutionary work may be seen clearly, for instance, in the double destruction of Jerusalem and the temple and their single reconstruction in the resurrection. Ellul notes how Christ replaces both city and temple because he gives himself as a full substitution for them.[40] In spite of external appearances, Christ's work in our stead is a finished accomplishment so that nothing remains the same anymore in principle. The accusation of Satan must yield to the intercession of Jesus, who asks for grace "because he took the place of the one who ought to be condemned." Or, as Ellul expresses it in another manner, he who lived among us was the absolute truth; death had to let its victim go and the resurrection took place, not just spiritually or in the faith of the disciples, "but in the most concrete way."[41]

On the basis of Christ's vicariousness, Ellul follows Barth in a movement toward universalism. Indeed, at this point he seems to be ready to go further than his mentor. Whereas Barth studiously does not commit himself, Ellul opts for universalism at least as pious opinion, if not as dogma: "It seems to me that the universality of salvation is implied by the fact that the totality of condemnation fell on Christ."[42] In this light he hesitates to see eternal judgments in Old Testament condemnations. Judgment undoubtedly fell on Joram and the officer, but this does not "necessarily imperil the salvation of these two men for whom Jesus also dies; they are put outside God's work, but not his love." When people reject God's call, God also rejects them, but he does not send them to hell.[43]

On the surface Ellul might seem to be engaging in double-talk here. Yet the section in *The Ethics of Freedom* where he espouses universalism makes it plain that this is not so. He tries to avoid either an automatic salvation on the one side or a salvation dependent on giving oneself in faith to Christ on the other. This for him is an unacceptable alternative. He distinguishes instead between salvation and freedom. Since Christ bore the condemnation of all, it seems to him that in spite of "the theological and biblical difficulties which this opinion involves," salvation "is a gracious gift to all men and all ages by the God who is love." Only by faith, however, can one enter into and practice the freedom with which Christ in his lordship has made us free.[44] Perhaps in the long run Ellul does not differ here very much from Barth's belief that all people are in fact justified by God but the possibility still remains—even to all eternity—that some will deny this truth and live as though they were not.[45]

This distinction between salvation and freedom enables Ellul to portray the present situation in much the same way that Barth does. The decisive victory over Satan has been irrevocably won and yet for a little space, and to a limited degree, the rule of Satan continues. Satan can no longer win but "the powers defeated by Christ are still at work . . . and are struggling more violently than ever," so that when man thinks he can defeat them alone, his bravado is ridiculous and grotesque.[46] A new component has entered the world scene—the triumphant Word of God. Yet history is still being made by the liar, the deceiver, and the disrupter, who can "upset the course of history . . . foil God's work in detail . . . set man against man . . . impose the crushing weight of necessity on man . . . [and] plunge him into an ambiguity of life from which there is no exit."[47]

Satan's continuing power does not alter the fact that after Jesus' birth "history is no longer the same; . . . there is a qualitative distinction of the times." What it does mean, however, is that "the new creation has not yet come." Indeed, it has not even "begun at the level of civilization, of human works." The kingdom of God is not being built now with our hands. Satan still has strength and he derives it precisely from the fact that, while men are saved, they have still to work out their salvation in the freedom which Christ alone can give them. Hence Christ's lordship, while universal and radical in principle, remains as yet hidden and suspended—a lordship of the glorified one who is also suffering servant and slain lamb. Christ's lordship has been established already; to this extent Ellul espouses a realized eschatology. It must still be brought to its fulfillment; to this extent he holds to a futuristic eschatology. The decisive battle has been fought, but the war is not yet over.[48]

The time of the "Not Yet"—in which space is given for human freedom—ties in with a central theme in Ellul's theology, namely, that of the relation between God's sovereignty and man's freedom. Significantly, a thought of Barth's offers Ellul his own basic insight in this area. As Barth puts it, a free determination of man is enclosed in the free decision of God.[49] Since God's sovereignty is not a tyranny—wherein everything is accomplished at a stroke from above—Ellul sees no conflict between human freedom and divine sovereignty. God's purpose is always achieved, but it does not constitute for man a fate or necessity. Man still has room for working out the freedom given in Christ; in fact God's activity invests human action with a history and a future.[50]

Ellul uses the stories of the Second Book of Kings to illustrate the interplay of divine lordship and human freedom. God's will is done; it is accomplished, however, by human beings and they do it in very different ways. Wicked peoples like the Assyrians serve as God's instruments even while pursuing their selfish ends. Jehu can act wickedly even in a conscious fulfillment of the prophetically revealed will of God. In these cases judgment will finally fall, for the acts of such people are acts of autonomy and not of authentic freedom. In contrast, Hezekiah performs an act of genuine freedom when in answer to the Assyrian threat he enters the temple to pray. In this case God then acts directly to raise the siege and destroy the invader.[51]

Ellul never accepts uselessness in human decision. He insists on leaving for man a sphere of free decision and therefore of authentic freedom. He is fully aware that all people do not decide freely; even many decisions we think to be free are in reality determined by the forces controlling human life. Ellul never minimizes these. As he says, "necessity still obtains in the course of history. . . . History and society are still very much subject to constraints." All the same, a power of freedom "was unleashed at the cross" enabling man to perform acts of real freedom, ones which will fall, of course, within the divine freedom.[52]

This freedom is received exclusively in Christ, making the gospel essentially one of liberation. Here again is a theme that recurs constantly in Barth's *Church Dogmatics,* and Ellul takes it up with vigor. Liberation, he thinks, provides the present age with a better figure of salvation than redemption does.[53] He does not suggest, of course, that preaching the Gospel can be equated with achieving political and economic liberation by a change of government. The problem goes deeper than that. Under any government man lies in subjection to forces that enslave him. In this tragic situation philosophers prattle about freedom, theologians utter empty platitudes, and revolutionaries suffer from the delusion that they are achieving liberation even as they serve historical determinations; but only Christ, who displayed his own freedom in the temptations, can bring true emancipation. As Ellul insists, we ourselves, trapped in the sociological determinations of life, are "booked to die." Our liberator must come to us from beyond the determinations and beyond death. Jesus Christ and he alone is this liberator through whom we are given, not an attribute or state of freedom, but a new being in freedom.[54]

The theme of living out this freedom forms the substance of *The Ethics of Freedom.* In discussing it, Ellul follows Barth most closely vis-à-vis freedom for God or freedom for the service of God. This aspect of freedom, he says, at first glance seems to be very true but far too restricted. In this regard Ellul gives the momentary impression that he is going to differ sharply from Barth. But this is not so; he moves on at once to argue that failure at this point undercuts all else that we might try to do, including social action. Freedom, as the obedience of free man to the free God, means first and foremost freedom for God.[55] When he comes back to discuss this in detail, Ellul acknowledges that "Karl Barth has dealt very thoroughly with the matter at various points in the *Church Dogmatics*, and since . . . I am in full accord with his presentation, there seems to be no point in repeating it." He thus restricts himself to "a brief summary." Freedom for God, Ellul says, must be regarded as the first and foremost freedom because, as the freedom of free obedience, it cannot be the false freedom of autonomy. This is, of course, the main point in Barth.[56]

As regards the forms of freedom for God, Ellul adopts the same course he did with the freedom of the Word. He quotes Barth's own theses and then appends some comments of his own.[57] Thus freedom for God is first of all freedom for prayer— real prayer not under the constraint of need or fear. In it "man accepts a life by grace and hence a life in gratitude which is the most complete form of freedom. . . . [Praying man is authentic man] naked before God with nothing in his hands. . . . Only liberated man dare see himself thus. . . . [Praying is] an act of final authenticity." Freedom for God is also freedom for confession, a turning to man and telling him "something about God and from God." Only free men dare take this risk.[58] And freedom for God is freedom for a sabbath day. Ellul sees satanic absurdity in the fact that the day designed to free us from the fetters of daily routine should become filled with constraint and boredom. The holy day is a day of liberation from the bondage and alienation of work. It is also a day of resurrection, that is, of liberation from the final necessity of death, from the enslaving forms of leisure as well as work. Finally, freedom for God is freedom for the reading of Scripture, a divinely given freedom to understand it, a freedom not to read Scripture "as a paper pope or a law," but to actualize it as Word and to pass it on to others as such. And throughout these illustrations of freedom Ellul insists on the over-riding thesis of Barth: "Human freedom cannot encroach upon divine freedom. Always and in every respect the latter precedes the former. Yet, on the other hand, divine freedom cannot destroy and suspend human freedom."[59]

SOCIOLOGY

Much of Ellul's dependence on Barth patently derives from the twofold fact that he is not himself a theologian in any technical sense and that he finds Barth the most helpful and impressive of all theologians. Ellul, however, has his own field of expertise—the history and sociology of institutions. By virtue of his mastery in this area he has made an important contribution. One need not be surprised, then, that when Barth enters this field—as he does in his chapter on the ethics of creation—a striking reversal of roles takes place.[60] While Barth had a long history of social concern and action—so that in early days he could even be known as "the red parson of Safenwil"—in this whole area he is the amateur and Ellul the master. Thus Ellul's occasional and almost apologetic theological disagreement with Barth gives place to what can be very severe, if still respectful, sociological criticism. One may observe this in various works but it comes out most succinctly in *The Ethics of Freedom*.

A first criticism stems from Barth's confusion of the state and politics. For Ellul, recognition of the state's validity and political participation are two very different things. To think that by recognizing political authority one necessarily engages in politics is to be "in the world of political illusion." As he sees it, a theology of the state and the derived activities of prayer and obedience have no immediate bearing on political action. From

Ellul's perspective, Barth confuses matters when "he lumps together obedience to the state, service of the state, and participation in political life." Along the same line, Barth's argument that since we are to pray for the state we must also take part in politics has no cogency. "There is a world of difference," Ellul writes, "between praying that God will give rulers a spirit of wisdom and justice and joining a political party which is designed to support or to attack the government." This does not mean that Christians should keep out of politics. They are taking part already, not as a duty but as an order of necessity, and they should learn to do so in freedom. This will not mean espousing a supposedly Christian form of government, as Calvin and Barth do, nor will it mean trying to christianize the state. It involves a Christian presence in politics and the relativizing of politics.[61]

Ellul, of course, does not reject everything that Barth has to offer in this field. In particular he approves of Barth's point that "Christians should never be the enemies of their opponents, not even in the sphere of the state." He recognizes a necessary relativizing in which Christians can be "a cooling and peace-making factor among other men" and, shunning false conflicts, devote themselves to "the best possible management of the common patrimony."[62] Christians, of course, should participate in political movements that aim at human freedom in general; and here again Ellul appreciates Barth's argument that the church's witness must include a basic concern for the freedom of those lacking it.[63]

On a related matter, Ellul surprisingly parts company with Barth, and also with Calvin and many others, in not making religious freedom essential for good government. The Christian is free already; hence it is not necessary that he fight for political, economic, domestic, or even religious freedom for himself. All that Ellul would ask of the state is that it impose no "obligatory intellectual, religious, doctrinal, or metaphysical truth." Beyond that, Christians have no claim to special privilege but must be ready to share the common lot. If they struggle for religious freedom, it should be for the freedom of others and should always involve the recognition that freedom can never be achieved with final success.[64]

But Ellul's most forthright criticism of Barth occurs when he turns to various contemporary issues. He brings a double accusation: first, Barth talks too abstractly about concrete issues; second, he has lost touch with the realities of modern life. The way Barth handles choice of career offers a good illustration of Ellul's complaint. It would be excellent, he argues, if Christians had the choice that Barth presupposes. In the main, however, his guidance is a purely academic hypothesis which applies only "to a liberal and individualistic world, to nineteenth century society." A few people may still be able to make a genuine vocational choice, but for most of us selection is merely an illusion in view of such constraining factors as qualifications, quotas, propaganda, environment, bureaucratic control, market pressures, discrimination of different kinds, and a permanent degree of unemployment. From a practical standpoint, then, Barth's discussion can only be labeled "anachronistic."[65]

The same objection applies to Barth's more general treatment of work.[66] Except, perhaps, for the tendency to rate work too highly, Ellul has no difficulty in agreeing with the general criteria which Barth sets up for work from a Christian angle. The only problem—but it is a decisive one—arises from the total impracticability of these guidelines in modern technological societies. If, for example, Christians refuse to do any work that preys on human folly, a collapse of whole sectors of the economy might well result. Again, resistance to unworthy work would find no help from non-Christian employers, while Christian employers could well go out of business and increase unemployment if they tried to follow this standard. Barth's suggestions, then, might still be relevant in some parts of a small country like his native Switzerland, but elsewhere they presuppose a situation which "was already out of date when he wrote this chapter on ethics shortly after the Second World War. . . . Man is hardly able to express his freedom in respect of work along lines such as these."[67]

And at a deeper level Ellul cannot agree with Barth's contention that the concrete sociological conditions of work do not constitute a determination of human life. Barth argues that such a perspective implies fatalism. Ellul replies that a distinction must be made between metaphysical fatalism and sociological determination. The environment has a more decisive impact than Barth admits. While the person who is freed by Christ can escape determination, it is totally unrealistic to deny that it exists. Here Karl Marx is nearer the truth for Ellul than is Karl Barth. Ellul can thus accept the analysis of Marx.[68] Nevertheless—and here Barth is right for him—freedom is possible, because determination is not fatalism as Barth supposed. The possibility of freedom arises, however, only as freedom "is introduced by grace into a world of necessities." Freedom is possible as "the freedom of Christ." Therefore, determination must be realistically faced, but concrete freedom "lived out in man's reality" need not be denied.[69]

Conclusion

Barth's influence on Ellul hardly needs listing as a conclusion, as though a debatable thesis had now been sustained. The fact of this influence is openly accepted by Ellul himself; it thus forms the basis of this essay. The statements quoted from Ellul establish its reality.

It should be noted, however, that for the most part only in the area of biblical exposition and dogmatics does Ellul lean heavily on Barth. Even here, indeed, the nature of the relation varies. Sometimes Ellul borrows material directly from Barth. On other occasions he finds a starting point in Barth but then engages in original and constructive work of his own. This is particularly true in biblical exposition but it applies to theology, too (as in the expansive development of the theme of Christian freedom and in creating a theology of the city for which there are no counterparts at all in Barth). Only rarely, however, does Ellul challenge Barth at the theological level, and when he does so—as in the matter of the mythical genre in Scripture—he recognizes that the real dispute may lie elsewhere, in this instance in the definition of myth rather than its theological evaluation.

The drastic divergence from Barth comes in the area where Barth and not Ellul is the amateur, namely, the sociological analysis of contemporary society and living in freedom on a practical level within it. Even here Ellul has no particular quarrel with the theological criteria that underlie Barth's concrete recommendations. He complains instead that as Barth aged in small and conservative Switzerland he lost touch with the rapidly emerging world of technocracy, so that his ethical recommendations, however sound in principle, were almost completely unworkable in practice. Not even Ellul's admiration for Barth could prevent him from opposing to Barth's theorizing his own realistic appraisal of the contemporary scene and the dilemmas it poses for concrete manifestations of freedom.

The sociological divergence, of course, can have theological implications, too, as the difference regarding sociological determination exemplifies. For Ellul, enslavement in the determinations does not mean subjection to fate but bondage to sin in its corporate dimension. Thus liberation in the deepest sense—not as liberation from certain surface forms but as release from the determinations themselves—constitutes for Ellul the Gospel's substance in terms which the contemporary world can understand. Barth, too, presents the Gospel as liberation, so that even here a similarity and measure of overlapping exist. In Ellul it means liberation also from the necessities imposed by corporate structures, so that, whether or not the structures are changed, Christians can know and practice an authentic freedom in spite of them. Grounded in the liberty of God himself, here is the glorious liberty of God's children.

NOTES

1. *Ethics of Freedom*, p. 8; French ed. 1970.
2. *Ibid.*, p. 175.
3. *Politics of God and Politics of Man*, p. 14; French ed. 1966.
4. *Ethics of Freedom*, p. 457.
5. In return, Barth appreciates the quality of Ellul's work. Referring, for example, to his *Theological Foundation of Law* (French ed. 1946), Barth quotes and approves Ellul's description of the covenant as a "contract of adherence (cohesion), i.e., a contract in which one of the parties makes the arrangements and the other simply agrees," in *Church Dogmatics*, vol. IV, pt. 1, p. 25.
6. *Politics of God and Politics of Man*, p. 15ff., 21, 12, n. 2.
7. *Judgment of Jonah*, p. 14ff.; French ed. 1951.
8. *Meaning of the City*, pp. xvii-xviii; English ed. 1970.
9. *Ethics of Freedom*, p. 177.
10. *Meaning of the City*, p. 7.

11. *Church Dogmatics*, vol. I, pt. 2.
12. *Ibid.*, vol. I, pt. 2, p. 673ff.; *Ethics of Freedom*, pp. 63–64ff.
13. *Ethics of Freedom*, p. 66.
14. *Politics of God and Politics of Man*, p. 12.
15. *Meaning of the City*, p. xvii.
16. *Ethics of Freedom*, p. 166.
17. *Politics of God and Politics of Man*, p. 12, n. 2.
18. *Ethics of Freedom*, p. 175.
19. Regarding exegesis, an interesting disagreement arises between Ellul and Barth. The latter, as is well known, would not include myth among the literary genres used in Scripture (cf. *Church Dogmatics*, vol. III, pt. 1). Ellul candidly admits: "I hesitate to use the term myth" and Barth's reservations are obviously the reason for this hesitation (*Meaning of the City*, p. 18, n. 3). Yet Ellul uses "myth" all the same. Barth's criticism, he thinks, has validity "only for a relatively minor part of the different possible meanings." On his own definition, myth "does not destroy the historical reality of the event but . . . gives it its full dimension." He thus finds the mythic category a useful one in certain cases, although this does not make him any less resolute in opposing the demythologizing of Bultmann. The latter's audacious exegesis, Ellul writes, issues from the bad conscience which alters and softens revelation, attempts syncretism, and seeks an exegesis which will satisfy modern man in order to to get him to "lend an ear—however careless—to what we are saying" (*Ethics of Freedom*, p. 255).
20. *Ethics of Freedom*, pp. 166–67.
21. *Politics of God and Politics of Man*, pp. 12–13.
22. *Meaning of the City*, pp. xvii-xviii.
23. *Ethics of Freedom*, p. 179.
24. *Meaning of the City*, pp. xvii-xviii.
25. Thus, if we take in all literalness the saying about not giving children stones for bread, our understanding may be crass, "but at least we know what it is about." It is not true, at this level, that "there is a ditch that some cannot get across."
26. *Ethics of Freedom*, p. 181.
27. *Meaning of the City*, p. 183ff.
28. *Ethics of Freedom*, pp. 181–83.
29. *Judgment of Jonah*, p. 15.
30. *Ibid.*, p. 102ff.
31. Cf. W. Vischer, *Witness to Christ in the Old Testament;* cf.

Church Dogmatics, vol. II, pt. 2; *Politics of God and Politics of Man*, pp. 9, 11.

32. *Politics of God and Politics of Man*, p. 189.
33. Cf. *Meaning of the City*, pp. 42ff., 81ff., 111ff., 113–46, 185ff., 207.
34. *Ibid.*, p. 209.
35. *Politics of God and Politics of Man*, p. 65.
36. *Ibid.*, p. 11.
37. *Ibid.*, p. 54.
38. *Judgment of Jonah*, p. 102.
39. *Meaning of the City*, p. 208.
40. *Ibid.*, p. 138.
41. *Ethics of Freedom*, p. 80.
42. *Ibid.*, p. 82.
43. *Politics of God and Politics of Man*, pp. 54–55; cf. 2 Kings 6.
44. *Ethics of Freedom*, pp. 77–79ff.
45. *Church Dogmatics*, vol. IV, pt. 3.
46. *Meaning of the City*, pp. 164–66.
47. *Ethics of Freedom*, p. 81.
48. *Ibid.*, p. 79ff.; *Meaning of the City*, p. 164ff.
49. Cf. esp. *Church Dogmatics*, vol. III, pt. 3; *Politics of God and Politics of Man*, p. 15. Or, to adopt another phrase of Barth's, freedom for Ellul is the obedience of free men to the free God (*Ethics of Freedom*, p. 108ff.).
50. *Ethics of Freedom*, p. 14ff.
51. *Politics of God and Politics of Man*, p. 173ff.
52. *Ibid.*, p. 187.
53. *Ethics of Freedom*, p. 66ff.; cf. also *Politics of God and Politics of Man*, p. 199.
54. *Ethics of Freedom*, pp. 23ff., 35, 49, 51–53, 69–72.
55. *Ibid.*, pp. 105–9.
56. *Ibid.*, p. 120. If there is any disagreement here with Barth, it can only be one of nuance. Barth, he thinks, sometimes seems so to emphasize the divine sovereignty that free obedience displays too much of the element of submission. Ellul, in contrast, would see on God's part more of a loving self-limitation in respect of "his decision, judgment, and influence" (*ibid.*, p. 121).
57. Cf. *Church Dogmatics*, vol, III, pt. 4, and *Ethics of Freedom*, p. 162ff.
58. Oddly, Ellul comments, those who say that confession is impossible are the very ones "who have the most to say in public" (*Ethics of Freedom*, p. 128).

59. *Church Dogmatics*, vol. I, pt. 2, p. 710.
60. *Ibid.*, vol. III, pt. 4; cf. *Ethics of Freedom*, pt. 4.
61. *Ethics of Freedom*, p. 374ff.
62. *Ibid.*, p. 383.
63. *Ibid.*, p. 398, n. 29; cf. *Church Dogmatics*, vol. II, pt. 4, p. 503.
64. On this whole issue see *Ethics of Freedom*, p. 435ff.; on the divergence from Barth, p. 435.
65. *Ibid.*, p. 457ff.
66. *Church Dogmatics*, vol. III, pt. 4.
67. *Ethics of Freedom*, p. 461.
68. *Ibid.*, pp. 23–27.
69. *Ibid.*, p. 75.

Chapter 3

Ellul and Kierkegaard: Closer Than Brothers

Vernard Eller

Although Karl Barth and Karl Marx had the earlier and more immediate influence on Ellul, it is Søren Kierkegaard for whom Ellul shows the most empathy. Ellul's opinion of Marx with respect to Kierkegaard is clear from the following quotation.

> Such is the state into which the three geniuses [Marx, Nietzsche, and Freud], humanity's great malefactors, have thrown us. They represent the opposite of mercy and love. I venture that, in spite of their science . . . they are charmers who have bewitched the soul and the intelligence of mankind by focusing our attention on problems which are fundamental but without any possible answer. . . . With regard to this trio, we would have to perform the same operation which Kierkegaard performed on the Hegelian myth, for let us remember that it was Kierkegaard, and not Marx, who was able to rise above Hegel and relocate man. . . . What Kierkegaard did, we should be able to do again. But he was able to do it only with strict reference to the revelation in Jesus Christ; that is to say, in committing the reality of the intellectual operation he was undertaking to the freedom of action of one more powerful than himself. All depends on that.[1]

Ellul, here, certainly is not retracting all the sociological insights he has picked up from Marx. But what is implied (to become abundantly clear as we proceed) is that Ellul considers only his Christian thought essential and that, consequently, no non-Christian thought, system, or thinker can be of decisive significance for him.

On the other hand, in this quotation he gives Kierkegaard a decisive enough place virtually to establish our thesis. For Ellul, Kierkegaard has not only "relocated man" into a true anthropology, he also has shown *the way* to think about human existence, the way upon which "all depends." Ellul makes no similar statement about any other thinker outside the Bible.

In this regard, we need to clarify *which* Kierkegaard we are relating to *which* Ellul. Kierkegaard's works fall into two distinct categories: the pseudonymous materials which build upon philosophical (including aesthetic) premises; and religious works, largely under his own name, which build upon explicitly Christian premises. Ellul's writings also fall into two distinct types— although without any hint that he was consciously emulating Kierkegaard: his sociological studies (including the history of institutions); and his theological works.

Both authors make clear the relationship between the two halves of their authorship; and they turn out to have a great deal in common. Kierkegaard says:

> [What] requires no explanation at all is the last section, the purely religious work which of course establishes the point of view. . . .[2] In a Christian sense simplicity is not the point of departure from which one goes on to become interesting, witty, profound, poet, philosopher, etc. No, the very contrary. *Here* is where one begins (with the interesting, etc.) and becomes simpler and simpler, attaining simplicity.[3]

Similarly, Ellul says of *his* own work:

> I have sought to confront theological and biblical knowledge and sociological analysis without trying to come to any artificial or philosophical synthesis; instead, I try to place the two face to face, in order to shed some light on what is real socially and real spiritually. That is why I can say that the reply to each of my sociological analyses is found implicitly in a corresponding theological book, and inversely, my theology is fed on socio-political experience. But I refuse to construct a *system* of thought, or to offer up some Christian

or prefabricated socio-political solutions. I want to provide Christians with the means of thinking out *for themselves* the meaning of their involvement in the modern world.[4]

James Holloway, perhaps the first theological analyst of Ellul in this country, explains further:

His sociological and political analyses are written under the demands he knows as a Christian, and it is precisely because of this commitment that he judges it dishonest as well as meaningless to introduce "Christianity" as an authority for these writings. Instead, his sociological and political analyses are a pole for his theological and biblical writings—"compositions in counterpoint," he calls them. These "compositions in counterpoint" are in no sense a Tillichian "theology of *correlation*." Rather, Ellul is composing a "theology of *confrontation*"—the biblical message written to confront the developments (especially the technical developments) in modern society. His work, he explains, has from the first turned on "the contradictions between the evolution of the modern world [notably the technical evolution] and the biblical content of revelation."[5]

Both Ellul and Kierkegaard have structured their authorships over a grand dialectic, putting one group of books against another. But we must note particularly which pole each chooses as being normative for his thought, namely, a rigorous and thoroughgoing version of biblical Christianity. Thus, even though it could be shown that Kierkegaard had some very percipient insights regarding the coming society which Ellul has analyzed as "technological," we do not propose to compare Kierkegaard's sociology with Ellul's, or Ellul's aesthetics with Kierkegaard's. Their understanding of Christianity is central for both men, and here the parallel between them is especially striking.

Their agreements produce a profile of that broader tradition within the church characterized as "radical Christian discipleship."[6] Almost every point of likeness between Kierkegaard and Ellul can be located within the radical tradition.

DIALECTICS

Our two thinkers are not only dialectical in their overall pattern of authorship, but also very much so in the way their theological method actually operates. Yet surely many other thinkers (including both Marx and Barth) also have been characterized as "dialecticians." So the notable fact is that Kierkegaard and Ellul agree on what they mean by "dialectic" *against* the more common understanding of the term (see Ellul's own contribution to this volume). Ellul posited the distinction thus: "The dialectic of faith is an intellectual one. It is impossible to prevent theological dialectic today from becoming ultimately an expression of the Hegelian dialectic. We shall try to show that the movement of hope is also dialectic, but that, in contrast to the dialectic of faith, it is inescapably a dialectic of the concrete. The reason is that hope cannot be systematized. It implies action in the tangible as a condition of its very existence."[7]

When Ellul says that the dialectic of faith is "an *intellectual* one," I understand him to mean the dialectic of faith as commonly presented. He would not deny that Scripture provides a dialectic of faith that is thoroughly existential. And when he says that "*theological* dialectic" inevitably must become Hegelian, I understand him to be using "theological" in the narrow sense that identifies a systematic type of thought dealing exclusively in terms of intellectual concepts. He clearly does believe in the possibility of maintaining "dialectics of the concrete" which do not become Hegelian. And when Ellul specifies that *his* dialectic "cannot be systematized," he is pointing toward the place where he parts company with Barth in order to go with Kierkegaard.

The difference is basic: because Hegelian dialectic deals only in formal, intellectual concepts, synthesis (the creation of a new, third "idea" that combines elements of the first-stage thesis and antithesis) becomes not only a possibility but itself the very goal of the process. On the contrary, because it deals in concrete realities rather than ideas, existential dialectic cannot arrive at synthesis, firmly resists any effort to synthesize, and takes as its goal the finding of one's life within the tension between the dialectic's unsynthesized poles.

Thus Holloway can speak of Ellul's "theology of confrontation" (refusal to synthesize) as against Tillich's "theology of correlation" (which is nothing other than synthesizing). And Ellul himself can talk about "the *contradictions* between the modern world and the biblical revelation," about not "trying to come to any artificial or philosophical synthesis" and refusing to provide a "system" or "solutions." And what Ellul has done in this is to choose Kierkegaard's understanding of dialectic rather than the popular definition inherited from Hegel.[8]

THE BIBLE

We need at some point to suggest the basic choice that sent Kierkegaard and Ellul together in a direction quite different from that of modern Christian thought in general. It has to do with their commitment to what Ellul in the quotation above calls "the biblical content of revelation." As he writes in *To Will and To Do:* "The criterion of my thought is the biblical revelation, the content of my thought is the biblical revelation, the point of departure is supplied by the biblical revelation, the method is the dialectic in accordance with which the biblical revelation is given to us, and the purpose is a search for the significance of the biblical revelation concerning ethics."[9] And Kierkegaard said: "Was I not in the right, and am I not, in saying that first and foremost everything must be done to make it perfectly definite what is required in the New Testament for being a Christian? The New Testament indeed settles what Christianity is, leaving it to eternity to pass judgment upon us."[10]

Further, Ellul likes to theologize in the form of biblical exposition. His books, *The Judgment of Jonah, The Politics of God and the Politics of Man, The Meaning of the City,* and *Apocalypse* are all of this genre; and the rest of his theological works are strong in their orientation toward Scripture. Likewise, the bulk of Kierkegaard's edifying and religious discourses (which constitute the largest category of his works) take the form of biblical exegesis.

Yet, of course, any number of theologians make use of the Bible. Where Ellul and Kierkegaard stand with one another against the trend of current theology is in letting the Scriptures dictate the metaphysic, epistemology, and method of their thought, rather than in striving to form a synthesis between the biblical material and some philosophical system of modern currency. Ellul spells out the difference:

> What we are proposing is obviously the direct opposite of what Bultmann has been sponsoring. Bultmann begins by affirming the given realities of the world, e.g., science or

history, and then proceeds to criticize, not just the modes of explanation, but the very core of what is passed on to us by the Bible. When the Bible has been stripped in this way, all that finally remains is myself in relation to a God to whom I have given existence. The same applies to the attempt of Tillich to find common ground between culture and revelation. What is more clearly needed here is the either-or which is more consonant, I think, with Scripture, not the synthesis or reconciliation which each attempts with new methods and which gives no help to those who famish through appeasement and toleration.[11]

Ellul and Kierkegaard are very close, not only in the fact that their thought is very much biblically oriented, but as well in the way they use the Bible.[12] Notice that Ellul has claimed even his method of existential dialectic as being of biblical derivation.

EXISTENTIALISM

In attributing to Ellul an existential dialectic, and in Ellul's own accusation that Bultmann leaves only "myself in relation to a God to whom I have given existence," the question of existentialism has been raised. Ellul and Kierkegaard need to be compared on this crucial score.

Kierkegaard, of course, is widely known as "the father of existentialism"; but the question is whether or not the children are legitimate. Certainly there is a sense in which both Kierkegaard and Ellul must be called "existential," namely, that their discourse is life-centered rather than thought-centered, concerned with historical realities rather than with intellectual theory, and pointed toward changing behavior rather than defining doctrine. In this sense, also, the broader tradition of radical discipleship is entirely "existential."

Yet what commonly goes by the name of "existentialism" is something quite different, namely, systematic philosophies dealing in concepts of existence (concepts which are just as far from being existence as are concepts of any other sort). There is no evidence that Kierkegaard would have had any time for such "existentialism"; all sorts of evidence indicate that Ellul does not.

Ellul makes no use of, and only occasional reference to, the existentialist philosophers. Sartre is mentioned more than any other, though not in the way of providing positive help to Ellul. There might seem to be more promise in going to existentialist Christians, that is, theologians of the company of Tillich and Bultmann; yet Ellul turns out to be not much more friendly to them. On that front, Ellul is more aligned with Barth than with Tillich or Bultmann. We saw above how he rejected Tillich and Bultmann for their synthesizing Scripture with modern world-views (notably existentialism). He also scored Bultmann for his existentialist reduction of reality to "myself in relation to a God to whom I have given existence." Now he focuses on the concept of "freedom" which is so basic to existentialist thought: "Naturally I accept Kierkegaard's analysis of decision as an expression of freedom, but only in its strict form and not in terms of the theory of decision of post-Heideggerians or Bultmann."[13]

"Naturally" he accepts Kierkegaard, but, just as "naturally," that is something quite different from accepting "existentialism." So we must proceed with great precision on this point. It would be false to both Kierkegaard and Ellul to compare them without pointing out the profoundly existential character of their thought; yet it would be just as false to let this imply any sort of substantive connection between them and existentialism. Ellul resists this; Kierkegaard did too—although he was handicapped in having to resist before existentialism even was invented.

SUBJECTIVITY

The topic "existentialism" leads to the topic "subjectivity," one particularly important to our study, because it impels Ellul and Kierkegaard into a separation from Barth on the right as well as from Bultmann and Tillich on the left. Ellul sets the framework for our discussion:

> In this catastrophic situation [of God's silence toward the modern world] there are two reactions. One is to objectify the Word of God (a charge to which Barth was vulnerable). Objectivication says that there is no need to turn the Word into an experience. The Word *is*. That is all there is to it, and it never changes. The other reaction is the radical subjectivication of the Word of God (a charge to which Bultmann was vulnerable). Subjectivication says that there is no

need to ask oneself whether or not there is a God who speaks. The important thing is "living as though."[14]

Ellul neglects to say here who hit upon the dialectical relationship that avoids the one-sidedness of either objectivication or subjectivication; but he knows and will give us the answer a bit later. Neither does Ellul tell us just *how* vulnerable Barth was to the charge of objectivication (probably not so much as the subjectifiers would like to make us think). It is sufficient to note that, on this matter, Ellul chooses Kierkegaard over Barth. It seems clear that he does not mean to imply a symmetry that would make Barth as far off the truth on the one side as Ellul considers Bultmann to be on the other.

Yet the relationship to Barth can be explored a bit farther. Ellul quotes and cites Barth much more frequently than he does Kierkegaard. However, as the previous chapter suggests, a growing number of these Barthian references are points of reference from which to develop new ideas rather than points of agreement. In this regard, it is interesting to observe that in his citations of Barth, Ellul regularly gives the specific locus of the idea, usually from the *Church Dogmatics*. With citations of Kierkegaard, quite the contrary: there is rarely a direct quotation nor even mention of a specific book. What we get, rather, is a reference to or a paraphrase of some Kierkegaardian idea. Ellul, it would seem, keeps Barth on his desk but Kierkegaard in his head (or in his heart).

It could well be that Ellul has come to Kierkegaard *through* Barth, that he has worked his way beyond (behind) Barth to Kierkegaard, and that, accordingly, he actually stands closer to the early Barth—the Barth who had not yet repudiated Kierkegaard—than he does to the author of the *Church Dogmatics*. In any case, we serve the purposes of this chapter best by noting specifically how Barth and Ellul compare on this matter of "subjectivity."

Ellul opens his *Hope in Time of Abandonment* with an apologia for the fact that he is going to treat hope with considerable subjectivity. He declares that he already had written a good deal about hope and then says: "This didn't cause much of a stir, which was normal. It was merely a case of being intellectually correct in a 'good' [i.e., Barthian] theology, because it was all there in Barth. But I didn't know what I was saying. There is an intellectual formalism which, in the very act of communicating the word richest in meaning, empties it of meaning. In our day one is tempted to call 'orthodoxy.' "[15]

Here is brought to focus not only the issue of subjectivity but also Ellul's earlier pleas for a "dialectic of the concrete," for an emphatically "existential" mode of thinking, for a truly biblical metaphysic. Here is definitely a move away from Barth—although not, by that token, a joining of forces with the subjectivication of Bultmann and Tillich. After all, speaking of his book *The Ethics of Freedom* (written after *Hope*), Ellul could still say: "It has to some extent been inspired by the theology of Karl Barth. I do not deny this, although I have never been an unconditional 'Barthian.' "[16]

It would seem accurate to say that Ellul wants to be Barthian *with a corrective;* and the corrective turns out to be the person who explicitly offered his thought as a corrective. "Subjectivity" is Kierkegaard's own term and concept, posed as a corrective, both to the objectivication that makes God's action so objective that the believer's action and experience are beside the point, and to the subjectivication that makes the believer's subjective action and experience so central that the objective subsistence of God and his acts are beside the point. "Subjectivity," then, is a dialectic relationship toward a totally objective action of an objective (Wholly Other) God which, nevertheless, is without decisive effect until it has been appropriated as a subjective experience of the believer himself. As Kierkegaard put it:

> Christianity exists before any Christian exists, it must exist in order that one may become a Christian, it contains the determinant by which one may test whether one has become a Christian, it maintains its objective subsistence apart from all believers, while at the same time it is the inwardness of the believer. . . .[17]
>
> The historicity of the redemption must be certain in the same sense as any other historical thing, but no more so, for otherwise the different spheres are confused. . . . The historical factual assumption necessary for the redemption must only be as certain as all other historical facts, but the passion of faith must decide the matter.[18]

The Individual

"Subjectivity" leads directly to Kierkegaard's key idea, "*den Enkelte*" (the individual).[19] Although in both Kierkegaard and Ellul this idea is polemical in the extreme against the crowd, or the public, or society, there is no similar intention that it be polemical against "the *community* of faith." It may be that both Kierkegaard and Ellul are vulnerable to the charge of not adequately emphasizing the biblical sense of community. Yet, with both men, the defect probably derives from the fact that they never experienced intimate Christian community. It clearly is *not* to be understood as any sort of necessary implication from their concepts of "the individual."[20]

The seminal article that introduced Ellul the theologian to many of his American readers gives pointed attention to a theme that has been pervasive with him since:

> This double movement [for which Ellul is calling] involves on the one hand, the creation of new forms (political, moral, religious, aesthetic), and on the other hand the struggle against structures (technical, economic, bureaucratic and also mental). In both cases we can only start with the individual; that is to say, the present movement is so radical that it is only by going back to the root—which is always the individual human being—that it will be possible to mend matters. . . . When I speak of the individual I have in view neither individual religion or enterprise, neither classic democracy or individualistic philosophy. When I speak of the individual as the source of hope I mean the individual who does not lend himself to society's game, who disputes what we accept as self-evident . . . who questions even the movement of this society. . . . This radical subjectivity will inform also the three human passions which seem to be the essential ones—the passion to create, to love, to play. But these mighty drives of the human heart must find a particular expression in each person. It is in the building of a new daily life, in the discovery of things, acts, situations utterly different from those that society would fasten on us, that this subjectivity can express itself. . . . I am convinced that Christians are absolutely the only ones who can attempt it—but here too on condition that they start from zero. Kierkegaard, it seems to me, alone can show us how to start. . . . If we are to question our society in so

> radical a fashion, we must adopt a point of view essentially different from that of society's—one that we cannot arrive at by starting from our human wisdom. It is precisely because [the Bible] speaks of a Wholly Other that the revelation provides us with a point of view and a point of departure that are essentially different.[21]

Here Ellul expressly identifies his position with Kierkegaard's, bringing in, at the same time, the related themes of "subjectivity" and "passion."

Let us speak, then, of "passion," or "the passions." Both Kierkegaard and Ellul have been notable in their efforts to give these theological significance.[22] The thought follows naturally from the whole point of view we have seen developing; it is part of the attempt to get away from the detachment of objective orthodoxy and involve the totality of the individual's historical existence in the gospel's "dialectic of the concrete." To me, the most impressive statement Ellul has made on the topic comes from the article quoted above:

> The passion to play: this alone must be the basis for anyone's participation in a group. However serious an enterprise, however important the stakes and the values to be realized, these must not induce us to participate (in political life, for instance). All that in fact is part of the very technical structures that must be opposed! But if, on the contrary, participation is prompted by the passion to play, then it is free; it gives life to the group and at the same time permits the individual to express himself.[23]

Yet more significant than anything either Kierkegaard or Ellul has said about the passions is the fact that both have done theology passionately. Far from constructing intellectual systems out of their heads, they have written out of their hearts (with a proportionate deterioration of academic footnoting) from a gut-level concern for God and the people. Indeed, Ellul's aforementioned defection from Barth was nothing other than his desire to make "hope" a passion rather than a concept.

Nonconformity

A theme upon which Kierkegaard and Ellul are fully in accord, a theme as fundamental to the tradition of radical discipleship as any characteristic could be, and one just as fundamentally a mark of New Testament Christianity, is "nonconformity to the world," the polemical stance of the gospel toward the standards and valuations of society at large. And with our thinkers this polemic applies not only to our technological society but, as well, to our political society, our violent society, our economic society, and, as we shall see, our religious society. Across the board, nonconformity is a root principle of the basic Kierkegaardian/Ellulian orientation—and one, by the way, which puts their thought into stark contrast with that of the theological world in general.[24]

One aspect of the world to which our men find the gospel not conforming is its "religion" (whether in the church or outside it); and it is here, again, that our two stand in sharp dissent from present theological fashion. Theirs, of course, is a *Christian* "religionlessness" consonant with Bonhoeffer's use of that term, although not premised on the questionable assumption that man has come of age. Ellul puts the matter bluntly:

> But it seems to us that this "religious" something which inspires morality, which builds it or conceals itself within it, is in no way an expression of the will of God. It is indeed a "religious" something in the human sense of the word; that is to say, it is a part of man's overall attempt to scale the heights of heaven, to lay hold upon God and to bring him into submission, or again, to acquire divinity for himself— in any case, to substitute something else for the will of God.[25]

Kierkegaard's most pointed critique of religion is *The Attack upon Christendom;*[26] Ellul's is *The New Demons*—with its twin themes: that modern man is as religious as they come; and that Christianity is *not* a religion. Kierkegaard was addressing a world which, in his day, was claiming to be Christian, and Ellul, one which claims to be secular; but given that difference in situation, the two books are voicing an identical critique.

Conclusion

Our study could be extended indefinitely by tracing the agreement of Kierkegaard and Ellul to more and more specific and detailed items. However, many of these would indicate nothing more than that they speak from a common background of Christian orthodoxy. We have chosen, rather, to spot the commonalities which establish the fact that they share a fundamental point of view distinguishing them from other theologians and thinkers past and present, thus making them "closer than brothers."

Both Kierkegaard and Ellul, however, have felt it their calling to be "apostles to the intellectuals," and neither has had appreciable success (as if success were something in which an "apostle" would be interested). Kierkegaard, finally, was heard by the intellectuals, who promptly appropriated his thought to pervert it into existentialism. It is too early yet to say what ultimately will happen to Ellul's message; but there is no perceptible rush of intellectuals to be doing what Ellul talks about. Yet it was Ellul himself who—to the charge that "all this is entirely utopian, and in fact it is an illusion to believe that the establishment of such organisms would be possible"—retorted: "I have never said that it *is* possible. I have only indicated what I consider to be the basic condition for social and political life and the *only* way to escape the political illusion [and all others]. If one does not want to follow it, so be it. The future is clear enough under such conditions [namely, the kingdom of God will come anyhow]."[27]

NOTES

1. *Hope in Time of Abandonment*, pp. 52–54; French ed. 1972.
2. Søren Kierkegaard, *The Point of View for My Work as an Author* (New York: Harper Torchbooks, 1962), p. 42.
3. *Ibid.*, p. 144.
4. "From Jacques Ellul" in *Introducing Jacques Ellul*, ed. James Y. Holloway, p. 6.
5. "West of Eden," *ibid.*, p. 20.
6. See my *Kierkegaard and Radical Discipleship* [hereafter referred to as *KARD*] (Princeton, N.J.: Princeton University Press, 1968), as my effort to relate Kierkegaard to this tradition. In much less extensive fashion I have suggested Ellul's relationship to the tradition in "Jacques Ellul, the Polymath Who Knows Only One Thing," *Brethren Life and Thought*, 18 (Spring 1973), 77–84, and "Four Who Remember," *Katallagete*, 3 (Spring 1971), 6–12. Ellul himself read this last-listed article and had some approving things to say about it—which is what got us into personal contact with

one another. He is quite aware of what I explicate here as the nature of the relationship between his thought and Kierkegaard's.

7. *Hope in Time of Abandonment*, p. 87.

8. Regarding Kierkegaard's dialectic, see Eller, *KARD*, pp. 144–45.

9. *To Will and To Do*, p. 1; French ed. 1964.

10. *Attack upon "Christendom"* (Princeton, N.J.: Princeton University Press, 1968), pp. 25–32.

11. *Ethics of Freedom*, pp. 68–69.

12. Regarding Ellul's hermeneutic, see Vernard Eller, "How Jacques Ellul Reads the Bible," *Christian Century*, 89 (29 Nov. 1972), 1212–15. Regarding Kierkegaard's, see Paul Minear and Paul Morimoto, *Kierkegaard and the Bible* (Princeton, N.J.: Princeton Theological Seminary, 1953), and Eller, *KARD*, pp. 408–23.

13. *Ethics of Freedom*, p. 113n; French ed. 1970.

14. *Hope in Time of Abandonment*, p. 126 (parentheses Ellul's).

15. *Ibid.*, p. vi.

16. *Ethics of Freedom*, p. 8.

17. Søren Kierkegaard, *On Authority and Revelation: The Book on Adler* (Princeton, N.J.: Princeton University Press, 1955), pp. 168–69.

18. *The Journals of Kierkegaard*, ed. Alexander Dru (New York: Oxford University Press, 1938), no. 602. For further analysis of Kierkegaard's "subjectivity," see Vernard Eller, "Fact, Faith, and Foolishness," *Journal of Religion*, 48 (Jan. 1968), 54–68; and *KARD*, pp. 356–74.

19. For an explication of Kierkegaard's concept, see Eller, *KARD*, pp. 101–200.

20. For Kierkegaard's explicit protection of himself in this regard, see Eller, *KARD*, pp. 335, 342–52. I cannot point to any such specific discussion in Ellul; however, his constant eschatological perspective—expressed most plainly, perhaps, in *The Meaning of the City* —makes it evident that his view of history has salvation focusing upon the human community rather than upon discrete individuals. Although regarding subjectivity, the individual, passion, etc. our two are very much in step with the broader tradition of radical discipleship, regarding "community" they are weak precisely where that tradition is conspicuously strong.

21. "Between Chaos and Paralysis," *Christian Century*, 85 (5 June 1968), 747–50. See *Presence of the Kingdom*, pp. 79–95.

22. Regarding Kierkegaard, see Eller, *KARD*, pp. 143, 149, 179–82.

23. *Ibid.*, p. 749. Notice that his was written before the "theologies of

play" appeared and that Ellul has an entirely different context and thrust.

24. For Kierkegaard on the subject, see Eller, *KARD*, pp. 213–31. For Ellul, all his books deal with nonconformity, although *Hope in Time of Abandonment*, p. 148ff., does constitute a specific treatment (and with specific mention of Kierkegaard).
25. *To Will and To Do*, p. 273, n. 11.
26. For an analysis, see Eller, *KARD*, pp. 328–33.
27. *Political Illusion*, p. 223; French ed. 1965.

Part II

SOCIOPOLITICAL
ISSUES

The Uncertain Hobbesian: Ellul's Dialogue with the Sovereign and the Tradition of French Politics

John L. Stanley

Certainly one of the most interesting aspects of Jacques Ellul's thought is found in the political concerns that pervade his writings. At present, he says, the greatest problem we have to face is "the citizen in the clutches of political power."[1] A constant theme found in both the theological and secular works of Ellul is his fear of the immense, all powerful, and tutelary sovereign which in all countries denies the individual his freedom, and, worse, undermines his desire to exercise it.

But not content merely to describe things as he sees them, Ellul confronts this dreary picture with a more appealing ideal. Against what he takes to be the overpowering reality of contemporary society, Ellul juxtaposes a vision of "true politics" rooted in social, political, intellectual, or artistic bodies, associations, and interest groups. As depicted in Ellul's utopia, these organizations must be completely independent not only materially but also intellectually and morally.[2]

It is perfectly proper to oppose ideals to reality in any system of political theory, but the manner in which Ellul proceeds to establish this opposition between the ideal of pluralism and the supposed reality of centralized power has led to confusing and contradictory tendencies in his thought. In taking a stark, pessimistic, almost Hobbesian view of the real political world, Ellul has misconstrued the nature of political power, and the consistency and clarity of his own ideals and his own solutions to the problem of power have suffered accordingly. On the one hand, in his earnest desire to excise the "political illusion" from our thought, Ellul eschews any compromise with the body politic, preferring instead an attitude of "total confrontation." On the other hand, convinced of the necessity of action despite the totality of modern power, Ellul at times asks us to become a part of that very totality.

Ellul has made a choice which, he argues *inter alia*, derives from the necessities of realism. Political power as it actually exists is viewed in terms of hierarchy, domination, and rule. It is not seen as he would like it to be, that is, as the process of the coming together of a plurality of men. Ellul's perception of power as it functions in the present world is therefore closer to the views of Augustine or Thomas Hobbes than to those of the Romans, Locke, Montesquieu, or Madison. For Ellul agrees with Hobbes and shares with the majority of modern thinkers the view that political power is rooted in the naturally violent propensities of mankind. With Hobbes, Ellul regards modern domination as having developed from the premise that "only an absolute, all-powerful state, itself using violence, could protect the individual against society's violence."[3]

The consequences of Hobbes's assumptions are familiar: to prevent violence and to assuage the fear of violent death, men alienate their natural powers and assign them to a sovereign who consequently establishes an absolute, stable political order ruled from a single source, whether by one man, a few, or a majority. This politically established power is by definition unitary, so constituted that there is no force superior to it. Having arisen from the violence of men, it is "men and arms, not words and promises, that make the force and power of the laws."[4] Violence is the cause of the state, and its monopolization by the state defines the locus of political power.

The Hobbesian view of political power has been criticized as a "grossly over-simplified and even hollow one. The power to act required only the elimination of hindrances rather than the active enlistment of the private power and the support of citizens."[5] However, as the late Hannah Arendt noted, many modern political theorists have adopted the Hobbesian viewpoint and have thus obscured the necessary distinctions between "force," "violence," and "power." To Arendt, power means to act in concert and is never the property of an individual; it belongs only to a group and it remains in existence only as long as the group remains together. "Power and violence are not the same, but opposites. Violence appears only when power is in jeopardy, but left to its own course it ends in power's disappearance. This implies that it is not correct to think of the opposite of violence as non-violence; to speak of non-violent power is actually redundant. Violence can destroy power; it is utterly incapable of creating it."[6]

In the present volume, Kenneth Konyndyk asserts that Ellul shares the common confusion of coercive acts with violence and violence with power. But while such a confusion may be shared by political theorists in many cultures, in a quite different respect, Ellul reflects the unique political experiences of his own millieu. As he states in the introduction to the American edition of *The Political Illusion*, France has become the Hobbesian nation par excellence. Her tradition of centralized government stemming from the time of Louis XIV makes the French easy converts to the Hobbesian viewpoint. On the other hand, Ellul may be confusing specifically French problems with those of political life in general, and in doing so his "solutions" take on a peculiarly Gallic character. In the face of an extreme and simplified concept of political power as it supposedly exists in present societies, Ellul puts forth an alternative vision that at times is just as extreme in the opposite direction. The Hobbesian interpretation of contemporary power means that in order to adopt a non-violent position, Ellul is compelled to become, as he says, an "anarchist" of the sort deeply rooted in the Proudhonian tradition. But in order to prevent this anarchism from degenerating into violence, a "dialogue" is necessary. Such a dialogue appears to have elements that make Ellul's call for anarchism a confusing one, for Ellul envisions some sort of "coercive" relations in his desire to affect the behavior of the sovereign. Ellul's ambiguities would be less troublesome were he to adopt a more conciliatory approach to political power in the non-Hobbesian sense, that is, by accepting the present reality of divided and plural power which he very much desires, but which he sees as being almost completely absent from politics as it is actually practiced.

I

Ellul shares Hobbes's view of sovereignty in two ways: He generally denies the possibility of divided sovereignty and, like Hobbes, regards as meaningless the distinction between a lawless and lawful ruler. Ellul inherits much of this view of power by way of the Marxist tradition and, indeed, continues to share it with many Marxian contemporaries.

Like many modern theorists, Hobbes's view militates against the idea of mixed government. It is quite true that Hobbes allows for monarchy, aristocracy, or democracy as legitimate expressions of sovereignty, but the idea that the two elements might be combined in a system of divided sovereignty is for Hobbes a contradiction in terms. More important, since government resides not in laws but in the swords behind them, the distinction between lawful and lawless government that is basic to political thought since antiquity is dismissed by Hobbes as "another error of Aristotle's *Politics*."[7] The difference between a lawful aristocracy and a lawless oligarchy, for example, is merely a matter of opinion, so that "those who are displeased with aristocracy call it oligarchy."[8]

This logic (even if it does not include all the principles of the *Leviathan*) has gained such widespread acceptance in modern social thought that it requires little elaboration to demonstrate it. Max Weber's assertion that "today the relation between the state and violence is an especially intimate one" and his view that the state is defined by virtue of its "monopolization of the legitimate use of physical force"[9] are regarded by many as little more than truisms. Even a "pluralist" observer like Tocqueville believed that a mixed government was impossible.[10] Although the author of *Democracy in America* is widely discussed in the literature of political theory, his view has provoked little controversy.

Ellul, too, dismisses the idea of mixed government, or any divided power, as casting ambiguity on the state. The assumption that a state can live with divided power "was the monumental mistake of Montesquieu."[11] Similarly, the difference between lawful and lawless states is mainly a matter of appearances. The "great difference" between the democracies and the "so-called totalitarian" states is that the latter have become conscious and desirous of ways in which technique can be harnessed to political power. The rule, for them, is to use means without limitation of any sort. Although democracies are inhibited by traditions and judicial affirmations and the like, through which a "facade" of public and private morality exists, such scruples "are without force or reality. They are merely verbal smokescreens, and thus democracies disregard them everytime it is necessary to do so. . . ."[12] The technocratic hierarchy in the United States resembles the Soviet system more than it resembles the early American Republic.[13] In one state after another the same "totalitarian" logic prevails.

Now it may be argued that Ellul has gone much further than Hobbes, whose definitions are broad enough to allow for diverse forms of government. Indeed, the sovereign bases his power on the consent as well as the interest of the subject—something largely missing from the subject of Ellul's autonomous technique. But the question here is not of faithfully representing Hobbes in all aspects of his thought, but in sharing his view of power once it is established—that is, once consent has been given and the life of the subject preserved. Even assuming that Ellul has gone beyond Hobbes, he is only exacerbating the difficulties involved in the Hobbesian position.

More important, once the logic of sovereignty has been established, one moves easily from power based on consent to a purely autonomous view of power, partly because of the rather hollow basis of Hobbes's view of consent, which is deemed legitimate even if given under coercive conditions.[14] The "interest" of the subject is thus reduced to sheer preservation.

Finally, Hobbes himself makes the transition from sovereignty based on interest to technical autonomy when he depicts the rational world as being analogous to a machine. As Michael Oakeshott puts it, "Hobbes' philosophy is, in all its parts, preeminently a philosophy of *power* precisely because philosophy is reasoning, reasoning the elucidation of mechanism and mechanism essentially the combination, transfer and resolution of forces.

The end of philosophy itself is power—*scientia propter poten-tiam*."[15] The possibility that Ellul has surpassed even Hobbes by associating power and technique is furthered when we recall that, in Hobbes, the association of machine and power is largely metaphorical (Oakeshott argues that Hobbes is a scholastic, not a scientific mechanist). To Ellul, however, the metaphor has not only been actualized, but extended beyond the limited realm of machinery and technology. For Ellul, the Hobbesian analogy is now made concrete in the world of *Staatswissenschaft*.

The transition from power based on interest to power without agency is also found in the Marxian literature, to which Ellul owes so much. It is certainly true that when Marx and Engels assert that "political power so-called is merely the organized power of one class for oppressing another,"[16] they are basing their argument on class interest. At other times Marx and Engels regard the state as taking a mediating role between classes—especially in transition periods. But when Engels attacks Bakunin on the need for authority under socialism, he separates political power from the autonomous power of technique at least for ana-lytical purposes. Like Hobbes, Engels associates power with the will. Engels calls this exercise of the will "authority" and defines it as "the imposition of the will of another on yours; on the other hand, authority presupposes subordination." It is mistaken, ac-cording to Engels, to read that the advocates of a future commu-nist society foresee a diminution of subordination. "Supposing a social revolution to have dethroned the capitalists. . . . Will au-thority have disappeared or will it only have changed its form?" Engels takes as his example a cotton-spinning mill whose product must pass through at least six stages before it becomes thread. These procedures, he argues, are the same under any political system. The hours of work and the activities of operatives are regulated according to the procedures of production itself. "All the workers, men, women and children are obliged to begin and finish their work at the hours fixed by the authority of the steam, which cares nothing for individual autonomy. . . .At least with regard to the hours of work, one may write upon the portals of these factories, 'Leave ye that enter in all autonomy behind!' If man by dint of his knowledge and inventive genius has subdued the forces of nature, the latter avenge themselves upon him by subjecting him, insofar as he employs them, to a *veritable despotism independent of all social organization.*"[17]

The striking resemblance between Engels's and Ellul's views in regard to an autonomous sovereign technology may be one reason so many humanist Marxists attempt to dissociate Engels's views from those of Marx. But if Engels is indicted for his "positivism" and "scientism" by neo-Marxists who attack the technocratic society for its totalitarian tendencies, the Critical School which had led this attack does not escape the clutches of Engels's confusion of authority, power, and coercion. Herbert Marcuse, for example, is a theorist who, along with Ellul, argues that "neither nationalization nor socialization alter *by themselves* this physical embodiment of technological rationality. . . . The power which technological society has gained over man is absolved by its efficacy and productiveness. If it assimilates everything it touches, if it absorbs the opposition, if it plays with contradiction, it demonstrates its cultural superiority." Marcuse indicts this "one-dimensional" society in a manner not unlike Ellul. He condemns its "totalitarianism," its mystification of new techniques in which the ideology emanates from the process of production itself.[18]

Yet the Engels spirit survives in Marcuse, who appears to ignore Ellul's warnings that most solutions to the totalitarianism of technique involve the improvement of these very techniques. Thus Marcuse takes refuge in the idea of planning: "Technological society, stripped of its exploitative features, is the *sole* standard guide in planning and developing the available resources for all. Self-determination in the production and distribution of vital goods and services would be wasteful. *The job is a technical one,* and a truly technical job; it makes for the reduction of physical and mental toil. In this realm, centralized control is rational if it establishes the preconditions for meaningful self-determination."[19]

Ellul rightly grapples with the problem of whether "self-determination" is at all compatible with "centralized control." But the question remains as to whether Ellul's own solutions are adequate. Has Ellul, in accepting Hobbes's definitions, given us impractical and unrealistic solutions to the problem of the dangers to freedom in the modern world? Or conversely, is Ellul the true realist because he has only defined power the way so many others in the modern era have defined and practiced it?

II

The answers to these questions are partly obscured because Ellul himself is torn between defining power in the way it is viewed by his countrymen and extending this definition to all industrialized countries. On the one hand Ellul argues that the Hobbesian view of the state is a universal one whose definitions have become self-fulfilling. "Every modern state is totalitarian; it recognizes no limit either factual or legal."[20] Although, as we shall see, Ellul's use of the term "totalitarianism" is rather loose, his view of modern power appears plain enough. As Hobbes's solution to the war of all against all is the pacification of society, so the barbarism of early techniques amidst the anarchy of capitalist competition has been pacified by the despotism of the technocrats. The result is, in Tocqueville's horrific phrase, "an immense and tutelary power, which takes on itself alone to secure our gratifications and watch over our fate, a power that is absolute, minute, regular, provident and mild."[21]

Much worse, according to Ellul, is that the ghastly character of modern rule is revealed to us because no heterogeneity is tolerated. Since the state exists to eliminate resistance, a détente is produced, a relaxation of the will in which the vitality of society is sapped and all parties become homogeneous. In such a world, "there is no longer any exchange and entropy will prevail."[22]

To confront this power, Ellul becomes a Hobbesian in reverse. Instead of recognizing, as Hobbes does, the all-pervasive character of *homo lupis* as legitimizing any government that does not threaten life, Ellul argues that "no state in the modern world is legitimate."[23] Consequently, Ellul calls for groups to present themselves as counterweights to the sovereign power—not as negating the state, which is impossible, but as "poles of tension" confronting the state, creating a condition of equilibrium in which "we are not trying to absorb one factor by means of another."[24] As a replacement for violence, these groups "deny that the nation is the supreme value and that the state is the incarnation of the nation."[25] Such a denial will open up what Ellul later calls the "dialogue with the sovereign," in which critical tension is sustained and communication kept open. Ellul asserts that such a dialogue can be fruitful for political action, since "there can be no true politics outside him who acts and him who speaks (i.e., speaks the true word), between him who has force and him who represents justice and love. . . . On the one side, the state acts with force, whereas on the other the Church speaks about justice and love."[26]

But while Ellul's characterization of modern power appears to be universal in its application, his theory does not square perfectly with an earlier self-characterization of the "political illusion" as pertaining primarily to French politics. The nature of Ellul's solutions to the problem of power sometimes appears to be a hearkening back to the earlier French traditions of anarchism and syndicalism. Ellul's view of power has driven him to a "radically negative attitude." The state, he argues, has become so powerful that the kind of action that can initiate dialogue and which "best expresses Christian freedom, is involvement in anarchy."[27] Only in such a self-excluded movement can the true tension necessary for freedom be assured. Such a tension is a "condition of life itself. . . . The point of departure for all culture." For Ellul, public liberties are resistances. "To exist is to resist."[28] That is why Ellul has no desire to see anarchism in full triumph; its victory would be as bad as the present system. What is needed instead is a system of "federalism" which reminds us of the philosophy of Pierre-Joseph Proudhon. It is Proudhon who is credited with the term "anarchism." It was Proudhon, too, who started with a Hobbesian view of human nature, but who converted the theory of sovereignty into a species of "federalism" that would balance the claims of the central power with the claims of self-constituted economic and cultural groups. In *La guerre et la paix*, Proudhon idealizes war and struggle as a means for averting social entropy, only to reject it at the last minute, arguing that it is dishonored in practice, however noble in theory. Most wars do not embody the principle of creative tension because they usually involve struggles between two highly unequal forces driven by greed. War is transformed into justice only when economic activity replaces war as the arena for struggle. Proudhon argues that if justice is practically impossible in the realm of the *droit de force*, it is possible in the realm of *droit économique*.

It was Proudhon's economic sublimation of war that helped to inspire Georges Sorel in *Reflections on Violence* to argue for a continued tension and struggle between classes in a state of equilibrium. Like Sorel, Ellul sees a wholly new realm of freedom outside political life as it is commonly understood. Ellul shares with Sorel and Proudhon a contempt for the vulnerabilities of intellectuals in politics, a dismal view of the lack of vitality in the modern world and, in Professor Clark's words, a "myth of agonistic combat." To Sorel's *Illusions of Progress*, Ellul gives us the political illusion, and to *Reflections on Violence*, Ellul gives us reflections on violence from a Christian perspective which are not too different from Sorel's.

Like Sorel, Ellul sees violence as opening the breach between classes and sustaining a tension between them. Despite his opposition to violence, Ellul understands its attractions and articulates them in surprisingly Sorelian terms: Violence "can bring about the disorder that is necessary when the established order is only sanctimonious injustice. . . . Violence is undoubtedly the only means for exploding facades, for exposing hypocrisy and hidden oppression for what they are; only violence reveals reality. It forces the 'good boss' or the humanist politician to show himself in his true colors—as a savage exploiter or as an oppressor who does not hesitate to use violence when he meets resistance."[29]

Though he recognizes the appeal of violence, Ellul rejects it by insisting that Sorel's ethic of violence is a failure. It is, he says, based on hatred and exalts violence into a value.[30] Yet Ellul's assertion that to "exist is to resist" is not very far from Sorel's definition of violence as "rebellion against the existing order which is aimed at destroying that order while force is what is used to impose the established system of minority rule."[31] The similarity of Sorel's and Ellul's views on the nature of power becomes all the more striking in light of Sorel's definition of violence as rebellion of almost any kind. But while Sorel is by no means a pacifist, he specifically disdains both sabotage and the rhetoric of hatred. For it was the slaughter of the French Revolution that Sorel's philosophy of "violence" is designed to avoid. He would certainly have included passive resistance under his definition of violence along with the general strike, though both are coercive.

Yet Ellul cannot possibly avoid all coercion in his own philosophy. Ellul argues that Christians "may have to force the gate in the interests of the state that has need of dialogue. Two speakers are necessary."[32] But how then can dialogue with the sovereign be initiated without producing the very thing he wishes to avoid? "Forcing the gate" would seem to be a form of coercion, and coercion is, in Ellul's view, a form of violence that he has repudiated.

The point here is not to assert that Ellul's view of violence is identical to Sorel's, but to suggest that both figures are over-reacting to French centralization. Both regard the creation of autonomous groups outside the conventional political system as the only proper response to sovereignty without replacing it with the brutality of an even more powerful revolutionary state. The "violence" of syndicalism was a way of restoring vitality in society without recourse to the power of the state.

The attempt made by Sorel to find a means of resisting the state without reenforcing its power is continued by Albert Camus in his book *The Rebel,* which was influenced by his compatriot, Sorel. The comparison between Camus's and Sorel's attempts with that of Ellul to "force the gate" without using force is instructive. In place of Sorel's distinction between violence and force, Camus distinguishes between rebellion and revolution. For Camus the political revolution "starts from doctrine and forceably introduces reality into it," while rebellion is the "negation, to the benefit of reality, of bureaucratic and abstract centralism."[33] The political revolution is both utopian and historicist. It has an end vision, the pursuit of which justifies any means and is in turn justified by a philosophy of historical and technical progress. The logic of "progress" requires the revolution to "mutilate man more and more and to transform itself into an objective crime."[34]

As distinct from political revolution, true rebellion denies "a future of reconciliation" in which social unity is achieved and problems resolved. The Sisyphusian struggle of Camus's rebel avoids both utopias and despair. True rebellion embodies both freedom and limits by insisting on the primacy of human liberation over justice. The progressive illusion that the means justify the ends because the ends are certified is replaced by a rebellion in which the end becomes the means. Since rebellion is an act of realized freedom itself, the very act of rebellion must be based on the respect for freedom. Rebellion therefore limits its excesses by restricting one's freedom in the face of the freedom of others. True rebellion "says yes and no simultaneously."[35] Mere affirmation or negation terminates in a continuum of quietism or murder. But when both are combined in rebellion, they moderate each other as well as rebellion itself. Moderation consists in a continued tension between affirmation and negation; moderation is in fact "nothing but pure tension. . . . But its smile shines brightly at the climax of interminable effort. . . . Moderation born of rebellion can only live by rebellion. It is a perpetual conflict, continually created and mastered by the intelligence. It does not triumph either in the impossible or the abyss."[36] As in Sorel, the rebellious movement is everything, the end is nothing. Revolution must not anticipate realizing itself in some future utopia "but in terms of the obscure existence that is already made manifest in the act of insurrection. This rule is neither formal nor subject to history, it is what can best be described by examining it in its pure state—in artistic creation." Thus to Ellul's "exist is to resist" Camus says "I rebel, therefore we exist."[37] Camus's paradoxical assertion that violence is never justified but is sometimes necessary is resolved by insisting that the rebel himself must be guided by a moral rule to balance the amorality of "history" which must consist partly in the realization that violence must be viewed as a moral and individual responsibility.

It is the idea of personal responsibility for one's acts that produces problems for Ellul's own view of rebellion. Camus's rebel can and does accept responsibility and punishment for deeds of terror, partly because he has made a distinction between rebellion and revolution that Ellul does not make. Since Ellul tends to collapse the distinction between coercion, violence, and power, the Christian must reject all violent activity except violence to himself, i.e., in a willingness to face martyrdom. But even here, Ellul wants to "force the gate." By explicitly recognizing the Camus-like link between victim and executioner, compulsion enters in. Martydom thus shows "how the victim can *compel* the executioner to become a man by recognizing his victim."[38] This Ellul calls the violence of love, a supreme spiritual violence that triumphs over the necessity of death.

Ellul disdains all other violence because it justifies itself on the basis of necessity or on the basis of pity. He criticizes "radical chic" Christians who reject martyrdom in favor of violence, "justifying their hatred of oppressors by their love for the oppressed."[39] Ellul's position is echoed by Hannah Arendt's own view of the role of pity in the French Revolution. It is pity, she argues, that "has proven to possess a greater capacity for cruelty than cruelty itself." Since pity constitutes a sort of passion for the oppressed, it shares a character of boundlessness in common with most passions. "Since the days of the French Revolution, it has been the boundlessness of their sentiments that made revolutionaries so curiously insensitive to reality in general and to the reality of persons in particular whom they felt no compunctions in sacrificing to their 'principles.'"[40] After hypocrisy had been unmasked and suffering exposed, it is rage, not virtue, that triumphs.

Such rage, in Ellul's eyes, is not dialogue and indeed prevents it. Arendt notes that the innocence of Herman Melville's hero Billy Budd "cannot be supported by the given word, which can be a lie. Billy Budd could have spoken with the tongues of angels and would not have been able to refute the accusations of the 'elemental evil' that confronted him; he could only raise his hand and strike the accuser dead."[41] Ellul adopts a similar perspective in rejecting both the pity and the principles of the *enragés*.

III

The self-evident need for speech raises the question as to the nature of the dialogue in situations that do not lead to martyrdom. What, in short, is the nature of Ellul's "true politics"? For Ellul, the state possesses neither the severity, virtue, nor integrity of Billy Budd's judge, Captain Vere. Its despotism is often in the guise of the syrupy humanitarianism that Sorel's syndicalists disdained.[42] Though he does not accept the Sorelian philosophy of violence, Ellul shares with Sorel the idea that an "absolutely negative position" is necessary in regard to the state in order to avoid the seductive blandishments of the political illusion. Ellul even alludes to nineteenth-century syndicalism as a prime example of the process of negation.[43] But this leads to the problem of how such an intransigent position can be reconciled with the kind of dialogue Ellul requires.

Hannah Arendt, who shares Ellul's concern about technological dominance (which for her takes the form of the domination of laboring man) and the loss of freedom in the modern state, also sees voluntary groups of a revolutionary nature as a realm of true politics and an alternative to sovereign rule. In *On Revolution*, she asserts that soldiers' and workers' councils—soviets in the original sense of the term—which have emerged in the course of nearly every modern revolution, reveal in this century the development of a new form of government, a new political realm, in which argumentative speech based on interest arose among men.

On the other hand, she notes that these movements soon gave way in every instance to the economic activity of "workers' management," which negated the very political activities that brought them into being in the first place. "The same men, entirely capable of acting in a political capacity, were bound to fail if entrusted with the management of a factory. . . . For the qualities of the statesman or the political man and the qualities of the manager or administrator are not only not the same, they very seldom are to be found in the same individual; the one is supposed to know how to deal with men in a field of human relations, whose principle is freedom, and the other must know how to manage things and people in a sphere of life whose principle is necessity."[44]

It is at this point that one might easily compare Arendt's portrayal of the failure of political man at the hands of *animal laborans* to Ellul's nearly fatalistic view of the omnicompetence of technique. Yet, precisely because Ellul extends technique into the political realm itself, he fails to make Arendt's distinction between political and managerial functions. In the course of his discussion of the nature of Christian political activity, Ellul attempts to combine Arendt's two distinct personality types into one. How, he asks, do we as Christians participate in political life when there is no scriptural support for it? How do we as Christians shatter "the solitude of power" in order "that political balance may be preserved?"[45]

Ellul conflates the two modes of activity, politics and administration, by giving one the character of the other. At first he appears to assign highly political and even diplomatic roles to Christians who have before them the task of "mediation and reconciliation." They must work as "intermediaries" in order to "lessen hostility" and "reduce class conflict," and act as "reconcilers" to "build a bridge between the different groups and opposing factions."[46] These conciliatory tasks seem well within the scope of traditional politics. As such, the Christian's role in politics is to soften doctrinal differences, and, as participants in all movements and parties, to "de-ideologize" politics. The attempt to reconcile hostilities is hardly exceptional in itself, since most skilled legislators are involved in these tasks, whether or not motivated by Christian principals. Yet Ellul appears to confuse "de-ideologization" with the reduction of politics to mere technique. Thus, astonishingly, he argues that "we have to work hard to get it admitted, by ourselves first of all, that politics is an honest concrete exercise in administration and management, but that it has no spiritual ideological or doctrinal content." De-mystifying matters in this way is synonymous with transforming politics into something which becomes "simply a matter of handling our common patrimony well, there is no need for passionate debate." Christians, he continues, must set an example. "They have to show that these *technical* (and not ideological) tasks must be taken seriously. . . ."[47] Unless I have misunderstood Ellul, it appears that among the tasks he assigns Christians is the duty of becoming committed technocrats, that is to say, using Ellul's definitions, committed participants in totalitarian domination. At any rate, it seems scarcely to resemble "involvement in anarchy." Even more curiously, however, Ellul juxtaposes these "technical" tasks with a stance that imitates the ideologues. He appears to jettison the conciliatory qualities in order to ask Christians to become "true ambassadors of the Wholly Other and not just participants in the power of the sovereign." Ellul asks the "ambassador" to become a militant because, as he puts it, "only militants can engage in dialogue." A dialogue with the sovereign can be initiated "only on the basis of the greatest possible intransigence, for power today is completely alien to any discussion . . . totally deaf to the individual."[48] But then what kind of dialogue is this? Indeed, the difference between the intransigent and the ardent technocrat managing the common patrimony can be seen as an internal dialogue between two halves of a personality. In such a case the dialectical relationship means that the

Christian plays the double role of conciliator and militant.

The double role is more reflective of the society in which Ellul lives than he may suspect. On the one hand, the Christian is asked to "work within the system," while on the other, he adopts an intransigence that more than a little resembles Sorelian anarcho-syndicalism or at the very least smacks of the tactics of the ideologues in French politics, which Ellul condemns. The general administration of things is set against a sort of Christian general-strike mentality, a trade unionism of the soul. As such, the Christian body appears more and more to resemble the division of the French polity between the *corps administratifs* and ideological parties.

IV

The question remains to what extent Ellul's solutions, though apparently contradictory at points, provide the only "realistic" response to the modern condition. As Sheldon Wolin has argued, we live in a society in which "office politics" within bureaucratic organization has replaced the old public realms: "we seem to be in an era where the individual increasingly seeks his political satisfactions outside the traditional area of politics. This points to the possibility that what is significant in our time is the diffusion of the political . . . the absorption of the political into nonpolitical institutions and activities."[49] By reducing the political association "to the level of other associations" (and vice versa), a process culminating in the "depreciation of the politicalness of the political order" has been achieved.

Ellul's thought seems both to understand and to reflect the ambiguous nature of modern organization. Not only does he ask us to work within the system and resist it at the same time, but he argues that the state is simultaneously omnipotent and merely supervisory; that in any case it is not political. In *The Technological Society*, he asserts that "there is no longer any question of a state in the classic sense. To think otherwise is a laughable error on the part of the majority who talk about the state. . . ." The state is "an amalgam of organizations with a greatly reduced organism for making decisions, reduced because, in the interplay of techniques, decision-making has less and less place. The situation is comparable to the elimination by an automatic machine of the individual, who retains no function except that of inspecting the machine and seeing that it remains in working order."[50] His view here is closer to a "withering away" of the state rather than its strengthening, which is implied in most of Ellul's other writings.

In any event the new organizational society is not rooted in a genuinely public space in which equals engage in speech and action, but in bureaucracy, the antithesis of politics. The blending of organizations based on necessity with a pseudo-politics places the locus of decision-making in a twilight realm which is neither truly public nor truly private and which Arendt calls "the social." The misunderstanding and confusion of political and social is, in her view, rooted in the confusion of "politics" and "rule" itself.[51] The victory of society over politics is the victory of Hobbes turned inside out. "A complete victory of society will always produce some sort of 'communistic fiction' whose outstanding political characteristic is that it is indeed ruled by an invisible hand, namely by nobody. What we traditionally call state and government gives place here to pure administration—a state of affairs which Marx rightly predicted as the 'withering away of the state,' though he was wrong in assuming that only a revolution could bring it about, and even more wrong when he believed that this complete victory of society would mean eventual emergence of the 'realm of freedom.' "[52]

In asking us to preserve the common patrimony, Ellul is not only recognizing, but to a certain extent accepting the "reality" of Arendt's socio-bureaucratic order and of the "rule by nobody," which is perhaps the most oppressive of all sovereignties.

In contradistinction to Wolin and Arendt, who insist that only a genuine politics gives us a realm of freedom, Ellul seems to suggest that accommodation can be made with a social realm in which some kind of politics can survive. An autonomy of sorts is seen as being present in society at large, a society that is neither simply bureaucratic nor ruled by government in a totalitarian manner but whose "sovereignty" is dispersed rather than concentrated. In fact, in his most recent work, after specifically identifying the sovereign with the state,[53] Ellul shifts his definition of sovereignty and asserts that "the people is now the true sovereign," and "it is to the sovereign that we must speak."[54] Furthermore he divides that sovereignty and says, "We cannot imagine reaching the people, since the people does not exist as an entity and in any case vast numbers of them are not interested. . . . Only groups specifically oriented to the various problems can speak."[55] Here Ellul's point of view seems to revert to a species of Madisonianism, that is, to the American group theory of politics. Such a theory is certainly a reasonable one, but it is neither "anarchistic" nor disdainful of the "errors" of Montesquieu.

It is an open question as to whether Ellul's extraordinary and exceptional lapse in terminology and acceptance of pluralism have any meaning for his generally stated view that the union of technique and political power is totalitarian. Sheldon Wolin argues that in the modern age, the political dimension of human activity has been revived mainly in the context of totalitarian regimes who have destroyed the autonomy of groups and replaced it with highly coordinated general policies. However, Langdon Winner, one of Wolin's students, has stated the problem somewhat differently. Winner assumes that even if and when intermediate groups are themselves victims of technique, and their existence is dominated by the same technological imperatives that dominate bureaucracy, the total convergence of techniques is not an inevitable consequence. In order to meet their own self-determined ends most efficiently, Winner suggests that the various subsystems of technocratic society resist full-scale integration with the state—or even with higher intermediate stages of integration.[56] Full-scale nationalization of agriculture, which has hardly shown itself to be a more efficient alternative to California agribusiness, for instance, provides an example of this sort of limit. Agribusiness may itself be highly centralized but since the autonomy of technique reshapes the ends of the technique itself, it is pure metaphysics to argue that such an end will inevitably culminate in nationalization or centralized control, even though Ellul has rather imprudently suggested such an inevitability.[57] As Winner notes, the very end a technique has set itself may serve as a resistance to the highest stage of integration: "The stage *immediately before total interconnection* poses a powerful barrier to this final step."[58] If this is so, then one would expect a *"dispersion of power"* into the functionally specific large-scale systems of the technological order."[59] Such a resistance is itself a "pole of tension" with the state, and the traditional political actor, serving as a sort of "broker" among the various subsystems, is not eliminated.[60]

Not only does the logic of Ellul's dialogue with the sovereign require some sort of pluralism—possibly on this line, possibly on more traditional lines—but his vision of the sovereign state is a gratuitous one. As noted at the outset, Ellul seems at odds with himself as to whether this vision is universal, or specific to his own traditions. I believe that the latter is the case; but this does not mean that the definition of power and authority cannot become self-fulfilling. As he states in the Preface to *The Political Illusion*, "I do not say that things are necessarily unfolding in other countries as they are here. But that face to face with the same necessities, the political powers run the risk of ending up traveling along the same road."[61] Nothing in our day appears to discourage this view, although the step to final integration, to the ultimate sovereign, may still require political interference rather than exclude it.

NOTES

1. *Political Illusion*, p. 11; French ed. 1965.
2. *Ibid.*, p. 222.
3. *Violence*, pp. 87–88; English ed. 1969.
4. Thomas Hobbes, *Leviathan*, ed. Michael Oakeshott (Oxford: Basil Blackwell, n.d.), chap. 46, p. 447.
5. *Politics and Vision* (Boston: Little Brown, 1960), p. 285.
6. Hannah Arendt, *On Violence* (New York: Harcourt, Brace and World, 1970), pp. 43–44, 56.
7. *Leviathan*, p. 448.
8. *Ibid.*, chap. 19, p. 121; cf. p. 447.
9. H. H. Gerth & C. Wright Mills (eds.), *From Max Weber: Essays in Sociology* (New York: Oxford University Press, 1958), p. 78.
10. Thus he argues that England, long thought to be a mixed government, was really an aristocracy. See *Democracy in America*, trans. Henry Reeve and ed. Frances Bowen and Phillips Bradley (New York: Vintage Books, 1957), vol. I, p. 270.
11. *Ethics of Freedom*, p. 393; French ed. 1970.

12. *Technological Society*, pp. 287–88; French ed. 1954. Cf. *Ethics of Freedom*, p. 397.
13. *Political Illusion*, p. 10. In *The Betrayal of the West* (French ed. 1975) Ellul does argue that "liberal" or "democratic" regimes (he puts the words in quotation marks) do not seek power at the expense of individuals and that "there are varied and divergent opinions in the liberal countries" of the West which express a concern for oppressed miniorities that is lacking elsewhere (pp. 99, 105, 121). But he adds, such regimes are "vanishing" and the world that produced them is "finished," betrayed as much as anything by the failure of the left to carry out its mission as the conscience of western civilization. The left has followed Christianity and liberalism in being corrupted, its inadequacies revealed by the challenge of power. "By bringing power to its highest degree of importance, efficacy and abstractness, the West thus created the means of its own negation and condemnation" (p. 131).
14 See *Leviathan*, chap. 20, pp. 130, 132, 133; *De Cive*, II, 16.
15. Oakeshott, Introduction to *Leviathan*, p. xxi.
16. *Communist Manifesto*, Sec. II (last two paragraphs).
17. "On Authority," in Marx and Engels, *Selected Works* (Moscow: Foreign Languages Publishing House, 1958), I, 636–37.Engels argues that the "social authority of the future would restrict authority solely to the limits within which the conditions of production render it inevitable. . . . The public functions will lose their political character and be transformed into the simple administrative functions of watching over the true interests of society." Cf. Ellul, *Technological Society*, p. 279.
18. Marcuse, *One-Dimensional Man* (Boston: Beacon, 1964), pp. 22, 84–85, 189.
19. *Ibid.*, p. 251 (emphasis added).
20. *Ethics of Freedom*, p. 396.
21. *Democracy in America*, II, 336.
22. *Political Illusion*, p. 209.
23. *Ethics of Freedom*, p. 396.
24. *Political Illusion*, p. 215.
25. *Ibid.*, p. 222.
26. *Ethics of Freedom*, p. 391.
27. *Ibid.*, p. 395.
28. *Political Illusion*, pp. 217, 222.
29. *Violence*, p. 132.
30. *Ibid.*, p. 91.
31. *Reflections on Violence*, trans. T. E. Hulme and J. Roth (London:

Collier-MacMillan, 1950), p. 171.
32. *Ethics of Freedom*, p. 387.
33. Albert Camus, *The Rebel*, trans. Anthony Bower (New York: Knopf, 1969), p. 298.
34. *Ibid.*, p. 246.
35. *Ibid.*, p. 251.
36. *Ibid.*, p. 301.
37. *Ibid.*, p. 250.
38. *Violence*, p. 167.
39. *Ethics of Freedom*, p. 393.
40. Hannah Arendt, *On Revolution* (New York: Viking, 1965), p. 85.
41. *Ibid.*, p. 82.
42. *Reflections on Violence*, chap. 2, Sec. II.
43. *Political Illusion*, pp. 217–18.
44. Arendt, *On Revolution*, p. 278.
45. *Ethics of Freedom*, p. 386.
46. *Ibid.*, pp. 379–82.
47. *Ibid.*, pp. 382–83 (emphasis added).
48. *Ibid.*, p. 397.
49. Sheldon Wolin, *Politics and Vision*, p. 353, chap. 10 *passim*.
50. *Technological Society*, p. 279.
51. Hannah Arendt, *The Human Condition* (New York: Doubleday Anchor, 1958), p. 27. She notes that "the profound misunderstanding expressed in the Latin translation of 'political' as 'social' is perhaps nowhere clearer than in a discussion in which Thomas Aquinas compares the nature of household rule with political rule: the head of household, he finds, has some similarity to the head of the kingdom, but, he adds, his power is not so 'perfect' as that of the king." Arendt argues that it is almost self-evident that the rule of the tyrant is less perfect than that of the *paterfamilias* because "absolute, uncontested rule and a political realm properly speaking were mutually exclusive" (Arendt, p. 27, citing *Summa Theologica*, ii, 2. 50. 3.).
52. *Ibid.*, p. 41.
53. *Ethics of Freedom*, p. 385.
54. *Ibid.*, pp. 388, 394.
55. *Ibid.*, p. 394.
56. Langdon Winner, *Autonomous Technology, Technics-out-of-Control as a Theme in Political Thought* (Cambridge: M.I.T. Press, 1977), p. 241.
57. *Technological Society*, p. 310: "Only through state collectives can technical progress be fully realized and technical means exploited

without fear of financial setbacks." This is a big step forward from the agricultural price supports that exist in most industrial countries.

58. Winner, *Autonomous Technology*, p. 255 (his emphasis).
59. *Ibid.*, p. 261 (his emphasis).
60. *Ibid.*, p. 262.
61. *Political Illusion*, p. xxi.

Chapter 5

Technology and Power: Technique as a Mode of Understanding Modernity

C. George Benello

The Technological Society is a powerful but also tenebrous work which, despite its great detail and scholarship, operates more in terms of auras and impressions than clearly defined ideas. It seeks to prove that technique has become a monster whose means now dominate ends, with man simply another mechanical part in the vast ensemble of techniques. Technique for Ellul is more than technology: it is the "organized ensemble of all individual techniques which have been used to secure any end whatsoever." The book proceeds to analyze this phenomenon in three areas: economic technique, political technique (technique of organization), and human technique (the manipulation of man through brainwashing, propaganda, advertising, and the like).

Characteristics of Technique

For Ellul, technique is characterized in a number of ways. First, it is *self-directing*, being guided by the single criterion of efficiency. Human choice has therefore little to do with technique, since technique prescribes always the one best or most efficient way in all things. Second, technique is *self-augmenting*, since its growth is automatic and irreversible, developing according to laws of geometric progression. The technical approach creates technical solutions. But these solutions in turn create even more problems which in turn demand ever more technical solutions. A situation of positive feedback or self-reinforcing cycles has been set up. Third, technique implies *monism*. One cannot, according to Ellul, disassociate the good uses of technique from the bad, the useful from the destructive. Once the technical orientation has been adopted, an automatic cycle begins which brings into existence all possible results of technique. There is no possibility of accepting some and rejecting others. Fourth, techniques in different fields of necessity become *linked together:* economic techniques require political techniques, which in turn require propaganda techniques, and so on. Finally, the commitment to technique implies *universalism* and *autonomy.* Technique has become a universal language, a universal determinant of human culture. And it has become autonomous, a closed system determining the conditions of social, political, and economic change, rather than being guided by imperatives developed independently of it. Admittedly, modern industrial societies manifest this most clearly, but it is evident that all other societies are also moving in this direction.

Technique in this view is clearly totalistic, but it is not the totalitarianism of terror. This totalitarianism resembles Huxley's *Brave New World* much more than Orwell's *1984*, since its ultimate technical accomplishment is to manipulate people into believing that they want to do what the state demands of them. For this, mind probes and propaganda are of more use than cattle probes and gas ovens. Ellul correctly sees that the domination of technique has little to do with different political ideologies. Both the Marxist and liberal-democratic versions of progress are equally uncritical of technique's domination, although at this point thinkers on both sides of the Iron Curtain are beginning to question the assumption that progress can be equated with technological advance, and some powerful countercurrents are beginning to emerge.

Ellul's analysis is valuable because it deals with the major feature of all contemporary industrial societies: the extent to which the instrumentalities have gotten out of hand, and have taken on the autonomy and self-directing character that Ellul emphasizes. This feature is reflected in the popular consciousness as a recognition of technology's dark side, represented by the myth of Frankenstein, the Sorcerer's Apprentice, and countless science-fiction stories. But in Ellul this sense of the runaway character of technique remains for the most part on the level of mythical description. It is only since *The Technological Society* was published that a body of literature has arisen which explicitly challenges, in the name of ecological thought and steady-state economics, the assumptions of unlimited technological advance.[1]

AUTONOMY OF TECHNIQUE

As an example of the autonomy of technique, Ellul cites the decision to develop the atomic bomb, which was dictated, he says, by the fact that atomic physics had reached a stage where such a possibility existed: once the possibility was there, the bomb had to be developed; and once it had been developed, as historians have pointed out, it had to be used. Although such an analysis leaves out some important elements, the important thing here is the dialectic of development, which moves from technical possibility, to research and construction, then to actual use as a weapon of war. This dialectic becomes a necessary one since it follows an internal logic, free from the element of human choice. As Ellul points out, to argue for selectivity in this process is to argue against obvious trends.

This autonomous movement occurs for several reasons. First, as given technologies are developed, they create problems which require more technology for their solution. Second, certain technologies, when completed, require for their efficient utilization other technologies. The technique of mass production requires the development of an efficient technology of transportation, and this in turn requires a technology of efficient communication. Finally, as with the atomic bomb, when such a vast technological apparatus has been assembled, with its training schools and engineers, physicists, and technicians, it is inevitable that this vast commitment of human resources will result in the maximum utilization of what is produced, and will, moreover, continue on, of its own accord, to produce bigger and better atomic bombs. Thus the weapons establishment becomes on its own a major factor in the shaping of armaments policy, just as the automotive-industrial complex (the automobile manufacturers, the oil companies, and the highway-construction companies) dictates transportation policy.

What is involved for the individual is a type of training which results in "tunnel vision," a narrow focus on instrumentalities with little or no attention paid to ends or long-term consequences. However, here we begin to perceive the limitations of Ellul's analysis: nowhere in his treatment do the human dimensions of technique really appear. Ellul's description of how technique historically came to dominate human society is extensive and revealing, but it fails to deal with the existential and intellectual reasons *why* technique has overwhelmed the human imagination. There is no treatment of the intellectual histories of pragmatism and Marxism, philosophies associated with the two nations most committed to the domination of the technical. Yet both these philosophies have their roots deep in the western intellectual tradition that derived from the Enlightenment. The critique of this tradition has been a major preoccupation of the Frankfurt School—Horkheimer, Adorno, Marcuse, and Habermas, among others—and this has led in turn to a sizeable literature which seeks to critique that instrumental reason which stands in opposition to substantive rationality.[2] An important element in this analysis, and one not found in Ellul, is the recognition that an obsessive preoccupation with instrumental reason leads to contradictions because it represses fundamental elements in human nature.[3]

Perhaps an even more important failure of Ellul's analysis is that by exclusively focusing on technique's autonomy, he does not understand this failure as a psycho-social phenomenon, one vitally linked to powerful human motivations. The very term "technique" connotes a disassociation from the human subject. In that sense, technique is distinguished from the term "instrumental reason," since the latter implies a type of rationality inhering in human beings. Instrumental reason allows for a dynamic operating on its own power, subjecting human beings to the demands of a system which has become autonomous. But, to pose the question dialectically: How can human beings become the agents for a social and technical system which then overwhelms its creators and subjects them to its own imperatives, so that, in the end, no one is in control? Although Ellul's description of technique is avowedly dialectical, he never carries his dialectical analysis into this crucial area, hence his argument floats in an existential vacuum, open to the criticism (which he disavows) that it is both deterministic and pessimistic. This weakness is not, however, one of attitude—and this is the level on which criticism of Ellul is most often made—but rather is a failure to provide a complete analysis.

Although Ellul develops his conception of technique dialectically, perceiving how a single element of social reality can grow to dominate the whole, his model of society is polarized and non-dialectical. Thus he is unable to relate the dynamics of technique to its roots in individual behavior or to the internal dynamics of the human psyche. But sociology and social theory have been plagued since their beginnings in Auguste Comte by a dualism which splits subjectivity from objectivity, and the realm of individual behavior from that of social events. Even dialectical thought itself, in some of its major manifestations, has emphasized the domination of the whole over its parts, while failing to recognize the way in which parts act back to reinforce the whole.[4] But when this happens, the determinism of matter is replaced by a determinism of idea, and in both cases the vital element of human freedom is submerged within overall necessity, whether described in Hegelian or Marxist terms.[5]

Ellul defends himself against the accusation that he is deterministic, and hence a pessimist. He sees himself, he says, as a realist, rigorously committed to analyzing the situation as it is. As described in more detail in chapter 8 herein, realism for Ellul is a necessary stage preliminary to making prescriptions for any sort of change. He claims that to accuse him of pessimism is in fact to operate from concealed metaphysical assumptions. However, when he states that his own method of description is based on a sociological assumption, unfortunately his own metaphysics creeps in. As he puts it: "To me the sociological does not consist of the addition and combination of individual actions. I believe that there is a collective sociological reality, which is independent of the individual. As I see it, individual decisions are always made within the framework of this sociological reality, itself preexistent, and more or less determinative."[6] Ellul, in his treatment of technique, dichotomizes collective sociological reality and individual reality. It is one thing to accept the existence of a collective reality; it is quite another to see this as "independent of the individual." But this "sociologism" is characteristic of present social theory. However, does not properly constituted dialectical sociology see individuals interacting with the institutions which they create, influenced by them but also able to act upon and change them?[7] It is precisely the reification of social constructs, resulting in the false consciousness that perceives these constructs as outside human action and possessing a facticity similar to the constructs of nature, which leads to a sense of pessimism and powerlessness.

It is possible—and accurate—to view contemporary social reality as reified, a system of unresponsive institutions independent of the human will and hence dehumanizing. But the reification is only mystified if it is perceived as a product of laws entirely outside the scope of human intervention, or as the result of some metaphysical dichotomy between the *civitas dei* and the *civitas terrena* (St. Augustine's terms) which ordains that human institutions will inevitably be corrupt and that morality will always appertain only to the individual, never to collective action. Ellul seems to espouse such a view since he renounces the possibility of meaningful collective action, and suggests that only a revolution of the individual consciousness can combat the domination of technique. A more properly dialectical view would argue for a necessary relationship between the personal and the political. Recent dissent—the feminist movement, for example— has been very much concerned with dialectics of this sort, so that changes in personal consciousness and relationships would accompany transformations on a broader and more political scale.

Such a dialectical view would see the development of the atomic bomb as one wherein the imperatives of technique (the perspective of instrumental rationality) gave way at times to genuine debate. In examining the series of decisions involved in that development, we begin to grasp the underlying motive which coexists with and supports instrumental reason. The atomic bomb was conceived as a unique form of power for those who possessed it. It was made initially out of fear that the enemy would develop it first, which would have allowed atomic blackmail. Then, when it became apparent the United States was in the lead, the bomb was constructed to ensure that power accrued to this country. At the time the bomb was first successfully tested, a debate developed as to whether it should be dropped in the sea as a test demonstration or used directly on the Japanese. The official reason for the latter choice was to save American lives by shortening the war; but an underlying reason was that the United States wanted to finish the war before the Soviet Union entered, in order to maintain its hegemony in the Pacific. To understand atomic power as a product of pure technique is tempting. What is more efficient in a destructive sense than the atomic bomb? It can be argued that the technological possibility of developing the bomb led inevitably both to its building and use, but power-political explanations run counter to this. If the Soviet Union had clearly intended to stay out of the Pacific, would the United States still have used the bomb? The imperatives of technique seem to be balanced by power-political imperatives, even if one does not accept the official explanations. Underneath the rhetoric lie the real reasons for the development of the technology of destruction—the search for security, for power, and for political domination.

The "Power Urge" and Technique

In general, recourse to the logic of technical rationality is used both as a refuge and as a justification for power-political activities. This holds not only for war and foreign policy, but also in the fields of business, science and technology, and bureaucratic administration. Although the resort to instrumental reason in these basic areas of human activity is the product of the urge to dominate, there remains the paradox that the net extension of human power over nature by using instrumental reason has left individuals powerless in important ways, and has locked societies into crippling systems where the domination of instrumental reason has resulted in an overall irrationality. This paradox of power leading to powerlessness can be understood both as a psycho-social phenomenon and as an organizational-ecological one.[8] We shall deal first with the manifestations of the power urge in its relation to instrumental rationality—and hence to technique—and then indicate how this leads to powerlessness.

Any history of the development of western science and technology is fatally skewed without the recognition that the urge to dominate nature forms the basis of the epistemological quest. Bacon's dictum "Knowledge is power" was the rationale for the desire to understand nature not in an empathic sense, but to control it. In the process, nature was desacralized and stripped of its full reality in order that it could be quantified—a process integrally linked with the development of what Ellul calls technique. What resulted was an abstract system of laws, following the Newtonian model, which did not seek to reveal essences of nature, but abstracted those aspects of natural processes which allowed man to make use of them. Organism and entelechy were rejected in favor of mechanism and reductionism. In the process an epistemology was developed which rejected essences in favor of operationalism. Knowledge became defined in terms of the operations that could lead to accurate measurements of behavior.

This same phenomenon took place in the social sciences as well as in the physical sciences, and the result was the disintegration of a philosophical anthropology (a theory of man as such) in favor of a number of truncated subdisciplines which renounced any pretensions to holistic understanding of the human condition. Social science confined itself to "problems" which were "scientific" in the same reductionist and mechanistic sense as did the physical sciences.[9] Indeed, the physical sciences have continued to be the model for the social sciences, with the positivist ideal that once enough is known, human behavior can be predicted completely. The science of man has been replaced by a science of manipulation, posited on a biologistic and ultimately mechanistic view of human nature.

There have been reactions against such mechanism and reductionism. Systems theory has moved at least a few steps away from mechanism, while humanistic psychology and sociology have tried to develop a more integral view of human nature. Phenomenological sociology has sought to recombine subjectivity and objectivity, closing the gap between individual and collective action which Ellul assumes to be unbridgeable. But the physical and social sciences do not exist as pure disciplines. Instead they are subordinated to the demands of the techno-industrial system, which rewards knowledge that will increase the opportunities for domination and thus reinforces the mechanistic assumptions on which this view is based.

Along with the discovery of techniques for the manipulation of nature, organizational systems for the manipulation of man have developed apace. A large and important field for sociological study is bureaucratic administration. Two approaches to the subject exist—the mainstream one which sees bureaucracy as the epitome of efficient rationalized administration, and a dissenting approach which perceives bureaucracy as a system dedicated not to efficiency as such, but to efficient control. This countertrend is slowly beginning to develop a body of empirical evidence which indicates that hierarchic bureaucratic systems are far from what we normally perceive as paradigms of efficiency, and that their real purpose is maintaining authoritarian control.[10] Even Max Weber, the sociologist of bureaucracy par excellence, understood that bureaucratic administration was not ultimately a neutral and purely rational means of management, but a system which rationalizes domination. In his own words: "Every administration requires some kind of domination, since, for its direction, some commanding powers must always be placed in someone's hands."[11] And further, "Bureaucratic domination thus inevitably has at its apex an element that is at least not purely bureaucratic."[12]

In the writings of the Frankfurt School—particularly those of Adorno, Horkheimer, and Marcuse—we find the further recognition that just as instrumental reason really serves the domination of man over nature and of man over man, so does appealing to instrumental reason conceal the real nature of this domination. In the words of Herbert Marcuse:

> Domination is transformed into administration. . . . Within the vast hierarchy of executive and managerial boards extending far beyond the individual establishment into the scientific laboratory and research institute, the national government and national purpose, the tangible evidence of exploitation disappears behind a facade of objective rationality. Hatred and frustration are deprived of their specific target, and the technological veil conceals the reproduction of inequality and enslavement.[13]

Because bureaucratic authority is rule-bound and ostensibly rational, it is not perceived as an arbitrary exercise of power, nor is responsibility for decisions easy to locate within it; it seems indeed possessed of a logic quite apart from its human actors. The genius of bureaucratic organization lies precisely in its capacity to conceal the exercise of power through its appeal to imperatives of rationality and efficiency, even though in its structure and overall goals it may well be both irrational and inefficient.

In the last decade a literature has developed centering on a critique of Taylorism which unmasks bureaucracy's claim to efficiency and shows instead that the technology of production has not evolved according to criteria of efficiency, but as a result of interest in perpetuating a managerial class, maintaining control over the workforce, and reducing skill levels so that minimal wages could be paid.[14] The objective of Taylorism was to separate intellectual work from manual work so that by a monopoly on technical expertise, which remained in the hands of the managers, workers could become maximally replaceable, and control would remain in the hands of the managers. Hence jobs were subdivided and simplified so that they could be performed mechanically and with as little skill as possible. The type of work that resulted was highly routinized and boring, and made machine tenders out of workers.

It is understandable that given this steady trend away from craft skills to mechanized labor, workers would have little interest in their jobs and little sense of responsibility. This then served to perpetuate the myth that workers were naturally irresponsible and should be treated like children. However, Taylorism went further than simply characterizing the organization of work. This explanation focused on the nature of production machinery, creating assembly lines, machines which required a minimum of skill, and a productive process in which each worker had only the smallest possible part. Thus it was possible to make the system appear as if it were the result of technological imperatives alone. As a result, the specialization and mechanization of work have become so embedded in the technology of production that it becomes difficult to visualize what a production system would look like which had as its objective the humanization of work and the development of responsible worker control. One finds in our typical explanations of the technology of production the supreme manifestation of the myth that efficiency dictates organization and content of the production process.

Yet, in an overall sense the system lacks efficiency. In the first place, where efforts have been made to increase worker responsibility over the production process and to develop a system of worker participation in production decisions, productivity has improved. It is, in short, impossible to define efficiency in purely mechanical, that is, Tayloristic, terms, without taking into account the psychology and motivation of the worker. Second, where efforts in the above direction have been made, it has become evident that supervisory personnel can be greatly reduced as workers take on enhanced responsibility.[15] This is why participation schemes have often failed when instigated within conventional corporations. Where they have been successful, they have shown that supervisory personnel and lower-level management were unnecessary, thus arousing strong opposition from those whose jobs were threatened.[16]

Enough has been said to suggest that the development of instrumental reason resulting in the hegemony of technique did not take place without the underlying incentive of expanding human power, both over nature and over other men. The usage of this power has been concealed and legitimated by arguing that the resulting bureaucratic administration was necessary if the products of instrumental reason were to be enjoyed. And, despite Ellul's necessitarian emphasis, as Victor Ferkiss suggests, technique does not dictate the use to which it will be put: "The new powers that man possesses are capable of many uses. Some of these uses are contradictory: biological and medical research can be used to produce germ warfare or to cure disease. And some of them, in practice at least, are mutually exclusive: the resources devoted to the space race cannot be used to create a 'Great Society.'"[17] If technique is perceived as everywhere dominant, this is not because it possesses an autonomous force completely dissociated from human motivation and decision. Rather, technique is an instrumentality which has led to the aggrandizement of power and wealth, and hence has been at the service of interests—not simply the general interest, but equally, special interests as well.

Nevertheless, the power of Ellul's analysis derives in part from the recognition that even if technique has been a vehicle for the pyramiding of power, it has also come to dominate even the most powerful. Neither nations nor individuals are free from the domination of means which instrumental reason has produced. To understand this domination as a human process rather than as a product of an unrelated dynamic inhering in technique itself, it is necessary to understand the nature of the power urge, both as a psychological process and as a social dynamic. Otherwise it is easy to accept Ellul's description of sociological determinism, wherein the only possible opposition is that of the individual will, isolated and powerless to alter the course of events.

What is involved is a dynamic recognizable in a number of areas of human behavior. The "technological fix" is similar to drug addiction. The appeal of the new vistas that open through the use of instrumental reason initiate a craving for increasingly more power and control. But as this orientation comes to dominate human consciousness, other equally important aspects of human nature are suppressed and are lost from consciousness. The resulting perspective becomes one-sided and monolithic, losing a sense of the full scope of human possibilities. The sense of community, of aesthetic appreciation, of relatedness to larger realms of value are all subordinated and sacrificed to the single-minded and one-dimensional desire for power, seen as power over nature. This power orientation in turn comes to define social relationships and organization as well, so that power over nature inevitably leads to the urge for power over man.

As the environment is shaped by the imperatives of power, the suppression of the other elements in human nature leads to a sense of deprivation: community is lost and nature in its full dimension recedes. And depriving other elements of human experience reinforces the power urge, just as addiction, by destroying the other elements of human life, reinforces itself by creating an escape from what is lost. As Wellmer puts it, in speaking of the seminal work of the Frankfurt School, "The Dialectic of the Enlightenment":

> Horkheimer and Adorno (who knew their Freud) emphasized that "the power of control over non-human nature and over other men" was repeatedly paid for by the "denial of

nature in man." This very denial, the nucleus of all civilizing rationality, is the cancer-cell of a proliferating mythic irrationality; with the denial of nature in man, not only the goal of the external conquest of nature, but the goal of man's own individual life is distorted and rendered unintelligible.[18]

The phenomenology of domination is classically analyzed by Hegel, in his description of the relation of master and slave: the relationship enslaves the master as it does the slave.[19] Depth studies of the psychology of domination have shown that the power-oriented personality is characterized both by authoritarian submissiveness and by the urge to dominate. Such personalities find a natural home in hierarchic systems which serve those above them and dominate those below.[20] Thus the psychology of domination enslaves, creating people with a single urge, unable to choose freely from among the real alternatives. The objective is always to render secure and increase power, while the purpose to which this power is put becomes irrelevant. The means to power, and the successful serving of power, become all-important and glorified as the only end. This accords with the dominating tendency in instrumental reason. If power is the goal and techniques are in fact techniques of domination, then the exclusive focus on techniques of domination leads in turn to the domination by techniques.

Just as Ellul fails to understand that instrumental rationality in its various organizational and technological manifestations serves both to conceal as well as to express the power urge, so he fails to notice the contradictions that lie inherent in the uncontrolled commitment to instrumental reason in the interests of domination. It is unwise to predict, as some have, that these contradictions will of themselves lead to an optimistic resolution which will free man from his bondage to technique.[21] However, the present debate over energy—whether to adopt what the physicist Amory Lovins has called a "soft" energy technology rather than a "hard" one—indicates that a significant choice-point may be developing which could have significant implications for the whole power-technology complex.[22] Soft technology is based on renewable energy sources (photosynthesis, sun, wind, and tides) and hard technology, on nuclear fuels and coal. Soft technology is inherently decentralizing, founded on the belief that "small is beautiful," while hard technology requires centralized power networks and vast capital commitments. The choice between the two, in other words, does not have simply technological but also power-political implications. Yet neither course involves the rejection of technology as such and neither course is necessary or fated. It provides an example of an area where technique alone does not dictate, and where even power-political imperatives may have to give way to the realities of resource conservation and the limits of growth.

CONCLUSION

The validity of Ellul's analysis of technique lies in the fact that vast magnification of human power resulting from technological advance—in turn a product of the discovery of the power possibilities inherent in the use of instrumental reason—has created unparalleled opportunities for the exercise of the power urge. If instrumental reason is in control, it is because the opportunities it affords for mastery over nature lead naturally to a power orientation which is expressed through social domination as well. The one leads to the other, both psychologically and organizationally. The machine organization of production leads easily and naturally to the machine organization of human beings, and it is in this sense that a seeming inevitability is discerned. But a social system based on domination is neither natural nor efficient. It operates only at enormous social costs, underlying which are the equally significant psychological costs of people constrained to perform dehumanizing work or to experience economic and social dislocation.

We cannot accept Ellul's claim that technique is coterminous with efficiency except in the narrowest and most mechanistic sense. But the rejection of this claim allows us to grasp how instrumental rationality, rather than being the autonomous and self-directing force it seeks to be, is in fact fraught with contradictions and with the irrationality of seeking to impose an order upon human affairs that flies in the face of the natural expression of human purposes. To understand the contradictory and flawed nature of instrumental reason is to allow for an optimism which Ellul's monolithic view of technique excludes. It suggests that Ellul has too easily accepted the rhetoric of those who uphold the system of instrumental rationality—the technocrats and bureaucrats, the upholders of Taylorism, mechanized efficiency, and automatic progress—in a fashion that is detrimental to his own basically critical view of the hegemony of technique, as well as others like him who would like to see a broader humanism prevail over the tunnel vision of the technocrats.

NOTES

1. Important works in steady-state economics include William Ophuls, *Ecology and the Politics of Scarcity* (New York: W. H. Freeman, 1977), and *Managing the Commons*, ed. Garret Hardin and John Bader (New York: W. H. Freeman, 1977). A landmark in ecological thinking was the Club of Rome's report *The Limits to Growth*, ed. D. H. Meadows *et al.* (New York: New American Library, 1972). See also *A Blueprint for Survival*, ed. Edward Goldsmith, *et al.* (Boston: Houghton Mifflin, 1972).
2. For a clear introduction to the Frankfurt School, see the introductory essay in *Critical Sociology*, ed. Paul Connerton (New York: Penguin Books, 1976). See also Martin Jay, *The Dialectical Imagination* (New York: Heineman, 1973), and Albrecht Wellmer, *Critical Theory of Society* (New York: Seabury Press, 1971).
3. For an analysis of the contradictions arising between instrumental reason and substantive reason, see Max Horkheimer and T. W. Adorno, *Dialectic of Enlightenment* (New York: Seabury Press, 1974).
4. In addition to the works of the Frankfurt School, discussed in detail in the American journal *Telos*, the critique of Hegelian and Marxist dialectics is found in the work of Georges Gurvitch. See especially his *Dialectique et Sociologie* (Paris: Flammarion, 1962).
5. For a critique of historical determinism (and for a broader view of Marxism than is found in Ellul) see *Existentialism versus Marxism*, ed. George Novack (New York: Dell, 1966). The article in this volume by Leszek Kolakowski, "Responsibility and History," is directly relevant.
6. *Technological Society*, p. xxviii; French ed. 1954.
7. A major work which avoids "sociologism" and instead develops a dialectical theory of social construction is Peter Berger and Thomas Luckmann, *The Social Construction of Reality* (New York: Doubleday, 1966).

8. For an understanding of how power as an orientation leads to powerlessness, see Paul Goodman's "Getting into Power," in his *Seeds of Liberation* (New York: George Braziller, 1964). For insight into the organizational-ecological aspects of power and powerlessness, see Berger and Luckmann, *The Social Construction of Reality*, and Mancur Olson, *The Logic of Collective Action* (Cambridge: Harvard University Press, 1965).

9. For a significant but dissenting history of the development of science as the quest for power, see Theodore Roszak, *Where the Wasteland Ends* (New York: Doubleday Anchor, 1973), chaps. 5 and 6 esp. For an excellent history of the fragmentation of the social sciences after the original Enlightenment vision of a unified social science, see Ernest Becker, *The Structure of Evil* (New York: George Braziller, 1968).

10. For an introduction to the extensive literature on self-management, see *Self-Governing Socialism*, ed. Branko Horvat *et al.* (White Plains, N.Y.: International Arts and Sciences Press, 1975). See also Paul Blumberg, *Industrial Democracy: The Sociology of Participation* (New York: Shocken, 1973), chap. 5 esp.

11. Max Weber, *Theory of Economic and Social Organization* (New York: Oxford University Press, 1947), p. 607. Quoted in Herbert Marcuse, *Negations: Essays in Critical Theory* (Boston: Beacon, 1968), p. 220.

12. Weber, *Theory of Economic and Social Organization* p. 127, quoted in Marcuse, *Negations*, p. 221.

13. Herbert Marcuse, *One Dimensional Man* (Boston: Beacon, 1964), p. 32. Much of Marcuse's thought in this work derives from Horkheimer and Adorno, *Dialectic of Enlightenment*.

14. The major work in this literature is Harry Braverman, *Labor and Monopoly Capital* (New York: Monthly Review Press, 1975). But see also the writings of Andre Gorz in his *The Division of Labor* (Atlantic Highlands, N.J.: Humanities Press, 1976).

15. See James Gillespie, "Toward Freedom in Work," in *The Case for Participatory Democracy*, ed. C. G. Benello and D. Roussopoulos (New York: Viking, 1971), pp. 73–94, for an example of the cutting out of unnecessary levels of supervision.

16. Andrew Zimbalist, "The Limits of Work Humanization," *Review of Radical Political Economics*, 7 (Summer 1975), pp. 50–60. The *Review* has also periodically carried articles on the themes of Taylorism and managerialism dealt with by Braverman and Gorz (see n. 14 above).

17. Victor Ferkiss, *Technological Man* (New York: George Braziller, 1969), p. 35.
18. Weller, *Critical Theory of Society*, p. 131.
19. G. W. F. Hegel, *The Phenomenology of Mind* (London: Allen and Unwin, 1966), pp. 229–40.
20. T. W. Adorno *et al.*, *The Authoritarian Personality* (New York: W. W. Norton [1950], 1969). See also the subsequent literature by Christie, Jahoda, Rokeach, and Laswell.
21. Traces of this optimism are found in the thought of Marcuse. See his *Eros and Civilization* for a view of technological advance as essential to liberation. See also "The Triple Revolution: Cybernation-Weaponry-Human Rights," in Goodman, *Seeds of Liberation*.
22. See Allen Hammond, "The Hard and Soft Technology of Energy," *New York Times*, 28 Aug. 1977, Sect. 4, p. 5.

Chapter 6

Mass Communications and Propaganda in Technological Societies

Michael R. Real

With broad, well-placed strokes, Jacques Ellul has painted a striking picture of the power of modern communication systems, and on the same canvas, has sketched details of why the more usual approaches to media draw up short intellectually. That picture of media and technique warrants wider recognition. This chapter assesses Ellul's place in the study of mass communications and propaganda by locating his work within the context of media research and theory. It compares his judgments with those of academic communication generally, and seeks, from *Propaganda* and other essays, some permanent lessons for an overall comprehension of the media's role in contemporary technological societies.

Ellul's synthesis of the media-society nexus is a contribution that stands alongside those of pioneers in the field—Lasswell, Lazarsfeld, Berelson, and Merton. His analysis of communications patterns and effects parallels the findings of major experimental researchers in media—specialists such as Hovland, Klapper, Tannenbaum, and Katz. Ellul's comprehensive overview suggests the works of the great synthesizers of media —Schramm, Gerbner, Halloran, Comstock, McLuhan, and Williams. And his assessments of media evoke the harsh critiques of Orwell, Marcuse, Schiller, Hall, and others.

However, two factors have restricted Ellul's impact on the study of media. First, he refuses to treat communication forms as isolated phenomena. Instead, his concern is society and human life as a whole; for him the mass media combine with education, religion, law, politics, economics, and human relations in holding technological society together. In the preface to *Propaganda*, his most media-oriented book, Ellul cautions that he has deliberately excluded the mass media as a focus of analysis, along with four other subjects found in most propaganda studies.[1] A second factor limiting Ellul's impact on media research is his tendency, even when writing specifically of media, to assume a wide-ranging frame of reference which overflows disciplinary lines. As a generalist, he refuses to stay within the confines of the usual literature, authorities, topics, methods, and vocabulary that provide the standard definitions for a single field such as communication. Growing from his fundamental analysis of technique as the dominant—but ultimately lifeless—central characteristic of modern life, Ellul refuses the compartmentalization that distinguishes the parameters of media research or any other recognizable disciplinary area. As a result, surveys of media and culture acknowledge Ellul's position, but the standard media journals, textbooks, graduate programs, research projects, government policies, and public understanding provide little evidence of an explicit debt to his work.[2]

The following examination of the dominant traditions of media analysis and research, especially as these have developed among American social scientists, will reveal the specific reasons for Ellul's lack of recognition by communication specialists, and will indicate the gaps in our standard wisdom which Ellul's analysis helps to fill.

ELLUL ON THE PRESENT CHARACTER OF MEDIA AND PROPAGANDA

While an appreciation of Ellul's breadth and complexity requires returning to his original texts, his central theses on media and propaganda revolve around a few identifiable points:

a. One term, "technique," organizes all of Ellul's thought.[3] Thus, while Ellul focuses on the media, he simultaneously has a larger frame within which media can be evaluated.

b. "Propaganda" is Ellul's term for the dominance of technical means over the flow of information through society. Departing from the typical definition of propaganda as biased persuasion, Ellul redefines it as a universal condition which pervades all individual lives in industrially advanced societies, and which intensifies as societies become more totalitarian.

c. The preconditions for propaganda are industrial societies composed of isolated individuals torn loose from cohesive family, subsistence, and neighborhood groupings, and subjected to the uniformities of mass education, mass media, an average level of culture, and an average standard of living. The resulting society is simultaneously individual and mass, interconnected by propaganda.

d. The most easily recognized—but least important—expression of propaganda is the demagogue, the political leader vertically agitating downward to the masses with irrational appeals for change. In contrast, modern propaganda is sociological as well as political, and the bulk of current propaganda aims not at agitation for change but at the integration of individuals into the established order. Similarly, the horizontal flow of propaganda between individuals establishes group norms, peer pressure, and similar collective standards which can be far more persuasive than the vertical action of a leader down to the people. Moreover, irrational falsehoods characterize only simplistic forms of propaganda, while rational propaganda overwhelms individual and group life with true but selectively edited knowledge, information, statistics, figures, and facts. Rational, horizontal, integrative, sociological propaganda—categories not identified in classical and especially American classifications of propaganda—are in fact the hidden persuaders dominating contemporary life.

e. The three great propaganda blocs today are the Union of Soviet Socialist Republics, the People's Republic of China, and the United States of America, though no modern or modernizing society is without propaganda.

f. Propaganda systems are presently total in scope, (involving all varieties of mass and interpersonal media), continuing (leaving no gaps and having no end), organized (orchestrated to bring individuals under the physical influence of organizations), and aimed at orthopraxy (bringing conformity in action [*praxis*] not just ideas [*doxis*]).

g. Psychologically, propaganda has the effect of providing heroes for the impotent, friends for the alienated, and simplified attitudes for the uncertain. Propaganda's sociopolitical effects include a partitioning of groups from one another and the destruction of democratic self-determination.

Under these seven propositions Ellul thoroughly redefines propaganda and in the process provides a new intellectual framework for understanding media and related forces in our society. His theses are not without problems. A certain ambiguity allows the old term and its new definition to convey connotations which are intriguing but also confusing. Usually propaganda is morally suspect because it depicts evil intent and persuasive manipulation by others, with Hitler and Goebbels as the prototype propagandists. Ellul's redefinition eliminates this intentional manipulation as a necessary component of propaganda, but retains the negative moral connotation associated with the word. As a consequence, the reader tends to transfer his feelings of shock and moral outrage at Nazi atrocities to the normal conditions of industrial society everywhere. This is especially complicating in the English language, where the term "propaganda" has maintained a definition more narrow and negative than in many continental European languages and in many other parts of the world—most notably Marxist countries, where propaganda is taken as a genuinely positive term. In fact, there is virtually no plural English equivalent of the very title of Ellul's original French book *Propagandes*. These ambiguities may serve the purposes of the generalist favorable toward powerful literary connotations, but they foreshadow the problems encountered when Ellul's contribution is placed within the context of more specialized research on mass communications.

ELLUL AND STANDARD MEDIA RESEARCH AND THEORY

Ellul challenges the standard assumptions anchoring many empirical studies and journalistic theories of media. An academic field such as media analysis grows around a core of research questions and theoretical conclusions grounded in assumptions about science, society, reality, human nature, and epistemology. Despite scientific criteria of objectivity, on a deeper level such assumptions are historically and culturally relative, as Thomas

S. Kuhn, Alfred North Whitehead, Claude Lévi-Strauss, and others have explained in their quite different ways.[4] As a consequence, the ultimate validity and usefulness of any discipline depends on the epistemological-metaphysical accuracy and historical-cultural appropriateness of these choices as much as on any internal standards unique to the discipline or the methods of science. It is on this deeper level that Ellul challenges many specialists in media as well as those in law, politics, theology, and other disciplines.

The evolution of media understanding in the twentieth century illustrates Ellul's general thesis that technical means tend to obliterate all other considerations in the modern world. Between World War I and World War II, the study of mass media emerged as "a crossroads where many pass but few tarry," in the words of Wilbur Schramm. Since mid-century, communications has established itself as an identifiable field with its own range of journals, scholarly associations, vocabulary, sub-fields, accepted authorities, leading schools, and other accoutrements of academic respectability. As in countless other fields, the twin forces of specialization and empiricism spearheaded communication's movement toward academic acceptance and prestige. Specialization and empiricism are, of course, extensions of technique; as such, they suggest problems for Ellul even as they facilitate academic development.

For example, broad questions of media policy have been debated under the specialized heading "freedom of the press." The two dominant theories of the press, capitalist and communist, are currently debated within the daily press as well as among media theorists.[5] Both capitalist and communist proponents claim objectivity and freedom in their respective press systems.[6] Each side tends to ignore or define with bias the epistemological and semantic bases of the debate. Ellul rejects the questions asked and insists on a universal truth: "There is no such thing as purely objective information."[7] Instead of joining either side in the debate, Ellul collapses the two categories into the more fundamental point that media are less free and objective than power-serving—whether power is the concentrated political power maintained by media in the communist states, or the consolidated economic power of privately owned and multinational conglomerates in the capitalist system. Thus Ellul categorizes media policy questions not under the heading of narrow ideals such as "freedom of the press," but under the broad reality of power propaganda.

Ellul has similarly shifted the assumptions underlying the two main traditions (empirical and aesthetic) of mass communication research and theory.

Empirical /Administrative Research Traditions

No question has been more central to the history of mass communication research than "Do the media persuade?" Ellul disagrees with the most widely accepted generalizations by answering that media indeed persuade, in many ways and under a variety of conditions. Popular intuition and a great deal of *prima facie* evidence support his position but, as documented below, publicized research on media effects has tended in the opposite direction. This research has insisted that media are not omnipotent and that numerous conditions obstruct media persuasiveness. Behind these differing judgments lie substantial disagreements over methodology, principles, and political-economic arrangements. Ironically, as media research has become more specialized and empirical, general axioms about media effectiveness have become more confused. At base, the media industries sponsoring the research and publicizing its results have themselves played a role in obfuscating the issues.

Media-effects research and theory-building have evolved for more than a half-century but are relatively young as disciplined human endeavors. As recently as 1921 Walter Lippmann could write in his classic study *Public Opinion*: "No American student of government, no American sociologist, has ever written a book on news-gathering. There are occasional references to the press, and statements that it is not, or that it ought to be, free and truthful. But I can find almost nothing else."[8] However, due to controversies over propaganda in World War I and the rapid rise of radio, media-effects research developed quickly in the 1920s and after. Soon, the effectiveness of radio advertising, the pervasiveness of Hollywood movies, the saturation of daily newspapers and weekly magazines, and the masterful use of media by Roosevelt, Hitler, and other politicians gave birth to the common "hypodermic needle" belief in the direct effectiveness of media for injecting messages into the body politic. A simple stimulus-response theory from behavioral psychology reinforced such impressions. Orson Welles's broadcast, "Invasion from Mars," on October 30, 1938, illustrates the high-water mark in the sensation of media omnipotence. While Ellul reflects more accurately than other current analysts the partial truths of that era, his position betrays none of its simplistic psychological and sociological premises. Yet current critics regard Ellul's position—as well as the hypodermic-needle theory—as having been destroyed by subsequent media research.

Countering such direct-response theories, research in the 1940s by Paul Lazarsfeld, Bernard Berelson, Hazel Gaudet, Robert Merton, and others associated with Columbia University identified a "two-step flow" in media influence.[9] They argued that because the "less active" sectors of the populace sought out "opinion leaders" who consumed more media, this latter elite placed an interpersonal communications system as a buffer zone between media and public. While this research revived an interest in personal linkages related to media effect and abolished some simplistic one-step explanations of media persuasion, the emphasis on personal influence within this research tradition then or since has never disproven media effectiveness. Ellul emphasizes, in fact, the necessarily complementary role of macro-communications and interpersonal micro-communications through media in creating a cohesive, organized, propagandized society. His definition of propaganda transcends the individualistic definitions in this research orientation[10] by emphasizing the integration of social groups into a manipulative propaganda apparatus.

As sociological research clarified these complex communication linkages, psychological research in the 1940s and 1950s increasingly emphasized the importance of individual personality variables in the acceptance of messages. Similar to earlier work by Kurt Lewin, the Yale Program of Carl Hovland and Irving Janis found, in numerous laboratory experiments, that identical messages affect different receivers in different ways or affect the same receiver in different ways under varying conditions.[11] This individual "judgment" theory was paralleled by the "uses and gratifications" analysis that approached media effects not in terms of the messages transmitted but from the point of view of the receivers' motives.

An important aspect of all these functionalist theories, whether sociological or psychological, is the assumption of an *a priori* system or balanced state. This assumption became most explicit with Leon Festinger's dissonance theory, in which messages were implemented or avoided according to the equilibrium present in the cognitive-attitudinal state of the individual.[12] It is precisely this prior given—against which the new message is measured and may be said to lack effect if rejected—that itself may be the effect of other media messages, as Ellul constantly emphasizes in his large-scale sense of propaganda. In a review of attitudinal-effects research, Wilbur Schramm draws conclusions similar to Ellul's, noting the more profound quiet effects of media: "Because they accumulate and are in a constant process of being added to, clarified, revised, and confirmed, they do not invite the kind of short-term change studies that attitude researchers like to do."[13]

Research on content analysis, public-opinion polling, political campaigns, news gatekeepers, the agenda-setting power of media, and other areas of media organization is sometimes construed, like the above traditions, as evidence that mass communications do not persuade. However, each on closer analysis serves only to outline a more complex process of influence spreading from transmitters to mass media audiences.

Ellul's assertions here come into sharper focus in Appendix I of *Propaganda*, where he attacks the empirical-effects research tradition.[14] He states as its most serious fault: "They preserve the old notion that the effect of propaganda manifests itself in clear, conscious opinions and that the propagandee will respond in a specific way according to the propagandists' slogans."

On the conceptual level, Ellul warns first that "we cannot find a 'zeropoint' from which to begin," since propaganda is by nature continuing, reinforcing, cumulative, and pervasive. Second, the complexity of entire situations and the intensity of individual effects always complicate measurement: "Propaganda tends to affect people in depth, and not just with respect to certain circumscribed actions." Third, he objects that election campaigns

—where voter decisions can be studied by organizations such as the University of Michigan Survey Research Center—involve the least significant cases of propaganda: "The objective is insufficient, the methods are incomplete, the duration is brief, pre-propaganda is absent, and the campaign propagandist never has all the media at his disposal." Fourth, on the methodological level, he objects that "*laboratory experiments* mean nothing because they do not reproduce the true milieu of real propaganda or its methods." Fifth, Ellul insists that surveys cannot be used in totalitarian societies or with oppressed minorities because trust is lacking, and the battlefield-like intensity of real propaganda situations prevents accurate findings. Finally, he states that the mathematical method—universally used in surveys or experiments alleging to "measure" propaganda—is "not just debatable, but wrong." This method removes facts to be quantified from their essential contexts, reduces their complexities to a simple state, and considers external phenomena only. Even worse is the tendency to assume that whatever cannot be quantified does not exist and that quantifications produce truth itself.

Ellul further warns that applications of the so-called objective scientific method are seldom unbiased. He cites conflicting studies by American and Nazi researchers on the effectiveness of each side's propaganda. A more recent example of Ellul's point is the well-funded and much-publicized research on television's effect on children, which was sponsored by the United States Surgeon General and published in 1971. At major steps in the process—the selection of researchers, the editing of research reports, and the summarizing of findings through press releases—the vested interests of the television networks were influential in watering down potential results. Despite clear evidence in the research of a causal connection between television violence and violent behavior (for specific categories of youth, though not for all) the *New York Times* headlined their report "TV VIOLENCE HELD UNHARMFUL TO YOUTH."[15]

Ellul's critique is not itself without flaws. He perhaps overstates the case against effects research even though his exaggeration is more than offset by the lack of self-criticism within this research tradition itself. When Ellul explains why the intensity of opinions held "cannot be measured by opinion analysis," his opposition applies only to superficial one-shot surveys for in fact intensity can and has been measured.[16] His criticism of field surveys, laboratory experiments, and mathematical methods fails to acknowledge their immense usefulness in providing information for numerous purposes just short of ultimate holistic propaganda analysis proper. He mounts an ethnomethodological attack on standard social psychology, but outlines only the simplest alternative formulations and rules of evidence. His arguments against social scientism are largely pragmatic when the roots of its shallowness and bias are more philosophical, historical, and political[17]—roots which Ellul traces elsewhere and which could have been briefly restated here. Of course, ambiguities inevitably appear in any attempt to match propaganda effects in general with media effects as such.

Nevertheless, to summarize the conclusions of empirical research on the persuasive effects of media, some of the more skeptical researchers within the tradition support Ellul's general approach. Lazarsfeld and Merton assert that mass media—despite their limitations—can confer status, enforce social norms, channel or even monopolize attention, and act as social narcotics.[18] White, Breed, and others have established how the media act as gatekeepers of information and agenda-setters for public discussion.[19] *The Effects of Mass Communication* by Joseph Klapper is often cited as denying media effects. But even that minimal review acknowledges that mass communications are typically "a contributory agent, but not the sole cause, in a process of reinforcing the existing conditions." And, Klapper adds, "It must be remembered that though mass communication seems usually to be a *contributory* cause of effects, it is often a major or necessary cause and in some instances a sufficient cause."[20] A final challenge to those skeptical of media effectiveness is the fact that advertisers spend perhaps $20 billion each year to persuade the American public via media. In 1976 U.S. presidential candidates alone spent $113 million, with the bulk of that sum going to media. The Proctor and Gamble corporation spends more than $260 million each year on television advertising. While much advertising and campaign-effects research are not publicly available, it is inconceivable that such amounts are spent on only a "hope" of effectiveness with no solid empirical evidence as justification.

Aesthetic and Critical Media Analysis

A distinct tradition of media study has developed alongside empirical social science and is currently organized around the headings of mass culture and popular culture. This tradition has been less confined to the collection and processing of measurable effects data. Instead, its methods and concepts are drawn from the humanities and arts with strong infusions from broad-based social theories, historical analyses, and political and economic critiques. Ellul's work obviously borrows from and contributes to this tradition more directly than to the empirical tradition.

Lazarsfeld made a distinction in the early 1940s between *administrative* and *critical* communications research.[21] The administrative type accepts the frame of reference of media industries themselves and the support structure of advertisers, agencies, and government. Since World War II, economists, political scientists, and anthropologists, as well as sociologists and psychologists have been drawn into this administrative market research, which, as Dallas Smythe writes, "is typically designed to make the mass media function more efficiently toward their objectives as business enterprises."[22] In contrast, critical communications research, much less lucratively supported, seeks a basic understanding of the economic organization, cultural content, and political implications of mass-communications structure and policy. Where administrative research has been concerned with the bullet-like technical efficiency of message delivery from sender to audience, critical theory has emphasized the human ends and means of the entire communications process in its mythic configurations and its aesthetic and ideological implications. As James Carey observes, administrative research has been most practiced in North America, critical theory in Europe.[23] Here in this humanistic and normative critical tradition Ellul's work has major importance, but remains only partly formulated and recognized.

The forerunners of critical media theory were the early sociologists of mass society—Comte, Spencer, Tönnies, Durkheim, and, in their own distinct ways, Marx and Weber. The current applications of critical theory to media divide into at least two streams. The more cautious right current contains Charles Wright, Melvin DeFleur, Sandra Ball-Rokeach, Douglass Cater, and the multitude of anthologies and textbooks on mass media and society (excluding, of course, those exclusively administrative and/or empirical). Similarly, certain literary humanists evaluating popular culture—Gilbert Seldes, Russel Nye, John Cawelti, Horace Newcomb, Ray Browne—apply "critical" theory primarily in the sense of aesthetic criticism; McLuhan is the most provocative, but confused, in that stream. The less cautious left current in critical media theory contains socialists and Marxists like Leo Lowenthal, C. Wright Mills, James Halloran, Raymond Williams, Herbert Marcuse, Herbert Schiller, and Stanley Aronowitz. Western European critics well represent this critical current also.[24]

Where does Ellul line up in these trends? He clearly works in the critical rather than the administrative camp, but—restrained by his preferences for democracy, the individual, and Christianity—he refuses to embrace a fully Marxist or leftist position *in toto*.[25]

As summarized above, Ellul's positions on technique, propaganda, mass society, and totalitarianism are acceptable to most critical theorists. Many write, as Ellul does, of the detrimental effects of the greater concentration of ownership and control of the mass media. Ellul asserts, "A state monopoly, or a private monopoly, is equally effective." Data compiled in the 1970s by Raymond Nixon on reduced competition among American daily newspapers, by Allan Pearce on the economic domination of American television networks, by Nicholas Johnson and *The Atlantic* on baronies built from print and electronic media, by Anthony Sampson on multinational electronics monopolies—all these and more confirm Ellul's warning a decade earlier about the accelerating concentration of control which makes "the situation increasingly favorable to propaganda."[26]

Ellul also sides with the bulk of critical theory against bourgeois suppositions in asserting that mass education and the leadership of intellectuals do not prevent propaganda but in fact coincide with its spread. Americans have been commonly instructed since the 1930s that education and intellectual analysis detect propaganda and immunize the citizenry against it. Instead, Ellul sees education as a necessary precondition for propaganda and the intellectual as the most propagandized member of society because of his access to overwhelming amounts of information, his need to have an opinion on every subject, and the conviction "of his own superiority."[27]

Ellul and Marxist critics likewise agree that Americans who decry regimentation in Communist countries represent the new, standardized mass man. Ellul's critique of advertising, for example, describes the process as "involuntary psychological collectivization."[28] Advertising's focus on behavioral effects—buying the product whether one likes or even recognizes it consciously—illustrates Ellul's emphasis that propaganda aims at "orthopraxy" (uniformity in action) more than "orthodoxy" (uniformity in doctrinal attitudes and thought).

As Ellul describes propaganda and its effects, several updated examples come to mind. For example, Ellul anticipates the difference between the Richard Nixon on public media and on White House tapes: "He cannot escape the mass; but he can draw between himself and that mass an invisible curtain, a screen, on which the mass will see projected the mirage of some politics, while the real politics are being made behind it."[29] He anticipates the entire Watergate team when describing the alienated people one meets everywhere who "filled with the consciousness of Higher Interests they must serve unto death, are no longer capable of making the simplest moral or intellectual distinctions or of engaging in the most elementary reasoning."[30] In fact, the 1972 reelection campaign was classical Ellulian propaganda.[31] The United States is one of Ellul's favorite examples of socio-logical, integrational, horizontal, and rational propaganda. Throughout *Propaganda* the problems between France and Algeria foreshadow the American debacle in Vietnam, in which propaganda, both domestic and foreign, played such an important role.

In another area, Ellul agrees with Marxists that democracy has virtually disappeared in an age of mass propaganda; but he retains the ideal of democracy. *Propaganda* concludes with that dilemma: Democracy cannot survive without propaganda but the utilization of propaganda makes democracy "as totalitarian, authoritarian, and exclusive as dictatorship."[32] Propaganda, even if supporting democracy, makes the citizen a totalitarian man—draining him "of the style of democratic life, understanding of others, respect for minorities, re-examination of his own opinions, absence of dogmatism."[33]

On Third World issues in propaganda, Ellul seems to remain between camps. Against the "free flow of information" arguments by American industry and administrative researchers, Ellul's position maintains that the flow is of propaganda, and "the world of pictures from the technological apparatus overruns man."[34] He would seem to oppose Pool, Lerner, Pye, and others proposing foreign media for development, and to side with Schiller, Nordenstreng, and UNESCO declarations in noting the cultural dependency and imperialism inherent in the global electronic invasion by multinational conglomerates.[35] But, on the other side, Ellul would reject the solution proposed—aggressive maintenance by Third World countries of independent national cultural policies or national communications policies. That too would be propaganda and, therefore, to Ellul, would deny the principles of democracy and humanity.

It is here, on the questions of public policy for both domestic and international communications, that Ellul's analysis parts with the Marxists and becomes ultimately immobilizing. Ellul emphasizes that modern society must turn away from domination by technique and propaganda, but their power overwhelms any alternatives; in fact, utilizing technique and propaganda to improve society would be internally self-contradictory and its own negation. The Marxism of Lenin, Mao, and current theorists rejects Ellul's puritanism and insists that if propaganda and technique can improve the concrete conditions of human life (both material and mental), then it should be so used. In contrast to such realism, there is an irony in Ellul's own work: he enters persuasively into the mass media (primarily books and periodicals) disseminated in France and internationally in order to attack national and international mass persuasion.[36] Is there an absolute distinction between the small-scale intellectual essayist and large-scale monopolistic persuasion, a distinction ethically and programatically sufficient to make the former a worthy lifelong vocation and the latter an unqualified evil?

In a related matter, while critical theorists have no uniform position on the People's Republic of China, most would object to Ellul's unrelenting criticism of Mao's China vis-à-vis propaganda. He sometimes reads like Cold War rhetoric and he tends to use China only to illustrate his general theses—total propaganda, orchestrated persuasion, integrating mass media and face-to-face discussion, the religionizing of the political—without directly confronting all the realities of old and new China. Specifically, in arguing for other values, Ellul tends to slight and almost deny tangible material measures of the quality of life. For example, American congressional reports such as the Mansfield Report (hardly pro-Communist propaganda) document the tremendous improvements in nutrition, clothing, housing, employment, women's rights, respect for children, medical care, mental health, care for the aged, education, agriculture, and other areas of daily life that have occurred since the revolution and the revolutionary use of persuasion in China.[37] China is not a simple question, but it seems dangerous for outsiders to argue against important amelioration of pre-revolutionary misery, and ignore such evidence as the Mansfield Report on the grounds that the techniques of change are apparently collectivistic.

However, in spite of such specific reservations, Ellul has contributed substantially to critical theory. In the process, he has been reinforced by critical theorists of media in his evaluations of the limitations of empiricism, the reality of mass society, the dangerous concentration of control in media, the propagandistic potential of education and intellectual leadership, the nature of advertising, the decline of liberal democracy, and the international domination of the Third World by modern technology and propaganda.

Ellul sharply separates from the more Marxist critical theorists by rejecting any application of media propaganda for positive mobilization of the people and building a humane socialism, such as efforts in modern China. He slights positive potential in institutions, material life, or social structures, preferring instead to emphasize the individual, the internal, and traditional democracy. But, in general, Ellul has provided the most challenging overview of media persuasion in the modern world. Even though Ellul does not have the single overall answer to all our questions about media and society, he has generously contributed to solving the central need of mass communication research and theory identified by George Gerbner as a need for "historically inspired, empirically based, institutionally oriented, comparative and critical theories adequate to the study of the cultural role and public policy significance of the mass media."[38]

ELLUL'S CONTRIBUTION

> Day after day the wind blows away the pages of our calendars, our newspapers, and our political regimes, and we glide along the stream of time without any spiritual framework, without a memory, without a judgment, carried about by "all winds of doctrine" on the current of history, which is always slipping into a perpetual past. Now we ought to react vigorously against this slackness—this tendency to drift. If we are to live in this world we need to know it far more profoundly; we need to rediscover the meaning of events, and the spiritual framework which our contemporaries have lost.
>
> —Jacques Ellul[39]

As a social historian, a cultural critic, a generalist, a media analyst, and even a prophet, Ellul and his work must await the judgment of history as much as the evaluations of his contemporaries. Simply put, he has provided a holistic connection between the fragmented experiences of modern life, one which explains the dangers, causes, and antidotes to technical specialization and propagandized alienation. These issues are crucially important to mass communication theory and research.

Because techniques of research do not easily lend themselves to measuring the nature of large propaganda systems or evaluating profound but subtle effects of media, the analyst surrounded by empiricism and specialization is tempted to erase such questions from his own consciousness as well as from the research agenda. At the opposite extreme, the rigorous demands of observation and logic used to complement data and quantification cannot become excuses for merely vague or groundless generalizations. Ellul avoids both pitfalls; he exemplifies the serious intellectual directly investigating the most important questions and developing his answers through the best evidence available to both concerned citizens and specialized researchers.

Of course, Ellul's work is not immune to criticism, as I have indicated. His analysis of mass communication tends to be reductionist, tracing all issues to the fundamental problem of totalitarian domination through technique. Even as it maintains the priority of a fundamental question, this slights other issues. As a generalist, he sometimes lacks familiarity with specialized studies, opinions muscle aside evidence, and unfounded generalizations result about the role and effect of a particular individual medium or research method. Also, Ellul understandably hesitates to place his own positive positions self-critically alongside those he attacks, thus leaving himself open to objection as a veiled partisan apologist. Yet he remains above any total identification with a single school of thought or narrow commitment, an individualistic position difficult to evaluate but demanding respect.

One of Ellul's most valuable contributions as an intellectual is his willingness to take value stands and to justify them. Unwilling to hide behind the mask of pseudo-objectivity, he steps into the value vacuum of academic analysis with "must" and "should." Throughout *Propaganda* he insists on "the *possibility* of choice and differentiation, which is the fundamental characteristic of the individual in a democratic society."[40] He repeatedly argues for critical independent judgment, decrying our typical abasement of thinking to a "superfluous exercise" rendered useless because individual human action has become exclusively determined by techniques and sociological conditions.[41] In being prescriptive as well as descriptive, he reduces the gap between theory and action (a problem especially for critical media theory).[42] Even in his pessimism over the power of propaganda, Ellul insists there remain rocks to cling to amid the rapids: "Basically a high intelligence, a broad culture, a constant exercise of the critical faculties, and full and objective information are still the best weapons against propaganda."[43] He demands of those who would criticize society and who would direct human life, nothing less than a "reason for living adequate to sustain life and an answer really satisfying and clear."[44]

The ultimate difficulty in assessing Ellul's contribution to mass communication research and theory is the complex profundity of his own personal point of origination. Even those who do not share his theological vision and personal faith can nevertheless learn from his testaments and indictments. Seldom has the depth of the mystic been so profoundly united with the breadth of the scholar. Jacques Ellul is himself the fulfillment of the vocation of "awareness" to which he exhorts us all. Though this is only one of his many important canvases, his powerful brush strokes have created a picture of media and propaganda that clarifies and expands our vision of mass communications in specifics and in general.

NOTES

1. *Propaganda*, p. xiii; French ed. 1962.
2. As a partial exception to this, my own *Mass-Mediated Culture* (Englewood Cliffs, N.J.: Prentice-Hall, 1977) was profoundly influenced by Ellul, yet it clearly acknowledges that influence in only a few places.
3. See Clifford G. Christians, "Jacques Ellul's *La Technique* in a Communications Context." The previous chapter in the present volume by George Benello also shows technique's centrality.
4. Thomas S. Kuhn, *The Structure of Scientific Revolutions* (Chicago: University of Chicago Press, 1967); Alfred North Whitehead, *Science and the Modern World* (New York: New American Library, 1948); Claude Lévi-Strauss, *The Savage Mind* (Chicago: University of Chicago Press, 1966).
5. One may prefer other labels. These are used in the classic paradigm of Fred S. Siebert, Theodore Peterson, and Wilbur Schramm (along with their historical antecedents—libertarian and authoritarian), in *Four Theories of the Press* (Urbana: University of Illinois Press, 1956).
6. *Ibid.*, p. 105.
7. *Technological Society*, p. 364; French ed. 1954.
8. Walter Lippmann, *Public Opinion* (New York: Free Press, 1922), p. 203.
9. See Elihu Katz and Paul F. Lazarsfeld, *Personal Influence* (New York: Free Press, 1964), for bibliography.
10. Especially those definitions of Lerner, Doob, and Lasswell. See Ellul, *Propaganda*, esp. pp. 1–87.
11. Carl Hovland and Irving L. Janis, *Personality and Persuasibility* (New Haven, Conn.: Yale University Press, 1959).
12. See, e.g., Leon Festinger, "Behavioral Support for Opinion Change," *Public Opinion Quarterly*, 28 (Fall 1964), 404.

13. Wilbur Schramm, *Men, Messages, and Media* (New York: Harper and Row, 1973), p. 233.
14. *Propaganda*, Appendix I, esp. pp. 259–77. Ellul expands and updates his criticism of empiricist research in "Problems of Sociological Method," *Social Research*, 43 (Spring 1976), 10–11.
15. Douglass Cater and Stephen Strickland, *TV Violence and the Child: The Evolution and Fate of the Surgeon General's Report* (New York: Russell Sage Foundation, 1975); Robert Cirino, *Power to Persuade: Mass Media and the News* (New York: Bantam Books, 1974), p. 21.
16. Robert E. Lane and David O. Sears, *Public Opinion* (Englewood Cliffs, N.J.: Prentice-Hall, 1964), chap. 9.
17. Jay W. Jensen, "Perspectives in Communication Research: A Critique," paper delivered to the Association for Education in Journalism, Pennsylvania State University, 31 Aug. 1960.
18. Paul F. Lazarsfeld and Robert K. Merton, "Mass Communication, Popular Taste, and Organized Social Action," in *The Process and Effects of Mass Communication*, ed. W. Schramm and D. F. Roberts (Urbana: University of Illinois Press, 1971).
19. David Manning White, "The Gatekeeper: A Case Study in the Selection of News," *Journalism Quarterly*, 27 (Fall 1950), 383–90.
20. Joseph T. Klapper, *The Effects of Mass Communication* (New York: Free Press, 1960), p. 8.
21. Paul F. Lazarsfeld, "Remarks on Administrative and Critical Communications Research," *Studies in Philosophy and Social Science*, vol. 9, no. 1 (1941), 2–16.
22. Dallas W. Smythe, Preface, in Herbert I. Schiller, *Mass Communications and American Empire* (Boston: Beacon, 1971).
23. James W. Carey, "Communication and Culture," *Communication Research*, 2 (Apr. 1975), 2.
24. For example, Hans Magnus Enzenberger, Kaarle Nordenstreng, and Stuart Hall. Donald Lazere's "Mass Culture, Political Consciousness, and English Studies," *College English*, 38 (Apr. 1977), 751–67, provides an excellent summary of the positions of Marxist and critical theorists.
25. The Ellul-Marxist relationship is developed along these lines in greater detail by David Menninger in chap. 1 herein.
26. *Propaganda*, pp. 102–3.
27. *Ibid.*, p. 111.
28. *Technological Society*, p. 407.
29. *Propaganda*, p. 122.
30. *Ibid.*, p. 174.

31. Real, *Mass-Mediated Culture*, "CRP Media Campaigning: All the President's Ad Men," chap. 5.
32. *Propaganda*, p. 249.
33. *Ibid.*, p. 256. Clifford Christians has forcefully detailed this conflict in "Jacques Ellul and Democracy's 'Vital Information' Premise," *Journalism Monographs*, Aug. 1976.
34. *New Demons*, p. 207; French ed. 1973.
35. See, e.g., Herbert I. Schiller, "The Appearance of National Communications Policies," *Gazette*, 21 (1975), 2.
36. Similar to McLuhan's writing books about the death of book culture.
37. Senator Michael Mansfield, "China: A Quarter Century After the Founding of the People's Republic," A Report to the Committee on Foreign Relations of the United States Senate (Jan. 1975).
38. George Gerbner, "Mass Media and Human Communication Theory," in *Sociology of Mass Communication*, ed. Dennis McQuail (Baltimore: Penguin Books, 1972).
39. *Presence of the Kingdom*, p. 138.
40. *Propaganda*, p. 255.
41. *Ibid.*, pp. 170, 179.
42. For details on Ellul's way of integrating theory and action see the second half of chap. 1 herein.
43. *Propaganda*, p. 111.
44. *New Demons*, p. 108.

CHAPTER 7

The Politics of Man, the Politics of God, and the Politics of Freedom

Jay M. Van Hook

Jacques Ellul has referred to the whole of his work as "a composition in counterpoint" in which sociological investigation is confronted with biblical and theological interpretation.[1] In both his sociological and theological studies, politics is a central and recurrent topic. As a sociologist, he analyzes the subjugation of politics to technique and, concurrently, the politicization of every sphere of modern life. As a theologian, he focuses upon the sacralization of politics and the state in the modern world, the politicization of the church, and the issue of Christian political responsibility. In what follows I shall explore Ellul's conception of the relationship between politics and technique, then examine his political theology, and finally, consider his views concerning responsible political involvement.

TECHNIQUE AND POLITICAL ILLUSIONS

Ellul sees modern society as characterized increasingly by "technique," which he defines as "the totality of methods rationally arrived at and having absolute efficiency in every field of human activity."[2] Technique, in this view, is not simply technology; it is the mind-set of an age wholly preoccupied with means and efficiency. We are beyond the point, he thinks, where the end justifies the means; in a technical society "the means justifies itself."[3]

Technique is neither neutral nor subject to the control of man; it is, rather, a self-propelled, amoral force spinning a completely deterministic web: "Technique never observes the distinction between moral and immoral use. It tends, on the contrary, to create a completely independent technical morality. . . . Not even the moral conversion of the technicians would make a difference. At best, they would cease to be good technicians."[4]

As Robert Nisbet has noted, however, it is not just technique in general, but *"political* technique with which Ellul is most concerned."[5] For Ellul, the modern conjunction of technique with the state creates the totalitarian society—totalitarian in that it attempts to absorb the citizen's life completely. This is not to say that Ellul believes that modern society is headed toward an Orwellian nightmare. Nor does he think that the atrocities of Hitler are necessarily characteristic of totalitarianism. The technical society he envisages

> will not be a universal concentration camp, for it will be guilty of no atrocity. It will not seem insane, for everything will be ordered, and the stains of human passion will be lost amid the chromium gleam. We shall have nothing to lose, and nothing to win. Our deepest instincts and our most secret passions will be analyzed, published, and exploited. We shall be rewarded with everything our hearts ever desired. And the supreme luxury of the society of technical necessity will be to grant the bonus of useless revolt and of an acquiescent smile.[6]

The convergence of the state and technique furnishes the context in which Ellul discusses what he calls the "political illusion." This illusion is occasioned by two factors: first, the domination of the state and the political process by technique; and second, the politicization of all areas of life.

Technique has changed the character of the state and with it the nature of politics itself. The modern state is no longer primarily a political organism, but is "an organization of increasing complexity which puts to work the sum of the techniques of the modern world. Theoretically, our politicians are at the center of the machinery, but actually they are being progressively eliminated by it."[7] Politicians depend upon bureaucrats—the technicians of government—to give them their information in manageable doses and to guide them toward the most efficient possibilities. Confronted with what is technically the best, the politician is left without significant choice. He would be unreasonable not to choose "the technician's solution, which is the only reasonable one."[8] His power of genuine decision-making is thereby weakened and confined mainly to the ephemeral area of current events. Thus, while bureaucratic administrators remain subordinate to the political leaders in principle, "in reality, the state is gradually being absorbed by the administration"[9] and is becoming "an enormous machinery of bureaus."[10]

One effect of technique's domination of politics is the obliteration of concerns with theory and principle.[11] The differences among modern technical states are becoming less significant in spite of variations in their ideological rhetoric. Ellul thinks that the United States is now more similar to the Soviet Union than to the United States of half a century ago. While the rhetoric of capitalism and communism differ, both states are fundamentally governed by technique. The political parties of democratic nations also evidence the eclipse of principle. The government's basic programs remain the same regardless of which party is in power. The bureaucracy continues to expand, government spending increases, and power becomes more centralized.

But the subordination of politics to the technical machinery of government is only one aspect of the political illusion. Another is that at the very time when genuine political activity is being reduced to little more than spectacle, all facets of life are being politicized. Personal, social, and moral problems have all been brought within the sphere of politics. We tend to think that "all problems are political, and solvable only along political lines."[12] We expect the political process, and finally, the state, to guarantee truth, justice, and freedom. The state is obligated to secure physical and mental health, and to provide for the security and happiness of all its citizens from infancy until death.

Ellul has two fundamental objections to the politicization of the whole of life. The first is that while politics can handle administrative problems, it cannot and should not concern itself with "man's personal problems, such as good and evil, or the meaning of life, or the responsibilities of freedom."[13] The transformation of private concerns and responsibilities into political matters enables the individual to evade his own duties. Further, Ellul does not think that "justice can be attained by a political organization of any kind."[14]

Ellul's second objection to wholesale politicization is that it requires the extension and centralization of the state's powers and contributes, thereby, to the development of totalitarianism. Ellul's concern here is based not so much upon some political ideology of his own as upon his realization that man's freedom and humanity are jeopardized by the expectation that government should provide for all material and spiritual needs. His political realism wants to warn us against self-deception. We cannot have it both ways. It is unreasonable to demand that government be responsible for everything and at the same time expect the state to decentralize, reduce bureaucracy, and decrease its spending.[15]

There is more, however, to the political illusion. Citizens accept the state's assumption of increased power largely because they think they can influence the state by means of their own participation in the political process. They believe that political activity can prevent the state from becoming a mechanism divorced from the will of the people and hostile to humanity. Political involvement is thus regarded as intrinsically virtuous. Ellul says, however, that "it is precisely here that the political illusion resides—to believe that the citizen, through political channels, can master or control or change this state."[16]

The state benefits from this illusion and nourishes it through propaganda. The widespread conviction that states govern by the consent of the governed requires the government to take public opinion seriously. But no state can base its actions on public opinion because that opinion is too varied and changes too rapidly. Hence the government itself must shape public opinion. As Ellul puts it: "One must convince this present, ponderous, impassioned mass that the government's decisions are legitimate and good and that its foreign policy is correct. The democratic state, precisely because it believes in the expression of public opinion and does not gag it, must channel and shape that opinion if it wants to be realistic and not follow an ideological dream."[17] The public must not only *accept* what the government does; it must *will* government's actions as its own. "The point is to make the masses demand of the government what the government has already decided to do."[18]

Thus, the citizen's political participation is largely illusory and passive. The information he receives is carefully managed for his consumption and designed to evoke from him the appropriate responses. Television coverage of political affairs, for instance, enhances the illusion because it gives the citizen the feeling of being in the center of action and in direct personal contact with the state's power. He fails to realize that televised politics is a staged spectacle and that the real structure of power remains hidden from him.

"Tensions" as a Solution

Ellul's analysis of technique and its implications for society and politics has led him to be regarded rather widely as a pessimist. Victor Ferkiss, for example, sees in him "a despair so profound as to render resistance hopeless."[19] This is an understandable, if superficial, reaction; Ellul often does write in a pessimistic vein. But he intends to challenge people to action rather than to encourage a fatalistic resignation. The following comment shows this clearly: ". . . as long as men believe that things will resolve themselves, they will do nothing on their own. But when the situation appears to be absolutely deadlocked and tragic, then men will try and do something. . . . Thus it is that I have written to describe things as they are and as they will continue to develop as long as man does nothing, as long as he does not intervene. . . . Consequently, it's kind of a challenge that I pose to men. It's not a question of metaphysical fatalism."[20]

What then should man do to escape from the clutches of the technical state? Ellul insists, first of all, that withdrawal from political concerns into those of private life can be no solution. One does not escape politics by becoming apolitical: "To become apolitical is to make a political choice, and as a result apoliticism hides some very definite political choices."[21] If a solution exists, it must lie instead in placing some control upon the state's totalitarian tendencies; and it is a mistake, he thinks, to believe that such control can be found within the state itself. On the contrary, "the state will retreat only when it meets an insurmountable obstacle."[22]

Ellul's solution requires groups of "citizens organized independently of the state" and possessing a "truly democratic attitude in order to depolitize and repolitize."[23] The purpose of these groups is to introduce "tensions" into society by declaring their independence and demonstrating that there are areas of life which cannot be absorbed into the state. These tensions are not intended to destroy the state; they aim instead to create a political life free of illusion. He sums up his proposal:

> . . . it is important above all never to permit oneself to ask the state to help us. This means that we must try to create positions in which we reject and struggle with the state, *not* in order to modify some element of the regime or force it to make some decision, but, much more fundamentally, to permit the emergence of social, political, intellectual, or artistic bodies, associations, interest groups, or economic or Christian groups totally independent of the state, yet capable of opposing it, able to reject its pressures as well as its controls, and even its gifts. These organizations must be completely independent, not only materially but also intellectually and morally, i.e., able to deny that the nation is the supreme value and that the state is the incarnation of the nation. . . . What is needed is groups capable of extreme diversification of the entire society's fundamental tendencies, capable of escaping our unitary structure and of presenting themselves not as negations of the state—which would be absurd—but as *something else*, not under the state's tutelage but equally important, as solid and valuable as the state.[24]

Ellul seeks a plurality of groups and interests within the state, yet independent from its monolithic structure.[25] Presumably, each of these groups would be organized politically. Ellul does not attempt to do away with politics, but to free it from the technical state. He frequently warns against confusing politics with the state. Unfortunately, however, he gives us little guidance as to what he considers to be the structure or functions of a properly formed state. Ellul is so concerned to control the totalitarian tendencies of the modern state that he fails to shed light upon what, concretely, a state should be.

The question remains whether Ellul's solution is at all feasible. "I have never said that it *is* possible," he responds. "I have only indicated what I consider to be the basic condition for social and political life and the *only* way to escape the political illusion."[26] One reason why Ellul is reluctant to speak about the workability of his solution is that *The Political Illusion* approaches the problem only from the perspective of sociological observation. An investigation of his theological works, however, soon makes it clear that he views the political problem as fundamentally a religious one, and that he is dubious about the possibility of any final remedy which originates within the framework of secular society. Our discussion must turn, therefore, to a consideration of Ellul's political theology.

HUMAN AND DIVINE POLITICS

Ellul's position as developed in his sociological studies appears to be that technique in conjunction with the state corrupts politics. If politics can be freed from technique, and if tensions can be introduced to restrain the state's totalitarian tendencies, then good politics may again become possible. Technique, it seems, is the *bête noire* of politics. An examination of Ellul's theological reflection on politics, however, casts doubt upon such a simplistic interpretation. In this context he often speaks as though politics is essentially characterized by coercion, manipulation, and lust for power; and he frequently implies that political activity is pretty much an illusion always, even apart from the technical state.

An appropriate starting point for a consideration of Ellul's political theology is his *Politics of God and the Politics of Man*, which he has called the theological counterpoint to his *Political Illusion*. This book's setting is far removed from the modern technical state. It consists of essays on the Second Book of Kings and deals with incidents during the reigns of various kings of Israel. A recurrent theme is the vanity and futility of the political activities of these kings and God's judgment upon their actions. The tone of these mediations is anticipated in Ellul's introductory comments on the story in which the Israelites demand a king of Samuel. He depicts this demand as an example of sociological conformity: Israel wants to be like the most advanced nations of the world. As the story unfolds, God objects to this form of government but finally capitulates to the persistent request of the people after issuing a stern warning. Ellul's interpretation of this story, beginning with the divine warning, follows:

> We are given an extraordinary description of what centralized political power inevitably means: more taxes, military conscription, arbitrary police, the impossibility of limiting power. This is the price the people will have to pay to have efficient political power and to reach the level of progress of other nations (for is it not inadmissable that God's people should be the most retrograde and should be the representative of antiquated political structures?). In spite of the divine warning the people is obstinate. . . . God does not press the point. He accepts this disobedience. . . . But still God does not give up. He does not give up saving the people in spite of itself. He does not give up remedying the progressivist infatuation of this people.[27]

This passage says much about Ellul's theological perspective on politics. First, he judges Israel's mistake in wanting a king to be that of trusting in a political mechanism to solve the nation's problems. This trust not only exemplifies conformity to the world; it is idolatorous in relying upon something other than God and his providence. The idolatrous character of this faith is amply illustrated in the rest of the book. The kings repeatedly engage in all sorts of futile political maneuvers and alliances while simultaneously turning a deaf ear to the prophets who come with a word from the Lord.

Second, it is apparent that Ellul views human political activity and governmental power as essentially coercive and exploitative. If Israel chooses the way of politics, she will have to pay the price —not because God is vindictive or punishes by giving her especially corrupt and inept kings, but because all these evils belong to the very nature of her political choice. Human politics *is* domination, violence, and manipulation; kings simply *are* that way. Every state, Ellul says elsewhere, "is founded on violence and cannot maintain itself save by and through violence."[28] And again: "There is no such thing as a good ruler (not even the sovereign people or the proletariat!). . . . Satan controls this power and he grants it in order that men should subjugate one another."[29]

Further, God's way of dealing with his people—the "politics of God"—is a striking contrast to man's way of dealing with his fellows—the "politics of man." The politics of God uses the means of love, grace, and persuasion. God does not coerce. He respects man's choices and adjusts his own plans in order to take human decision into account. Insofar as God does intervene, it is not to enforce his will upon man but to work for man's good and salvation. He uses the new situations which men create outside his will in order to actualize his grace and love. But in all of this, man's independence is respected. "God does not mechanize man. He gives him free play. . . . Man is at the time independent. We cannot say free. . . . He is under the burden of his body and his passions, the conditioning of society, culture, and function. He obeys its judgments and setting. He is controlled by its situation and psychology. Man is certainly not free in any degree. He is the slave of everything save God. God does not control or constrain him. God lets him remain independent in these conditions."[30] Thus Ellul sees man as determined rather than as free; but he is determined not by some form of divine predestination, but by biological, psychological, and sociological factors. Man is in bondage to the world, but he is independent in relation to God. In spite of his roots in the tradition of French Calvinism, Ellul seems to have no qualms about opting for a sociological rather than a theological determinism. We shall return to this topic later; but it is already clear that divine politics is distinguished from human politics mainly in being characterized by freedom rather than coercion.

The issue of technique and politics as posed in *The Political Illusion* can now be seen as merely the tip of the iceberg. Ellul is basically trying to uncover the religious phenomenon of idolatry as it is manifested in man's attitude toward politics and the state. And idolatry is neither exclusively ancient nor modern. It is the error not only of Israel and her kings, but also of Constantine and medieval Christendom,[31] and of contemporary democratic, monarchistic, and socialist states. There is nothing inherently wrong with either monarchy or any other form of government;

the evil lies in the deification of the state. As a result of the onslaught of scientific positivism and skepticism, the values of a past Christian culture have been thoroughly desacralized. But it is characteristic of desacralizing forces to reconstitute something else or even themselves as objects of veneration. For Ellul, the state, politics, and technique are especially sacred in our era. Of politics he says: "The *religious* legacy of Christianity is taken over by the great political currents and by politics. . . . Politics, after having been dominated as a subordinate sphere by the religious phenomenon, gained its independence from organized religion, and has been making a triumphal entry into the religious for a half a century. It is the supreme religion of this age."[32]

When man puts his faith in politics, technique, and the state, he becomes a slave to them and loses his capacity for critical judgment. "It is not technology itself which enslaves us, but the transfer of the sacred into technology." And it is the state's "sacral transfiguration . . . which makes us direct our worship to this conglomerate of offices."[33]

What started out as a political illusion has become, in Ellul's political theology, the religious problem of idolatry. When idols take on power, they become demons. Where at first it seemed that only the spell of an illusion needed to be broken, it now appears that nothing short of exorcism will suffice. Ellul calls the task one of "desacralization." The first step toward a responsible politics must be the desacralization of politics and the state. Their implicit and explicit claims to be absolute must be relativized. The biblical writers consistently maintain, Ellul contends, that politics has only relative worth. It is this relativity, as we shall see, that Ellul believes Christians must demonstrate in their efforts to be politically responsible.

Ellul's position that politics is essentially coercion is certainly open to debate. Many thinkers, both inside and outside the Christian tradition, would argue that coercion is a distortion rather than the essence of human politics. Like Luther, Calvin, and, more recently, Barth, Ellul takes a radical stand on the fall of man. But his view is even more extreme than those of the Reformers (although his position seems to have more affinity, finally, to that of Luther than to that of Calvin) in that he considers the fall to be a total break with God in which virtually nothing is left of God's image in man. Expressed theologically, the fall places man in bondage to sin; stated philosophically and sociologically, it puts man in the grip of a biological and cultural necessity. Man no longer knows anything of God's will, and his works are all corrupt and worthy of divine judgment. Political activity is by no means alone in this situation. Ellul regards the city, and with it culture generally, as fundamentally rooted in rebellion against God. All cities are "Babylon," and there is no hope for their reform.[34] Natural law, morality, and theology fare no better. "Natural law, then, becomes part of this tremendous effort at reconciliation beyond grace. It is just one part of this effort, along with natural theology and Gnosticism, natural morality, and the absolute value of reason. All are designed to permit man to escape from the radical necessity of receiving revelation in order to know what is goodness and what is truth."[35]

Even taking into account Ellul's Christian convictions, it may be argued that his position concerning the fall is too extreme. While conceding that Ellul's emphasis on the fall is welcome in a theological climate which has tended to ignore this basic Christian teaching, many of his fellow believers would maintain that the image of God is seriously damaged in the fall, but man retains, nevertheless, a sense of justice, the use of reason, and some capacity for natural goodness. And they might go on to insist, along with a significant portion of the Christian tradition, that human activities and institutions—law, morality, politics, and the state—are not simply products of the fall but also provisions of divine grace in order to enable fallen man to live with a modicum of sanity and stability. Finally, Ellul's Christian critics could go further and argue that it is not even proper to consider such things as politics primarily in relation to the fall, but that politics is thinkable, both before the fall as part of the structure of creation, and after the Kingdom of God has finally been established in its fullness.[36]

Ellul may be understood, in part, as reacting against the influence of "immanence" thinking in current theology and religious ethics. He sees such movements as Bonhoeffer's religionless Christianity, Cox's secular city, liberation theologies, and the activities of the World Council of Churches as presumptuous claims that the Kingdom of God can be established in history by man's works. Ellul always emphasizes that the Kingdom of God will be built by God rather than man. He shares Eric Voegelin's opposition to the "immanentization of the *eschaton*," although Voegelin would undoubtedly view Ellul's theological position as unduly parochial. Ellul is correct, I believe, in his consistent opposition to any glorification of human endeavor; at the same time, however, he risks minimizing the extent to which God may choose to establish his Kingdom through the agency of man.

In addition to his understanding of the fall, Ellul is led to a dim view of man's ability to know any truth about law, morality, and political good, by his insistence on the freedom of God. His peculiar understanding of divine freedom places him in the camp of philosophical nominalism and voluntarism.[37] Ellul opposes freedom to structure. Since God is free, his will cannot be codified in a system of law or morality. The divine will can be known only through revelation; but "revelation is an act ever new which cannot be systematized,"[38] and no general principles can be derived from it. Thus there can be no Christian philosophy, ethics, political party, or system of government. For Ellul, the will of God "never becomes an abstract law of the presence of the one who puts it forth. It never becomes a philosophic or moral principle from which we would be free to draw conclusions, and which would remain as the origin of Christian reflection or conduct. There are no Christian principles."[39]

It is not surprising, therefore, that Ellul's critics are often disappointed in his failure to propose concrete measures for remedying the ills of society which he has so forcefully diagnosed. But such specificity is virtually precluded by his theoretical framework.[40] Since God's will is revealed only to individuals in particular situations, no structure, program, or action can be promoted as inherently compatible with that will.

If Ellul's analysis of politics as a factual reality in the modern technical state seems gloomy, his theological interpretation of the meaning of politics is certainly no less so. And while he would not oppose any efforts in the direction of the solution outlined in *The Political Illusion*, it is significant that his own recent political reflection focuses more and more on the problem of the Christian's political responsibility. One might expect him to urge his fellow believers to wash their hands of any involvement in politics; but he does not do so—first, because he is convinced that politics cannot be avoided in modern society, and second, because he believes that faith must be lived in all areas of human life. Ellul is acutely cognizant, however, that in addition to being susceptible to illusions of their own, Christians are subject to the same political illusions which affect other men. He is concerned, therefore, to force Christians into an awareness of a distinction between true and false modes of Christian political action. In portraying this distinction, he combines the analytic skills of the social scientist and theologian with a tone reminiscent of the biblical prophets.

The Politics of Christendom and the Politics of Freedom

Ellul is often harsh in his criticism of the past and present political behavior of Christians. He regards much of what transpires in the name of Christian political action as misguided (a "false presence") both politically and theologically. A false presence in politics often proceeds from conformity to the standards of the world—as, for example, in attempts to establish a Christian power structure—or it may simply be the result of well-intentioned but ill-informed bungling in the political arena.

Ellul has always stressed the importance of realism as a prerequisite for work in politics; but he believes that much Christian involvement in that sphere is naive. He chides Christians for leaping to political action without understanding social reality, for "joining struggles that are virtually over,"[41] and for being "pushed from behind by the movement they think they are propelling."[42] He depicts them as being "very susceptible to propaganda"[43] and "at the mercy of every fad."[44] Failing to grasp the illusory quality of politics in the technological society, they have unrealistic expectations of what can be accomplished politically. At the same time, their exaggerated view of the import of their political flourishes for the establishment of the Kingdom of God betrays their theological puerility.

Besides lacking realism, the politicized church or individual Christian commits the error of reducing Christianity to political action, and thus, of conforming to the standards of the world. Such churches and Christians, Ellul maintains, "are defined by their sociological milieu."[45] In his view, many of the recent political discussions and pronouncements of church organizations are examples of such conformity. As Ellul states it: "One need only read Protestant newspapers and magazines to realize that they contain, six months later, exactly the same treatment of hunger, overpopulation, decolonization, unionism and mass culture that one can read anywhere. Eighty percent of their articles have to do with social and political problems, stated in exactly the same terms in which the world states them."[46] Similarly, the involvement of Christians in protest rallies is seen as another instance of their tendency to get on the world's bandwagons. While Christians so engaged often do so with worthy intentions, their Christian motives are completely lost on the other participants and observers, and in the media which report the protest. The result is that the Christian "presence" is merely absorbed into a secular cause.

Perhaps the most vicious form of false presence, however, is what Ellul alternatively refers to as "Constantinism" or "Christendom." Constantinism is not only "an acceptance of the state and an agreement with the political power," but also a desire "to win over to Christianity the rich, the powerful, and control centers."[47] It seeks to Christianize, but also to appropriate, worldly power and influence. For Ellul, the state is properly secular. Christians should not try to establish a Christian society or acquire special privileges for themselves from the secular state. For all its pious rhetoric, the politics of Christendom remains the politics of coercion. He considers any attempt to impose some supposed Christian structure or value upon secular society to be a violation of Christianity, the essence of which is free response to the free action of God.

Ellul realizes that the flagrant Constantinism of medieval Christendom is held in contempt by most liberal religious leaders. But he sees a subtle revival of the motives of Christendom in the contemporary political church which tries to influence political events toward some end implicity regarded as the Christian way. On both the right and the left, he argues, "we are seeing the same identification between Christian truth and political option. On the one hand there is extolled the anticommunist crusade in defense of Christendom, and on the other hand there is the claim that socialism is the hope of mankind, which the Christian should support."[48]

In contrast to the modes of false presence which are conformed to the world and fail to transcend the coercive politics of man, the true presence is a manifestation of divine freedom in the political realm. Christ breaks the chain of necessity and frees man from bondage. As a result, politics is infused with a new hope which comes from a transcendent source. Ellul challenges Christians to live out of the freedom received in Christ in their political engagements. To the extent that they do so, their politics becomes a reflection of divine politics—a politics of freedom.

The politics of freedom is, first of all, a politics which pays careful attention to the means it employs. It does not imitate the technical state or Christendom by assuming that ends justify means. It avoids means which negate freedom: violence, hatred, and deception. Ellul calls upon Christians to employ only the means of freedom—honesty, openness, and nonviolence—in their political action. "The means of freedom are the means of liberal organization which does not create in its members a spirit of orthodoxy, nor demand of them a total commitment, but trains them in the practice of concrete freedom and criticism, acting by means of this freedom and not by means of a systematization of action and thought."[49] Can a politics so scrupulous about the means it uses, however, be effective? Will it bring about the desired results? Ellul maintains that these are wrong questions. In order to pursue the politics of freedom, men must be freed from their bondage to efficiency and from their compulsion to get results. "Why are we so concerned about utility? Why do we regard what is not useful as worthless? In reality, we are obsessed at this point by the views of our age and century and technology. . . . To be controlled by utility and the pursuit of efficacy is to be subject to the strictest determination of the actual world. To want to attain results is necessarily not to be a witness to the free gift of God. . . . To do a gratuitous, ineffective, and useless act is the first sign of our freedom and perhaps the last."[50]

The politics of freedom requires, then, the relativization of politics. Such relativization implies that political decisions should not become a matter of ultimate concern. The choice between various political parties and actions "cannot be made for Christian reasons" and should not be justified by "theological arguments."[51] What Christian freedom needs, Ellul contends, is "not a Christian political doctrine, but a Christian life-style in politics."[52] The task of Christians is to eliminate anguish from politics and to be "a cooling and peace-making factor among other men."[53] The specific forms of Christian political activity will, of course, vary from situation to situation. Ellul thinks that in our own time a valid form of Christian political involvement may well be work for anarchy. He does not regard anarchy as "an intrinsic or permanent Christian attitude";[54] but he does consider it imperative to challenge the absolute and totalitarian character of the modern technical state.

Another basic political responsibility for Christians is to plead the cause of the weak, the poor, and the oppressed. It is important, however, that Christians seek out the genuine poor, and before their cause becomes celebrated in the secular media. He rebukes Christians for their tendency to defend the "interesting" poor—the poor whose cause has already become fashionable and who, therefore, are no longer the truly oppressed and neglected because they "already have millions of champions."[55]

The relativity of politics does not imply, for Ellul, its unimportance. He says: "Christian freedom ought to lead us to treat seriously these very relative problems . . . and to view grandiose proclamations and doctrines with humor. We know that the results will be half good and half bad. No revolution will bring about the change desired. All the same, even if their results can only be provisional, these little works of politics should be well done."[56]

Ellul's final word about politics is not a message of pessimism or despair, but one of hope. He is convinced that the Christian faith provides a power to restore politics to health. Thus he transcends his vision of politics as a force merely destructive of freedom. The politics of fallen man is coercion; but Ellul challenges Christians to put aside the politics of violence and to develop a style of political involvement which reflects the politics of freedom.

Ellul's political vision will undoubtedly be unattractive and unconvincing to those who do not share his theological perspective. His analysis of politics in the technological society will perhaps be seen as merely another attempt to lay the groundwork for a Christian apologetic. Perhaps, too, he underestimates the resources within contemporary society to use technique and politics for the well-being and freedom of man. If secular society wishes to participate in the politics of freedom, however, Ellul will insist that it must begin by desacralizing the state, technique, and political action.

Considering the widespread cynicism about politics evident in much of western society today, Ellul's call for a desacralization of politics and the state may appear to be wholly gratuitous. But perhaps part of the reason for our despair about contemporary politics lies precisely in the fact that we have come to expect from the state and political action the solution of all problems and the inauguration of the great society. It is profoundly disquieting to see one's gods tumble from the heavens or to catch them in paltry crimes.

Notes

1. "Mirror of These Ten Years," *Christian Century*, 18 Feb. 1970, p. 201.
2. *Technological Society*, p. xxv; French ed. 1954.
3. *Presence of the Kingdom*, p. 69; French ed. 1948.
4. *Technological Society*, p. 97.
5. "The Grand Illusion: An Appreciation of Jacques Ellul," *Commentary*, Aug. 1970, p. 41.
6. *Technological Society*, p. 247.
7. *Ibid.*, p. 254.
8. *Ibid.*, p. 259.
9. *Political Illusion*, p. 142; French ed. 1965.
10. *Ibid.*, p. 141.
11. In his *Political Illusion*, Ellul seems to regret that ideology is obscured when politics becomes subordinated to technique. In *Ethics of Freedom*, however, he defines politics as simply a "concrete exercise in administration or management" which is without "spiritual, ideological, or doctrinal content" (p. 382).
12. *Political Illusion*, p. 185.
13. *Ibid.*, p. 186.
14. *Ibid.*, p. 191.
15. Nicholas Wolterstorff has stated well the dilemma which Christians face in attempting to limit the totalitarian tendencies of the state: "We seem to have to choose between blinking our eyes to the deprivation of social justice, and acquiescing in the monstrosity of

the comprehensive service state." See his "Contemporary Christian Views of the State: Some Major Views," *Christian Scholar's Review*, vol. 3, no. 4 (1974), 322.
16. *Political Illusion*, p. 160.
17. *Propaganda*, p. 126; French ed. 1962.
18. *Ibid.*, p. 132.
19. *Technological Man: The Myth and the Reality*, p. 137.
20. Interview with David Menninger, 24 Oct. 1973. Quoted in Menninger, "Jacques Ellul: A Tempered Profile," *Review of Politics*, 37 (Apr. 1975), 235.
21. *Political Illusion*, p. 201.
22. *Ibid.*, p. 202.
23. *Ibid.*
24. *Ibid.*, p. 222.
25. Ellul's position here appears to be similar to that outlined by Wolterstorff, "Christian Views of the State," pp. 322–26.
26. *Political Illusion*, p. 223.
27. *Politics of God and Politics of Man*, pp. 17–18; French ed. 1966.
28. *Violence*, pp. 84–85; English ed. 1969.
29. *Ethics of Freedom*, p. 55; French ed. 1970.
30. *Politics of God and Politics of Man*, p. 16.
31. See Ellul, *The New Demons*, pp. 1–17; French ed. 1973.
32. *Ibid.*, pp. 166–67.
33. *Ibid.*, pp. 206–7.
34. *Meaning of the City*, esp. chaps. 1, 2; English ed. 1970.
35. *Theological Foundation of Law*, p. 11; French ed. 1946.
36. This position is fetchingly argued by Richard Mouw in his *Politics and the Biblical Drama* (Grand Rapids, Mich.: Eerdmans, 1976), chaps. 2, 6.
37. For a discussion and critique of Ellul's nominalism and voluntarism, see Arthur Holmes, chap. 10 herein.
38. *To Will and To Do*, p. 204; French ed. 1964. The logic of Ellul's argument is faulty in this passage. From the premise that God is free, it does not follow necessarily that there can be no moral system. God could, conceivably, choose to express his will in a moral system. And from the premise that God's will can be known only through revelation, it surely does not follow that revelation cannot be systematic or that no general principles can be derived from it. God might well choose to reveal a system of general principles. And Ellul can deny this only by himself limiting the freedom of God, the very thing for which he so severely chides his opponents.

39. *Ibid.*
40. See Arthur Holmes, chap. 10 herein, for a more detailed exploration of this issue.
41. *Violence*, p. 153.
42. *Ethics of Freedom*, p. 291.
43. *Violence*, p. 153.
44. *Ethics*, p. 291.
45. *False Presence of the Kingdom*, p. 47.
46. *Ibid.*, p. 49.
47. *New Demons*, p. 214.
48. *False Presence*, p. 135.
49. *Ethics*, p. 408.
50. *Politics of God and Politics of Man*, pp. 197–98.
51. *Ethics*, pp. 375–76.
52. *Ibid.*, p. 385.
53. *Ibid.*, p. 383.
54. *Ibid.*, p. 396.
55. *Violence*, p. 153.
56. *Ethics*, p. 383.

Chapter 8

Ellul on Solution: An Alternative but No Prophecy

Clifford G. Christians

Ellul readers typically complain that he offers no solution, that his fatalism destroys his value as social analyst. The objection appears in several forms, but uniformly as a device to discredit him. *Time* magazine writes, for example: "Jacques Ellul is a French historian noted for his pessimistic view of man's works and a lay theologian who mirrors the deep Calvinism of his French Reformed Church."[1] Some seek understanding from biographical paraphernalia. Harvey Cox speculates whether Ellul became wounded by the "endless humdrum of the Paris suburbs, the glacial immobility of the French bureaucracy, the traffic of his champs."[2] Others picture him as beleaguered and revengeful. Two Europeans put it this way in a conversation with Stephen Rose: "Ellul [is] just a frustrated man who [has] never been accepted and who [spends] most of his time railing against this fact."[3] Lewis Mumford forgoes psycho-history, but deplores his "ingrained fatalism."[4] Edward Shorter is "disturbed"[5] and Robert Johnston "disappointed" by Ellul's silence "on what shape a more positive reconstruction" might take.[6] Rupert Hall stings Ellul's *Technological Society* continually, declaring for example: "Ellul lives on black bread and spring water. . . . The prophet whose cry is only 'Woe, ye are damned' walks unheeded. Ellul is such a prophet. . . . If he is right, his book is useless."[7]

Such status denigration prevents insightful analysis. Dismissing Ellul as an impoverished pessimist is as irresponsible as calling Tocqueville and Ortega "aristocrats" and reading no further. One must decry such superficiality, and lay that common folly aside in order to deal more fundamentally with Ellul's view of solution. Otherwise academic work on this matter remains trapped in an external game, with Ellul complaining that he is not being read[8] and his critics (erroneously, I believe) insisting that he is inconsequential.

"Pessimist" as an *ad hominem* epithet for Ellul almost always appears without careful attention to meaning. The context and intent of Ellul's critics, however, indicate that "pessimism" connotes for them a view of life as basically futile, history as without discernible meaning, and man's capacity for change as nonexistent. But anyone who implies that Ellul sees life in this fashion—that he views it as intrinsically self-defeating—simply misunderstands him. Ellul does not express Spengler's dogmatic cultural pessimism nor does he fall within the tradition since Schopenhauer that history is blind will. His purpose, instead, is to reflect modern predicaments accurately. "I have no mechanical, fatalist, or organicist view at all," he declares; "I only say that most of the time, in our day, things are that way."[9]

Certainly he is a sober analyst, but nowhere categorically deterministic and devoid of solutions. Only if each of us limits himself to a "trivial existence," Ellul contends, *only then* will everything happen "as I described it and these determining forces be transformed into inevitabilities."[10] "I am convinced," he declares straightforwardly, "the situation is not completely hopeless."[11] In fact, Ellul's delineation of "pessimism *in hope*" serves as an explicit retort to all who condemn him as irremediably disheartened;[12] and the first volume in his projected ethical trilogy, *Ethics of Freedom*, begins with hope in order to counteract man's faltering desire to live. Crisis and melancholia never function in Ellul as independent motifs rooted in pure negativism and disillusionment. As Paul Pickerel concludes: "You want to believe that the completeness of the argument is simply paranoid. . . . But unfortunately these hopes perish of malnutrition."[13]

ELLUL'S SUGGESTIONS ABOUT SOLUTION

"Pessimism" may be dismissed as a lightweight accusation which misjudges Ellul's spirit and objective. Ellul frequently offers an alternative. He speaks clearly about the overall shape of a solution and often pointedly about details. These major statements appear over several writings and the focus of each varies, but throughout his essays and books Ellul emphasizes essentially three major themes.[14] They appear with different accents and in various combinations, but together they constitute a solution with range and substance. Certainly they defy any charge of pessimism. The following schema will provide an easily accessible description of Ellul's suggestions.

1. Ellul insists on establishing from the start a fundamental realism.[15] All roads to prosperity begin for him with penetrating insight. Where the utter harshness of our contemporary predicament nudges us toward superficiality and retreat, Ellul crusades instead for ruthless honesty. Realism is the attitude on which he wishes to build reliable analysis.

He introduces the term "desacralization" in *The New Demons* as something comparable to realism. We must smash our modern idols, expose false claims, demythologize today's illusions, stand squarely before the bloody face of history. We imbue technology, education, and politics with an aura of holy prestige, and it is this sacral transfiguration which enslaves us.[16] Our promotion of revolution as a moral imperative must start with a drastic assessment which shatters all grandiose claims by the technological and bureaucratic domains.

We commonly assume that intellectuals must further such awareness, and Ellul shares this desire. While unwilling to enfranchise any elite as saviors, he persistently cherishes the hope for "an authentic . . . tension between the intellectual and political realms."[17] He describes his own scholarly motivation as arousing "the reader to an awareness of technological necessity and what it means, . . . calling the sleeper to awake."[18] With that objective, he strips away our simplistic epithets. (Ellul's *Critique of the New Commonplaces* shows how incensed his polemic can become.) Moreover, his personal abandonment of several movements for not being sociologically astute indicates that he takes this role seriously. Intellectuals must be watchmen on the walls, heralds of warning; but regrettably, they seem as vulnerable to sociological propaganda as anyone. The crushing invasion of technique into all areas, "also into the sphere of intelligence," co-opts academics into the system and forces them to incant mythologies as "explanations" for current events.[19]

Ellul opposes that farrago of cheap solutions offered by the accommodationism of mainstream World Council churches and academic liberals. Christianity, caught in Constantinism by the fourth century and "mongrelized since the seventeenth," marries the status quo and thereby does not lead the rescue.[20] Ordinary democratic liberalism makes statism the means to salvation and vaunts its pride in scientific progress. Using Dostoevsky's "Grand Inquisitor" as his framework, Ellul demonstrates that sociopolitical activism does not represent true love for man in any sense, all claims notwithstanding. It does not bring about a new state of affairs.[21] Man's "wild cry for freedom" cannot be integrated into the necessary course of events. The rhetorics of mainstream relgious or political liberalism ultimately offer only cul-de-sacs.[22]

Religious and political liberals speak easily of "revolution" and there is some movement at the margins and on the surface. But Ellul insists that "the forces which are of decisive importance in our world situation, . . .the constituent elements," are nowhere touched.[23] Most turbulence, he contends, does not produce worthwhile changes, but only entrenches existing institutions and canonizes the powerful. Both eccelesiastical and political reform are futile, because by dealing with images on the periphery they dissipate their energies over fictitious disputes.[24] Technique removes mankind's ancient constraints, but it does not make man free. Destruction of technique rather than control of technology must be the starting point of change.[25] Thus Ellul cuts with a heavy sword; he seeks mightily to "give all activists pause, to pull us back from our relentless plunge into frenetic activity in the world."[26] The result of such fanaticism is to entrench society's predictable course even more. "What a fraud, what a swindle," Ellul says with scorn, "when the only decisive result is the relentless strengthening of the State" under the guise of liberating oppressed peoples from tyranny.[27]

But realism does not mean capricious iconoclasm just for indignation's sake; rather it means we must resolve to seal off misleading exits. Authentic revolutions cannot occur until all reasonable possibilities are blocked, Ellul declares, and unless we recognize that conciliation is impossible.[28] If we believe we can alter societies by reducing their pace, we will choose such a route. If we assume that we only need to eliminate defective parts, or more tightly organize the social order, or balance political and economic disproportions, or fill visible gaps, we will pursue these reforms rather than seriously engage the pervasive malaise of our time.

Our mass media accentuate this reluctance to revolt. If the burgeoning state and industrial order embody technique supremely, communications systems are that order's "innermost and most elusive manifestation." The media, Ellul argues, prevent increasing administrative organization "from being felt as too oppressive and [persuade] men to submit with good grace."[29] As sociological and integrational propagandas, they standardize our actions and motivations. As a result, man makes a "virtue of necessity"; he equates the media's universe with reality. Immersed in the efficiency motif, he convinces himself that he is "really free."[30] Man's attempt to surround himself with rationalizations and cover-ups, Ellul contends, was already noticed by Marx in "his theory of the false conscience and ideology."[31] The tendency to rationalize increases as networks of information multiply and numb our powers of independent criticism.

Therefore, while his critics charge him with being "unremittingly anticulture,"[32] Ellul actually promotes realism as a crucial dimension in accomplishing something worthwhile. What others castigate as negativism is really Ellul's pushing us nearer bona fide revolution, arguing that when we come up with "a few minor transformations" we only "tranquilize our fitful slumber."[33] Fixing the boundaries tightly accentuates the existential seriousness of human decision. Only through skilled diagnosis, he claims, can we "achieve a genuine consciousness of the problem."[34] This "transformed awareness" issues into "deliberate and premeditated attitudes"[35]: accurate, information-filled confrontation with the established order, perceptions which recognize inescapable dilemmas rather than present artificial options.

2. When we have rejected false answers and inadequate definitions of the problem, we emerge into phase two—the transformation of ourselves. Once we face up to the fallenness of contemporary culture, then trustworthy moves toward restoration become possible.

Ellul does not promote a desperation sociology, but, in fact, these two phases—realism and transformation—must go togeth-er.[36] Scathing realism is merely rebellion if it stands alone; de-stroying shelters and closing escape routes will simply drive most people toward nihilism. Those who attack Ellul's pessimism fail to realize that his vigorous desacralization is but one element in a larger perspective, the first step in a longer journey. Ellul's exposé of crisis does not focus on doubt and despair, but on salva-tion. "Desacralizing," Ellul writes, "can be done only if, along with it, one supplied a reason for living adequate to sustain life, and an answer really satisfying and clear."[37] We must break the impasses we have created; we must finally resolve the questions we have raised.

All appearances to the contrary, Ellul is searching for an ameliorative option capable of "communicating good and grant-ing life . . . a *true* change which would put things right."[38] He suggests that a revolutionary solution is grounded in metamor-phosed life, in persons with utterly different sensitivities from the technicized social order as a whole. People with illumined consciousness are the solitary channel through which to realize social change. A single, spectacular seizure of power will never bring about change. Only a resuscitation and expansion of the private realm can destroy technique's tyranny.[39] Ellul starts with individuals rather than political ideologies, economic systems, or institutions such as education or government. The individual must dispute society's game and refuse to honor the self-evident. Such a pioneer stands on his own feet, banking on inner resources for his decision-making and sense of judgment.

Thus Ellul cries out for individuals who have come to grips with a social order that turns all ends into means. He seeks people who can provide examples of effective living and demonstrate genuine personhood. "Non-conformists who without heroics or hysterics will decisively give themselves to setting men free" can act as leaven in today's society.[40]

Therefore, the important question for Ellul is not doing, but being. Man should not merely be incited to noble activity, but encouraged to achieve some end. In Ellul's vision, "the end has been established and all our means must represent it." Ellul does not demand a struggle for peace, but insists that "we have our-selves to be peaceful." The end, authenticated supernaturally, is miraculously available so that we live in its power; we can "be" rather than act. It is not "a question of doing good but of embodying faith, which is fundamentally different." Forces supremely revolutionary arise outside of technicized nature and move in an opposite direction; they "belong to another city," have "another Master."[41] Only a decisive power—achieving fruition within man yet originating beyond him—can transform the contemporary environment. Anything less cannot penetrate overwhelming technique. A spiritual reality cannot be restored by material means. And when addressing a Christian audience, Ellul uses explicit theological terms: "Only in the light of Jesus Christ's sacrifice of himself can man be compelled to live as man"[42]; the intervention of God's Spirit, resurrection power, enables us to incarnate freedom and overcome evil.

For Ellul authentic solutions require remade persons, a new mode of being. As renewed humans combine into new patterns not under technique's tutelage, this reordered consciousness will begin eliminating monolithic structure. Infusing the contemporary world with significance and curbing efficiency arise finally, for Ellul, from new men occupying new social ground. Thus he prescribes a radical alternative; in so doing, however, he is not recommending that we abandon all interest in the *res publica*, "but on the contrary . . . achieve it by another route, come to grips with it again in a different way, on a more real level, and in a decisive contest."[43]

Ellul thus places himself in that powerful tradition of moral philosophy, self-realization ethics, where a life of rectitude is considered an achievement as singular as an artist's creation. Though he often characterizes his principles in explicitly Judeo-Christian terms, his larger framework emphasizes the handcrafted life. We must fight "at the level of the citizen's virtue," he writes; we must start with "critical renewal."[44] He summons us "to the most difficult of all tasks, to revolutionary nonconformity as individuals disdaining the illusory warmth of the mass."[45] He asserts that our social order requires great humans who enrich the common life of mortals, not by rage or condemnation alone, but by demonstrating a reformed conscience. The issue for him is character, cherished holiness, valid moral behavior, a reconciled life. Effectiveness emerges only from opinions fundamentally altered, lives nourished deeply at a fresh source, fullness provided solely by divine being itself.

3. The first two elements in Ellul's solution—realism and renewed personhood—obviously reflect his counterpoint motif, that double-sided, sociological-theological mode of argument which is a basic strategy in his work.[46] Once these first two types of awareness are exhibited, a third phase is possible—concrete action. Ellul viciously condemns activities conducted for their own sake, but whenever he sees defiant realism and transformed life,[47] he anticipates tangible acts which *ipso facto* circumvent the socio-technological order. Ellul is not as simplistically antipolitical as often assumed.[48] As long as our actions arise from these two roots, Ellul writes, "it will be possible to mend matters."[49] Contrary to the charge that he shows no concern for "making a troubled world more decent,"[50] he eagerly seeks creative nonconformity and spontaneous movement within the proper guidelines.

Ellul is very careful here: our choices are always existential ones, since we determine their precise content freely at each new moment of decision. Prefabricated programs may simply be another realm of necessity, preventing us from achieving a liberated lifestyle. Thus Ellul steadfastly refuses to construct fixed models of conduct, insisting that we must think out for ourselves "the meaning of [our] involvement in the modern world"[51]: "This is something people find difficult to understand in my books. They expect me to give them a plan, but I refuse to do that. My purpose is to oblige the reader to choose *for himself* a course of action. I don't want disciples or people who obey me. I want to incite people. . . . I can't list what is *necessary* to be free."[52] Therefore, Ellul's ethics are only indicative. Any body of doctrine too easily becomes "the organization of a workable moral life in abstraction from grace." Ellul always guards himself here, so that when finished, he has not "enclosed a cistern instead of opening a spring."[53]

Surrounded with these warnings, Ellul suggests several concrete possibilities, not for our blind imitation, but as illustrative of activities unannexed to technique.

He recommends, for instance, exercising the "passion to play."[54] He refers not to revelry for its own sake nor cheap parody, but to reclaiming festivals and rituals which reinvigorate our social life. In our highly functional and trivialized age, Ellul encourages us to restore the sabbath motif.[55]

He also advocates centers of opposition and debate. He commends American blacks, for example, for providing an opposition group who "challenge technicized society" and "call for a new cultural orientation."[56] Ellul does not imply that all their claims are meritorious, but does see some hopeful signs.

Ellul further urges us to promote pluralism. He seeks all kinds of subcultures "which diversify our society's fundamental tendencies" and present themselves "not as negations of the state, but as something else not under [its] tutelage."[57] Together these subcultures can provide a new infrastructure, a fresh web of interlocking relationships. As a guarantee for such pluralism, Ellul suggests that "we become neighbor to someone," that we "rediscover him socially."[58]

Several authors exhibit a formal similarity to such suggestions.[59] Wendell Berry, for example, promotes "thinking little," an exhortation that the enormously complicated issues not prevent us from attempting some personal and manageable achievement.[60] Berry's attempt to discredit faddish "Think Big" mentality nurtured by glamorous short-term pragmatics corresponds directly to Ellul's phase one. Laying a "Think Little" basis—that is, depth, personal responsibility, vision—describes in other terms what Ellul means by substantive activity here in phase three.

In a similar vein, E. F. Schumacher loathes our bearing toward giantism and argues for "appropriate scales." He, with Ellul, rejects material growth as the chief measure of social progress, and urges us to base attention on people instead of goods, "production by the masses, rather than mass production."[61] Ivan Illich likewise recognizes the failure of our industrialized order and introduces "conviviality" as a useful guideline with at least external similarity to Ellul. He challenges us to invert the present deep structure of tools, to limit tools in order to free people.[62]

One label for Ellul's strategy is radical nonviolence, a careful decision to withhold some vital part of self, a conscientious exclusion of all physical and psychological violence. The critical matter for Ellul, as it was for Weber, is withstanding a preemption, protecting man from "the parcelling out of his soul, from the supreme mastery of the bureaucratic way of life."[63] He does not advocate ideological or pietistic pacifism, but a deliberate resistance to monolithic apparatus.[64] Ellul does not condemn involvements as such, only those which fail to meet this nonviolent guideline.

Certainly some frustration regarding Ellul's three-phase solution is inevitable. Recovering it in a coherent fashion requires an elaborate content analysis of his entire body of work. Ellul understood the problem at an early date, but only recently has he begun to recognize the solution with equal clarity.[65] Those who only read his pre-1971 writings might be easily misled, for his most famous works, which appeared before then, contain little suggestion of any solution.[66]

Nor does Ellul's dialectical mode always function unerratically. In *The Meaning of the City*, for example, Ellul uses an overarching dialectic between Babylon and Jerusalem. Yet his emphasis throughout rests on the first pole. Not until the final pages does the "City of God" receive its due, and our modern tension between the Yes and No is virtually nonexistent anywhere in the book.[67] Thus the tendency of readers to find judgment without grace arises at least in part from Ellul's method. In *Ethics of Freedom* he concentrates on solutions which come from individual awareness and never reconciles them with social and collective awareness very well, although he mentions these about halfway through the book.[68] Moreover, his sometimes peculiar definitions (such as the activistic flavor he gives to prayer, waiting, and the incognito) can easily be misinterpreted as doubletalk.[69]

On that basis, Robert Merton speaks for many when he concludes: "Ellul often formulates his ideas in an unqualified fashion. . . . His formulations [are] extravagant and undisciplined."[70] Others even view this existentialist as a "supreme rationalist" who never "splutters off into unreason or what for him would be the ultimate self-betrayal, illogic."[71] Labeling him a "rationalist" is certainly inaccurate and usually arises from those fixating on one side of his argument. Yet Ellul himself does not always help matters; his sweeping scope tends to downplay the nuances and countervalance.

However, the real problems with Ellul are neither imbalance nor overgeneralization—either imposed or actual—but a fundamental mind-set against him. He speaks of solution, but we are deaf. Ellul's distinctive paradigm is incommensurable with that of his critics, therefore nothing comes through. Ironically our attachment to the very naiveté which he detests makes us reject him for the sake of our own self-preservation.

Humanists who carry a decided bias against his religion oppose Ellul;[72] they reject the demand for renewed personhood as a condition for solving anything. Secular humanists prefer an alternative like Lewis Mumford's resourceful continence: "The next move is ours," Mumford concludes; "the gates of the technocratic prison will open automatically, despite their rusty hinges, as soon as we choose to walk out."[73]

Ellul, in contrast, admits that revolution is so difficult, "the effort required so unending, that it is not possible save as one can lean on something other than oneself."[74] He insists that elevated activity does not happen naturally, and Christianity rates as the strongest source he knows. In effect Ellul revives that great debate initiated by the Reformation and the Renaissance. As the former celebrated the renewed emphasis on man, so does Ellul; he believes with the Reformers that only by retaining the God-principle can we protect all other humanistic values.[75] History has certainly proved the Reformation correct on this point; without a personal absolute, society consistently erects arbitrary ones. However, instead of engaging in debate over this significant issue, humanists prefer to ignore it. Since Ellul does not believe in history as a series of open doors, they accuse him of being an inexorable determinist. And in spite of Ellul's unending disgust with institutional religion, they dismiss him on those grounds anyhow.

Ellul is opposed further by a scientific mode which does not like his holism, preferring neat statistical categories instead. Ellul rejects that exploratory universe.[76] He asserts, as Robert Nisbet would in a different way, that *Sociology [is] an Art Form*. He is more concerned in grand European manner about getting the problems straight and not just surrendering to a utilitarian penchant for immediate answers. Once again, Ellul—who can only think of phase three as one element in process with the other two —is rejected by a superficial methodology which finally entrusts social change to "the manipulative care of a superior technician."[77]

In any case, if debate about solution proceeds on the foregoing terrain, I contend that Ellul is clearly the victor. Serious study of his work indicates that he fares well when criticism is directed on this level against his pessimism. Those excoriating his melancholia must admit that the darkness so accentuated in Ellul exists only as the reverse side of redemption. Contentions that he is devoid of solution must be recognized finally as paradigmatic deafness. Ellul's work warns us that liberal-humanist-scientific modes of inquiry lend themselves to the propagation of technique and allow their very analysis to be shaped by technique's demands (demands for action rather than contemplation, work rather than play, easy solutions rather than the clarification of problems).

On a deeper level, however, there is another issue which must be resolved if Ellul's permanent significance is to be achieved. The following section sets that larger problem in focus as a matter for Ellul himself or second-generation scholarship to consider.

WHERE HAS THE PROPHECY GONE?

Ellul does provide a multidimensional and wide-ranging solution, but substantiating it raises an even more fundamental question: Is Ellul prophetic in this area?[78] Granted that he does suggest possibilities for action, are these as overpowering as his analysis of the problem? Ellul's concept "technique" is typically hailed as an extraordinary description of society's malaise, several critics notwithstanding. Ellul has helped set the terms of our debate about technology, politics, and the mass media. Now the harder question: Is that also true of solution? Is his work in this area once again too trenchant to be ignored?

Ellul's insights emerged a generation ago when virtually everyone else assumed that technology was advantageous and that technical problems require technical responses. His prophetic voice has cut against the grain of accepted opinion; his understanding of the modern dilemma has been unmatched.

Now the mood has shifted substantially. The sleepers still have not fully awakened, but they are stirring. Groups at virtually all socioeconomic levels sense that an era is over, a historical phase ended. Daniel Bell and Norman Birnbaum have documented the arrival of a "Post-Industrial Age" to the point where the term is increasingly a commonplace.[79] Maybe no great ruptures are yet visible in the system, but a new skeptical temperament appears everywhere. Ellul presently stands as only one voice among a growing chorus. A host of intellectuals now express doubts about technology—John McDermott, Robert Heilbroner, Lewis Mumford, Siegfried Giedion, Rene Dubos, Theodore Roszak, Charles Reich—to name only a few popular ones.[80] Euphoria over the scientific enterprise is ebbing; its demigodhood is crumbling.[81] The large literature on alienation, the studies of the social "pathology of mass society, the soaring statistics of crime, delinquency and divorce, all give the lie to the liberal belief in Progress."[82]

Ellul has played a critical role in elucidating the crisis. In fact, "his Amos-like ministry to the technological society is [still] very much needed."[83] But as Ellul himself writes: "Historically [our] society became possible only when a massive cultural shift, called the Enlightenment, prepared men's minds to test every social activity according to the norm of efficiency."[84] Though we still live on its capital, such Enlightenment days have died in principle. The discordances are increasingly obvious everywhere.[85] And if being prophetic means speaking the truth so forthrightly that it emanates an aura of eternal verity, we will simply have to address this macro level. Previously we did not see the problem; today a growing number—although focusing on different nuances —recognize our plight and request a means of escape. Their analyses meet Ellul's first criterion for solution, although sometimes their critiques are intuitive rather than fully articulated statements. While Ellul did not father all these observations, he is being more readily comprehended. For Ellul to imply that our attitudes are still unchanged in the 1970s, that he still sees "no breach in the system of technical necessity," is disingenuous to the extreme.[86]

Ellul's prophetism cannot be maintained solely from a thoroughgoing analysis of our social bearing in the first half of the twentieth century. Prophets in the decades ahead will have to address our rising concern about lifestyle, deliberately intentioned alternative societies, genuine community, body life. And for all the worthwhileness of Ellul's three-dimensional approach, it does not seem sufficient to meet that challenge. Ellul's suggestions for solution need to be anchored in a sociology of community in order to become prophetic. Outstanding social analysts such as Ellul are not necessarily powerful social theorists. Nor may we necessarily expect that more onerous task of them. However, in Ellul's case, only a generative theory of society will ensure his prophetism. He needs a fundamental framework for solution, a well-argued core developed from the nature of being and social reality.

Ellul's Kierkegaardian roots predispose him toward solitariness instead.[87] God-oriented individuals, in Ellul's vision, can alone withstand the forces of efficiency which characterize our present agenda: "Freedom can be demonstrated only by individual acts in individual cases."[88] In order to protect himself, he adds (as noted earlier) a social referent and neighborly love. He does mention a community (the church), where we live out freedom as a body.[89] These are fleeting glances, however; the social dimension remains virtually undeveloped. Societal transformation, in Ellul's own definition, "comes only by the accumulation of a vast number of individual decisions."[90] Nonetheless, while all moral decisions are personal and their crisis-moment significant, should they become individualistic, do we not overly accentuate our own happiness? Such individualism has led in the modern West to an unhealthy narcissism. How does Ellul's solution prevent an escape from that trend? He fervently desires to protect human beings from their increasing oppression. Can an I-oriented ethics accomplish that goal or does it become too easily co-opted by the very ideology it is designed to oppose? An anthropology built around the irreducible self often becomes a fallacious guide. Absorption in self-needs ironically blocks their fulfillment.

Even on Ellul's own grounds,[91] do the Scriptures not emphasize covenant, koinonia, a community called into being by the action of God? Is Ellul beckoning people to Christ or to a heavy individualism? One almost needs full acceptance of the latter, it seems, before he confronts the Gospel. And while the biblical message remains theologically debatable at points, Ellul certainly would find Reinhold Niebuhr's conclusion difficult to contradict: "Paul [emphasized] a cultural ethics. It had to be lived, moreover in the midst of societies evidently subject to the dark powers."[92]

I realize that by existentialist disposition and specific disclaimer, Ellul disavows all interest in theoretics. He deliberately refuses to go "beyond description" into abstract conceptualizations unrelated to the man on the street.[93] But I want from Ellul neither *a priori* elements in some sophisticated metaphysic, nor the building of unrestricted universals in Ernest Nagel's sense. I simply appeal for a systematic address to the perpetual problem of how societies are possible.[94] What principles emerge from man's long struggle to understand his relationship with other minds?[95] Though often yielding faulty collectivism, the quest for community is the western world's most "revealing preoccupation."[96] Covenant fraternity has long been a major theme of sociology, given lasting terminology by Tönnies, nurtured in Durkheim's assertions that man's concepts of God and the universe originated communally, and advanced imaginatively at early twentieth-century Chicago. Academics of virtually every kind have sought to articulate its dimensions, even until our own time as we witness "the erosion of public life" and wonder how the absence of a common culture can be overcome.[97]

At present, instead of locating himself within that continuing and invariably significant dialogue, Ellul works from historical nuance. His vast and complicated viewpoint arises fundamentally from a particular temporal circumstance wherein—following Engels's law—we face a qualitatively different world than did previous generations. In spite of our shifting era, technique is a powerful label and provides an excellent context within which to do our academic work at present. But it is inductionary, descriptive, and reflexive, in the sense that it summarizes an epoch, describes what is happening. Technique is not a generative concept which breaks new ground or rearranges our assumptions about reality, such as Charles Darwin's revolutionary naturalism did —an idea which laid hold of a static universe and gradually overturned western values and academic disciplines.[98] Ellul thus has had considerable explanatory success, but he provides description not generalization, simplification rather than discrimination and integration combined into a definitive theoretical statement.[99]

Ellul's solution appears at the far end of an unrelenting paradigm. If sovereign efficiency impounds everything under necessity, Ellul argues, liberation is the only alternative. "The problem is tyranny; opposing tyranny is freedom."[100] My call for a solution built on the nature of community demands from Ellul an explosive work which breaks loose from this one-piece analytical system.[101] In a major sense, Ellul's solution is presently entrapped by his unyielding framework, victimized by hardened categories and a measure of reductionism. His projected volume on relationship (*Ethics of Love*) might correct his weakness regarding community, but the fact that it appears near his life's conclusion symbolizes my complaint. And if it only presents the reverse side of the problem rather than a transitional book with considerably widened horizons, it will not suffice as prophecy.

Technique, the administrative animus, is a collective reality underlying observable situations. While that notion carries enormous capacity for understanding the modern mystique, it does not readily produce a meaningful pattern of social existence. Ellul is subject here to the same criticism often leveled against his mentor, Max Weber: his concept of rationalization is so abstracted that it fails to indicate the social content and institutional framework within which it operates.[102] Mighty figures contend in Ellul, but they are scarcely human. The moral architecture is clearly blueprinted, but stands "so isolated from any human context that it is difficult to see how it could possibly exist in the human world."[103] Bonhoeffer warns vigorously against offering up abstract Manicheanistic idols (such as freedom) when constructing "the responsible life."[104] If one focuses on underlying forces, as Ellul does—and then develops a solution within the same arena—a community-oriented eithic becomes impossible. The result instead is a monistic and universal contest, realms of light and darkness which have "the hollow sound and wooden substance of a morality play" divorced from actual situations and without worthwhile content.[105]

A sociology of community, carefully wrought and properly accented, likewise penetrates to fundamental issues but without the surreal dimension. It can yield instead a series of liberating distinctions which produce solutions immediately experienced in space and time. What distinctions would emerge in Ellul's case is beside my interest in this essay. But the principle should be uncontestable. Bonhoeffer's healthier sense of bodyhood produced "ultimate and penultimate" (*Die Letzten und die vorletzten*

Dinge), a copious guideline for moral behavior.[106] Joseph Gusfield distinguishes symbolic and instrumental politics; while Ellul argues accurately that the latter enhances paralysis, why should we discourage the former?[107] In both cases, human action takes on possibilities without the triviality Ellul deplores. It prevents one from pleading, as Ellul does in effect, that we escape from our civilization. Adding content to our solution also protects us from our own confining imaginations. Moreover, it produces enough sanctions so that we do not, as a matter of fact, idealize the past and call for its return.

Concluding Remark

I have argued that Ellul's solution—while worthwhile and provocative as presently formulated—will need to be re-anchored around an articulate sociology of community for him to remain prophetic. Given his individualistic bearing and penchant for infrastructures, such a modification entails some major reconceptualizations. While the scope of my essay only develops the framework, hinting at the revised shape of his three-dimensional solution may help verify the value of this new design.

The major shift in the proposed model will be in phase three—concrete possibilities. The illustrations Ellul now provides will be replaced by creative distinctions which serve as normative guidelines. Thus content will be given without fixed rules and prescribed answers; principles and sanctions will exist without a rigid system of casuistry. And even more fundamentally, a revised phase three will be placed in the forefront, not as an afterthought—"as when," in Niebuhr's striking analog, "a priest is sent to accompany a criminal on the way to the gallows."[108] These distinctions will then operate as sanctions to which one appeals and not as cheap options mentioned only on the rebound. Instead, the suggested possibilities will be honed out against man's ancient preoccupation with effective community. I believe with T. S. Eliot that a social observer's deadly sin is not heresy as much as eccentricity.

Ellul's second and most important phase—transformed being—will receive solider support. Detractors now tend to assume, though unjustifiably, that Ellul makes his choices "for essentially theological reasons, whatever their sociological disguise."[109] Ellul's audience is increasingly a Christian one and he assumes that role without reservation.[110] In the process, however, his confrontation with contemporary culture becomes less distinct and he can be relegated to the inconsequential fringes more easily. Nothing can prevent critics from typing him as an ideologue somewhere on the Christian spectrum, but a sociology of community will place the weight of his argument on cogency, not just theological assertion. When developing the problem, Ellul rooted his effort in sociology and moved from there to theology; one senses that his work on solution centers almost exclusively in that latter phase without adequate attention to the former.

While not materially altering Ellul's first dimension—his plea for realism—the new design puts his indictment of our age into slightly better perspective. It allows for countervailing factors more consistent with actual history. At present Ellul appeals only to those in a highly agitated posture and that limits him in a major sense to a "handful of scruffy malcontents"[111] near inward despair. Bonhoeffer rejected this approach as pointless and ignoble; in fact, the turbulence must subside periodically, he would argue, for any reflection to occur at all.[112] Certainly there is no guarantee, as Ellul assumes, that when we face the abyss we "automatically turn to what God can do."[113] Resigned acquiescence is more likely. Or, in another sense, a substantive solution helps those who realize the issues and want somewhere to turn.[114] It allows one to be angry and still be creative about a new pilgrimage. It would have significant implications for "breaking out of technological tyranny—one of the weakest links in his argumentative chain."[115] Ellul is presently susceptible to the charge that he invites an attitude which takes on a self-fulfilling prophecy: With the world so intensely diabolical, I can make no difference, so why not accede to the status quo?

This fresh perspective, in other words, should help satisfy the demands of both general validity and concreteness. Without it, mutually destructive antagonism will continue among Ellul and his detractors, the one side castigating him as a "one-eyed man . . . finding security in absolutes,"[116] and Ellul acting as though he must single-handedly suffer for the world's unrighteousness. No significant theoretical progress occurs in that environment.

My reorientation can temper the debate about hope and pessimism. And while perhaps not unhinging those with a mentality steeled against him, it can lift us from status denigration, keep the discussion suggestive, and provide a prophetic dimension for the coming decades.

NOTES

1. "Review of *Meaning of the City* by Jacques Ellul," *Time*, 7 Dec. 1970, p. 56.
2. Harvey Cox, *Seduction of the Spirit: The Use and Misuse of People's Religion* (New York: Simon and Schuster, 1973), p. 77.
3. *Introducing Jacques Ellul*, ed. James Y. Holloway, p. 129. See also an incident at a Genevan conference recorded by Donald W. Shriver, "Man and His Machines: Four Angles of Vision," *Technology and Culture*, 13 (Oct. 1972), 551. As a matter of fact, several of Ellul's involvements have turned into failures. Shriver notes, for instance, Ellul's quarrel with the World Council's "way of laying hold of problems" and his resignation from a French Reformed synod with its "ponderous apparatus" which precluded reform. As a result, Ellul complains, "I found myself on the fringe" ("Mirror of These Ten Years," *Christian Century*, 87 [18 Feb. 1970], 202).
4. Lewis Mumford, *Myth of the Machine* (New York: Harcourt Brace Jovanovich, 1970), II, 290–91.
5. Edward Shorter, "Industrial Society in Trouble: Some Recent Views," *The American Scholar*, 40 (Spring 1971), 334.
6. Robert Johnston, "Ellul, Easy Rider, and Hartford," *Reformed Journal*, Mar. 1976, p. 30.
7. Rupert Hall, "An Unconvincing Indictment of the Evils of Technology," *Scientific American*, 212 (Feb. 1965), 126–27.
8. For example: "Either Donnelly hasn't read my book or else he deliberately distorts it. Moreover, as the natural sequence to my *Technological Society*, I wrote a book on propaganda, where he could have found a detailed discussion of these matters. He would have done better to read it before talking" (*Christian Century*, 90 [27 June 1973], 706). Written in reply to Thomas G. Donnelly's "In Defense of Technology," *Christian Century*, 90 (17 Jan. 1973), 65–69.
9. *Political Illusion*, p. 34, cf. also pp. 29–30 (French ed. 1965); and *Technological Society*, p. xxviiff.; French ed. 1954.

10. *Technological Society*, pp. xxix, xxxi.
11. Interview with David Menninger, Bordeaux, Oct. 1973.
12. *Hope in Time of Abandonment*, p. 275 esp.; French ed. 1972.
13. "Heading toward Postcivilization," *Harper's*, 229 (Oct. 1964), 124.
14. Two introductory essays ("Between Chaos and Paralysis" and "Technique, Institutions, and Awareness") provide both perspective and three concrete suggestions each. "The Technological Order" outlines five necessary conditions for getting started. *Hope in Time of Abandonment* (pp. 258–306) advocates a compellingly written plan of action, though somewhat narrow in focus. *Presence of the Kingdom* (French ed. 1948) refers constantly to alternatives and chapter 4 presents a systematic statement. The last two chapters of *Political Illusion* recommend activities for making democracy healthy. Perhaps no more definitive statement on altering society exists than the last chapter in *Autopsy of Revolution* (French ed. 1969). Though addressed primarily to Christians, the second half of *Ethics of Freedom* (French ed. 1970) prescribes behaviors and attitudes for acting responsibly. And specific possibilities appear everywhere in "The Technological Revolution and Its Moral and Political Consequences."
15. His best discussions of realism are "Le Réalisme Politique: Problèmes de civilization, III," *Foi et Vie*, 46 (Nov. 1947), 698–734; *Hope in Time of Abandonment*, pp. 274–82; *Prayer and Modern Man*, chap. 3 (English ed. 1972).
16. Cf. *New Demons*, e.g. pp. 206–7, 228; French ed. 1973.
17. *Political Illusion*, p. 223, n. 3.
18. "Author's Foreword," *Technological Society*, p. iii.
19. *Presence of the Kingdom*, p. 108. For more details on Ellul's complaint about academics see *Propaganda*, pp. xvi–xvii, 11, 31, 40, 113, 121, 146, 160; *Presence of the Kingdom*, pp. 99–103, 108–11; *Political Illusion*, p. 202; *Technological Society*, pp. 335–87. For a summary, see my "The Vulnerable Intellectual," *Journalism Monographs*, Aug. 1976, 22–26.
20. *The New Demons*, chap. 1; *False Presence of the Kingdom* is entirely devoted to a critique of Christendom, especially French Protestantism.
21. "Love and Order," *Katallagete*, 9 (Summer 1976), 28–33. He attacks political liberalism particularly in *Autopsy of Revolution*, chap. 4.
22. *Autopsy of Revolution*, pp. 240, 248; throughout this book and

elsewhere Ellul is concerned to distinguish genuine revolution and misguided revolt. Cf. also *Presence of the Kingdom*, chap. 3; *Violence; Critique of the New Commonplaces*, pp. 54–66, 82–91, 196–201, 288–93.

23. *Presence of the Kingdom*, p. 33.
24. "Between Chaos and Paralysis," p. 748; cf. also "Technique, Institutions, and Awareness," p. 42, where he condemns the "technocratic model," the Leninist one, and all solutions issuing from central power.
25. Ellul categorically rejects a "technical humanism" which assumes that technology is neutral and can be used for good purposes (*Technological Society*, p. 340). He is even more emphatic in "Note on the Theme: Technical Progress is Always Ambiguous" ("The Technological Order," pp. 28–37).
26. David Gill, "Activist and Ethicist, Meet Jacques Ellul," *Christianity Today*, 10 Sept. 1976, p. 24. His special foe here is Teilhard de Chardin and others like him, who depend on automatic mechanisms whereby humanity fuses at Point Omega by simple evolution; cf. esp. "The Technological Order," p. 23ff.
27. *Hope in Time of Abandonment*, p. 278; cf. also "Between Chaos and Paralysis," p. 747.
28. *Autopsy of Revolution*, pp. 245–46; cf. also *Hope in Time of Abandonment*, p. 275.
29. *Propaganda*, pp. xvii–xviii; French ed. 1962.
30. Seymour Martin Lipset sees this as one of Ellul's great contributions, in "Facing a Free Choice," review of *Propaganda* by Jacques Ellul, *New York Times Book Review*, 6 Mar. 1966, p. 47.
31. *Hope in Time of Abandonment*, p. 275.
32. Richard L. Rubenstein, review of *The New Demons* by Jacques Ellul, *Psychology Today*, Nov. 1975, p. 18.
33. *Autopsy of Revolution*, p. 279.
34. "The Technological Order," pp. 25–26.
35. "Technique, Institutions, and Awareness," p. 42.
36. The relationship between phases one and two is developed more in *New Demons*, pp. 207–8.
37. *Ibid.*, p. 208.
38. *Presence of the Kingdom*, p. 31; and letter to Vernard Eller, 15 Sept. 1972.
39. Ellul's individualism is not a libertarian one; he realizes this is a "suicidal solution" in "Between Chaos and Paralysis," p. 748. He adds: "We need . . . a new spirit wholly distinct from traditional

individualism" (*Autopsy of Revolution*, p. 300). For all who criticize him as an individualist, see his retort in *Presence of the Kingdom*, pp. 82–85, 103.

40. Vernon Grounds, "Under Cover: Review of *Autopsy of Revolution* by Jacques Ellul," *His*, Jan. 1973, 23.

41. *To Will and To Do*, p. 217 (French ed. 1964); *Presence of the Kingdom*, pp. 33, 78–79, 81; cf. *Meaning of the City*, p. 119; English ed. 1970.

42. *Violence*, p. 167; English ed. 1969.

43. *Political Illusion*, p. 221.

44. "Between Chaos and Paralysis," p. 749.

45. Richard Schickel, review of *Autopsy of Revolution* by Jacques Ellul, *Harper's*, Apr. 1972, p. 101.

46. "Mirror of These Ten Years," p. 201.

47. In *Autopsy of Revolution*, he calls it a "spark of defiance and self-assertion," p. 300.

48. In the interview with David Menninger, Bordeaux, Oct. 1973, he insists: "I am not against politics in general." He disavows the idea that "technology and its products are evil and that man ought to shun them" (*Ethics of Freedom*, p. 190). And further: "It is not technology itself which enslaves us, but the transfer of the sacred into technology" (*New Demons*, p. 206).

49. "Between Chaos and Paralysis," pp. 748, 750; see "Technique, Institutions, and Awareness," p. 42. Or, as he says explicitly in *The Nation*, 24 May 1965: "I am still convinced that if we can be sufficiently awakened to the real gravity of the situation, man has within himself the necessary resources to discover . . . the path to a new freedom" (p. 568).

50. Rubenstein, review of *The New Demons*, p. 20.

51. *Introducing Jacques Ellul*, p. 6. He adds: "I am willing to engage in dialogue, to suggest a number of specific things [for those willing] to take the necessary steps themselves. . . . But I still wouldn't try to establish a total program of political action" (interview with David Menninger, Oct. 1973).

52. Interview with David Menninger, Oct. 1973. In another typical statement: "Every Christian must discover for himself the style and form of his action" (*Ethics of Freedom*, p. 300).

53. *Ethics of Freedom*, pp. 106, 510. We need to be constantly vigilant because we can easily become overtaken and reintegrated into society; cf. "Between Chaos and Paralysis," pp. 748–49.

54. "Between Chaos and Paralysis," p. 749.

55. Ellul is not suggesting quick cures. But as our sense of community shrivels, the importance of this suggestion increasingly occurs

among social observers. For an interesting summary of this issue, see "Rituals—the Revolt against the Fixed Smile," *Time*, 12 Oct. 1970, pp. 42–43. Rollo May documented (in *Love and Will*) that a society which suppresses ritual eventually produces all manner of magic and fakery with a vengeance.

56. "Technique, Institutions, and Awareness," p. 42. Daniel Berrigan's class on Ellul produced a similar example: "Someone spoke of the Buddhists in Vietnam, those who spend their time helping the wounded, resisting the draft and calling for a ceasefire as the primary step towards ending the war; then Dan smiled with empathy and nodded a vigorous affirmation. . . . It was a provocative and hopeful, if sobering indication of the concrete working out of such a perspective" (*National Catholic Reporter*, 22 Dec. 1972, p. 6).

57. *Political Illusion*, p. 222.

58. *Presence of the Kingdom*, p. 126.

59. I emphasize "formal similarity." Berry, Schumacher, and Illich are only illustrative of the kind of movement Ellul anticipates here in phase three. While each of them also begins with a crusading realism, and each calls for a radical change in attitude, they do not duplicate Ellul's theological orientation in phase two.

60. Wendell Berry, "Think Little," in *The Updated Last Whole Earth Catalog* (Menlo Park, Calif.: Nowels Publications, 1974), pp. 24–25. Cf. also "The Culture of Agriculture," *The CoEvolution Quarterly*, Spring 1975, pp. 38–40, and *A Place on Earth* (New York: Harcourt, Brace and World, 1967). Berry suggests that we plant a garden—an analog for each of us cultivating a garden in the contemporary cultural mix.

61. *Small is Beautiful* (New York: Harper & Row, 1973), pp. 60–61.

62. *Tools of Conviviality* (New York: Harper & Row, 1973).

63. Quoted from Max Weber in J. P. Mayer, *Max Weber and German Politics* (London: Faber and Faber, 1943), p. 128.

64. In the *Ethics of Freedom*, Ellul recognizes the value of anarchistic acts which open the system, though he never recommends sabotage as inherently good. Elsewhere he declares: "We are obligated to participate in many unjust but inevitable actions. . . . But in doing so we must remember that . . . these necessary actions are of the order of sin, and so I must repent and rely on the grace of God, even for that which I believe useful and indispensable on the political level" ("Correspondence: Ellul Replies on Violence," *Christianity and Crisis*, 19 Oct. 1970, p. 221). For further development of this matter, see chap. 9 herein.

65. In "Mirror of These Ten Years," Ellul notes: "I have come to a

progressively clearer view of my writings" (p. 200). In that sense, *Political Illusion* (eleven years after *Technological Society*) is the maturest description of technique.

66. Those focusing more on hope and solution appear after that time: *Autopsy of Revolution* (1971), *Hope in Time of Abandonment* (1972), and *Ethics of Freedom* (1976). However, his most important and popular trilogy appears before the more hopeful emphasis: *Technological Society* (1954), *Propaganda* (1962), *Political Illusion* (1965).

67. Vernard Eller has developed these themes in an unpublished paper, "A Response to Harvey Cox's Review of Ellul's *The Meaning of the City*." Ellul's dialectic operates best in his excellent essay, " 'The World' in the Gospels," *Katallagete*, 5 (Spring 1974), 16–23, and to a degree in *Presence of the Kingdom*.

68. *Ethics of Freedom*, e.g. p. 270.

69. *Hope in Time of Abandonment*, pp. 259–74, 288–95.

70. Personal letter from Robert Merton, 8 Dec. 1976.

71. Schickel, review of *Autopsy of Revolution*, p. 96.

72. Ellul's own, most lengthy, attack on humanism occurs in *Metamorphose du bourgeois*, e.g. pp. 267–75.

73. *Pentagon of Power*, p. 435.

74. "Between Chaos and Paralysis," p. 749. Or, as he describes it in his interview with David Menninger: "In order to engage oneself in combat with the problems of our time—the state, technique, and the like—one must have strong motives. And the strongest motives can be found in Christianity" (Bordeaux, Oct. 1973).

75. In Ellul's terms: "The heart of a revolution is the extra point, on the basis of which it is possible to view all the rest since it is transcendent . . . the never-achieved prospect in relation to which everything has its place" (*New Demons*, p. 211).

76. Ellul develops his criticisms most fully in *Social Research*, and in Appendix I of *Propaganda*. He complains, for example: "Some scientists think that the only guarantee of truth is methodological rigor," thus they deal with the "relatively secondary and nothing fundamental has been questioned" (*Social Research*, Spring 1976, pp. 13, 17). And further: "Anything this method can't handle isn't available to science," and when other non-amenable areas are probed, they are "considered amateurs or essayists, quite unlike true men of science" (p. 14).

77. "Technique, Institutions, and Awareness," p. 41.

78. Though poorly written and mis-oriented, Arend Van Leeuwen's book at least asks the right question: *Prophecy in a Technocratic Era* (New York: Scribner's, 1968). My definition of the prophetic

mode parallels that of Robert W. Friedrichs, *A Sociology of Sociology* (New York: Free Press, 1970), chaps. 3–6.

79. Daniel Bell, *The Coming of Post-Industrial Society* (New York: Basic Books, 1973); Norman Birnbaum, *The Crisis of Industrial Society* (New York: Oxford University Press, 1969). David Reisman's *The Lonely Crowd* (New Haven, Conn.: Yale University Press, 1950) can also be read historically as documenting the same shift. Though on a different level, Kevin Philips in *Mediacracy* (Garden City, N.Y.: Doubleday, 1975) uses sociological data to describe the present information age as differing in substance from the corporate-industrial era.

80. For a summary of some contemporary writers who have turned sour on "technophoria," see Leslie Sklair, "The Revolt against the Machine: Some Twentieth Century Criticisms of Scientific Progress," *Journal of World History*, 2 (1970), 479–89.

81. Cf. Hans J. Morgenthau, e.g. *Science: Servant or Master* (New York: New American Library, 1972).

82. C. George Benello, review of *The Technological Society* by Jacques Ellul, *Our Generation*, Mar. 1967, p. 107. See also Shorter's bibliographical essay in which he concludes that "the conventional wisdom of liberalism, of which we have been so confident over the last two decades, is leading us into the sand" ("Industrial Society in Trouble," p. 348).

83. Dale Brown, "Critique: New Demons," *Sojourners*, 5 (Nov. 1976), 37. An analysis still relevant even though the objects of Ellul's attack (the theological fashions and political activism of the 1960s) are virtually nonexistent at present.

84. *Technological Society*, p. 43.

85. Daniel Bell, *The Cultural Contradictions of Capitalism* (New York: Basic Books, 1976).

86. *Introducing Jacques Ellul*, p. 17. Rubenstein is harsh, but essentially correct: "In light of the outpouring of books and articles that deal with the deadly problems of technological civilization, Ellul's characterization of technology as the modern 'sacred of respect' can be regarded as nothing but the unsubstantiated opinion of a biased observer" (review of *The New Demons*, p. 18).

87. The well-known Kierkegaard scholar Vernard Eller takes exception to the typical condemnation of Kierkegaard's overwhelming individualism. Eller argues that Kierkegaard's notion of community, while not extensive, is very intensive, and while not a major theme, is an authentic one. Cf. Vernard Eller, *The Dunkers and the Dane*, chap. 11 esp.

88. *Ethics of Freedom*, p. 210.

89. E.g. *Ethics of Freedom*, pp. 210, 298; *Presence of the Kingdom*, chap. 4.

90. *Ethics of Freedom*, p. 478.

91. Ellul writes: "The criterion of my thought is the biblical revelation" (*To Will and To Do*, p. 1).

92. H. Richard Niebuhr, *Christ and Culture* (New York: Harper and Row [1951], 1956), p. 164.

93. *Technological Society*, p. xxvii. In *To Will and To Do*, he disassociates himself from a philosophy of values (p. 140). See also his sarcasm about "pretending to be deep" (*Presence of the Kingdom*, p. 77).

94. In effect, I use Ellul's own definition here: "Theory . . . is [that] rigorous intellectual activity which determines action" ("Technique, Institutions, and Awareness," p. 42).

95. William Ernest Hocking's phrase in *The Meaning of God in Human Experience* (New Haven, Conn.: Yale University Press, 1963).

96. Robert Nisbet, *The Quest for Community* (New York: Oxford University Press, 1953), p. vii.

97. Richard Sennett, *The Fall of Public Man* (New York: Alfred A. Knopf, 1977), p. 6; chap. 11 esp.

98. Explained with substance and detail by Paul F. Boller, *American Thought in Transition: The Impact of Evolutionary Naturalism, 1865–1900* (Chicago: Rand McNally, 1969).

99. Dudley Marcum has clarified this distinction for me in his work on Harold Innis.

100. Mitcham and Mackey, "Jacques Ellul and the Technological Society," p. 117.

101. In a formal sense, I am asking for a statement which makes the same inspired critical juncture as does *Hope in Time of Abandonment*. See James Holloway's perceptive review of this book in *Religion in Life*, Autumn 1975, pp. 379–81.

102. Jürgen Habermas, *Toward a Rational Society* (Boston: Beacon, 1970), p. 100.

103. Mitcham and Mackey, "Jacques Ellul and the Technological Society," p. 116.

104. *Letters and Papers* (New York: Macmillan, 1953), pp. 194–96. See also his *Ethics* (New York: Macmillan [1949], 1975), p. 3, for our tendency to create ahistorical villains and saints.

105. Hallock Hoffman, "The View from Hell," *The Center Magazine*, 2 (July 1969), 22; cf. also Benello, *Our Generation*, p. 112.

106. *Letters and Papers*, p. 79ff.; *Ethics*, p. 84ff. For a summary, see

The Place of Bonhoeffer: Problems and Possibilities in His Thought, ed. Martin E. Marty (New York: Association Press, 1962); from the chapter by George W. Forell, "Realized Faith, the Ethics of Dietrich Bonhoeffer," pp. 197–221.

107. Joseph R. Gusfield, *Symbolic Crusade* (Urbana: University of Illinois Press, 1963), chap. 7. For more development of the key concepts involved here, see Murray Edelman, *The Symbolic Uses of Politics* (Urbana: University of Illinois Press, 1964).

108. *Christ and Culture*, p. 240.

109. Douglas D. McFerran, "The Cult of Jacques Ellul," *America*, 6 Feb. 1971, p. 123. Cf. also Rubenstein's review of *The New Demons*, which calls that work a "religious diatribe" (p. 18).

110. For example: "I write mainly for those within the faith" (interview with David Menninger, Bordeaux, Oct. 1973).

111. Theodore Roszak's phrase in another context; *The Making of a Counter Culture* (New York: Doubleday Anchor, 1969), p. 44.

112. *Letters and Papers*, p. 146ff.

113. *Sojourners*, p. 36.

114. Isn't there increasing need for a *Guide for the Perplexed*, a recent title by E. F. Schumacher (New York: Harper & Row, 1978)?

115. Mitcham and Mackey "Jacques Ellul and the Technological Society," p. 119.

116. Lester DeKoster, review of *Meaning of the City* by Jacques Ellul, *The Banner* (16 July 1971), 25. Or, as Rubenstein puts it in his review of *The New Demons:* "I regret to report that he [Ellul] has little use for ordinary civility" (p. 20).

Part III

ETHICS
AND
THEOLOGY

CHAPTER 9

Discontinuity in the Ethics of Jacques Ellul

Gene Outka

Ellul's writings on ethics are widely assumed to perpetuate many of the distinctive claims associated with the "neo-orthodoxy" of an earlier generation. His corpus contains a number of favorable references to Karl Barth and Reinhold Niebuhr, for example, and standing behind them, to Søren Kierkegaard. This assumption, while vague and impressionistic, is partly correct, yet it has to be qualified. Certain differences, sometimes admitted, sometimes not, distinguish Ellul from these earlier thinkers (and these thinkers from each other). Ellul's corpus also contains lengthy assessments of contemporary (post–neo-orthodox) proposals in Christian ethics. He has attacked, for instance, the recent widespread endorsement of movements on behalf of revolution and liberation. His own ethics should be viewed within this contemporary setting and not only in relation to the earlier legacy.

I shall attempt a selective sketch of Ellul's reflection on ethical matters. For the sake of manageability, attention will be restricted to three of his books which address ethical questions: *To Will and To Do, Violence,* and *The Ethics of Freedom.* And I shall aim for comparison as well as exposition: we need to locate, however cursorily, the particular region Ellul occupies on a larger map of discussions in the modern period.

To study Ellul also affords an opportunity to consider some general issues about a program avowedly committed to "discontinuity." I find Ellul especially interesting because, like Barth most notably, he refuses to decode the Christian conceptions he describes. He joins forces with those who contend, whether they are believers or atheists (and thus whether they lament or welcome the prospect), that "to decode turns out to be to destroy."[1] Ellul insists that Christianity be accepted on terms internal to it, and not by an appeal to criteria authoritative for a secularized worldview. Indeed, he thinks believers have every reason to be aggressively critical of such criteria. They should choose "discontinuity" rather than "continuity." The following statements are representative.

> In my view, to reject what is specific in Christianity is the greatest delusion in our own generation [*Ethics of Freedom*, p. 254].
>
> An important decision has to be made here. Between the world and the kingdom of God, is there continuity or discontinuity? . . .
>
> In the former case, all men's works as such even though man does not know it, prepare the way for God's kingdom. They are as such prophecies of what God has in mind. Eros is a sign or prophecy of agape. What man calls justice, goodness, and freedom is a sign or prophecy of what God reveals as his own justice, will, and freedom. Man's religion is a sign and prophecy of revelation in Christ.
>
> My own belief, however . . . is that there is discontinuity. What man manufactures in these areas is illusion and self-justification, a means of escaping judgment and grace. As I see it, then, what man calls freedom is not a small part of the way to true freedom in Christ. It is not a beginning, a preparation and intimation, or a reflection of authentic freedom. It is the very opposite [*Ethics of Freedom*, pp. 272–73].[2]

Of course Ellul's version of discontinuity may appear on examination to be idiosyncratic or unduly obscure at crucial points. Even so, certain basic questions will surface periodically in reference to his work. For example, how are we to understand the insistence that a believer's freedom be wholly unprecedented? Why must the distinction—between worldly and Christian accounts of love, justice, goodness, and religion itself—not be elided in any way? *Can* such a program be executed successfully? Does

Ellul himself succeed, or do we find hints of continuity that the program officially forbids?

Let me try to achieve these interdependent aims by examining, first, Ellul's characterization of "worldly" morality, and then of Christian ethics. Finally, I want to discuss at greater length certain issues which seem especially important in assessing a program like the one Ellul offers.

I

What then of worldly morality? The first point to be noted is that Ellul appears austerely sociological and historical in comparison with most influential accounts in theological ethics. There is for him "no such thing as general or universal morality. There are actual moral systems and there is a morality which derives from revelation"(*Ethics of Freedom*, p. 361). That is all. Worldly morality is wholly devoid of "permanent content" (*To Will and To Do*, p. 118). To approach the subject of worldly or "natural" morality correctly is therefore to proceed at once to the study of "actual moral systems." The plural is obviously important. For Ellul, we can attend only to the actual moral code of each community in its turn. And our attention shows us that a given code will be necessarily tied to all the other economic, political, and cultural features distinguishing a given community. Ellul commends Karl Marx's insight. "It is surely one of the many merits of Karl Marx to have demonstrated the contingent character of morality, its connection with economic structures and class relationships, and its role in the interplay of social forces" (*To Will and To Do*, p. 291). Ellul does not shrink from applying this perspective in his occasional references to modern moral philosophy. Existentialism (especially as found in the writings of Sartre) is alleged to mirror twentieth-century developments in the West far beyond the conscious imaginings of its exponents (*Ethics of Freedom*, pp. 134, 142). Ellul doubts the importance, moreover, even in contemporary settings, of most theorizing about ordinary moral judgments. "Theoretically morality," as a self-conscious enterprise, is largely the creation of Mediterranean civilization (*To Will and To Do*, p. 128). The theorist has a prominent role to play only when he or she acts as a "recorder and catalytic agent" for social forces wholly outside his or her control (*To Will and To Do*, pp. 136, 139). Our attention shows us last that moral reflection remains always temporal and transitory. It is idle to search for a kind of cumulative moral wisdom or to hope to learn from some great thinker in the past what is morally decisive for us here and now. "Look at the greatest systems of moral thought and it will easily be evident how dated they are, the extent to which they belong to a time and to an epoch. To grasp them once again requires an effort. Never do they speak directly and openly to us as they were able to speak to their contemporaries. Only by extracting certain happy expressions, a few rare pearls out of the whole superseded mixture, can we still follow Socrates or Confucius" (*To Will and To Do*, p. 64).[3]

Ellul's wholesale concentration on discrete moral systems differs in an important way from several influential accounts of natural morality in theological ethics. The most conspicuous cases are theories of natural law which offer ontological pictures of a fully determinate and unalterable human nature. A strict relation obtains between person-time-place-invariant properties constitutive of the human person as such and a correlative series of fixed obligations.[4] Yet one also meets with less ambitious, more empirically based proposals, without commitments to any explicit ontology. David Little, for example, in his essay "Calvin and the Prospects for a Christian Theory of Natural Law," appeals to the findings of cultural anthropologists like Clyde Kluckhohn and Ralph Linton in an attempt "to establish a set of empirical generalizations about human nature that is constant, both spatially (cross-culturally) and temporally (historically)." He then moves from these descriptive generalizations to a set of prescriptions about how persons ought to act.[5]

Ellul disregards such nuances and briskly rejects, presumably on empirical grounds, every appeal to an "essential human nature" (*To Will and To Do*, pp. 52, 151).[6] And unlike Little on Calvin, he refuses to view the second table of the decalogue as a convenient summary of prohibitions to which all persons pay some kind of homage. Murder itself, for example, is generally but not always reproved cross-culturally; respect for life is by no means "a universal commandment" (*To Will and To Do*, pp. 118–19).

Reinhold Niebuhr shares Ellul's suspicion of any ambitious belief in natural law. He criticizes the certainty displayed by traditional Roman Catholic natural-law theorists who define and apply the principles of justice in every situation.[7] Moral reflection is too relative to a particular time and place and too tainted with self-interest to make such certainty credible. But Ellul's comment about murder goes beyond what even Niebuhr is prepared to allow. Niebuhr stops short of the radical discontinuity between actual moral systems which Ellul propounds. His sensitivity to cultural and historical diversity does not undermine his respect for those codes and principles of justice which he claims all communities strive in some measure to articulate and apply. It is wrong to dismiss these, Niebuhr insists, as "both secular and Reformation relativists" are inclined to do. For him the prohibition of murder possesses more than the limited validity accorded to rules which only certain societies or communities accept as binding. Similarly, equality and liberty as "essentially universal" principles of justice find expression in every major historical period.[8] They serve as "transcendent" reference points from which to criticize and reform status quo arrangements or any particular "system of justice."

How shall we understand this disagreement between Niebuhr and Ellul? It concerns in part which set of claims are factually well founded. Ellul's denial—that the prohibition of murder has quite the universal place or importance in moral codes which Niebuhr ascribes to it—appears to be based on empirical evidence. When he criticizes Niebuhr explicitly for failing to appreciate "the unbelievable variety of . . . content" which has been attached to the word "justice" (*To Will and To Do*, p. 292), the charge concerns a neglect of available sources. We might extrapolate and say that for Ellul, Niebuhr's assertion about universal principles of justice is too parochial (spatially) and too sweeping (temporally). The putative universality is ethnocentrism in disguise, given Niebuhr's nearly exclusive attention to western cases in point; and historical differences between Stoic, medieval, and modern depictions of equality and liberty do not receive their due. This part of the disagreement, resolvable perhaps in principle, remains inconclusive in fact. Neither Ellul nor Niebuhr, in the works referred to, provide the kind of empirical documentation of their respective claims which would allow some definite judgment to be made with any confidence.

In any event, I think the disagreement goes beyond anything we may settle by empirical evidence. Ellul objects to natural-law proposals for theological as well as sociological and historical reasons. Why should the believer as believer be concerned to stress spatial and temporal constancies? Ellul maintains that something corrupt is at work in this stress. For him human moral codes, what *we* call justice, goodness, and freedom, must not be taken as "signs," "prophecies," "beginnings," "preparations," "intimations," or "reflections" of the genuine articles. The latter we know solely by revelation. Now the language Ellul uses to mark this discontinuity is often distressingly vague. At numerous points the reader must be satisfied with blanket denunciations—of the urge toward "a single movement," for example, in Thomism, Hegel, and Teilhard de Chardin (*Ethics of Freedom*, p. 364). I take it he shares Barth's general concern to keep the witness of Scripture as the only source for the knowledge of God. Nothing else, no essentialist account of human nature, no worldview, no ideology, can dictate the conditions for, or contribute necessarily to, divine revelation. The assumptions about justice, goodness, and freedom bequeathed to our western minds must thus be scrutinized afresh in the light of what God reveals. In themselves (even provisionally or in terms of a presumption in their favor), they cannot serve as a semi-independent source of the knowledge of God's will, or furnish a set of criteria for distinguishing genuine from spurious divine commands. Yet matters grow more complicated when, as we shall see in the second section, part of what is bequeathed to us are Christian moral values now secularized. What status do *these* values have for the believer? Do they warrant some greater allegiance on his or her part then other moral values? If they do, then in what sense do they remain Christian, and in what sense are they now decoded? As it happens, such a line of questioning is not taken by Ellul nearly as far as I at least would wish. Our present concern, however, is with his theological objections to natural-law proposals. And on this subject, one comparison is worth drawing in more detail.

Ellul contends that "the doctrine of natural morality is an

aspect of heresy cropping up incessantly by which an accommodation is sought between grace and nature in the process of setting a value upon nature" (*To Will and To Do*, p. 52). This accusation is very serious, though the language in which it is couched is not commensurately precise. While positions like Niebuhr's and Little's may be rejected in part along the way, the major tradition which sets a value upon nature in a fashion Ellul resists is theism generally and Thomism specifically. Within this tradition, it has been thought to make sense to talk about morality as "a discipline which yields results which are true or false."[9] And further, it has been held that certain kinds of action—murder and treachery, for example—are wrong in themselves. That this is so does not require a reference to God's will to be established as valid. Rather, God and morally virtuous persons are understood to join together in condemning intrinsically wrong actions because they are wrong. The actions do not just become wrong because or when God condemns them. Eric D'Arcy summarizes the position well:

> God forbids certain kinds of action because they are wrong, not vice versa; God commends, commands, or forbids certain kinds of action and certain frames of mind because he is essentially holy, and they are intrinsically good, or evil; the connection between morality and the Christian religion is therefore intrinsic and necessary, though a connection of natural, not logical, necessity. If I had to summarize my reasons in a single phrase, I should say that they are packed into the Christian's notion of his God as being literally and unreservedly *worthy of worship*.[10]

Here one is asking about the onto-moral status of acts, about the things which make acts right or wrong. D'Arcy, appealing to Thomas Aquinas, sides with those who say that it is some property intrinsic to the acts and frames of mind themselves which makes them right or wrong; he rejects the view sometimes called "moral positivism" which holds that the thing which makes them right or wrong is precisely that God wills or forbids them.[11] A final claim is an epistemic one: in this life we have at least some limited access to what these actions and frames of mind are, independent of revelation.

It is this last claim in particular which Ellul finds theologically unacceptable. To be sure, he endorses what he calls "theological nominalism" where "commandment is not based on the divine essence but on the sovereign will of God" (*To Will and To Do*, p. 268), yet he does not elaborate on this endorsement. And he might ask whether the debate about the onto-moral status of acts is not idle speculation until the epistemological question is settled. One can locate two closely related objections to the last claim. First, Ellul believes such a view places inordinate confidence in the powers of practical reason. Something naive is mixed with something presumptuous. We live too incurably in a fallen world to suppose that our moral reflection can escape, fundamentally and for all time, ambiguity and defilement. Ellul goes further: "Whatever it is of the *imago Dei* which survives, that cannot in any case be the moral sense" (*To Will and To Do*, p. 42). And so the very origin of morality "is bound up with disobedience. Henceforth it forms part of the order of the Fall" (*To Will and To Do*, p. 41). The corruption referred to earlier seems to inhere in the cognitive process itself, in the sheer human ambitiousness displayed in the course of judging which actions are right or wrong in themselves. While these do not exhaust the options, there is perhaps in the end no peace between those who, like D'Arcy, see a necessary link between immorality as determined on independent grounds and sin as an offense against God and his holy law,[12] and those who, like Ellul, describe sin as "not the failure to obey a morality. It is the very desire to determine that morality independently of God, a desire which is, at the same time, concupiscence, the will to power" (*To Will and To Do*, p. 13).

A second consideration shifts the ground slightly from a concern over the capacity of fallen practical reason to one about the usurpation of God's sovereignty. In effect we go back to the sort of concern Ellul shares with Barth. If we claim that God forbids certain kinds of action because they are wrong in themselves and that we know about such wrongness (albeit in a limited way) independent of revelation, are we not then attributing a kind of secondary revelatory status to natural moral knowledge? This knowledge is independent of Scripture and yet informs us about that which God will never require. We are no longer strictly in a position where something must be told to us which we cannot tell to ourselves.

Finally, another kind of theological objection to natural morality should be mentioned. Some proponents of this morality have ascribed religious importance to de facto moral attainment. Consider D'Arcy's insistence that moral performance affects one's relation to God. "Catholic teaching has always insisted that substantial fidelity to morality is a necessary condition of enjoying God's favor. This is not to say, of course, that it is a *sufficient* condition of this: that issue has been a topic of lively theological dispute since the time of Pelagius and Augustine, and this is not the place to rehearse it. Not sufficient therefore; but necessary."[13] It seems too much like "preparation" or a "beginning" to claim that living a morally exemplary life is a necessary condition for enjoying God's favor. Adherence to any system of natural morality does not in itself, Ellul insists, bring one closer to God. To talk of a necessary condition is to raise the specter of "works righteousness"; a Protestant like Ellul is instinctively wary of the latter being masked as the former. How far such wariness should extend must remain unclear. It seems to apply to every version of the claim that only the serious moral person has the chance of grasping grace—where the moral life is, as it were, the narrow gate through which one must pass if certain religious and/or Christian questions or affirmations are even to arise or be possible.[14] Ellul, on the other hand, does not relish radical talk of "the paradoxical nature of God's way," where the knowledge that one is a sinner or immoralist is a necessary condition for enjoying divine favor. If "enjoying God's favor" is tantamount to "salvation," then for Ellul no conditions are attached: neither moral performance nor the acknowledgment of sin. He cautiously accepts the universality of salvation (*Ethics of Freedom*, p. 82), going further in this respect than Barth is explicitly willing to go.[15] Several implications of this acceptance will be considered in the pages ahead.

In light of such historical, sociological, and theological objections to most accounts of natural morality in theological ethics, what attitude should the believer take toward actual moral systems? Ellul does not commend an unrelievedly negative stance. There is a sense in which the believer may properly say Yes, as well as No after all.

While no permanent material content common to all moral codes can be observed, Ellul allows that every community finds it necessary to formulate a morality (*To Will and To Do*, p. 125). Why is this so? He gives a familiar answer, reminiscent of Thomas Hobbes and, in our own time, G. J. Warnock,[16] though his version is stated very cryptically. Some kind of moral code is required to overcome social chaos. "Life is possible within an ethical system. Apart from that it would be a constant warfare, and interpersonal relationships would be unthinkable. Therefore, we must respect this morality for its utility, since it is useful to man" (*To Will and To Do*, p. 80). Morality has to do with the meeting of "humble but essential needs": "air fit to breathe, sufficient nourishment, a harmonious order, the possibility of mutual relationships . . ." (*To Will and To Do*, pp. 80–81).

How then should the believer—the one striving to live in accordance with morality derived from revelation—assess the morality justified by its "utility"? A given moral code should be supported by the believer, for it possesses "relative validity" as "an element of the preservation of society" (*To Will and To Do*, p. 106). Ellul is prepared, moreover, to accept a large dose of determinism: believers will naturally, and it seems unproblematically, share the judgments of their contemporaries about many matters of morality, custom, and etiquette. "This morality, strictly human, relative, temporary, and temporal, which is not the will of God no matter what form it takes, is nevertheless necessary. The Christian who is aware of its limits has absolutely no right on that account to treat it as false or useless. . . . We are living on this earth at a given time in a given place. We are human beings like everyone else. . . . It is to be expected that, at the human level, we should judge to be good that which the people of this age call good" (*To Will and To Do*, p. 77). Or again, since "ethical systems are essential" to human beings, "from the Christian standpoint there can be no question of condemning or rejecting them, *no matter what they may be*" (*Ethics of Freedom*, p. 361, my italics).

We may distinguish a descriptive and a normative question at this juncture. What it takes to make a code a moral code is one question; why believers ought to accommodate to a moral code is another. Ellul's sole criterion, in answer to the first question, seems to be societal survival: a system is an ethical system if it contributes essentially to this end. And he assumes every community finds it necessary to formulate such a system. Thus far his general case reminds one also of the Reformers' defense of the "civil use" of the law.[17] Yet unlike modern figures such as Emil Brunner and Helmut Thielicke who attempt to carry forward Reformation themes,[18] Ellul refuses to undergird his account of natural morality with a doctrine of creation (*To Will and To Do*, p. 266). His preference for historical and sociological depiction of discrete ethical systems, furthermore, appears more minimalist than even Barth would find wholly satisfactory. The latter is prepared to refer in the singular to "the ethical question," and to maintain that it arises irrepressibly "in every age and place."[19] To be sure, theological ethics for Barth invades and takes over the sense of the question as well as its answer. Still, apart from this all-important invasion, Barth insists that ethics be kept distinct from custom, politics, and laws of historical development.[20] Due in large part to his indebtedness to Marx, Ellul is more willing to stress the connections between ethics and all the rest.

Ellul's answer to the normative question of why believers ought to accommodate to a moral code remains largely undeveloped. And so he does not face various well-worn difficulties. What of a conflict between the needs of certain individuals and the interests of the society at large? Should collective interests always override? Ought believers to accommodate this far?

To regard the promotion of societal welfare as a sufficient condition for an acceptable ethical system seems notoriously permissive. Consider the distinction offered by Christine Battersby in her paper "Morality and the Ik":

(i) a rule is a moral rule if it serves to promote the treatment of other human beings as ends-in-themselves;

(ii) a rule is a moral rule if it promotes the welfare of the society.

Obviously, (ii) is far more inclusive than (i). To show this, Battersby cites the following rules:

D. You should not give gifts to old and dying people;

D1. You should give gifts to old and dying people.[21]

How does the distinction apply to these rules?

> According to (i), D will not count as a moral rule because it
> does not protect the dignity of the old and dying, although
> D1 will count as a moral rule. According to (ii), both D and
> D1 could count as moral rules in differing circumstances. In
> the case of the Ik society, D will most certainly count as a
> moral rule as it is in the interests of the survival of the soci-
> ety that all available food should go to the young who still
> have the capacity to reproduce. From the point of view of
> the survival of the Ik society as a whole, the reproductive
> value of the old and dying is nil, so they are (on this criter-
> ion) properly ignored.[22]

Could Ellul accept such a conclusion? On his account, (ii)
qualifies descriptively as a moral rule. Why not then accommodate, if "from the Christian standpoint there can be no question of condemning or rejecting" ethical systems, "no matter
what they may be"? Should an elderly Christian living in the Ik
society conform with D by refusing all gifts and going off to die
rather than threaten the survival of the society? It may be so. But
should a Christian of reproductive age ignore the old and dying
without further ado? In short, can so strict a dichotomy be viably
maintained between natural morality, as Ellul construes it, and
Christian ethics? We shall be in a better position to speculate on
Ellul's own answers after his account of Christian ethics proper
has been considered.

II

It seems to me useful to approach most characterizations of theological ethics, including Ellul's, by disentangling at least three
broad issues. (A) One must determine whether there is an irreducibly distinct morality which derives from revelation. We have
noted already Ellul's belief in such a morality. The respects in
which it is distinct must be shown. This will require us to examine in Ellul's case the core notions of freedom, and the dialectic of freedom and love, for these have been especially prominent
in his account of Christian ethics to date. (B) Does such a morality include, in addition to these core notions (though perhaps as
their specification and application), more or less determinate and

fixed prohibitions and injunctions generated out of the Christian community's past experience of revelation?[23] Or are decisions to be made extemporaneously, relative to time, place, and circumstances, to contemporary perceptions of what is required and needed? We shall find Ellul sometimes unclear and inconsistent on whether such prohibitions and injunctions exist, or retain their authority. (C) To whom does the morality based on revelation apply? Is it relevant for believers only, or for all persons? Ellul goes to unusual lengths to limit the relevant application to those who *explicitly* believe, while he extends their range of responsibility. For he does more than insist that believers should not ask and expect of nonbelievers the same kind of behavior that believers ask and expect of themselves, and that believers have responsibilities and burdens which nonbelievers do not. He also thinks that nonbelievers themselves suffer when believers fail to meet such responsibilities and bear such burdens. This last belief is peculiar to Ellul and perplexing in its own right; it will be examined in due course.

What should be emphasized initially with regard to the first issue is that freedom does indeed occupy a central place in Christian ethics. Several explicit statements in *The Ethics of Freedom* leave no doubt (pp. 7, 104, 109). How, then, shall we understand the freedom which has so decisive a status? The question proves surprisingly difficult to answer, given the length—510 pages—of *The Ethics of Freedom*. It would be tedious and unprofitable, however, to compile a list of statements about freedom which are hard to reconcile and which constitute either momentary lapses or outright contradictions. It would mislead as well, for justice would not be done to the quality of much of the work as edifying literature. I do think Ellul makes his readers suffer unwarrantably in this book from repetitive and obscure passages. He too often opts for rhetorical effectiveness even when this results in intellectual obfuscation. Our time is thus better spent on several themes which do emerge and are important in themselves.

Early on he says that "freedom is the ethical aspect of hope" (*Ethics of Freedom*, p. 12). And "hope bears witness to us that there is a future. We can escape destiny. We have scope for life. . . . The worst man, the most lost, is not lost. Nothing has been definitely settled" (*Ethics of Freedom*, p. 18). Our biological, psychological, and social inheritance, the wrongs we have done or endured in the past, do not altogether dictate the outcome. "Freedom loosens up a tightly regulated mechanism. It is a little space where man can breathe in the midst of constraints. . . . It is the transcending of an imposed suffering or end" (*Ethics of Freedom*, p. 75).

The "transcendence" in question is never to be regarded as entirely "spiritual, metaphysical, or inner" (*Ethics of Freedom*, p. 290). Ellul denounces what he takes to be a "Stoical" escape from "the temporality of existence, living in the non-temporal logos . . ." (*Ethics of Freedom*, p. 96). St. Paul knows better:

> In my view one does not find in Paul the slightest dualism of body and soul, of the outer situation and the inner situation. He does not plead for an internal freedom no matter what may be the social or physical condition. In this regard he is no Stoic. He is solidly in the tradition of the Old Testament revelation, and . . . he constantly applies the freedom gained in Christ to the various departments and responsibilities of concrete life. We may thus say that Paul is not an innovator in his teaching on freedom. He follows the lines laid down by the God of Abraham [*Ethics of Freedom*, p. 99].

An antithetical error must also be avoided, Ellul argues, if one is to follow the general lines laid down by a "biblical anthropology." One must not insist only on "the fleshly or human aspect." Here he criticizes a contemporary attitude in the church which he thinks is inclined to bestow an uncritical blessing on whatever social developments present themselves: "The church of aggiornamento, the church which accepts the works of the world as the works of the Saviour, the church which justifies the world in its course and tries to put itself at the head of sociological movements that can get along very well without it—in all this we have another way of enslavement" (*Ethics of Freedom*, pp. 290–91). Ellul summarizes the two kinds of error involved: "In the preceding form the spirit is too pure to incarnate itself in reality. Hence reality is ignored or there is a pretence of ignoring it. This extreme purity leads to an ethereal freedom which is of no value to man. In the present form, however, there is no more spirit to incarnate. . . . A great deal is said to justify things as they are" (*Ethics of Freedom*, p. 291).

This account seems to sustain a view of the human person as a composite of two polarities, infinitude on the one hand and finitude on the other. Sickness accrues to the degree that the two are in disrelation. Yet there is no mediation or rational movement from one pole to the other; the two stand always in paradoxical tension. Thus on the subject of freedom as the ethical aspect of hope, Ellul is prepared to leave matters at a general dialectical level: freedom passes back and forth between the "spiritual" and the "material" without being exhaustively one or the other. Hope thereby retains an essential "totality" (*Ethics of Freedom*, p. 331). Beyond this general level, matters remain frustratingly indeterminate.

So let us try to improve our understanding of his account by altering somewhat the angle of vision. Ellul refers favorably to Martin Luther's *The Freedom of a Christian* (*Ethics of Freedom*, p. 109), and James Gustafson rightly finds affinities between Luther and Ellul in their general approach to believer-freedom.[24] Luther in that treatise sets down these two propositions: "A Christian is a perfectly free lord of all, subject to none. A Christian is a perfectly dutiful servant of all, subject to all."[25]

The first proposition points to a view of freedom which focuses on what I shall call an incessant readiness to step back: from wholesale assimilation into any culture, from permanent alliances with particular social, political, and economic arrangements, from bondage to natural desires. Here we arrive at some of the most important claims about discontinuity.

Ellul resists, together with many orthodox believers, various kinds of cultural pressures to assimilate. For example, he is quite prepared to affront those within academic circles who seek to acclimatize theology to the secular intellectual disciplines.[26] Theology as a discipline must keep its own counsels and legislate for itself which current academic enterprises to take seriously. Here Ellul reflects closely, I believe, a Barthian attitude. For Barth, Christian theologians and ethicists should never commit themselves unqualifiedly to single methods; they may use freely whatever conceptual schemes and philosophical writings are at hand, but only in an eclectic, fragmentary, ad hoc way, always with final allegiance to the kerygma alone.[27] This case on behalf of resistance to cultural and especially intellectual assimilation is obviously of central importance. The trouble is that Ellul's own writings are not the place to assess its cogency. For he appears unwilling to support such a program with independent and carefully wrought conceptual elucidation; we may well think that Barth has already achieved what is required in this respect. So, while a general congruity between Barth and Ellul here needs to be noted, I shall pass on to other matters about which Ellul himself has considerably more to say.

One of these has to do with the freedom from permanent alliances with given social, political, and economic arrangements, and the values such arrangements embody. Now occasionally this sense of freedom seems to be perpetual recoiling from "necessity" as such, that is, the constant breaking away from *any* contemporary arrangement, whatever it happens to be, merely because it consists always of a web of determinations. The practices and policies which express freedom will then prove to be exceedingly various. What is appropriate in one spatio-temporal setting may be wholly inappropriate in another. Indeed, rival or opposite courses may be extolled in different contexts. For instance, in the nineteenth century it was fitting to oppose individualism as the dominant cultural and social value, but in the twentieth century "we need to affirm the exclusive value of the individual" because now what dominates is an absorptionist and reductive collectivism (*Ethics of Freedom*, p. 296).

More frequently, however, Ellul ties freedom expressly to religious belief; believers are culpably unfree if they fail to introduce something specifically Christian into current trends and points of consensus (e.g., *Violence*, p. 28). The stress shifts from freedom as resistance to all current patterns of conformity as such to freedom as the continual introduction of a distinctive perspective which only believers can bring. And the practices and policies which express freedom need not be so various. On the contrary, as we shall see, they are sometimes strikingly uniform. In any case, they will be governed by something more than pure in-principled opposition to the established powers. Although the sense of freedom tied expressly to religious belief goes beyond such in-principled opposition, it nonetheless rules out permanent alliances of the sort which Ellul identifies as "the construction of a Christian system of economics, politics, society . . . in any form" (*Ethics of Freedom*, p. 341). Here too an important kind of discontinuity is indicated. How far it extends, especially with reference to the "values" which given arrangements embody, is a difficult question to which we must return.

Freedom consists, finally, in being lord over one's natural desires. This means provisionally and minimally that a person's conduct is not unavoidably subject to internal mechanisms of control, that it is possible to step back from given (first order) desires, to reach positive or negative (second order) evaluations of them, and proceed to act, or at least to want to act, accordingly.[28] While Ellul might welcome a minimalist account along these lines, his distinctive contribution lies in the theological status he ascribes to "nature" and the "natural," and the discontinuity between believer-freedom and "natural" liberty on which he then insists.

The place to begin is with his claim that "Christian ethics . . . should guard against . . . confusing man's own natural tendency with the will of God" (*To Will and To Do*, p. 282). This confusion occurs whenever positive religious significance is accorded to eros in the sense of natural tendency or natural desire. Eros, let us remember, is on continualist premises a "sign or prophecy of agape," a clue to "what God has in mind." And for Ellul it is always a theological mistake to join together erotic, instinctual, and religious motifs.

Certainly Barth also takes pains to guard against confusing natural human tendencies with God's will. Eros as "natural mysticism" must be opposed whenever it effectively denies that the command of God is alien to us, that it not only comforts but likewise humbles.[29] And romantic eros as the joining together of erotic, instinctual, and religious motifs is viewed as an artificial extravagance. It remains the sublimest, most dangerous human experience because here, more than anywhere else, we easily, arrogantly, prematurely assume that what we desire is bound to be what God wills. But once we draw back from all such presumptuous connections, once we undeify eros so that it no longer has the capacity to bridge heaven and earth, Barth is prepared to make positive room for it in his theological ethics. I have tried to show elsewhere that three quite distinct senses of eros may be found in Barth's writings, two of which he commends.[30] Neither of these positive commendations requires acceptance of continualist premises à la Ellul; Barth never treats eros as an unfailing sign of agape, or as a systematically authoritative source for knowledge of what God wills. Barth declines moreover to support the contention, often associated with Roman Catholic moral theology, that natural love or eros must at least complement what is revealed, and be capable of gratuitous elevation.[31] What he affirms is that a suitably chastened sense (or senses) of eros may find some legitimate though subordinate place in a Christian ethical scheme. There may even be a "sanctified eros."[32] And so natural desires in general are not to be viewed as simply opposed, without qualification, to believer-freedom.

Ellul, on the other hand, seems content to dwell, nearly without relief, on the opposition. This is especially evident in those passages where he sounds a somber chord—far removed from freedom as the ethical aspect of hope—by insisting that freedom is a burden to be borne.

> There is no worse present than freedom. . . . Freedom is the most crushing burden that one can lay on man. . . .
>
> We are not dealing, then, with a privilege, superiority, or dignity that has been conferred on Christians. The situation of Christians is, on the contrary, very dangerous, uncomfortable, harassing, and ambivalent. Christians are set very definitely in a situation which is "against nature" [*Ethics of Freedom*, pp. 92–93; see also *Violence*, p. 166].

The opposition goes further. Added to the discontinuity between freedom and other things is the discontinuity within freedom itself. That is, the burden of freedom is one which only believers can assume, for only in the context of explicit belief does freedom exist as a genuine possibility. On this point Ellul is quite emphatic: "With all humility and prudence we have to say that Christians are the *only* bearers of freedom" (*Ethics of Freedom*, p. 272). And so he often takes the discontinuity to be complete: "When we say that Christians are the *only* bearers of freedom, this means that what others call freedom is never more than a substitute and fabrication" (*Ethics of Freedom*, p. 272).

How does he support these extremely bold assertions? He maintains that apart from religious belief, freedom is neither universally desired in fact nor appraised as desirable as a value to which everything else should be subordinate. Freedom is not an innate capacity or a constitutive element in human nature (*Ethics of Freedom*, p. 103). The objects persons call "good" are various and mutable; we do not agree normatively that freedom ought to have overriding significance. Ellul sees evidence in Scripture that most persons prefer in fact a life of dull conformity, without individual responsibility (*Ethics of Freedom*, p. 92). He also stresses that freedom may be sacrificed willingly for the sake of other things. "Man is not so enamored of freedom as some have supposed. Freedom is not an inherent personal need. The needs of security, conformity, adaptation, happiness, economy of effort, and so forth are far more constant and profound. Man is completely prepared to sacrifice his freedom in order to satisfy these needs. . . . He fears freedom more than he desires it" (*Ethics of Freedom*, p. 35).

In connection with these claims, let me attempt a comparison with Kierkegaard's pseudonym Anti-Climacus, in *The Sickness unto Death*. If we regard the statement above as a descriptive report of the priorities to which a majority of persons subscribe, then it seems that Ellul and Anti-Climacus vaguely agree. Anti-Climacus speaks of "the sorry and ludicrous condition of the majority of men, that in their own house they prefer to live in the cellar, . . . that is, in the determinants of sensuousness."[33] Yet an instructive difference emerges, too. Anti-Climacus also speaks of "the soulish-bodily synthesis in every man" which "is planned with a view to being spirit, such is the building. . . ."[34] One interpreter takes this "plan" to be "the ineradicable propensity of the immediate spirit or self to liberate itself by metamorphosing its given nature."[35] The propensity is a datum which none of us can successfully ignore or disavow. For Anti-Climacus there is a penchant toward liberation which naturally characterizes all persons, not only believers, and the result of repressing it is far more serious than we find Ellul prepared to acknowledge. For the result is despair.

Extreme caution should be exercised with respect to this possible difference between Ellul and Anti-Climacus, however. Kierkegaard is after all one of the great opponents of theological schemes which stress continuity. For him, we are not all covert believers ("When everyone is a Christian, no one is a Christian"), and he certainly resists decoding the Christian conceptions he describes. Yet the legacy he has left is perceived by some to be ambiguous precisely on the points now before us—that the propensity to liberation is a natural endowment common to all persons, believers and nonbelievers alike, and that its repression is a decisive clue to an understanding of despair.

Barth admits that around 1920 and even later he himself may have succumbed to this part of the Kierkegaardian legacy. Whether Barth is right or wrong, fair or unfair, in ascribing to Kierkegaard a position Barth himself defines and repudiates, is a question I cannot address here. The position as Barth sketches it, and which he attributes to the young Brunner as well, is this:

> "The natural knowledge of God is neither a true knowledge of *God* nor a true *knowledge* of God". . . . All natural knowledge of God is . . . essentially a knowledge of the wrath of God. And being subject to the wrath of God meant the same thing objectively as a bad conscience or despair subjectively. The different degrees of the subjective consciousness point to the objective side. The "contact" made in the natural knowledge of God consists in the fact that it involves a "loss of certainty." The contact is made, not with something positive or neutral but with something negative. As regards the contents of the relations of God and man there is a discontinuity. Only as regards the formal fact of the relation is there continuity. . . . Hence the proclamation of the God revealed in Christ must always be at the same time an attempt "to show to the unbeliever the true character of his existence without faith, to show that despair is the 'fundamental condition' of existence."[36]

This indirect or negative "point of contact" involves knowledge we can have of ourselves about ourselves, the truth of which, and the ground for our believing in the truth of which, is independent of revelation. Ellul joins Barth in refusing to accord systematic theological significance to such self-knowledge. Christian theology and ethics court disaster when they obligate themselves in principle to make use of this knowledge. So the discontinuity between believer-freedom and every other kind—including the repressed freedom leading to despair—must remain intact. Whether the intactness is quite as complete as I have described it thus far is another difficult question to which we shall have to return in the final section.

It is time now to consider the second of Luther's propositions—"a Christian is a perfectly dutiful servant of all, subject to all"—as it points both to Ellul's dialectic of freedom and love and to his treatment of love as such.

This dialectic is as centrally important in Christian ethics as freedom itself. "At the level of human behavior one might say that the totality of the Christian life amounts to a dialectic of freedom and love. Everything leads up to the movement in which freedom is incarnated in love and love stimulates freedom. The whole of ethics consists in this dialectical movement, constantly renewed, from love to freedom and from freedom to love" (*Ethics of Freedom*, p. 206). We seem to find both a negative and a positive sense of "dialectic" if we assume that it means, among other things, "mutual implication." At times freedom and love are held to coinhere negatively: "There is no love without freedom. On the other hand . . . there can be no freedom . . . without love. The two mutually imply one another even though they are *contradictory*. Freedom *in itself excludes* love. Ministering love *excludes* freedom. But the whole of the Christian life can advance . . . only in the dialectical development of the two" (*Ethics of Freedom*, p. 112, my italics). Does such a statement suggest another instance of two things standing in paradoxical tension? It is hard to know, partly because elsewhere Ellul tells us that in Christianity "love and freedom are indissolubly united, not by a halting conciliation . . . but by the essential implication of the one in the other" (*Ethics of Freedom*, p. 207). This "essential implication" appears to go beyond negative coinherence. And the case for a positive sense is plainly made: "Scripture, however, maintains that there is no freedom where there is no love. The two realities are tied together so closely that to destroy the one is necessarily to destroy the other" (*Ethics of Freedom*, p. 200). Is it then coherent to assert at once (1) that each of two things in itself excludes the other, because they are contradictories, and (2) that if either of two things is destroyed, the other is destroyed as well, because they are so positively tied?

Ellul's answer to this question I find to be less than clear. Perhaps (2) characterizes what obtains in the case of Christianity and (1) refers to ordinary or secular usage. And in general we may say that despite the centrality he formally ascribes to the dialectic of freedom and love, his treatment to date is marked by a paucity of detailed discussion.[37] We should note also that he has yet to publish his comprehensive thoughts on love as "an ethics of relationship" (*Ethics of Freedom*, p. 7), and he may intend there to elaborate on what we currently have before us. I at least hope he will address at greater length the sort of question identified above, and amplify, too, a number of very suggestive remarks he makes, often incidentally, about the more specific material connections between freedom and love (e.g., *Ethics of Freedom*, pp. 200–201, 286, 411).

What of Ellul's account of love itself, once more, as we have it to date? One distinct theme is wholly personalist. That is, only "a neighbor or several neighbors" are addressed by love, for "it is an interindividual matter" (*Violence*, p. 34). The "neighbor" is not anyone or everyone affected by my actions; he or she is restricted to the ones with whom I may have significantly personal relations.[38] Love cannot be lived out except in direct personal relationships (*Ethics of Freedom*, p. 267). Ellul endorses Martin Buber's familiar contrast between I-Thou and I-It relations (*Ethics of Freedom*, p. 208).[39] But Ellul's own description is conspicuously unqualified. Consider this statement:

> Love cannot express itself in a framework of laws, constraints, and obligations. It is never the point-by-point realization of a program. It is never the execution of a law, however perfect this may be, nor the fulfillment of obligations. When law and morality come into play, love takes flight. Planning excludes love. In society law and morality uphold the social organism. They function between beings who do not love each other but have to live together. Where love is, however, all that is left behind and is not to be taken into account. Love implies the richness of instant free presence. A total person, in the fullness of his strength, is totally with you. For this person is free, has left all else on one side,

and has no ulterior motives or constraints or attachments which might cause division or restriction or pressure [*Ethics of Freedom*, p. 201].

To contend that love cannot express itself in the fulfillment of obligations, at least partially or on some occasions, goes further even than a proponent of "situation ethics" like Joseph Fletcher.[40] (And Ellul himself by no means always takes matters to these extreme lengths, as we shall see.) One naturally wonders if Ellul is being deliberately hyperbolic at times like these.

Yet speculation of this latter sort should not obscure what is a distinctive feature of his ethics. Explicit belief is judged to make an enormous attitudinal and behavioral difference; the moral efficacy of such belief is something about which Ellul remains exceedingly hopeful. Disallowed are pessimistic secular accounts of what transpires in interpersonal relationships. "If I think I am free in Christ, I can have no suspicion of others and must break with Freud, Marx, and Nietzsche. If there is freedom only in the reciprocity of love, I must lay down all weapons" (*Ethics of Freedom*, p. 212–13). Love actually makes realizable the "abnormal action" of effacing oneself, of putting "oneself so radically in the place and situation and 'skin' of the other that one knows what is good for him, what is in his true interests, because one is the other" (*Ethics of Freedom*, p. 200).

Such unqualified agent-availability has had various unhappy consequences which are familiar enough, and Ellul himself sometimes shows unease with it. He observes in a different context that love does not require the agent to go to perdition with others (*Ethics of Freedom*, p. 359), though if salvation is universal, this prospect seems literally impossible in any case. But further, "I cannot encounter the other unless I myself have become an I" (*Ethics of Freedom*, p. 328), and hence I appropriately attend to my own identity. Apart from this kind of (not unimportant) qualification on Ellul's part, however, what must be recognized is, first, that love is often depicted in exclusively personalist terms, so that social welfare activities—like overseeing a clinic which helps the sick or effecting social changes which improve the condition of children—fall outside its purview; and, second, that Ellul is extremely hopeful that such love can be realized here and now.

In light of the personalist theme as described by Ellul, we should not be surprised that he finds little or no room for justice in his account of Christian ethics. "To say that the establishment of terrestrial justice is a concrete way of expressing love and that power is a way to achieve it seems to me historically and politically untrue. Some fine approximations to terrestrial justice may be found which are the opposite of love, e.g., the admirable Roman system" (*Ethics of Freedom*, p. 369). Not only is it historically and politically untrue that terrestrial justice has expressed love, but it seems that normatively no positive material connections can be drawn between the two. And because love and freedom are so closely tied, it follows that there is "antagonism and incompatibility" between justice and freedom also (*Ethics of Freedom*, p. 403). In passages like these, where Ellul virtually banishes justice from Christian ethics, we find a view which differs from Niebuhr and even, I think, from Brunner.

On love and justice Niebuhr claims to be "dialectical."

> . . . the Christian conception of the relation of historical justice to the love of the Kingdom of God is a dialectical one. Love is both the fulfillment and the negation of all achievements of justice in history. Or expressed from the opposite standpoint, the achievements of justice in history may rise in indeterminate degrees to find their fulfillment in a more perfect love and brotherhood; but each new level of fulfillment also contains elements which stand in contradiction to perfect love. There are therefore obligations to realize justice in indeterminate degrees; but none of the realizations can assure the serenity of perfect fulfillment.[41]

Ellul refuses to appropriate this sense of dialectic. Furthermore, Niebuhr rejects as "sentimental" those versions of the love commandment "according to which only the most personal individual and direct expressions of social obligation are manifestations of Christian *agape*."[42] Many sectarian and Lutheran accounts which exclude justice from the domain of love yield, he maintains, to this sentimentality. Niebuhr criticizes Brunner for offering one such version. Presumably he would find the personalist theme Ellul advances another.[43] But it is difficult to say more. I have attempted elsewhere to show that modern discussions of love and justice in theological ethics would be conducted more fruitfully if greater pains were taken by the disputants to distinguish various senses of each notion.[44] I have also tried to demonstrate in another place that certain concepts ("need," for instance) sometimes serve as points of normative overlap for both love and justice.[45] When Ellul denies that love has anything to do with social welfare activities, for example, he neglects to consider sufficiently this latter possibility.

Ellul also endorses more than one sense of "love." I find a second theme, at any rate, which diverges from personalism, and I would argue that it constitutes one of Ellul's most distinctive and important contributions to ethics. The category "neighbor" is not always restricted to those with whom I may have a significantly personal, reciprocal relation. "In all this . . . the rule of conduct is not to be our own imagination or desire or conformity or adaptation to changing society. It is to be only our assessment of the best possible expression of our love for the poor and the stranger and the enemy, that is, for the neighbor" (*Ethics of Freedom*, p. 210). If the neighbor may include the poor, the stranger, and the enemy, Ellul approaches the view which holds that each person should be regarded as irreducibly valuable, before doing anything in particular which distinguishes him or her from others.[46] "Anything in particular" has usually been taken to refer to some special merit, claim, attractiveness, and the like. Ellul's originality lies in stressing another set of "particulars": specific political, economic, ideological viewpoints and affiliations. He fights for a sense of the neighbor that goes deeper than any of these particulars, that relativizes them all, and that ascribes dignity to each person irrespective of them.[47]

Ellul has formulated this distinctive version while critically assessing recent theological writings by both Roman Catholics and Protestants in support of revolutionary and liberationist movements. He believes that in these writings a "new predestination," for all intents and purposes, is invoked: "the poor being righteous and saved, whereas the politically and economically powerful are damned" (*Ethics of Freedom*, p. 424). Ellul objects to such a view on various grounds, not all of which are relevant to our present purpose.[48] That purpose is served most directly, I believe, by the following summary. He finds agape to be incompatible with the claim about predestination in at least two respects: the belief in the equality of all persons before God collides with "a theology of violence which calls for discrimination for or against certain men or groups of men" (*Violence*, p. 75); and the generic view of the neighbor as valuable *qua* human existent, independent of his or her (often) contingent socioeconomic conditions, stands against the claim that "Christ is not identified with man or men, only with the oppressed" (*Ethics of Freedom*, p. 425). Moreover, if universalist features of agape are accepted, Ellul thinks certain definite practices and policies follow which make relative all specific political, economic, and ideological viewpoints and affiliations, and which thus attest to the dignity ascribed to each person as human existent.

Love is held to generate a perpetual readiness to change sides. At a given time it may prompt support of revolutionaries who are justifiably protesting oppression (*Ethics of Freedom*, p. 433). But because one's neighbors are not to be limited solely to those who participate on behalf of the revolution (*Violence*, p. 47), one should be prepared at once, in the event the revolution succeeds, to identify with the defeated in the name of the same love (*Ethics of Freedom*, p. 433). The decisive test of whether a believer's participation in a revolutionary movement is motivated by a genuine concern for "the poor, the oppressed, and the disinherited" is whether he or she is willing to change camps, to support those who are now the victims and forever refuse to stay with the victors, whoever they happen to be (*Violence*, pp. 109–10, 138–39). And even in those times of justified alliance with a particular oppressed group, it is also urged that, "as Barth puts it, Christians should never be the enemies of their opponents . . ." (*Ethics of Freedom*, p. 383). For in the end, "there is no justice without reconciliation—that is the revolutionary message of the Christian within the revolutionary movement" (*Ethics of Freedom*, p. 418). Moreover, Ellul employs the dialectic of love and freedom to protest against conformist participation in revolutionary movements which focus selectively on groups he calls the "interesting" poor. Ignored are many others whose poverty and other suffering are at least as pronounced. Ellul, writing in 1968, proposes this list: "And then there are the 'uninteresting' poor, people who obviously are not worth troubling about: the Biafrans, massacred by the federal troops of Nigeria; the monarchist Yemenites, burned by napalm and bombed into obliteration by the Egyptian air force from 1964 to 1967; the South Sudanese, destroyed en masse by the North Sudanese; the Tibetans, oppressed and deported by China; the Khurds, perhaps 500,000 of whom were massacred in Irak and Iran between 1955 and today. These and many more in similar cases do not attract the interest of our violent Christians" (*Violence,* p. 67). Believers betray their allegiance to the dominant societal ideology whenever they fail to display independent concern about those virtually ignored by everyone else. Finally, believers should find their solidarity with one another in the community where they share the gift of faith (*Violence,* p. 57). That gift is what really counts. They should not *have* to acquire a sense of community in common revolutionary action. Indeed, basic solidarity should not be threatened even when they hold contradictory political views.

The second broad issue, let us recall, is this: in addition to the core notions of freedom and love, though perhaps as their specification and application, does a morality which derives from revelation include determinate injunctions generated out of the Christian community's past experience of revelation, or are decisions to be made extemporaneously, relative to time, place, and circumstances, to contemporary perceptions of what is required and needed? I am afraid Ellul's several answers constitute a bewildering pastiche of statements which support each of the alternatives . Yet the answers considered in their own right contain features of interest. Statements on behalf of extemporaneousness and relativity will be noted first, since they are perhaps more plentiful.

Sometimes Ellul flatly asserts that even the "moral values" articulated in earlier centuries—which *he* allows may be appropriately regarded as "Christian" (*To Will and To Do,* p. 74)—are now superseded completely. This is because "if it is a genuine ethic it was necessarily related to a certain social, political, and economic situation which is no longer ours. Their conclusions (if not their point of departure and their method) are thus entirely outmoded" (*To Will and To Do,* p. 225). Ellul is prepared to be very explicit: the moral reflections of, for example, Augustine, Ambrose, Luther, and Calvin are outmoded in precisely this way. And in this connection he draws a contrast between the theological task and the moral one (*To Will and To Do*, p. 225). Theological doctrines formulated in prior centuries possess an on-going authority and relevance for believers nowadays which previous moral judgments lack. I think the view that the moral conclusions of earlier Christian thinkers and communities are, unlike theological labors, dated and disposable is linked in Ellul's mind with the thesis that natural morality consists in spatially and temporally discrete codes. Even if these moral conclusions were distinctive by virtue of the Holy Spirit's guidance, they are transient and subsequently unbinding all the same. To sustain the distinction between the theological and the moral task, Ellul may have to cross swords with two kinds of critics. He will be asked by some why theological doctrines do not inevitably pass out of date for the same reasons that moral ones do. Why are they not also "necessarily related to a certain social, political, and economic situation which is no longer ours"? What precisely is it that makes them immune from the same kind of analysis which morality receives? And others will ask, as Barth is asked by John H. Yoder, "Why should it not be possible for a general statement in Christian ethics to have the same validity as a general statement within some other realm of Christian dogmatics?"[49] The spirit of Yoder's question is, "Why not indeed, on Barth's own premises?" For in Barth's theology, ethics is certainly a constitutive part of dogmatics. Barth's position on the second broad issue proves to be very complex, in ways I cannot explore.[50] But certainly ethics for Barth is too integral to dogmatics to allow him to accept Ellul's distinction as it stands. And Ellul himself ignores the distinction in many contexts.

In any case, Ellul's reasons for stressing extemporaneousness, relativity, contemporaneity, and the like extend far beyond what is implied by his thesis about natural morality. Explicitly religious themes prove in fact to be more determinative. And this should not surprise us. Earlier we noticed that Ellul regards as epistemologically presumptuous the claim that we have some access to what is right and good independently of revelation. To avoid this overweening contention we must hold that God can command what ordinary moral sensitivities find offensive. Ellul is prepared to treat the *herem* or the interdiction as an illustration. In a passage such as Deuteronomy 7:1–2, God asks the Israelites to destroy the Canaanite tribes. Ellul believes God issues this command "in order to show that the will of God can remove the ethical norms, or to show that the will of God is in itself the good in its entirety . . ." (*To Will and To Do*, p. 206).

Each of us must have a personal relation with God if we are to be dispositionally open to what he ordains. The conditions for personal relations preclude general moral principles and rules which "systematize": "There are no Christian principles. . . . That is . . . why the Bible never presents itself as a book of philosophy, but as a history. And when the will of God takes the form of a law, the latter always appears as a commandment. 'Thou' it says to the hearer. It is not at all a question of a general rule promulgated by a legislator, but the start of a personal dialogue. In this commandment God addresses a particular person at that moment" (*Ethics of Freedom*, p. 205). Ellul purports to see a theological heresy at work in the movement from the fifth and sixth centuries onwards "to take objectively good behavior into account in . . . understanding . . . revelation" (*Ethics of Freedom*, p. 241). What then occurs? The personal relation between God and the individual is abandoned for something far less arduous. One finally abdicates that primal responsibility which each individual has before God (*Ethics of Freedom*, p. 241).[51]

We encounter another source of statements on behalf of extemporaneousness and relativity whenever Ellul affirms what he regards as the Pauline injunction to reverence Christian freedom from the law. "The freedom won in Christ is alive, unlimited, without restrictions or obligations. It enables us to throw off all constraints and admonitions. It is true freedom: freedom to choose, to decide, to go where I want to go, to break that which dominates, to transgress prohibitions, to profane what man holds sacred, to conform, to enter into and to break free from commitments, to give and to take back again" (*Ethics of Freedom*, p. 186). For those concerned to extol freedom from determinate and fixed prohibitions, nothing more sweeping could be desired. It is possible to assume virtually any role, hold any ideological position, take any attitude toward Scripture. "Hence a Christian may be a monarchist or he may be a Communist, so long as being either the one or the other is an expression of his freedom in Christ. He may be a militarist or a conscientious objector on the same condition. In relation to Scripture he may be a literalist or a demythologizer" (*Ethics of Fredom*, p. 187). What greater permission could be given? It seems that there are no fixed or even presumptive criteria of what the Christian life must be.

In light of the above, readers are unprepared for statements on behalf of determinate prohibitions and injunctions. Yet they will not have to strain to locate them. Let us retrace our steps, beginning with the contention that the moral reflections of earlier Christian thinkers are entirely outmoded and that we should contrast the theological task with the moral one. In Ellul's *Violence* the reader expects to find instances of the attempt to apply to past Christian values a belief in historical discontinuity. Ellul does not always disappoint: he considers the doctrine of the just war as it culminates in the analysis by Gratian and Aquinas. After listing the seven conditions which must coincide if a war is to be just, he concludes: "Let us point out . . . that these seven conditions were formulated in a day when it was possible to see a war situation with relative clarity; but the phenomena of modern war—total war as well as wars of subversion—and the extent of the battlefields rule out utterly the *application* of these seven criteria and render them altogether inoperative" (*Violence*, p. 6). So far, so good: the reflections of Gratian and Aquinas seem "entirely outmoded." We could then go on to compare Ellul's project with twentieth-century endeavors by thinkers like Paul Ramsey and John C. Ford to apply just-war conditions to modern military circumstances.[52] While it cannot be pursued here, such a comparison might serve as a test of the thesis of historical discontinuity, and tell us much in its own right.

The difficulty which concerns me at the moment is simply that in the same book certain theological claims are made which seem to blur Ellul's distinction between the theological and moral task, and obscure therefore his account of historical discontinuity as applied to Christian moral values. Ellul begins by observing that we display historical ignorance when we assume that only *modern* believers adopt any of the three predominant stances he distinguishes: compromise, nonviolence, and violence. In fact, all the current "attitudes have had "their representatives, their theologians, their sects from the beginning" (*Violence*, p. 1).

"The casuistry of the just war," as part of the stance of compromise, finds formulation very early in the church (*Violence*, p.5). The posture of nonviolence has equally primitive origins and an unbroken line of subsequent defenders. Ellul cites St. Martin of Tours for one, "who, a soldier and a soldier's son, after his conversion refused to serve any longer and accepted death, explaining his position in terms that, theologically, are remarkable" (*Violence*, p. 11). Finally, modern Christian proponents of the "theology of revolution" erroneously suppose that they must operate without precedents. "Not so. At most, this theology represents a return to traditional currents of thought" (*Violence*, p. 23). Ellul concludes his survey by asserting that all three suffer from a common theological error: "monism" (*Violence*, p. 24). All three attitudes recur again and again, and they are always wrong. Their wrongness has to do with a misplaced and doomed zeal for an "accord" which human life in this world will never attain.

These three predominant stances serve to illustrate how difficult it is to keep the distinction clear between dispensable moral values expressed in the past and recurrent theological attitudes which retain their relevance. For ordinary usage at least, each of the stances has perduring "moral" implications. For Ellul, one of the stances should be binding on believers: "Freedom necessarily leads to an ethics of non-resistance" (*Ethics of Freedom*, p. 409; see also *Violence*, p. 159). This judgment seems to be relevant not only in the twentieth century; Ellul treats it as normative in every century. At the very least his dichotomy between the theological and the moral task proves to be too crude to accommodate much of what he wants to say.

When we turn to explicitly religious themes, further additions and qualifications appear. Whatever may be the correct interpretation of the *herem*, Ellul naturally regards as pernicious any conclusion that God is a despot or that his commands are incoherent, isolated, or absurd (*To Will and To Do*, p. 259). Believers are enjoined to trust in God's design, even if they can see it now only in part. And we find constancies in the divine command after all. "Without any doubt, God can will and decide anything at all. He can change his action as he pleases. But he does not do so. The very revelation which he grants us shows us a remarkable continuity in his decisions" (*To Will and To Do*, pp. 262–63). Once believers forgo the use of ethical judgments "as a way of being correct with God or of protecting ourselves from him" (*To Will and To Do*, p. 265), they may begin to attend to the continuity. Such attention does not obviate the "need for individual encounter," the requirement of personal consultations at every point. Yet Ellul may equivocate with respect to this latter requirement. On one interpretation it seems that personal relations can be guaranteed only if moral judgments are taken as intrinsically impersonal and thus as entirely problematical. God's will must remain systematically uncertain in advance and on every question, or else the need—that it "be spoken" and "received personally"—vanishes. On another interpretation, the objection to moral judgments is confined to showing how they are put to corrupt uses (for example, to justify oneself, to deny primal responsibility or avoid total commitment). If nonviolence is held to be always binding on believers, then God's will is not uncertain in advance for them on *this* question, and any zeal to vindicate personal consultations cannot, in consistency, alter matters. Sometimes Ellul may try to have both interpretations. But in the end, he must plump for one or the other, so a critic may plausibly charge, or risk incoherence.

An analogous difficulty arises when one finds qualifications attached to the Pauline injunction to reverence freedom from the law. In the earlier quotations cited from *The Ethics of Freedom*, we found the claim that freedom could be expressed by literally any attitude, opinion, or choice. But elsewhere in the same volume the reader meets with statements like these:

> True freedom is never linked with liquidation of what can build up personality and assure it continuity. It implies, presupposes, and demands durability of the personality [*Ethics of Freedom*, p. 241].
>
> The means of freedom are means that rule out violence, hatred, and lying [*Ethics of Freedom*, p. 405].
>
> Torture is always to be condemned. There is no possible justification for its use [*Ethics of Freedom*, p. 408].

Once more the obvious should be noted, and I shall again employ the example of violence: we have been told at different points that God issued the command for the Israelites to destroy the Canaanite tribes (which involves violent actions, given the vague and sweeping meaning which Ellul attaches to "violence"; see *Violence,* among others); that a believer may be a militarist; and that the means of freedom prohibit violence. Each of these claims is important in itself, and it is also instructive to ask which are compatible and which are not. But to try to put them all forward at once is to reach incomprehensibility.

Finally, note should be taken of other more random observations which cut against the claim that freedom could be expressed in literally any attitude, opinion, or choice. For one thing, if freedom and love are dialectically related in every time and place, then we should expect that freedom will be informed and constrained by what love enjoins. Ellul discusses sensitively the limits that the "weaker" members of the community of faith impose upon the stronger concerning actions which, in themselves, are religiously and morally indifferent, but which, if performed, will cause avoidable spiritual harm to some (the Pauline counsels on the eating of meat sacrificed to idols are cases in point) (*Ethics of Freedom*, pp. 198–99). In this context, a need-based criterion of love emerges as decisive. The personalist sense of love, moreover, is itself taken by Ellul to perdure and so to appear in various historical periods (*Ethics of Freedom*, p. 212). And then we are told that certain conceptions have appeared which Ellul applauds as recognizably Christian and which he thinks the believer is bound to take with special seriousness. He endorses, for example, Erich Auerbach's account in *Mimesis*:[53] "I know of no profounder analysis of the irruption of Jewish and Christian freedom into the intellectual and spiritual world. . . . Genetic thought is thus a product of Christian freedom" (*Ethics of Freedom*, p. 165; see also p. 275). The believer is told as well that certain institutional arrangements are relevant in that they protect and foster Christian insights. To cite another example, Ellul says this about democracy: "If democracy is this recognition of the relativism of politics, the validity of opponents, the limitation of political means, the worth of minorities, the legitimate difference of opinions, the general distribution of competence and truth, and the reduction of power, then precisely by the reason of its modesty this form of government offers a better chance than any other for Christians to take part as free men in Christ (*Ethics of Freedom*, pp. 384–85). Ellul contends too that "we certainly cannot associate with a movement whose aim is to destroy the Christian influence of the church, to liberate man from Christianity" (*Ethics of Freedom*, p. 401). In short, the theological and moral considerations Ellul himself counts as relevant go far beyond what the earlier, unqualified statements regarding freedom can encompass.

The third broad issue is this: To whom does the morality based on revelation apply? Is it relevant for believers only or for all persons? Ellul insists on a strict correlation between explicit belief and authentic freedom. Faith alone permits and enables one to realize Christian freedom (*Ethics of Freedom*, p. 93). And faith includes necessarily "an express confession" (*Ethics of Freedom*, p. 98). If we attempt "to increase freedom outside faith," we "simply increase the possibility of doing evil" (*Ethics of Freedom*, p. 428). The condition of explicitness rules out, as Ellul himself stresses, "the medieval notion of implicit faith" (*Ethics of Freedom*, p. 101). More modern versions of that notion presumably suffer a similar fate. An obvious example is Karl Rahner's vindication of the "anonymous Christian."[54] And Donald Evans's sympathetic depiction of "implicit faith" also comes to mind. God is at work wherever there is "liberation"; believers may "unconsciously resist" divine activity just as atheists and agnostics may be "unconsciously receptive" to this same activity: "basic trust" can be present without necessarily implying explicit religious belief.[55]

None of this appeals to Ellul. He claims instead that (1) the possibility of realizing authentic freedom exists only for believers who expressly confess their faith; (2) the injunction to realize freedom applies only to them; (3) whether or not believers realize freedom has collective consequences for all of humankind; and (4) believers are wholly responsible for these consequences, or at least for the consequences which follow from their own failures. Let us consider briefly each of these claims.

(1) We have already noted Ellul's extremely bold assertions concerning the effects of explicit confession: believers are the only bearers of freedom, and they are entitled to hope that a per-

sonalist sense of love will be realized here and now, protestations of the pessimists notwithstanding:

> The real point at issue when we speak of Christian freedom is ethics. Christians, like all other men, are still subject to pressures, temptations, determinations, and necessities. The Christian, like everyone else, obviously knows what it is to be hungry; he can be tempted when he is hungry. His distinctive gift, however, is that of participation in the secret lordship which enables him to give a different reply from that of all others in the same conditions, and which allows him to introduce a lever of freedom into the dense mass of constraints. We believe that this is possible for him alone because necessities have been overcome only once in Christ, and therefore this is a possibility only in express association with the work of Christ [*Ethics of Freedom*, p. 87].

Does Ellul's "therefore" obviously follow? Many theologians have failed to see why the positive working of Providence should depend so much on those who expressly associate with such work. And they might well ask precisely how Ellul's belief in universal salvation bears on matters here and now. His belief seems wholly incongruous with his "therefore." Believers alone exercise authentic freedom in the present, but nothing they do or fail to do has soteriological significance, either for themselves or others. Why then does Ellul lament the strategy of so many moderns who "are in the main prepared to be all things to all men, like St. Paul, but unfortunately this is not in order that they may save some but in order that they may be like all men" (*Ethics of Freedom*, p. 255)? This must be a different sense of "save" from the universal one. We need in general to know more about what believers should seek or expect when they witness to others in this life. Perhaps Ellul is allied with Barth once more, despite their disagreement concerning universal salvation. Barth distinguishes between a de jure state of affairs—the covenant as God's all-inclusive, pretemporal Yes which obtains for all persons—and de facto knowledge of it, which only believers possess.[56] Witnessing consists in the promotion of this knowledge (cf. *Ethics of Freedom*, p. 254).

Another sort of comparison may be ventured. I think Reinhold Niebuhr would find claim (1) unpalatable, though for complicated reasons. First, Niebuhr strives for an account of freedom as "self-transcendence" which characterizes the human person as such (and which, by his own admission, is very indebted to Kierkegaard).[57] This account of freedom prepares the way for his consideration of sin and guilt. Freedom must be related to our allegedly primal anxiety about finitude and our consequent inordinate self-assertion. These melancholy characteristics haunt all our personal and collective life in every time and place, whether or not we expressly believe, and despite his own less relativistic depiction of "natural" morality as discussed in the first section of this chapter. There is for Niebuhr simply too much "continuity in sin" between those who believe and those who do not to justify claim (1); sin remains too tenacious a datum to allow explicitness to make so large a difference. Human nature is therefore not so plastic in this respect as Ellul appears to suppose; Niebuhr offers more of an ontological picture that does not change. Second, one finds an openness in Niebuhr to "the facts of history" which he argues must and do confirm "the view of human nature" which the Christian faith articulates. Ellul, on the other hand, asks, "How can it be said . . . that freedom exists only in Christ and only for those who confess Jesus Christ . . . ? In spite of the experience of history, however, I do say this" (*Ethics of Freedom*, p. 90). Niebuhr is unwilling to discount "the experience of history" so readily. Contrition and humility follow when the self's own motives are soberly probed and when the rise and fall of tribes, nations, and empires ("Christian" and otherwise) are examined. Do we have adequate empirical grounds for claiming that explicit belief possesses the efficacy that Ellul ascribes? That is a test which Niebuhr counts as relevant and to which he would give a negative answer.

(2) Ellul maintains that "one of the essential rules of the Christian life is never to ask a non-Christian to conduct himself like a Christian" (*Ethics of Freedom*, p. 104). Freedom "is the core of ethics for Christians but has no meaning for anyone else" (*Ethics of Freedom*, p. 88). Prohibitions, like the one against violence, should not be demanded of nonbelievers which the latter "can neither understand nor attain" (*Violence*, p. 156). We are presented, then, with what is sometimes called a "believers' ethic": certain attitudes and classes of conduct are binding only among co-religionists—they lack intelligibility and significance

to those outside.[58] We must, however, avoid the impression that such an ethic always possesses the same features. For example, Friedrich Schleiermacher espouses a believers' ethic, yet his account of its relation to "natural" morality is distinctively irenic. Neither Christian ethics nor natural morality renders the other superfluous, and it is "impossible that what the one regards as moral, the other can regard as immoral."[59] Ellul, on the other hand, views with suspicion any uniform account of natural morality as the "product of common reason" extending to all of mankind. Furthermore, it seems that for Ellul nonbelievers are forced to acquire attitudes and perform actions which stand in opposition to the dictates of Christian ethics. Violence, for instance, appears endemic to that world of necessities from which there is no release or relief, except through an express confession of faith.

With reference to claim (2), Ellul diverges not only from Schleiermacher but also (ironically, though of course very differently) from Barth. Ellul does not object to the singularly narrow epistemological brackets marked by Barth, governed wholly by christology, and within which Christian ethics must be established. Yet inside these brackets, Barth seeks a referential expanse far wider than Ellul can endorse.[60] That is, Barth is not content to restrict Christian ethics to a "rather obscure sphere by its isolation from the sphere of reason, experience and human self-determination."[61] Christian ethics must speak with "universal validity" and not "only esoterically."[62] And so Barth substitutes for a peaceful coalition between Christian ethics and natural morality annexation "of the kind that took place on the entry of the children of Israel into Palestine."[63] Ellul seems typically more content with a dualism in which each territory is appropriately ruled by its own standards and the standards themselves are mutually incompatible.

(3) Something bizarre happens next. After drawing the boundaries so uncompromisingly, Ellul suddenly adds, in claim (3), that whether or not believers adhere to their own dictates will have momentous de facto effects "outside."

> It would be a grave error to think that we are independent
> of others, that we are free to take up this freedom or not,
> and that we alone have to suffer the consequences. What I

> want to show . . . is that, while the act of the Christian who takes up his freedom does not have to have collective consequences, the decision of the Christian (even if it be only by default) not to take up his freedom does have collective consequences and that historically these have been very tragic [*Ethics of Freedom*, p. 270].

> Hence every Christian decision is necessarily individual in origin and execution but also necessarily collective in its reference and consequences. There is no escaping this. The consequence of my Christian life is not my salvation but the orientation of all the groups within which I live, of the society in which I find myself, and in some sense of the world as a whole [*Ethics of Freedom*, pp. 270–71].

One would like to know more about the meaning of that patently slippery phrase "in some sense." Is more at stake here than a version of the biblical affirmation that believers are "the salt of the earth"? It would seem so. Ellul adds the odd claim that tragic consequences for the world follow necessarily when believers fail to take up their freedom, but that nothing positive follows necessarily if they do take it up (*Ethics of Freedom*, p. 273). Why do we find this asymmetry? No reasons, to my knowledge, are given. We are left with a vision that seems starkly pessimistic.

It is clear in any event that the negative stakes are exceedingly high. And the outcome remains genuinely uncertain, for believers may fail. Their freedom is not "an inalienable gift . . . a possession. It is not a quality which becomes a natural attribute. . . . We can become slaves again. We can destroy freedom by not living it out" (*Ethics of Freedom*, p. 236).

(4) How far does believer-responsibility extend when freedom is not lived out? Sometimes Ellul comes close to advancing the perverse claim that believers are solely responsible for the past and present evils in the world:

> What we have here . . . is a precise responsibility which can be calculated historically. Christians are responsible because they have not taken up the freedom which Christ gave them to live out. This is what has finally brought with it the sufferings of the working-class, the evils of colonialism, the scandals of dictatorship, totalitarianism, and concentration camps, and the triggering of technology [*Ethics of Freedom*, p. 287].

If violence is unleashed anywhere at all, the Christians are always to blame. This is the criterion, as it were, of our confession of sin [*Violence*, p. 156].

Do such statements require us to conclude that believers are the only actors on the world stage, that what they do or fail to do is all that counts, that others are wholly determined by outside forces and thus exempt from any responsibility for sufferings, evils, scandals, and the like? Can any such conclusion avoid ludicrous arrogance on the one side and fatalism on the other? Will it not prevent us from holding the Hitlers and Stalins of this world accountable for their actions? I find it hard to accept that Ellul really means to press such a conclusion. Earlier I speculated that his readers should be prepared to allow for hyperbole. And elsewhere we find more restrained descriptions. He writes at one point for example of how a believer who renounces his or her freedom is responsible "to others for not having represented freedom to them and therefore for having *aggravated* their bondage and alienation" (*Ethics of Freedom*, p. 94, my italics). This seems to lighten somewhat the extent of believer-responsibility. Moreover, to insist that believers acknowledge that their failures have harmed others is not in itself equivalent to a claim of exclusive responsibility for all past and present evil. Ellul confines himself, certainly most of the time, to the former insistence. Still, to assert that "if violence is unleashed anywhere at all, the Christians are always to blame" is to ascribe promethean importance to the actual lifestyle failures of those who expressly believe. It is also to announce some unexplained level of strict casual connectedness between these failures and that which happens to nonbelievers anywhere. Would violence simply vanish from the face of the earth if all Christians practiced nonviolence? If not, how is their blameworthiness established and why is it so sweeping? Claim (4) appears the least clear and attractive of all.

III

Earlier I suggested that the intactness of discontinuity between believer-freedom and every other kind might not be quite so complete as one had reason to think. Or perhaps the discontinuity should not be characterized as unceasing contrast and opposition. This possibility derives from occasional statements which jar any reader who expects interminable opposition. Here is one of them:

> Christian freedom is the limit of other freedoms. This does not mean that it hampers them. What is meant is that it is the ultimate point on which tendencies towards freedom converge. . . .
>
> There is a thrust, then, towards freedom from this side of freedom in Christ which can be a reflection of this freedom and a summons and aspiration towards it. On this movement of effort freedom in Christ casts a kind of light and benediction and approval [*Ethics of Freedom*, p. 410].

Now what are we to think? Convergence and benediction! Later on, too, Ellul writes that believer-freedom positively contains "within itself all other freedoms at all levels" (*Ethics of Freedom*, p. 438).

It is tempting to throw up one's hands and conclude that a point of diminishing returns has been reached in our attempts to exegete passages like these or to reconcile them with most of their predecessors and that we must simply pay our money and take our choice. Earlier I also expressed the judgment that Ellul in *The Ethics of Freedom* makes matters unjustifiably difficult for his readers. However, in the case of these two statements in particular a word may be said in his defense: a position like his *may* permit greater room for maneuver than is generally recognized.

In the case of each statement, Ellul immediately proceeds to qualify: there is also a freedom "on the far side" of Christian freedom which has no validity and receives no approval (*Ethics of Freedom*, p. 410), and no line runs the other way, *from* these worldly freedoms *to* Christian freedom (*Ethics of Freedom*, p. 438). This latter qualification in particular suggests that something quite determinate is meant by the "continuity" Ellul consistently rejects. Let us return to the language in the quotation cited at the beginning of this essay. Any worldly account of freedom is inadmissible if: it serves as a "preparation" for believer-freedom, that is, a necessary first stage or condition in some fixed sequence; or if it assumes the status of "prophecy," reliably anticipating or presaging what believer-freedom will prove to be, or stipulating either what it must or must not be. The two ideas are not the same, and the second includes very different senses of "prophecy" (anticipation and stipulation), but everything encompassed by the two must be excluded nevertheless. What I take all of this to mean is that nothing in fact can serve as a set precondition for believer-freedom. This "nothing" is certainly what I meant in my use of "unprecedented" at the beginning. The freedom Ellul affirms is distinguished because it is claimed to be a qualitatively new event; it must be understood on terms internal to itself; it retains its own integrity; it remains irreducible to anything else. In all these respects (and there are others), no line runs from any of the natural freedoms to Christian freedom.

The determinate meaning of the continuity which is always extruded appears then to be part of a larger campaign waged on a variety of fronts against natural theology and natural morality. But this campaign is wholly intramural. Believers ought not to commend *to one another* nonscriptural and nonrevelatory starting points.

Suppose, however, we ask about the appropriate attitude the believer should take, after he or she has begun to live out this irreducibly distinct freedom. Suppose, too, that he or she meets with certain worldly accounts of freedom which do not presume to be otherwise: no preparatory or prophetic claims are at issue. Will all such undeified accounts, viewed now from the side of grace, either be left behind, or indefatigably opposed? How far must a refusal—to decode the Christian conceptions one describes—extend? The refusal certainly makes criticism of secular notions always possible. The question is, does it of itself make criticism always necessary?

Here Ellul may oscillate. Sometimes it seems that God-given freedom always and only contradicts natural notions of and aspirations toward freedom (for example, *Ethics of Freedom*, p. 366). And Ellul is over fond of undiscussed, snap contrasts. Yet I have already cited quotations which authorize benediction and approval. Ellul's most considered judgment may well be found in a footnote on Barth's ethics: "On the different possible relations between the two moralities . . . neither an apologetic nor a compromise nor a distribution of roles. K. Barth opposes differentiating between the two on the basis of the criteria of the world's ethics. But we also accept Barth's attitude which considers that ethics should examine the problems, intentions, and motives of general ethics for what they are, in order to accept them or reject them. Ethics should adopt a comprehensive and not a negative attitude while remaining essentially critical" (*To Will and To Do*, p. 286). This standpoint makes criticism of secular notions possible but not necessary.

The possibility of criticism remains on the other hand sufficiently comprehensive to prompt reconsideration of the dualistic and the accommodative theses we have also found in Ellul's ethical writings. Earlier I remarked on a tension between a Barthian program to annex natural morality and a sometimes Ellulian acceptance of two mutually incompatible moralities, where nonbelievers are forced in the nature of the case to practice violence, and so forth. Similarly, though much earlier, I asked whether Ellul permits excessive accommodation when he regards the promotion of societal welfare *simpliciter* as a sufficient condition for an acceptable ethical system. The example of the practices of the Ik society should give one pause. It seems that from the standpoint of comprehensive criticism, a believer cannot viably sustain so strict a dichotomy between natural morality and Christian ethics.

The comprehensive standpoint is not merely critical, however. To claim that believers should be unwilling to exempt worldly morality from their normative assessment is, again, not equivalent to making criticism always necessary. It allows one to assume positive responsibility for exploiting whatever overlaps one finds, making the most of whatever agreements there may be, between the ethical judgments of believers and nonbelievers. Ramsey does this, for example, when he brings together historic Judeo-Christian ethical concerns and consent as a "canon of loyalty" between physician and patient.[64]

Can one exploit overlaps and yet resist cultural assimilation? How shall the limits be defined of what believers really have to protect if they are to retain their integrity? How much discontinuity is enough? Is refusal to decode or destruction of integrity their only alternative? Or is there a way to pass between the horns of this dilemma? To study Ellul is of great value because it compels one to face such fundamental questions.

About Ellul's treatment of love four highly general remarks must suffice. First, we seem to have at present two principal senses of love: intimately personal I-Thou relations, and efforts to help the poor and dispossessed everywhere. Again, there appear to be few positive material connections between love and the established moral and legal order—the sphere of justice. Yet even if one accepts (as I would not) that love's operations exclude such connections, one should be told how a personalist account of love and a nonideological account are themselves related. Do they possess features in common? Are there special conditions attached for intimate, personal relations? Should one of the senses have at least *prima facie* priority, in cases of choice?

Second, it is a commonplace to say that love can be effective only if we do not disperse our energies in all directions, that it is self-defeating to allow our lives to be cluttered by so many demands, obligations, and commitments or by so much changing of sides that we become "totally incapable of systematically and effectively loving any concrete human being."[65] Ellul would not disagree. He observes that fidelity "belongs to love constitutively, for it demands that the other be taken seriously. . . . One might prefer irresponsible roaming to committed and ongoing co-existence. But this does not mean freedom" (*Ethics of Freedom*, p. 241). Yet there still may be (I say no more) a psychological danger that this concern about effectiveness and staying the course with a limited number of neighbors will not receive its due in Ellul's perennially restless dialectic of freedom and love.

Third, we ought to notice that Ellul turns his back on various well-known adages, for example, that an implacable enemy is "needed" as one of the necessary conditions for a minimally cohesive revolutionary effort, that the more ambiguity is tolerated with respect to the "final" rightness of the revolutionary cause, the more difficult it is to have an inspired movement, etc. Furthermore, one finds no hint that Ellul would approve of a milder, less combative view, recently ventilated by Juan Luis Segundo, to the effect that "we are able to love our neighbors to the extent that we keep other human beings from showing up on our horizon."[66] This view does not require that we have enemies. Yet Segundo's discussion takes a worrisome turn. In order to prevent numerous human beings from being neighbors, he says,

> We resort to the familiar mechanism of treating them as *functions* rather than as persons; we reify them. We have time and energy to love our family, for example, thanks to the mechanism whereby we take no interest in the countless

> people who cross our path each day. We would consider it an improper intrusion if the baker, the butcher, or the telephone operator tried to get us interested in their *personal* history. Our inclination is to treat them in terms of the role or function they represent and perform.
>
> Now no one can doubt the fact that this mechanism *does violence* to the one and indivisible reality of those persons.[67]

While the "conditions of finitude" alone require every agent to limit the number of neighbors whose interests he or she can actively take into account, it is nonetheless hard to see why those whose interests are not considered have violence necessarily done to them. The issue of tangible help or harm may simply not arise. One could also say that even a human being whose relation to the agent is confined to the social role he or she happens to occupy is not, as Segundo implies, thereby merely a means to or a function of the agent's desires and purposes. Love may, for example, find expression in certain prohibitions which honor the humanity of the other, quite apart from any sharing of a personal history. The baker ought not to be raped, or the butcher murdered, or the telephone operator treated with derision. Such a line of reply seems to me persuasive as far as it goes. It suggests that Segundo badly exaggerates when he claims "that violence is an intrinsic dimension of any and all concrete love in history just as it clearly is an intrinsic dimension of any and all concrete egotism."[68]

Ellul's treatment suffers, however, from a contrary difficulty. For him, love must eschew violence altogether. And he is disinclined to accept any version of the historic distinction between violence and force (e.g., *Violence*, pp. 1–9). The result appears to be a lamentable absence of careful discussion of the question whether love provides definite guidance on those occasions (and they are many, even if not so many as Segundo believes) when the interests of persons unavoidably conflict. Ellul does not address at any length, for example, the standard challenge issued to the proponent of nonviolence, namely, how can it be more loving to refuse to defend, by force if need be, innocent third parties who are being unjustly attacked? Yoder has offered one such reply,[69] and one wishes Ellul would do so, for it is this challenge which is the point of origin for so much "just-war" thinking. Ellul simply bypasses this issue when he denounces the just-war tradition as hopelessly flawed because it seeks an "accord" which human life in this world will never attain.

Fourth, the important distinction one finds in Ellul—between the irreducible dignity of the neighbor and the particular ideology he or she endorses—requires more scrutiny than he has so far given. One would have to examine the way in which "ideology" itself is used, for obviously the word has no settled meaning.[70] And as we saw earlier, Ellul sometimes extols a ceaseless stepping back, certainly from a permanent alliance with any particular political ideology, so that, for instance, one should resist individualism in the nineteenth century and collectivism in the twentieth. Yet it seems too simple to leave matters at that. One naturally asks, is it feasible to be so indifferent to the content of particular political beliefs and affiliations? Are oppression by those in power and material deprivation not only severally necessary but jointly sufficient to warrant full if temporary support in the name of love? Suppose Ellul encounters a group each member of which is demonstrably oppressed and deprived. Suppose further that each member pledges unswerving loyalty to the principle that the state and not the individual person is the only basic subject of moral predicates,[71] that there is no such thing as right or law or personal meaning and significance apart from the collective and its own welfare. Suppose finally that Ellul knows with certainty that if these people seize power they will never relinquish it whatever catastrophes occur under their leadership, and that they will practice brutal oppression and deprivation, far worse than anything they themselves endured. What is Ellul to say? Is it enough always to be prepared to leap to the side of the newly defeated, whenever an overthrow proves successful? For what is contemplated is present support for an oppressed group with a fascist ideology. Can the substantive beliefs of such a group not have some relevance in determining the content and range of the support given? In fact, Ellul himself is not content for long to deny such relevance altogether. We have already noted examples of a more complicated analysis: if a group's ideology includes the aim of liberation from Christianity, then believers must remain outside; believers have a better opportunity of taking part as free persons in a social setting where the relativism of politics is recognized, the form of government is modest, and so on.

More generally, one will have to decide whether Christianity requires a doctrine of the individual person as a basic subject of moral predicates (in addition to, or rather than, the collective)— once again not only in the twentieth century vis-à-vis "collectivism," but in every century; and if it does, whether there is something at stake for the believer as believer in labors to make the ordinary moral, political, economic, and legal existence of the society at large embody and safeguard appropriate parts of that doctrine. Pope John Paul II seems to accept that there is indeed something at stake. He is reported to have told a cheering crowd of thousands in Mogila, Poland, in June, 1979:

> Christ will never approve that man be considered or that man consider himself, merely as a means of production, or that he be appreciated, esteemed, and valued in accordance with that principle. . . .
>
> Christ will never approve of it. . . . This must be remembered both by the worker and the employer, by the work system as well as by the system of remuneration; it must be remembered by the state, the nation, and the church.[72]

I have already identified hints of how Ellul qualifies the promethean responsibilities he sometimes ascribes to the failures of those who believe. Let us close by referring to one additional and far more formidable qualification. Indeed, it seems to alter decisively the estimate of what burdens any of us bear, whether we believe or not. It is found in the view that Providence works in the midst of human failure as well as human faithfulness, that God may not only override such failure, he may actually use it. Hope resides more in such providential working than in the exercise of believer-freedom. And the very content of the hope itself is transformed. However uncertainly it fits with many of his characteristic themes, Ellul shares this view: "According to his own will God uses the history which men make. He both hides himself in history and also reveals himself in it. In it he manifests his blessing and his cursing. . . . That God takes it up does not mean that he approves of it. He takes charge of it. He finally works it out in his own way and not in that which man has chosen. He transforms it, doing for man far more than he could ever have hoped" (*Ethics of Freedom*, p. 66).[73]

NOTES

1. Alasdair MacIntyre, "Can Medicine Dispense with a Theological Perspective on Human Nature?" *Knowledge, Value, and Belief*, ed. H. Tristram Engelhardt, Jr., and Daniel Callahan (Hastings-on-Hudson: Hastings Center, 1977), p. 36. See also MacIntyre and Paul Ricoeur, *The Religious Significance of Atheism* (New York: Columbia University Press, 1970), pp. 1–55.

2. So far as I am aware, none of the questions I raise or criticisms I make turns on issues about translation. Yet because this second quotation in particular is so central to the entire essay, reference to the French edition should at least be made: Jacques Ellul, *Éthique de la liberté*, vol. I (1970), pp. 309–10.

3. While Ellul does not aspire to be a professional philosopher, his own account of actual moral systems calls to mind modern philosophical discussions of historicism, ethical relativism, and conceptual relativism. It would be instructive to ask whether he could utilize such discussions to defend his view more clearly and rigorously, without introducing disastrous shifts in what he wants to say, or whether he could not profit from the wider discussion because his own account is too dissimilar. That possibilty is not one we can pursue here, however.

4. See, e.g. Paul E. Sigmund, *Natural Law in Political Thought* (Cambridge, Mass.: Winthrop Publishers, 1971); Yves Simon, *The Tradition of Natural Law* (New York: Fordham University Press, 1967); D. J. O'Connor, *Aquinas and Natural Law* (London: Macmillan, 1967), esp. p. 71.

5. David Little, "Calvin and the Prospects for a Christian Theory of Natural Law," *Norm and Context in Christian Ethics*, ed. Gene Outka and Paul Ramsey (New York: Scribner's, 1968), p. 176. James M. Gustafson, in *Protestant and Roman Catholic Ethics: Prospects for Rapproachement* (Chicago: University of Chicago Press, 1978), p. 76, thinks Little's project "must be commended as a major effort to formulate constants ('natural law') without grounding them in an explicated ontology (such as a traditional theory of natural law). . . ."

6. We know from his *Theological Foundation of Law* that Ellul finds them all theologically deficient; French ed. 1946.

7. Reinhold Niebuhr, *The Nature and Destiny of Man*, vol. II (New York: Scribner's, 1947), p. 253.

8. *Ibid.*, p. 254.

9. Richard Swinburne, *The Coherence of Theism* (Oxford: Clarendon Press, 1977), p. 201.

10. Eric D'Arcy, " 'Worthy of Worship': A Catholic Contribution," in *Religion and Morality*, ed. Gene Outka and John P. Reeder, Jr. (Garden City, N.Y.: Doubleday Anchor, 1973), p. 192.

11. *Ibid.*, pp. 191–2.

12. *Ibid.*, p. 197.

13. *Ibid.*, p. 185.

14. Perhaps Kant presents one such version. See Immanuel Kant, *Religion within the Limits of Reason Alone*, trans. Theodore M. Greene and Hoyt H. Hudson (New York: Harper, 1960); see also Allen W. Wood, *Kant's Moral Religion* (Ithaca, N.Y.: Cornell University Press, 1970).

15. Karl Barth, *Church Dogmatics*, vol. II, pt. 2, trans. G. W. Bromiley *et al.* (Edinburgh: T. & T. Clark, 1957), pp. 449–506.

16. G. J. Warnock, *The Object of Morality* (London: Methuen, 1971).

17. See the description by Edward LeRoy Long, Jr., "Soteriological Implications of Norm and Context," *Norm and Context in Christian Ethics*, p. 267.

18. Emil Brunner, *The Divine Imperative*, trans. Olive Wyon (Philadelphia: Westminster Press, 1947); Helmut Thielicke, *Theological Ethics*, vol. 1, ed. William H. Lazareth (Philadelphia: Fortress Press, 1966).

19. Barth, *Church Dogmatics*, vol. II, pt. 2, p. 516.

20. *Ibid.*, pp. 514–15.

21. Christine Battersby, "Morality and the Ik," *Philosophy*, 53 (Apr. 1978), 201–14.

22. *Ibid.*, p. 211.

23. See, e.g., John H. Yoder, *Karl Barth and the Problem of War* (Nashville, Tenn: Abingdon Press, 1970), p. 63.

24. Gustafson makes reference to these affinities in his review of *The Ethics of Freedom* in *Journal of Religion*, Jan. 1978, p. 77.

25. Martin Luther, *The Freedom of a Christian*, in *Martin Luther*, ed. John Dillenberger (Garden City, N.Y.: Doubleday Anchor, 1961), p. 53.

26. For discussions of this question, see *The Study of Religion in Colleges and Universities*, ed. Paul Ramsey and John F. Wilson (Princeton, N.J.: Princeton University Press, 1970), esp. the essays by Arthur C. McGill, "The Ambiguous Position of Christian

Theology," pp. 105–38, and Victor Preller, "Catholic Studies in the University," pp. 139–58; Ninian Smart, *Secular Education and the Logic of Religion* (London: Faber and Faber, 1968).

27. Barth's attitude is perceptively characterized by Hans W. Frei in his review article of Eberhard Busch's *Karl Barth,* in *Virginia Theological Seminary Quarterly,* 30 (July 1978), 42–47.

28. On the distinction between first-order desires and second-order evaluations, see Harry Frankfurt, "Freedom of the Will and the Concept of a Person," *Journal of Philosophy,* 68 (Jan. 1971), 5–20; Charles Taylor, "Responsibility for Self," *The Identities of Persons,* ed. Amélie Oksenberg Rorty (Berkeley: University of California Press, 1976), pp. 281–99; Taylor, "What is Human Agency?" *The Self: Psychological and Philosophical Issues,* ed. Theodore Mischel (Oxford: Basil Blackwell, 1977), pp. 103–35.

29. Karl Barth, *Church Dogmatics,* vol. III, pt. 4, trans. A. T. MacKay *et al.* (Edinburgh: T. & T. Clark, 1961), p. 130.

30. Gene Outka, *Agape: An Ethical Analysis* (New Haven, Conn.; Yale University Press, 1972), pp. 222–24. For example, there can be an eros as natural desire which constitutes one of the indispensable bases for marriage (together with mutual understanding and self-giving). See Barth, *Church Dogmatics,* vol. III, pt. 4, 219–22.

31. Outka, *Agape,* p. 184.

32. Barth, *Church Dogmatics,* vol. III, pt. 4, pp. 222–23.

33. Søren Kierkegaard, *Sickness unto Death,* trans. Walter Lowrie (Princeton, N.J.: Princeton University Press, 1974), p. 176.

34. *Ibid.*

35. Paul Dietrichson, "Kierkegaard's Concept of the Self," *Inquiry,* 8 (Spring 1965), 18.

36. Karl Barth, "No!" in *Natural Theology,* trans. Peter Fraenkel (London: Geoffrey Bles, 1946), p. 113.

37. Any serious discussion of dialectic would have to include consideration of the respective treatments of Hegel and Kierkegaard. Cf., e.g. J. N. Findlay, *Hegel: A Re-examination* (New York: Collier Books, 1962), esp. pp. 55–79; Robert C. Solomon, *From Rationalism to Existentialism: The Existentialists and Their Nineteenth-Century Backgrounds* (New York: Harper, 1972), pp. 39–68; Hermann Diem, *Kierkegaard's Dialectic of Existence,* trans. Harold Knight (Edinburgh: Oliver and Boyd, 1959); Vernard Eller, *Kierkegaard and Radical Discipleship: A New Perspective* (Princeton, N.J.: Princeton University Press, 1968), esp. pp. 144–45.

38. For the meaning of this latter interpretation of "neighbor," see Outka, *Agape,* esp. pp. 9–24, 34–42.

39. Martin Buber, *I and Thou*, trans. Walter Kaufmann (New York: Scribner's, 1970).

40. Joseph Fletcher, *Situation Ethics* (Philadelphia: Westminster Press, 1966); Fletcher, "What's in a Rule? A Situationist's View," *Norm and Context in Christian Ethics*, pp. 325–49; see also my characterization of the debate about situation ethics in Outka, *Agape*, pp. 93–122.

41. Niebuhr, *The Nature and Destiny of Man*, vol. 2, p. 246.

42. *Ibid.*, p. 251.

43. Emil Brunner, *Justice and the Social Order*, trans. Marty Hottinger (New York: Harper, 1945), pp. 128–29.

44. Outka, *Agape*, pp. 75–92, 291–312.

45. Gene Outka, "Social Justice and Equal Access to Health Care," *Journal of Religious Ethics*, 2 (Spring 1974), 11–32.

46. Again, I have tried to analyze the meaning of this sense of "neighbor," in *Agape*, esp. pp. 2–24, 260–74.

47. I cannot do justice in this essay (though I hope to do so in the future) to the significance of this fight. Ellul has put us all in his debt for making us aware of it.

48. For example, he thinks that an internal contradiction plagues the distinction between the poor and the powerful: "It might seem strange that people can simultaneously hold both . . . that the poor man represents Jesus Christ on earth, and therefore all the right is on his side, and he is the only one who must be considered; but at the same time, that poverty is a scandal, and we must do our best to get rid of this scandal and to put the poor into a 'normal' situation; that is, put an end to poverty" (*Violence*, p. 38–39).

49. Yoder, *Karl Barth and the Problem of War*, p. 61.

50. Some of these complexities I have tried to locate in *Agape*, pp. 229–33. For sensitive discussion, see William Werpehowski, "Command and History in the Ethics of Karl Barth" (forthcoming).

51. Ellul's passion to retain an account of the religious relationship where personal consultations are in place at every point, and his opposition to versions of morality which jeopardize that account, remind one in a rough way of Kierkegaard's pseudonym, Johannes de silentio in *Fear and Trembling*, trans. Walter Lowrie (Princeton, N.J.: Princeton University Press, 1974). See also Gene Outka, "Religious and Moral Duty: Notes on *Fear and Trembling*," in *Religion and Morality*, pp. 204–54; Edmund N. Santurri, "Kierkegaard's *Fear and Trembling* in Logical Perspective," *Journal of Religious Ethics*, 5 (Fall 1977), 225–247. There are also affinities with what I have called the "theological contextualism" of twen-

tieth-century figures like Barth; Dietrich Bonhoeffer, *Ethics*, ed. Eberhard Bethge (New York: Macmillan, 1955); Paul Lehmann, *Ethics in a Christian Context* (New York: Harper, 1963); H. Richard Niebuhr, *The Responsible Self* (New York: Harper, 1963). Ellul is, however, exceptionally emphatic on the self-justifying motives in so much moral striving. We pursue virtue and behave decently so that we can "put our minds at rest. God will not be *able* to condemn us" (*To Will and To Do*, p. 211, my italics).

52. Paul Ramsey, *War and the Christian Conscience* (Durham, N.C.: Duke University Press, 1961); Ramsey, *The Just War: Force and Political Responsibility* (New York: Scribner's, 1968); John C. Ford, S.J., "The Morality of Obliteration Bombing," *War and Morality*, ed. Richard A. Wasserstrom (Belmont, Calif.: Wadsworth Publishing Company, 1970), pp. 15–41.

53. Erich Auerbach, *Mimesis: The Representation of Reality in Western Literature*, trans. Willard R. Trask (Princeton, N.J.: Princeton University Press, 1974).

54. See, e.g. Karl Rahner, "Christianity and the Non-Christian Religions," *Theological Investigations*, vol. V, trans. Karl H. Kruger (Baltimore: Helicon Press, 1966), pp. 115–34; "Anonymous Christians," *Theological Investigations*, vol. VI, trans. Karl H. and Boniface Kruger (Baltimore: Helicon Press, 1969), pp. 390–98; "Atheism and Implicit Christianity," *Theological Investigations*, vol. IX, trans. Graham Harrison (New York: Herder and Herder, 1972), pp. 145–64; "Anonymous Christianity and the Missionary Task of the Church," *Theological Investigations*, vol. XII, trans. David Bourke (New York: Seabury, 1974), pp. 161–78.

55. Donald Evans, "Does Religious Faith Conflict with Moral Freedom?" *Religion and Morality*, pp. 348–88; *Struggle and Fulfillment: The Inner Dynamics of Religion and Morality* (Cleveland, Ohio: Collins, 1979).

56. Karl Barth, *Church Dogmatics*, vol. IV, part 2, trans. G. W. Bromiley (Edinburgh: T. & T. Clark, 1958), p. 511. See also Outka, *Agape*, pp. 243–47.

57. Niebuhr, *The Nature and Destiny of Man*, e.g. vol. I, pp. 170–71.

58. Cf. my distinction between agent-stringency and community-stringency in *Agape*, pp. 306–9.

59. Robert Munro, *Schleiermacher* (Paisley: Alexander Gardner, 1903), p. 256.

60. Outka, *Agape*, pp. 245–47.

61. Barth, *Church Dogmatics*, vol. II, pt. 2, p. 526.

62. *Ibid.*

63. *Ibid.*, p. 518.

64. For example, Paul Ramsey, *The Patient as Person* (New Haven, Conn.: Yale University Press, 1970).

65. Juan Luis Segundo, S.J., *The Liberation of Theology*, trans. John Drury (Maryknoll, N.Y.: Orbis Books, 1976), p. 159.

66. *Ibid.* It has not been feasible in this essay to consider whether Ellul's criticisms of the theologies of liberation and revolution are either accurate or telling. Those writers he mentions explicitly include Richard Shaull, "Revolutionary Change in Theological Perspective," in *Christian Social Ethics in a Changing World*, ed. John C. Bennett (New York: Association Press, 1966), pp. 23–43; Harvey Cox, *The Secular City* (New York: Macmillan, 1965); James H. Cone, *A Black Theology of Liberation* (Philadelphia: Lippincott, 1970). His references to Jürgen Moltmann, e.g. *Theology of Hope*, trans. James W. Leitch (New York: Harper, 1967), are more favorable.

67. Segundo, *The Liberation of Theology*, pp. 159–60.

68. *Ibid.*, p. 161.

69. John H. Yoder, "'What Would You Do If . . . ?': An Exercise in Situation Ethics," *Journal of Religious Ethics*, 2 (Fall 1974), 81–105.

70. See, e.g. Patrick Corbett, *Ideologies* (London: Hutchinson, 1965).

71. I adopt this phrase from an unpublished paper by Bernard Rosen entitled "The Nature of Ethics." He is not responsible for the use to which I put it here.

72. *New York Times*, Sunday, June 10, 1979, p. 1. Barth writes in a similar way, *Church Dogmatics*, vol. III, pt. 4, p. 423.

73. In writing this paper I have been helped enormously by suggestions and comments from Stanley Hauerwas, Paul Nelson, Susan Owen, Paul Ramsey, John Reeder, Edmund Santurri, Steve Siebert, Philip Turner, and William Werpehowski. I want also to thank the editors for their initial invitation and their patience.

Chapter 10

A Philosophical Critique of Ellul on Natural Law

Arthur F. Holmes

The specter haunting mankind, of a technological society dominated by political and economic structures with bureaucratic rules and managerial procedures, is a recurrent theme in Jacques Ellul's writings. While he develops it most fully in *The Technological Society*, he also includes a chapter on "Technological Morality" in *To Will and To Do*; and in *The Theological Foundation of Law* he warns against the dangers of "technological law." In this latter case, writing in the mid-1940s in the immediate aftermath of the Nazi perversions, he argues that it is impossible to return, as some wish, to the concept of natural law. Instead he proposes a "covenantal" understanding of law and justice appropriate to Christian realism.

I take this interplay between technological law, natural law, and Ellul's covenantal conception to be a crucial theme in his theology of law. In this essay, therefore, I explore his account of legal history in order to assess the problem with natural law as he sees it, then I examine his reasons for substituting a covenantal approach for the creationally based morality that underlies Christian natural law theories and similar approaches; and finally I show that a creational approach, though not necessarily a natural-law theory, provides a more adequate response to technologism than Ellul allows.

LAW IN THREE STAGES

Since the problem of technologism is a historical phenomenon, seeing its origins is essential. For Ellul the sociologist, moreover, law is first and foremost a historical fact, as is morality. All three —law, morality, and technology—have evolved under a variety of determining forces, such as biological and economic ones. In no case do theories shape them; theory, too, is historically determined and it reflects the concrete situations which give it birth.

Ellul describes how law has evolved through successive stages to its present state. First, it was given a religious basis: laws expressed the will of the gods. Law was formulated by the priest and given religious sanctions. In the second stage law became secularized. Arising spontaneously from a common sense of justice under the impact of social and economic circumstances, it had a common content affecting basic institutions like marriage and property that made social existence possible, and its authority derived from the conscience of the people in the circumstances where they live. Ellul calls this stage "natural law" in the tradition of the *lex gentium* of Roman jurisprudence, roughly analogous to the English concept of "common law." Thomas Hobbes approximates it also in his account of psychologically based "laws of nature" antecedent to the political contract. But Ellul draws a sharp distinction between the juridical concept of natural law as historical fact and the philosophical concept of natural law as an ethical ideal from which positive law is derived and by which it is to be judged. Ellul stands closer here to Roman jurisprudence than to Thomism, and closer to Hobbes than to Locke or Grotius.

But even natural law as historical fact is now, according to Ellul, a thing of the past. In the third and present stage, any underlying sense of justice disappears because the state has usurped that authority by creating its own laws, building its own juridical system (now hardened into legal codes), and operating by purely rational techniques remote from the spontaneity of any intuitive sense of justice. This is technological law, and it is decadent.[1] In a technological society, law becomes a managerial and logical skill related more to social expedience than to moral norms. We are accordingly ruled not just by outward organizations with sophisticated sets of procedures, but by an inner technological mentality supporting technological law. Like other technologies, it is at the disposal of whoever takes control and for whatever reason he chooses. In this fashion modern societies spawn dictatorships and bureaucracies. Nothing short of a revolution within the human spirit can free man from its tyranny.[2]

This account echoes with ideas from French philosophy. Ellul's three historical phases of law are reminiscent of Comte's three stages, but with major differences. Comte's first and third stages (the religious and the scientific) seem to correspond; but his second stage, the metaphysical, is not what Ellul has in mind. Even though he sees natural law as a historical fact, Ellul refuses to tie it to metaphysical theories of natural law, parallel though they be to the juridical fact. Moreover, Comte was optimistic about the positive or scientific stage of things, while Ellul is plainly pessimistic. He leaves no room for evolutionary optimism, least of all for optimism about the scientific and technological mentalities.

This in turn echoes Henri Bergson's rejection of the static and analytic in favor of an intuitive morality of spontaneous freedom. Ellul's notion of an intuitive sense of justice and the spontaneous birth of laws—in contrast with rule-ordered structures —suggests that Bergson is not forgotten. But the *élan vital* in Bergson's view is a creative evolutionary force inherent in nature and forever breaking the static bonds that contain it. For Ellul, the vitality of the human spirit, shattered by sin, provides no basis for optimism about the future. Man's hope lies elsewhere, outside himself.

Similar parallels could be drawn to Rousseau's notion of a common will (namely, a common sense of justice) and a noble savage free from civilization's taint, or to Marcuse's scathing indictment of the technological mentality. But Ellul again sees no hope for restoring human freedom by any human means including political revolution. The problem of technologism is symptomatic of something more: man's sin from which only divine grace can deliver. Progress, then, is not inevitable for Ellul. More recently than in *The Theological Foundation of Law*, he repudiated the idea that God would never let technological progress turn out badly, and the idea that human nature deserves more of our confidence. He also rejects Teilhard de Chardin's apparent claim that evolutionary mechanisms will automatically resolve the problem; nor will a new lifestyle and a new law emerge unless the human spirit, inwardly freed, shatters its oppressor.[3]

Ellul's concern, then, is to know what can deliver us from technological law by freeing man within. No teleology immanent within nature, man, or history can succeed. Herein lies the basis for his refusal of natural law. He cites three insurmountable difficulties that block its revival at this later stage in history. First, its individual human rights have since been subsumed into legal rights generally, granted and guaranteed by an all-pervasive state authority. The historical transition from Hobbes to Hegel and Marx cannot be reversed, for it reflects not just a theoretical difference but also and more basically a fact of juridical and political evolution. Second, law is now changed from a once-for-all abstract norm embodying rational moral ideals into a malleable sociological phenomenon: natural law is not a present fact any longer. Third, modern society presents legal problems and embraces legal domains (social legislation, labor laws, and liability, for example) of which natural law was ignorant and on which its common sense of justice is silent.[4] Scientific study, Ellul concludes, shows the futility of reviving natural law in a technological age.

It should not be thought that Ellul is simply capitulating to such philosophies of law as positivism or historicism. The positivist regards law as purely the state's work, whatever it lays down, and the historicist makes it dependent on social and economic conditions alone. But such accounts consider law to be far more relative than it is, for they fail to recognize the fundamental similarity of laws throughout the western world at every time and place—those, for example, that govern such human relationships as marriage, property, murder, and contracts. These resemblances cannot be satisfactorily explained on purely historical grounds, nor by any coincidental contact between different legislations. Ellul points instead to man himself, who refines the rules that arise from historical conditions and is guided in that activity by principles common to all men (basically their sense of justice).[5] This alone gives vitality to juridical concerns and accounts for spontaneous similarities between social and legal institutions everywhere.

For Ellul as for Hegel, theories of natural rights "are abstractions and formalisms filled with exactly the opposite of ethical vitality," yet it is this vitality and the freedom of the human spirit that account for historical affinities in positive law.[6] Natural law is not unchanging and eternal, nor primarily a theory about deducing laws from nature. It, too, is a historical creation of the human spirit. Thus technological law poses such a dire threat, for it stifles vitality in a maze of rules and structures and inviolable procedures. Even man's common sense of justice is of man's own making, and no rational explanation can justify its existence or its authority or its common content. It is a product neither of social and economic conditions nor of historical interactions, nor of philosophical theories, but of man's vitality. The worth of natural law is not absolute for Ellul, then, but neither does it stem simply from the historical conditions in which it arose nor from man himself. Something outside man and history gave man this vitality. Ellul feels that we must recognize that natural law was God's will for man at the historical stage. As God's will is the key to understanding morality and all of history, so it was with law.[7]

CREATION OR COVENANT?

Every theist, if consistent, regards God's will as the ultimate basis for moral obligation. This gives rise to two markedly different directions for ethics and for the theology of law. On the one hand, God's will is expressed in his creation, so that our own knowledge of the creation is indirectly an understanding of God's will. Christian natural-law theories—whether Thomistic or Lockean—are of this variety, providing the basis for a universal and unchanging morality that judges and proposes the laws men make. On the other hand, God expresses his will in a covenant of grace in Jesus Christ, so that our knowledge of him is itself a knowledge of God's will. In this tradition we find writers like Martin Luther, Karl Barth, and Jacques Ellul. What leads Ellul in this direction? Here our attention turns from natural law as a historical fact to natural law as a philosophical theory.

First, Ellul accepts no unchanging or universal human nature. Any theory of universals is to him a form of idealism in which man and the world are ruled by an immanent divine reason *(logos)* rather than by God's sovereign will. Thomas Aquinas's version of natural law is patently unacceptable. Moreover, idealism expects that man can be ruled by reason and its laws, a hope that Locke developed in his theory. But man for Ellul is not rational enough either to perceive or to do the good, and whatever else we know of his nature reveals nothing of consequence. Biology dictates the natural order of relations between men and women, Ellul suggests for instance, and one can deduce nothing at all from it.[8] In fact, moral theorists are simply the recorders of morals. Their morality is a product of society's changing values, changing less rapidly but nonetheless reflecting the influence of the social group. And each group develops the morality that it finds essential.[9] Nor does it help to identify natural law with the decalog and make it, as Calvin did, into a moral ideal for legislators to copy. This ignores the distinction between divine justice and laws of human origin, natural law included.[10]

There is no fixed order of creation, because God did not create a fixed universe once and for all. Creation is continuous, and God still acts. God is not bound to universal, rational, and moral ideals, but acts freely; consequently, there can be no universal moral law that he and we alike must follow. God's will alone is ultimately binding, and he decrees what he wills independently of any fixed forms of creation. Ellul is a thoroughgoing nominalist.

Second, sin has erased all trace of God's image in man. His creation form has been totally changed and his nature now is evil.[11] To speak of man's nature in any other way in unbiblical; it misunderstands the human predicament and ignores "the tragic separation created by revelation and grace." Natural law exalts the autonomy of man's reason and separates human law from any consideration of God's purpose in law: it is heretical.

All moralities stand in rebellion against God's will. Before the fall, man acted in a spontaneous fashion without duty or organizational constrictions. Now of necessity he is given the external restraints of morality and law for his own preservation and that of society. Human survival depends on our giving value to some things rather than others.[12] But there is nothing objective or absolute about these values. In fact today's technological morality makes normalcy the highest virtue and reinforces success-orientation—as if they will solve all our problems. Actually all such rules epitomize man's refusal to submit to God's will. Yet they still indicate that God wills to preserve his creation.[13]

Third, man is completely ignorant of God's will and of the good. This did not just result from the fall, for it has been true since creation. In fact, the forbidden fruit in Eden precluded man from any knowledge at all of good and evil. The tempter raised the question for the first time. Paul's statement about the Gentile conscience in Romans, chapter 2, does not help either; Ellul assumes that refers not to some universal natural law but to Gentile Christians whom the Holy Spirit directs to the will of God.[14]

Nor is man's ignorance relieved by the moralities we find in the Bible. The Mosaic law was not divine law, nor does it represent God's will today; it was man-made and therefore historically relative. The Sermon on the Mount is no unchanging divine law either, nor is Paul's moral teaching the universal will of God. Bringing such things into Christianity is to import the world's man-made moral systems. They bear witness to God's will, but they are not themselves his command. They point to what God demanded then, but not to what God wills for us.

Ellul's Barthian concept of revelation comes into focus here. As Professor Bromiley notes in chapter 2 herein, the Bible for Barth and Ellul does not give moral absolutes. It does not present God's unchanging rules for men, but rather a human witness to the fact that God's will is mediated differently to man in various situations. In Ellul's perspective, revelation is either a living, present word which cannot be systematized into a morality, or it is a dead letter no better than anything else for building an ethic. He opts for the former. The Bible, he says, is history and not a book of philosophy. God's will is not something universal and unchanging, but is addressed to us personally.[15]

God's will, then, is in general unknown. "There is only a personal relation for each person with God in which the good is revealed in its character as the will of God." That will cannot be an end to be attained nor an ideal to be emulated. Ellul considers it, instead, a task relating to the kingdom of God and a command to be obeyed.[16]

There are, then, no universal maxims, no unchanging basis in ethics for law. Ellul's ethic is purely situational and law is relative, too. The state does not have to apply the law of Christ or observe any moral code. It has only to serve the common interest as usefully as possible.[17]

Ellul grounds his situationism in the Hebrew terms for justice (*shaphat*) and righteousness (*sedeq*). The former is not a moral quality and does not refer to any moral attribute of God. It simply signifies a judgment. Divine justice is divine judgment; it finds expression in God's commands and in his determinations on the last day. Righteousness likewise is neither a moral quality of actions nor a moral attribute of God. It refers simply to fairness and equity in one's dealings. God's righteousness is expressed in unconditional grace, because thereby nobody has an unequal advantage. Accordingly, there are no ultimate moral ideals on which to base any universal ethic, and no known moral attributes of God from which to derive such ideals. God makes his judgments constantly, not once and for all like a tape recorder. He takes human justice and law into account, not because they are just in themselves but because he wills to use what man creates. He judges us according to our judgments.[18] A man for his part only knows that a good exists and that choices have to be made, but he is ignorant of that good and has no way of knowing God's will for him here and now. Knowledge is always an active involvement based on a decision, not some unchanging truth achieved once and for all. An action belongs to particular situations, and cannot be made universal, systematized, or even analyzed logically. One acts in spontaneous freedom out of his own relationship with God.[19]

By now the basics of Ellul's covenantal view have emerged. If no universal moral ideas exist as foundation for law, if universal goods are unknown, if the Bible does not teach an unchanging morality and is not propositional revelation—in the classic sense of teaching unchanging and universal truth—then what theological basis remains?

Ellul responds that God still has a purpose in history for human moralities and legal systems, the purpose of preserving the creation he acts to redeem. The purpose of his revelation is redemptive; the purpose of history is redemptive. It is all summed up in Christ. God's covenant of grace then adopts what man has made and works with that as he summons men to act in his Kingdom. The presence of that Kingdom calls not for ethical standards or systems or philosophies of law, but for loving action that attests the intercourse of man's action with God's.

Ellul spells out the bearing of this covenant on the three elements typical of human law: common institutions, common laws about human rights in relation to those institutions, and the common sense of justice.[20] Institutions, first of all, are bodies of rules oriented toward a common goal, constituting an enduring entity that exists independently of man's will. The Bible says God made institutions such as marriage and the state, but Ellul denies that God did it by creating universal tendencies in men. Rather, these institutions are historical developments willed by God for his own redemptive purpose. Their outward form may change, but the inner reality remains. Human rights likewise are not God-given at creation, fixed by virtue of the way we are made. Rather, God grants men certain rights for his own purposes. Ellul quotes Deuteronomy 16:19–20: "You shall not violate any of these rights . . . that you may inherit the land which the Lord your God gives you."[21] So, too, the sense of justice that gives to institutions and rights their particular historical forms. It is not an innate idea of some eternal moral ideal. It merely concerns the pragmatics of preserving the institutions and rights that serve God's purpose. Man's justice, like God's, is simply the making of judgments about the form things should take. It has no content or moral good in itself.

The theological foundation of human law, then, is found in God's will to appropriate for his purposes the juridical systems of men. At most, human law witnesses to this covenant of God and his grace.

PROBLEMS AND PRESUPPOSITIONS

I leave the reader to judge for himself about Ellul's view of Scripture and his novel interpretation of particular texts. Suffice it to say that I consider existential theology ill-grounded when it creates a disjunction between revelation as historical and personal and the humanly formed propositions that the Bible preserves. The biblical record of God's redemptive acts in history is interwoven with interpretative material about unchanging theological and ethical truth. Consequently fixed moral standards destroy neither an individual response to God's particular will for him nor the spontaneity of personal freedom. Rather, both are essential to the guidance of Christian liberty and the knowledge of divine will.[22]

We now turn our attention to Ellul's philosophical assumptions, for these are hidden under the surface of his writing and he appears not to give them sufficiently critical scrutiny.

1. Voluntaristic nominalism: the disjunction of will and intellect. Ellul's covenantal proposal, and his insistence that divine law is independent of any essential logos-structure in creation, plainly assumes—as we have noted—a voluntaristic position in the old "will and intellect" debate, and nominalism with respect to universals of any kind. He prefers a covenant to a creation order, law to logos, and the divine will to divine intellect as the basis for law and morality. No unchanging essences are allowed and he conceives of no universal moral principles. This kind of position is not novel: in a well-known essay on Christian influence in the rise of modern science, Michael Foster argues that Christianity's doctrine of creation encouraged voluntaristic nominalism in place of Greek rationalistic realism, and that this in turn encouraged the rise of empirical science.[23] William of Occam is the classic example, with his claim that the doctrine of archetypal forms deprives God of his freedom. Thus morality rests on what God wills, not on the essential nature of either man or God. Ellul stands in this tradition and his opposition to natural law arises from it. Paul Sigmund finds one critical assertion in all types of natural law theory: ". . . there exists in nature and/or human nature a rational order which can provide intelligible value statements independently of human will, that are universal in application, unchangeable in their ultimate content, and morally obligatory on mankind."[24] Every such claim Ellul repudiates. There can be no universal and unchangeable moral obligations and no natural law of that sort, because there is no unchanging rational order in nature or in man. The objectivity of values independent of the human will is at stake, if morality results from ideology and social conditions, not from either an essential nature of man or an essential attribute of God.

A voluntarism of this sort, applied to either God or man, has always encountered opposition. In the first place, if God's will is not governed by his attributes or his reason, then his will and law would seem to be arbitrary. Ellul's covenantal proposal tries to avoid this inference—what God wills relates to his redemptive purposes and such purposefulness is not arbitrariness. He works with human laws. Yet it still means that God's judgment and human morality alike are situational and relative, devoid of universal and unchanging moral principles. Why then could God not work his purposes as well with technological morality and technological law as with natural law (in the "historical fact" sense)? Why is technologism bad? And what does "bad" mean other than repression of man's inner sense of justice? Yet if God chooses for now to use that man-made sense of justice, then why is it bad to repress it? Surely God could use the rules of juridical technology instead. In effect, Ellul's voluntarism logically denies him any basis for the value judgments he constantly makes about man and society—the more so since he explicitly states that man has absolutely no knowledge of what good or righteousness really are. How can an ethical skeptic make moral judgments?

In the second place, voluntaristic nominalism defends God's sovereignty against the autonomy of Platonic ideals and of man's utopian efforts. But Ellul goes too far. Christian natural-law theorists, while retaining common ground of a limited sort, reject the optimistic idealism that Ellul fears. Jacques Maritain, while affirming God's sovereign right, still insists that human rights may be derived from natural law. But this imposes no obligation on God that he treat men a certain way, although God owes it to himself to act toward them according to the nature he gave them. Anything else would be self-contradictory.[25] And Dietrich Bonhoeffer, who agrees with Ellul in a number of regards, speaks more positively of nature. Creation, though fallen, remains open to God in Christ. In him, God enters created reality and reaffirms our right and obligation to be men before God. Our rights and obligations, moreover, relate to mandates God gave at creation concerning labor and marriage and implicitly concerning government as well.[26] Both Maritain and Bonhoeffer remind us that rights are prior to duties, so that our moral duties logically stem from the God-given right to be treated as the persons God made us to be. Ellul's voluntaristic nominalism forfeits such a basis, leaving God to covenant that he will go along with the rights we design on our own.

The question is whether there is anything both essential and universal about creation and man that is ethically consequential. Ellul thinks not. But if there are law spheres in creation that remain after the fall, if there are God-given human rights which do not limit God's sovereign freedom, if God's creation mandates to men have not been rescinded, then—real universals in the Greek sense or not—this is ethically significant.

Ellul makes a further move, however, by claiming that man's sin has altogether destroyed his original creation form. But this view, too, is challenged by many thinkers, including those who share Ellul's Reformed tradition. They do not agree with Ellul that man has radically lost his original humanness.[27]

Third, Ellul's voluntaristic nominalism commits him to all the assets and liabilities of a divine-command theory in ethics. There are, of course, various kinds of command theories. Those in which God decrees universal moral rules are the most common. But Ellul is atypical. His situationalism adopts an act theory rather than a rule theory, and he must face the problems that ethicists find therein.[28] Again, some command theories speak of God's will as the source of moral *obligation*, and some speak of his specially revealed will (in Scripture, for example) as the source of moral *knowledge*. Theists would all in some sense grant the first, but not all would grant the second, for here the question is whether God's will can be discerned from general as well as special revelation. Obviously Ellul regards God's revelation as our source of knowledge, but he is still atypical in that God's commands only reveal what action people are told to take in a particular situation; his enjoinders to us are not found in Scripture.

This divine-command theory faces a host of objections. First, is not the faculty psychology outdated that separates will from intellect (as the medievals tried in their debates) and poses a rivalry in which one must rule the other? Is personality not more holistic than that? Does Ellul's divine-command theory, then, impose on God a mistaken human psychology? In man, moral reasoning is itself a free activity constrained by the demands of consistency and honesty, and freedom is rather an inner-directedness than merely a property of will that commands. Nor is it necessary to separate God's will from the nature of his creation as if that were independent of his choice. This is not the only possible world, one which rational necessity imposed on God, but rather one out of many possibilities—the one he chose to create. Its nature, however unchanging, fixed, and ordered it be, arises from God's command as well as from his reason. And at creation he declared it good.

Second, if Ellul does not mean to separate will and intellect, but rather to say we only know what to do by virtue of God's situational commands, then he speaks not as a voluntarist but as an ethical skeptic. But are God's reasons totally hidden from men or does the creation order perhaps bear witness to God's law as well as to his existence? Ellul's exegesis of Genesis, chapter 1, and Romans, chapters 1 and 2, is at stake here, and he condemns natural-law ethics along with natural theology to the same pit as Gnosticism. Yet if we object to rationalistic overconfidence in ethics and philosophical theology, then is skepticism the only other option? If we oppose a rationalistic casuistry that hides the moral ambiguity of situations, the twistedness of moral judgments and agents, and the perversion of our social institutions, then again ethical skepticism is not the only option. Between dogmatism and skepticism lie a host of good reasons for making moral judgments of the universal sort. The good, like other things, may well be known in part and seen through a glass darkly, in relation to the intrinsic nature of the creation order and of the institutions like marriage and work that God ordained for men. In effect, then, neither the desire to preserve God's freedom nor the fallenness of man, nor nominalism, is sufficient to produce ethical skepticism by rejecting every creational basis for morality and law. Even if they were sufficient, Ellul could not hold the position he does; without knowledge of the good he still makes universal his value judgments about technological law and society.

2. Existentialism: the disjunction of fact and value. As chapter 3 herein emphasizes, Ellul is an existentialist in that he allows no essential nature to things and no intrinsic meaning or values. He wants to avoid the illicit optimism of an evolutionary idealism whose immanent teleology guarantees a good outcome to history. This understandably violates both his historical sensitivities and his theological convictions.[29] But Ellul goes too far

and denudes nature of all value. While his theological voluntarism leads him to reject legal positivism, he still accepts a world of bare, meaningless, neutral facts as the subject matter for a value-free empirical sociology. Natural morality, he writes, is not an expression of God's will but an effect of biological, social, historical, and psychological conditions. Natural-law ethic has nothing to do with the right and the good embedded in God's will. It simply rationalizes the morals which history and biology produce.

To his ethical theories and legal systems God for a while may attach some value when he chooses to use them for his purpose, but nothing has value apart from this. The will of God has no objectively perceptible content that remains the same once and for all. The positivist disjunction of fact and value is accepted intact. The world of fact is value-free; value is ascribed to it from outside with utter freedom. Men assign it value; so does God. But it has no value in itself and neither does man. This is Ellul's existentialism.

My objection is twofold: theological and phenomenological. I contend theologically that it distorts the biblical doctrine of creation as objectively ordered and having objective value. The divine value judgment in Genesis, chapter 1, "it is good," repeated after each successive phase of creation, suggests God made a world whose order is value-laden. Man's place in creation hinges on this as Psalm 8 and Hebrews, chapter 2, intimate. His value is related to God's purposes, to be sure, but that is tied to the essential nature of things initiated by the creator, rather than being independent of the way things are.

This, of course, is the point of Hermann Dooyeweerd's doctrine of law spheres, that all creation is subject to the law of God from its earliest beginnings and for all time, so that nature still exhibits law structure. Its value is neither independent of God in some quasi-Platonic sense, nor does God assign it value apart from the structured relationships he built into things. The essential nature of things is morally significant and consequential. Ellul, on the other hand, seems both to admit and deny this. He admits that basic social institutions like the family are divinely ordained, but not their law structure; that rather is man-made. Man is *homo faber*. God calls him to act; he is given intelligence, hands, and eyes—nothing more. He only knows that he must act and judge.

And he judges according to his own criteria, not God's. His rules of justice and his value judgments are entirely his own.[30] Whatever value the world has to God remains unknown to man. Man's world bears witness to no value but that of survival.

My phenomenological objection is related. Ellul sees only two options for relating fact and value: either the nihilism of positivists and existentialists which denies any natural relation at all and opts for *value-neutrality,* or the idealism that declares the goodness of all being and opts for the full *value-actuality* of things. Ellul chooses the former over the latter. But nihilism and idealism are not the only options. I propose that the *value-potentiality* of things is truer both to biblical theism and to the nature of values.

Two things are involved with values: some quality, achievement, or potential experience that ought to be valued (we therefore speak of values as concepts and think about them as ideals to pursue), and the act of valuing or loving it. Values, then, are not things in themselves like autonomous Platonic forms. All value is the value of something for someone. It is identified with some thing or event, and it requires a valuing being. The earth's fruit has value for me; some of it is actualized value—I already enjoy its beauty and its nourishment; some of it is potential value—I have yet to enjoy it. Indeed, some of that potential may well be frustrated so that I never enjoy it. Blight may kill the fruit or a storm may pound the harvest. Potential value allows for evil as well as good, evil that is the non-actualization of the potential value. Of course, if I value the fruit of the earth, I can do things to ensure enjoying at least some of its benefit. I can spray to protect the fruit and I can harvest before the storm. Valuing beings are active agents as well, who do not leave something unattended for better or for ill. They act to actualize the good they seek.

Several features arise in this simple phenomenology:

a. Everything within his life-world has potential for a valuing being. For God, then, all creation has value in terms of what possibilities in it he prizes and purposes to fulfill. Nature cannot have value either in itself or for itself, but only by and for the creator who gave it the possibilities he wants to accomplish. Value-actuality and value-neutrality are not then the only options.

b. Negative as well as positive values are possible, according to what is achieved. The very possibility of evil, in fact, depends on there being value-potential rather than either full value-actuality or full value-neutrality. With the former there would be no room for evil; with the latter it would not matter. Murder, adultery, theft, and every inhumanity can only be considered evil, because life and marriage and property are neither value-neutral nor fully value-actualized. Evil denies to their value-potentialities the actualization sought. Not everything automatically turns out all right in the end.

c. Value-potentiality is related to "action projects" of valuing beings. To have value either for God or for man, something must have potential in relation to its purposes and ends. But humans have action projects in common, areas of value and spheres of action that are universal: physical life and health, work and economics, sex and marriage. Here is an identifiable ordering of creation, and in each action-sphere certain value-potentialities are at stake. We act to preserve or improve life and health, we work for economic ends, we marry to achieve certain values. Common action-spheres identify value areas essential to man and facilitate the formation of moral rules that are universally binding. Value-potentiality leads to a creational ethic.

d. Values are not actualized by some inevitable process of nature or history. Ellul is right in rejecting immanent teleology. But the next step is not to reject teleological explanation altogether. Immanent teleology and a creationally unrelated covenant are not the only possible ways in which values might be achieved. In fact our phenomenology of fact and value suggests a "transcendent teleology," where value-potentials are actualized by agents who in some measure at least transcend the process, inject something new, and secure outcomes which in the normal course of events would not occur. Natural processes provide necessary conditions that make possible those good outcomes, but they are insufficient for their actualization. Such in fact is the precondition of both human action and divine.

Contributing to value-potentiality with a transcendent teleology is a vast amount of recent philosophical work which distinguishes between events and acts, or between process and action. The distinction is basic to Kant's ethics and his entire worldview. He distinguished empirical science with its study of natural processes from normative ethics with its laws of free human action.

Man from one perspective is an event in a process, but he is more fundamentally an agent who transcends that process to act freely out of moral duty. More recently the distinction has been developed by John Macmurray and analytic action theory.[31]

The point is that actions partake of both nature and freedom. Freedom is an active pursuit of values. Nature provides the necessary value-potential. Nature and values are therefore related, and this is made evident by human action. Man actualizes the value-potentiality things have for him, by transcending what might otherwise be the natural course of events and acting to achieve those ends which otherwise might never be actualized at all. Value-neutrality and full value-actuality, nihilism and idealism, are not the only options.

The application to law is plain. If nature and society exhibit value-potentialities that are essential to man and created by God, then law is not lacking divinely affirmed, universal values for its basis. Preserving the value-potential of men, society, and their environment and enhancing the actualization of values essential to a human quality of life are incumbent on all men and societies. Law is one important means of contributing to this task.

3. Empiricism: the disjunction of fact and theory. My objection to voluntaristic nominalism and the resulting separation of fact and value is rooted in the creational emphasis on an objectively value-laden order. But my demurral has epistemological bearings as well: is it possible in some sense at least to uncover that order and its value-potentiality? Whatever one thinks of natural-law ethics in traditional garb, something of a creational ethic at least seems mandatory. The epistemological issue concerns the practicality of such a view. Ellul denies that any such knowledge is possible. Yet talk of a creation order with value-potentiality creates expectations that it is possible. How can we get at the matter?

Ellul has high regard for our knowledge of fact, low regard for theory, and no regard at all for any logical relation between them. I think him mistaken. Factual knowledge is not so certain as he implies, nor theory so precarious; nor are the two unrelated. Theory, he says, is just ideology—an expression of the social and biological determinants with which the individual lives. Hence the great systems of moral thought are dated. "Only by extracting certain happy expressions, a few rare pearls out of the whole superseded mixture, can we still follow Socrates or Confucius."[32] Yet the facts of sociology, biology, and legal history are taken to be indubitable and clear.

Ellul's epistemology is consistent with his existential and positivist leanings. Since nature is a conglomeration of brute facts without any unchanging created orders, only bare factual knowledge is possible. But just as I have complained about his view of nature, so, too, I object to the resultant epistemology. Pure empiricism has come on hard times in philosophy in the last decades. Sense-datum theories have had to recognize the variability that different "observation conditions" produce, and empirical science has been forced to acknowledge that observation is theory-laden. In the history of science, Thomas Kuhn has focused attention on the role of paradigms and paradigm shifts in theory formation, while Michael Polanyi has shown that tacit personal factors profoundly influence scientific knowledge. Purely factual knowledge now seems an illusion.[33]

If this is the case, we should expect even Ellul's "facts" to be theory-laden, and it is not hard to identify elements of Marxism as well as neo-Kantianism in his thinking. The aim of law and government, he says, is public utility. This, apparently, is an observation drawn from the history and sociology of law. Yet to derive the aim of something from a purportedly empirical study of it presupposes all sorts of theories: in epistemology, empiricism; in metaphysics, nominalism, for example. Any principle based on bare utility, moreover, leaves open the question "useful for what?" Ellul seems to choose the survival of man and society. Yet this too is guided by theories that sound quite Hobbesian. Theories are simply unavoidable in empirical discussion. His appeal to theology doesn't avoid it either, for theology, too, has its theoretical assumptions, the philosophical included.

Perhaps the most significant supposition that influences his account is his Marxist theory about theories. We have noted his insistence that ethical and legal theories simply rationalize the status quo. A morality is determined by actual morals, and a philosophy of natural law by the stage of natural law in the history of jurisprudence. Knowledge, he says, is active involvement based on a decision, not a purely theoretical thing at all. Praxis is all there is, and theory is its prophet.[34]

Ellul takes all this for granted despite its highly controverted nature. I agree about the primacy of the practical, such that thought is itself human action related to action projects. But this does not mean that it is wholly determined like an echo by all the attendant circumstances surrounding the action. Reflective inquiry is one of the ways man transcends the process in which he finds himself, examines the process, and decides how to act in ways that make a difference. The transcendent teleology we referred to earlier entails this view.

The obvious rejoinder will be that man has no such freedom. And here may be the nub of the issue: the degree to which human action and reflection are controlled by rather than influence attendant circumstances. Is man still man or not? In his theory about theories Ellul implies that man is not. Of course, my response could simply be that if all thought is determined, so also is his—which means the end of reasonable discourse.

If fact and theory cannot be divorced, and if theory is not wholly shaped by circumstances but is in measure created by free reflective thought, what does this imply about the fact-value relationship? The options again are more varied than he seems to suppose. It is not a choice between apodictic certainty of a Cartesian sort, on the one hand, or sheer skepticism on the other. Ellul is led to the latter (I cannot say he "opts" for this theory, in view of his theory about theories) in regard to ethics and law. Instead of offering a theory of knowledge he calls us to a relation with God that reveals what we should do. About theories he is a skeptic (apart from his theory about theories). But I agree that the Cartesian alternative is impossible too. In addition, I find it neither necessary to the formation and evaluation of theories nor especially desirable.[35] Instead, what seems to occur all the time, even in Ellul's work, is an ongoing examination of the coherence of theoretical assumptions and conclusions with an eye to provisional and contextual justification.

In order to address this third option to the kind of theological concern Ellul so well expresses, let us revert to creation orders and law spheres. Both nature and man, I suggest, bear witness to their initiator by the intelligible order and value-possibilities they have been given. This is not a natural theology that constructs proofs of a foundationalist sort, but a creational theology that calls us to interpret the witness of nature and man, to examine those orders of things that are essential and universal to the nature of man, to identify the value-potentials inherent therein. This is not a natural-law ethic that derives its conclusions deductively, but a creational ethic whose logic is more informal. Theories are adduced as possible interpretations of things, refined to match actualities better, evaluated by their coherence with the whole of what we believe and by their explanatory power and good fit. There is room to construct a theory of human rights, to ground those rights in what else one believes about God and creation of man, and to see a right as a claim to the sanctity of certain God-given value-potentials in man.

A Final Observation

Ellul's epistemology, akin to positivism, is itself a kind of scientism. He resists the technological mentality of scientism by adopting the epistemology of scientism. And he accepts the philosophical assumptions of the technologism he rejects (nominalism, the separation of fact and value, and scientific empiricism). His critique is not radical enough. His avoidance of these philosophical issues has weakened his cause. Perhaps natural-law theories in the traditional sense are too optimistic to stand much of a chance today in the face of history, theology, and epistemology. But for the Christian theist a creational ethic offers a surer basis than existentialism and empiricism.

Notes

1. *Theological Foundation of Law*, pp. 17–20; French ed. 1946.
2. *Ibid.*, pp. 31–36.
3. "Between Chaos and Paralysis," *The Christian Century*, (5 June 1968), 747–49.
4. *Theological Foundation of Law*, p. 10.
5. *Ibid.*, pp. 26–30; cf. pp. 8–9, 36.
6. Georg W. F. Hegel, *Natural Law*, trans. T. M. Knox (Philadelphia: University of Pennsylvania Press, 1975), p. 132.
7. *Theological Foundation of Law*, pp. 70–74.
8. *To Will and To Do*, p. 45; French ed. 1964.
9. *Ibid.*, pp. 134–36, 162–63.
10. *Theological Foundation of Law*, pp.20–26.

11. *Ibid.*, pp. 60–63, 70ff.
12. *To Will and To Do*, chap. 4.
13. *Ibid.*, p. 74.
14. *Ibid.*, chap. 3.
15. Cf. *ibid.*, chaps. 5, 12.
16. *Ibid.*, pp. 83–85.
17. *Ethics of Freedom*, p. 385; French ed. 1970.
18. *Theological Foundation of Law*, chap. 1.
19. *To Will and To Do*, pp. 7–14, chap. 12.
20. *Theological Foundation of Law*, chap. 3.
21. *Ibid.*, p. 80.
22. Cf. Arthur Holmes, *Faith Seeks Understanding* (Grand Rapids, Mich.: Eerdmans, 1971), esp. chaps. 3–6.
23. M. B. Foster, "The Christian Doctrine of Creation and the Rise of Modern Science," *Mind*, 43 (1934), 446; 44 (1935), 439; 45 (1936), 1. See also G. C. Berkhouwer, *General Revelation* (Grand Rapids, Mich.: Eerdmans, 1956), p. 196 *passim*. Ellul also recognizes this assumption in *To Will and To Do*, p. 268, n. 1.
24. Paul Sigmund, *Natural Law in Political Thought* (Englewood Cliffs, N.J.: Winthrop Publishers, 1971), p. viii.
25. Jacques Maritain, *The Rights of Man and Natural Law* (New York: Scribner's, 1943), p. 65ff.
26. Dietrich Bonhoeffer, *Ethics* (New York: Macmillan, 1955), pt. I, chaps. 4–5, and pt. II, chap 3. See also Arthur Holmes's previous essays on natural law: "The Concept of Natural Law," *Christian Scholar's Review*, vol. 2, no. 3 (1972), 195–208; "Human Variables and Natural Law," in *God and the Good*, ed. C. J. Orlebeke and L. B. Smedes (Grand Rapids, Mich.: Eerdmans, 1975), pp. 63–79. This latter essay discusses Ellul's theological objections to natural law without examining his positive proposal.
27. Cf. G. C. Berkouwer, *Man: The Image of God* (Grand Rapids, Mich.: Eerdmans, 1962), where he reviews Reformed views of man and the effects of the fall.
28. See, e.g., W. Frankena, *Ethics*, 2nd ed. (New York: Prentice-Hall, 1973). He discusses the command theory on pp. 28–30 and act theories on pp. 23–25 and 35–37.
29. Reinhold Niebuhr made this point effectively in *The Nature and Destiny of Man* (New York: Scribner's [1943], 1964).
30. *Theological Foundation of Law*, p. 90ff.
31. See John Macmurray, *The Self as Agent* (Salem, N.H.: Faber and Faber, 1957), and Stuart Hampshire, *Thought and Action* (New York: Viking, 1959).

32. *To Will and To Do*, p. 64.
33. See Thomas S. Kuhn, *The Structure of Scientific Revolutions* (Chicago: University of Chicago Press, 1962); Michael Polanyi, *Personal Knowledge* (New York: Harper, 1964) and *The Tacit Dimension* (New York: Doubleday, 1966); also Norwood Hanson, *Patterns of Discovery* (New York: Cambridge University Press, 1958), and Peter Winch, *The Idea of a Social Science* (Boston: Routledge and Kegan Paul, 1958). On a more popular level, see Nicholas Wolterstorff, *Reason within the Bounds of Religion* (Grand Rapids, Mich.: Eerdmans, 1976), and Holmes, *Faith Seeks Understanding* chaps. 1–3.
34. *To Will and To Do*, p. 7; David Menninger details this connection between act and knowledge in chap. 1 herein.
35. On this see Arthur F. Holmes, *Christian Philosophy in the Twentieth Century* (Nutley, N.J.: Craig Press, 1969).

Chapter 11

Violence

Kenneth J. Konyndyk

Violence has always been a problem for reflective men. On the one hand, violence is morally repugnant; no one doubts that it would be eminently desirable to have a world without violence. Yet some situations seem to require the use of violence in order to do justice, to protect the innocent. This dilemma is not merely a fine reflective puzzle; it is a practical problem which touches everyone's life. May I use violent force to repel an attack on myself or my family? May I be a soldier or a policeman and perhaps even kill "in the line of duty"? Should I permit force to be used to protect myself and my neighbors? Can a state justifiably wage war? May I and my neighbors revolt against an oppressive and tyrannical government? Such questions most of us must face in some form. Must we opt for one horn of the dilemma or the other? Or are there some distinctions and guidelines which will enable us to steer between the horns and preserve our moral integrity at the same time?

The mainstream western Christian traditions (Reformed, Lutheran, and Roman Catholic) have maintained that there is a just and proper use of violence. But the position of nonviolence has always had its defenders within the Christian tradition as well. Jacques Ellul, though a member of the National Reformed Church of France, rejects that Reformed tradition at this point and affirms a nonviolent view. While defending nonviolence is nothing new, Ellul thinks there is something distinctive about his support of nonviolence. He seeks to escape the failings of the typical advocacy of nonviolence, and simultaneously avoid the errors in traditional Christian defenses of violence.

In this essay, I will examine Ellul's position and his supporting arguments as these are presented in his book *Violence*. Although he has insightful things to say about violence—particularly when he urges us to be realistic about it—I think he fails to make his case successfully. I will try to show that his perspective is inadequately developed and that the arguments he advances for his position are not persuasive. Although many aspects of Ellul's thinking fall within mainstream Christianity, his position on violence and the underlying reasons stand outside that tradition.

THE TRADITIONAL POSITIONS

Ellul wants to distinguish his viewpoint from the traditional positions which he rejects. Although he stands within the pacifist tradition in an important sense, he charges conventional pacifism with certain errors which he wants to avoid. Thus he does not consider himself an ordinary pacifist.

The characteristic Christian views as Ellul distinguishes them are: the "compromisers," who condone legitimate uses of violence by the proper authorities; nonviolent Christians, who think that Christians should not use or sanction violence; and "Christians for violence," who hold that violence by an individual may sometimes be legitimate without the authorization of higher officials.

Ellul's classification of the usual positions may seem to parallel Roland Bainton's, but I think there is a noteworthy difference. Bainton classifies the three attitudes as just-war theorists, pacifists, and crusaders. His just-war theorists are the same as Ellul's "compromisers" and Bainton's pacifists parallel nonviolent Christians, but there seems to be a genuine divergence of opinion about the third class. Bainton describes a crusade as "a holy war fought under the auspices of the Church or of some inspired religious leader, not on behalf of justice conceived in terms of life and property, but on behalf of an ideal, the Christian faith."[1] Later he adds that the difference between this crusade view and the just-war view is essentially a matter of degree: "The crusade differed from the just-war primarily in its intensely religious quality."[2] He goes on to find a crusader mentality in such figures as Thomas Muenzer and Oliver Cromwell. Although Ellul includes these figures in his third class ("Christians for violence"), he characterizes their views differently: they hold that "aside from any question of authority, violence *on the part of* the individual may be legitimate."[3] He distinguishes this outlook from the just-war theory because it fails to require the authorization of some higher earthly power for the violent acts of individuals. In developing examples of this view—some of which also serve Bainton as illustrations of his "crusaders"—Ellul tries to show that their concern is primarily with social and political matters, and not with the spiritual issues which are prominent in their "justifications" for their actions.

Differing historical interpretation, however, may not be the only reason for Ellul's variance with Bainton. One of the chief reasons for Ellul's interest in this issue of violence seems to be his desire to oppose the so-called "theologians of revolution."[4] These advocates of revolutionary violence in support of the poor and oppressed for Christ's sake do not fit very well into the crusader classification as described by Bainton. Ellul's rubric comprehends this view and shows its affinity to a group of previous similar perspectives. On the whole, I think Ellul's way of characterizing the crusader/Christians-for-violence tradition shows superior insight over Bainton's, though I am less than fully sympathetic with his almost casual dismissal of some persons' stated reasons for their actions.

Ellul concludes that this third view has the least warrant in Scripture of the three traditional options. Its advocates usually have argued that some prominent practice was contrary to Christianity—for example, oppression of the poor or tyranny—and then, that violence was necessary and proper for correcting the situation. Ellul has two main objections against individuals taking the law into their own hands in such situations. First, he accuses such persons of caring much more about social and political matters than about genuine Christianity. Second, he thinks these persons improperly regard themselves as God's agents for ushering in his kingdom all at once. They are, like Jacob and Rebeccah, taking steps to secure the promised birthright, instead of waiting for God to work in his own way.

Ellul considers just-war theory the position of compromise. According to this belief, there is a distinction between force and violence, or, we may say, between justified violence and unjustified violence, authorized and unauthorized violence. The state is a distinct sort of entity from individual man, and this different nature authorizes it to bear the sword. The theory specifies various criteria for properly using the sword—the cause being pursued must be just, for example, and violence must be used only as a last resort. Although this view is usually associated with waging war, Ellul observes that it is actually broader. Not only may the state rightly use violence to protect itself and its citizens from external enemies, it also may properly use violence to repel internal threats. The state may rightly enforce its laws by coercive force if necessary, and it may rightly quell organized attempts by revolutionaries to overthrow its authority.

Ellul has essentially two reasons for regarding this position, long dominant in western Christianity, as a compromise of the Christian viewpoint. First, it compromises by conceding that violent force is permissible. It implies that violence can be used justly, whereas Ellul believes that to be impossible. Second, in conceding this right to the state, this position implies that the state is a legitimate institution.[5] Although Ellul admits that the state is ordained of God, we must regard it as Babylon, the *civitas mundi*.

The pacifist, the Christian proponent of nonviolence, holds the second major position within the Christian tradition. Ellul recognizes that there has always been a certain amount of diversity among those within this position. Some have based their case on the Sixth Commandment ("Thou shalt not kill"), taking it to be an absolute prohibition of any violence against anyone. Others claim love as the Christian objective and any use of violence as incompatible with this. In *Violence* Ellul is concerned primarily with this latter attitude. He sees an advocacy of nonviolence not as an end in itself, but as a means—a superior means —not only of expressing one's Christian love but also of changing the world, achieving political and social objectives. He argues that this is a mistaken reason for advocating nonviolence. For one thing, nonviolence does not always work. Gandhi in India is often cited as an example that nonviolence can be effective. Ellul responds that Gandhi's tactics worked by taking advantage of the moral sensibilities and traditions of the British, and he suggests that Gandhi would not have lasted long in the Russia of 1925 or the Germany of 1933. Ellul also objects to viewing nonviolence primarily as a means for political struggles because nonviolence becomes politicized so easily. Once a man chooses sides, he tends to ignore the violence used by others in his camp while he vigorously protests the violence of the other side.

In addition to such individual objections to each of the traditional positions, Ellul thinks they have some important errors in common. All three see their position as the right way of establishing justice and proper social order here on earth; they are all trying to "bring in the kingdom." Their common error, according to Ellul, is thinking that "there must be a Christian 'solution,' a valid way of organizing society and the world."[6] Thus they are led either to compromise between Christ's demands and the world's necessities, or to demand that the world change so as to become satisfactory to the Christian. Both types of "solutions" fail to accept the fact that the world is radically evil, and therefore no solution is possible.

ELLUL'S POSITION

Ellul begins the presentation of his own position in the last two chapters of *Violence* with the advice that Christians must be "completely realistic" about violence. He characterizes his own perspective as Christian realism, by which he means seeing things as they are and knowing what one is doing. In contemplating using violence or dealing with it, one must be under no illusions about what will happen and must understand the phenomenon thoroughly. At the same time, Ellul calls his view Christian radicalism. He means by this that he wishes in no way to compromise the demands of the Christian faith and calling.

Using violence is always sinful, according to Ellul. He believes that this is the position implied by his realism and his radicalism. He does not affirm nonviolence merely because he considers nonviolence the most effective means of pursuing Christianity's goals; that position is insufficiently radical and is unrealistic. But he does not regard violence as unnecessary either; to do so is also unrealistic.

One of Ellul's main reasons for looking at violence realistically is that Scripture does not spell out explicitly what view we should take: "If we want to find out what the Christian attitude toward violence should be," he writes, "we cannot proceed by deducing the consequences of Christian principles or by enumerating Biblical texts."[7] Thus if we want to formulate a clear and Christian position on violence, we must understand exactly its nature and role. We must realize that violence is universal and necessary. We must harbor no illusions about being able to avoid the kinds of problems which have plagued past users of violence.

The first question, then, would seem to be: What is violence? But, strangely, Ellul does not address it. He appears to assume that we all know and agree on a definition of violence. Of course, he regards physical coercive force as violence; perhaps this is the core. But in his discussion he adds a broad list of examples: "psychological manipulation, doctrinal terrorism, economic imperialism, the venomous warfare of free competition, as well as torture, guerrilla movements, police action."[8] Are all of these properly regarded as forms of violence? There is the hint of an answer in *The Political Illusion*, which comments on the transition from physical forms of violence to psychological ones: "This force, which for a long time was purely physical, has taken on a new dimension in our day—it has become psychological force or violence. When the state utilizes propaganda—'violates' the masses and insidiously determines the citizen's behavior—it exercises repressive coercion, but on a larger scale."[9] This passage implies that its coercive character makes a violent act violent; this is the aspect that violates a person. We might say, then, that for Ellul violent behavior is coercing someone in a way that violates his personhood. The coercion involved need not be physical.

I think two cautions are in order with respect to this characterization. The first concerns the pejorative nature of the definition. If Ellul wishes to define violence in a way which guarantees that violence is always wrong, he is free to do so. But this in itself will not settle the question or resolve our quandaries about violence, but merely relocate the problem. Now the issue will no longer be whether violence is wrong, but whether the act in question fits Ellul's definition of violence. A second caution concerns the adequacy of his characterization itself: I am doubtful that it will suffice. It seems clear that some acts of violence—which we sometimes describe as cases of wanton violence—are not coercive and have no coercive intentions associated with them. Beating someone for the fun of it or committing suicide are examples. Likewise, it seems that certain coercive acts which violate someone's personhood are not violent. Intensively questioning someone for a long period and depriving him of normal amenities in order to extract information from him is an illustration. Perhaps Ellul can explain away these cases, but in doing so he will have to make his representation clearer and precise enough to be more readily usable. My caution here is merely that the present characterization needs such clarification.

Even if Ellul's depiction is less than adequate and clear, this need not prevent us from understanding and evaluating what he says about violence. For we all can think of many obvious examples of violence, and we can partly evaluate what he says by how well his definition fits those examples. Let us turn, then, to his description of how violence works.

Ellul says that violence is universal, occurring everywhere and at all times. Every state establishes and maintains itself through violence. The free enterprise system is a form of violence. Indeed, modern social life is riddled with violence; "violence is the general rule for the existence of society."[10] Ellul argues that if we look at violence honestly and objectively, we will see that it is necessary. Violence is only a part of the order of necessity; some other examples which he gives are eating, toiling, struggling with nature, providing for the future, and dying. Man is compelled to do these things: they are inevitabilities.

Ellul notes that such activities have an order and inner logic of their own, one which the person who engages in them will be unable to escape. To illustrate this in the case of violence, Ellul offers five laws of violence:[11]

a. Violence is habit-forming. Once a person starts using it, he cannot get away from it. (The law of continuity.)

b. Violence always provokes more violence. The violence of the attacker provokes the violence of the victim. Those who are violent will suffer violence. (The law of reciprocity.)

c. All kinds of violence are alike. No legitimate distinctions can be made between justified and unjustified violence. Condoning violence in one case commits one to condoning violence in all cases. (The law of sameness.)

d. Violence begets nothing but violence. Good results will not come of evil means, and the end cannot justify the means.

e. Users of violence always try to justify it and themselves. But hatred always goes with violence, and thus violence always always provokes hypocrisy.

These "laws" constitute an important set of warnings to any man considering the use of violence to attain his ends. They call to our attention a certain dynamic which is often at work when violence is used. But in what sense are they *laws?* Do they describe a necessary order or inner logic of violence? Ellul's analogy with gravity suggests that he thinks obeying these laws is like "obeying" laws of nature.[12] But the latter are not violated even when they appear to be, and obedience to them is morally indifferent. I find the suggestion that these laws are like laws of nature badly mistaken, and I will return to this point later when I consider Ellul's main argument against violence. And the third "law" simply begs one of the central questions at issue between Ellul on the one hand and John Calvin, Thomas Aquinas, and hosts of other theologians and philosophers on the other.

Ellul insists that the Christian has been called from the order of necessity to the order of freedom and his present role is to "shatter" necessities. The order of freedom is the order of Christ, while the order of necessity is that of separation from God. According to Ellul, prelapsarian Adam was perfectly free; he "knew nothing of necessity, obligation, inevitability."[13] Necessity comes with the fall and only then becomes part of the order of nature. An absolute opposition exists for Ellul between freedom and necessity, and in the Christian life necessity must give way to freedom: "But when God reveals himself, necessity ceases to be destiny or even inevitability. In the Old Testament, man shatters the necessity of eating by fasting, the necessity of toil by keeping the Sabbath, and when he fasts or keeps the Sabbath he recovers his real freedom."[14] In the New Testament, Christ shatters even the necessity of death.

Since Ellul sees the role of the Christian as shattering necessities, he warns against acquiescing in them. If Christians do, they simply step outside the realm of obedience to God. Some violence may be inevitable and necessary (indeed, it is important to recognize this), but by virtue of the very fact that it is necessary, it stands outside the Christian's calling and is forbidden to him. Every time he engages in or supports violence, he does wrong; he disobeys God.

Thus Ellul holds that the Christian's rejection of violence must be radical. Violence must be rejected "root and branch" as incompatible with the Christian life. The Christian must be intransigent on this point. If he finds violence necessary and uses it himself, he must proclaim that he is sinning. No exceptions can be made, either for himself or anyone else. He must condemn every kind of violence, not just physical violence. Clearly, too, he will never offer any justifications for violence and he will attack those which are offered. Anything short of absolutely affirming "Thou shalt not kill"—and all that Ellul thinks it implies—is accommodation and essentially a denial of Christianity.

This position against violence is stated uncompromisingly and in absolute terms. But it would be surprising, given the long history of differences of opinion among capable scholars, if the question were so easily answered even in theory. Is Ellul's case as conclusive as his attitude suggests? I shall argue that it is not.

Ellul's Arguments for His Position

Ellul gives two arguments for his position of nonviolence, one quite traditional and one original with him (as far as I know). I wish to examine these arguments carefully.

The argument which is original with Ellul can be stated simply and is implicit in some of the preceeding exposition:

a. Violence is of the order of necessity.
b. The Christian's role is to shatter necessity and to reject all necessities (to reject anything of the order of necessity).
c. Therefore, the Christian must reject violence.

This argument in one form or another is repeated several times in the opening section of chapter 4 of *Violence*. A Christian is supposed to reject violence just because violence is necessary.[15] Ellul denies that the necessity of violence in any way implies its moral legitimacy.

Let us now concede that in the above argument the conclusion follows from the premises. This is not sufficient to render the argument acceptable; it is also necessary that the premises be true. Ellul's argument, sadly enough, does not satisfy this latter requirement.

In order to judge whether or not the premises of this argument are true, we must first understand them. What does Ellul mean in claiming that violence is of the order of necessity? We must find out what kind of necessity Ellul has in mind, and we must see what the *order* of necessity is.

Ellul defines necessity as "what man does because he cannot do otherwise."[16] In the same passage he offers as synonyms "obligation" (by which he appears to mean lacking a choice and being forced to do something) and "inevitability" (which for Ellul carries the implication of being law-governed and predictable). The opposite of necessity is freedom, which he takes to imply alternatives, possibilities, and spontaneity. However, necessity is not fate or determinism. These latter views Ellul explicitly rejects.[17]

When Ellul speaks in his definition of man, he means man in a collective rather than individual sense.[18] He does not mean that each individual person must or will participate in these activities he calls necessities, but that at least some men and probably most men must engage in them. They are necessities for the species even if they are not necessities for each individual. Also, when Ellul speaks of man, he means man in his fallen condition, not man as originally created. Necessity—apparent in the use of money, preparing for the future, eating, and dying—appears after and as a consequence of man's fall.

What sort of necessity is this, then? Obviously it is not *a priori* or logical necessity. But it does not seem to be a natural or causal necessity either. Not all the examples he cites are causally necessary for the survival of the individual, nor are they all necessary for the survival of the race. Ellul's example of the use of money plainly does not count as necessary in any of these senses, even though it is an activity that arises naturally in societies and whose development does follow predictable patterns. Perhaps we can best describe this sense of necessity in terms of a law-like pattern of development and a kind of statistical regularity (which seems necessary from the standpoint of practice). Ellul himself says,

"When we consider the structure of a society and the constituent elements of our world . . . we note that everything happens as though in obedience to imperious necessities which in practice are unavoidable, since the same developments take place, the same trends come finally to expression, and there are regularities which at the very least we have described as tendencies."[19] It is by no means obvious to me that a single, clear sense of necessity will fit all of Ellul's examples and descriptions.

Violence, according to the first premise of Ellul's argument, is of the order of necessity. An activity can only be of the order of necessity if it is inevitable, obligatory, and inescapable in practice for the human race. This does not mean, as Ellul has noted, that any particular instance of someone's engaging in that kind of activity is necessary in the sense that it could not have been avoided. Rather it means that we are under an unavoidable compulsion to engage in that kind of activity, even though any particular instance of our actual involvement may be avoidable.

But Ellul has more than this in mind when speaking of an *order* of necessity. He also implies that these necessary actions form a system which behaves in a law-like way. He speaks, as we saw earlier, of *laws* of violence. Although it is still not clear to me that these are laws in any usual sense, Ellul's point is plain enough: The use of violence usually follows predictable patterns and thus can be said to constitute an order. These compulsions, for example to eat or to use violence, will produce predictable consequences whenever we succumb to them.

Let us now consider the second premise of Ellul's argument: The Christian's role is to shatter necessity and to reject all necessities. Why does Ellul think this is true? Because he believes the order of necessity is the order of separation from God. As observed earlier, necessity results from the fall of man. God did not create us subject to compulsions; he created us free. When we follow our compulsions, we are not acting freely, but we have subjected ourselves to necessity. To become a Christian in Ellul's terms is to become free and to demonstrate what a life of freedom is like. These necessities are not intrinsically evil or immoral; we do not refuse to participate in them on that account. Christians must avoid them because they are outside the Christian life.[20]

The idea that necessity results from the fall seems questionable at the outset. Are eating or breathing or sexual intercourse results of Adam's fall? Or is our "inescapable compulsion" to eat or breathe or use money or prepare for the future a result of the first sin? I find this very hard to believe. But perhaps Ellul does not mean that the existence of these activities results from sin, but that the way we engage in them and experience them as necessary are the consequences of sin.

What then does it mean to claim that the Christian's role is to shatter these necessities? What does rejecting them entail? Ellul writes:

> In the Old Testament, man shatters the necessity of eating by fasting, the necessity of toil by keeping the Sabbath. . . . The institution of the order of Levites likewise shatters the normal institutional order of ownership, duty, provision for the future, etc. And this freedom is fully accomplished by and through Jesus Christ. For Christ, even death ceases to be a necessity: "I give my life for my sheep, it is not taken from me, I give it." And the constant stress on the importance of giving signifies a breaking away from the necessity of money.[21]

Notice that in no case is the necessity supposed to be shattered by having all God's people forgo it entirely; in fact this would be quite impossible. In no cases are these necessities declared immoral, forbidden, wrong, or outside the will of God; this would be preposterous. In none of the examples does Ellul say that Christians should refuse to justify eating, using money, dying, and the rest, and that if we engage in them we should repent; such a claim would be ridiculous. Rather, in each case the necessity is shattered or rejected by a refusal of all or a segment within the Christian community to follow the necessity on a given occasion. But I do not find any biblical support for the suggestion that one behaves as a Christian only when fasting and not when eating, or that one follows the Lord only when resting and never when toiling. Indeed, this suggestion lacks any serious claim on our attention. Thus, I take the shattering of necessity to consist in some kind of demonstration by the Christian community that it is not bound by these compulsions and a testimony that things will not always be this way. Only in this sense do I find it plausible to say that at least part of the Christian's role is rejecting necessities.

But what of Ellul's conclusion? Does it follow that the Christian must always forgo violence, or that if he ever acts violently, he acts outside his Christian calling? Does it follow that he must refuse to justify any violence and repent when he falls into it himself? We have construed the premises of his argument so as to make them appear plausible, but his conclusion *as he appears to understand it* does not follow. What we should conclude is that perhaps we might shatter the necessity of violence by forgoing it at certain times—for example, during Sundays, holy days, and Lent, or by having a certain segment of the Christian community, such as the clergy, forgo it. If we understand the premises—particularly the second—so as to yield the conclusion he draws, the second premise is false. So understood, the second premise would not be true of the other examples Ellul gives of necessities. It would yield the conclusion that Christians must *never* eat, use money, and toil, and that they should repent whenever they find themselves falling into such necessities.

Ellul's second and more traditional argument against the use of violence is based on the Sixth Commandment: " 'Thou shalt not kill' (as Jesus explained it) is to be considered not a law but a guiding principle in accomplishing the supreme task of *man.* . . . 'Thou shalt not kill' expresses the true being of man. All the demands implied in these words—faith in Jesus Christ, love of enemy, the overcoming of evil by love—must be affirmed, taught and lived with the most absolute intransigence."[22] Ellul makes it clear that he takes these words to forbid participation in violence of any kind and that he regards this position as radical, presumably getting down to the commandment's root.[23] Unfortunately we cannot describe Ellul's presentation here as an argument, since argumentation is lacking at precisely the crucial point.

Throughout the history of the church, Christian pacifists have sought to argue for their position on the basis of the Sixth Commandment. The trick has always been to show how one gets from the commandment which every Christian accepts to the conclusion that killing—in the sense of *any* taking of human life for any reason or under any circumstances—is forbidden by this commandment. The crucial argumentation is lacking here with Ellul also. And it hardly needs to be pointed out that such exegesis of the commandment is dubious at best and has not been accepted by mainstream churches. That in itself does not show the inference to be faulty; it does indicate to me, however, that the burden of proof is on those who would have us draw this inference. Ellul has nothing to offer beyond the assertion that the Sixth Commandment implies radical nonviolence.

Actually Ellul has asserted something stronger than the claim that absolutely all *killing* is forbidden by the Sixth Commandment; in fact, he claims that this commandment forbids all *violence*. This is an extraordinarily strong declaration, especially when we recall that Ellul refuses to distinguish between violence and force, preferring to regard both as violence.[24] Even if the commandment clearly forbade absolutely all takings of life, a large step would still remain before the conclusion that all uses of violence and force are forbidden by it.

Ellul has singled out the Sixth Commandment as expressing "the true being of man." But this is hardly an obvious truth. Certainly failing to kill does not distinguish man from *all* other animals. In fact, keeping the Sabbath seems to be a better distinguishing mark of this sort. And even if it did express the true being of man, would it then follow that violence is totally forbidden to Christians? Once again Ellul's reasoning is too thin: we have no acceptable argument for nonviolence here either. Indeed this was a strange place for Ellul to look, given his earlier remark that we cannot deduce the Christian view of violence from a few Christian principles or biblical texts. That is the reason Ellul gives for employing his first argument about violence being of the order of necessity. And if that reason is valid, then basing his second argument on the Sixth Commandment is most inappropriate. Both of Ellul's arguments for violence fail to persuade.

ELLUL AND THE CHRISTIAN LIFE

One of the central themes of the Christian faith is Christ's lordship. There is no area of life exempt from his headship, no domain which is not to be brought under his rule. This implies, I think, that no aspect of life—government, education, economics, business, or whatever—is irredeemably evil. While evil permeates them all, no Christian ought to withdraw from any if he wants to lead a life of discipleship. There are necessary and proper functions which institutions in each area should carry on. All the mainstream branches of Christianity have held that the state is necessary and legitimate, ordained by God for good, and assigned certain functions which it appropriately exercises. Furthermore, it is proper and even desirable for Christians to serve in this institution.

Ellul's view of the state and politics implies that Christians who are genuinely living as Christians have no business there. Christian statesmen and a Christian state are impossible, for the state is founded by violence and maintains itself by violence. Thus involvement in politics means becoming caught up in violence. Ellul obviously is not suggesting that there are no Christians involved in politics or that no Christians have ever been statesmen. But he suggests that the role and obligations of a politician are incompatible with those of a Christian. To put his view somewhat paradoxically, a truly Christian statesman could not be a good statesman.

On the basis of remarks he makes about other areas, I think Ellul would draw similar conclusions about involvement in economics, since the use of money necessarily leads to evils and abuses. Even normal life in society seems to be incompatible with Christian living, since violence is necessarily the form that societal relations usually take, acording to Ellul.

Ellul accuses traditional Christians of mistakenly thinking that some political or economic or societal problems have Christian solutions, and are so important that Christians must take action to solve them, using violence if necessary. He feels that this "mistake" betrays a lack of faith: although there are no genuine solutions to these problems which Christians can produce, this does not mean that God cannot solve them. But these areas, then, are irredeemable in an important sense: Christian action will not transform them. Sinfulness necessarily results from participation in politics, in buying and selling, and, apparently, even in normal societal relationships. There is, therefore, no possibility of transforming these areas by direct involvement in them.

But there are, Ellul says, Christian responses to problems such as poverty and oppression even if there are no Christian solutions. Since the Christian has been called from necessity to freedom, he must not compromise with necessity or he will find himself subject to it. He must contend with the spirits and powers of darkness; he must fight spiritual battles. He is a sentinel as Ezekiel was; he is like Moses holding up his hands in blessing during the battle with the Amalekites. The role of the Christian in society is that of advocate and mediator for the poor and oppressed. He must be careful to see that he always sides with the genuinely poor and oppressed. Ellul even goes so far as to suggest that the Christian must change sides as soon as the poor and oppressed he has been supporting win out. The upshot, then, of Ellul's view is that Christians are barred from direct action in the usual areas of life. They do not pursue their ends in the same ways as unbelievers. Indeed, it may appear to unbelievers that Christians are not doing anything at all, but that is because unbelievers cannot perceive the forces actually at work.

So far as the political, social, or economic struggles are concerned, the Christian in Ellul's view is reduced to the role of partisan spectator; or perhaps on some occasions he may be a cheerleader. He cheers for the success of this or that oppressed group, and then once they gain the upper hand, he cheers for their opponents. But he may not get into the game. He must fight like Moses—holding up his hands in blessing. He may not fight like Joshua did, wielding a sword. He is permitted to contend with the spirits, but not their incarnations.

But we may ask why Moses is the only character in this biblical story whom we should emulate. Did the Lord approve only of Moses' actions and not those of Joshua and the rest of the people? It seems to me that if it was wrong for Joshua to kill the Amalekites, it was also wrong for Moses to hold up his hands in blessing on that killing. But if this is so, then Ellul is wrong in claiming that the Christian must follows Moses' example and that if he imitates Joshua, he is following necessity and must repent.

How has Ellul fallen into this error? I have suggested it is due mainly to the strange view he has taken of *necessity* and his identification of necessity with separation from God. This view of necessity derives much more from Marx than it does from Scripture. This does not deprecate Marx; rather, I assert that the view does not make good sense in itself and it does not treat Scripture adequately.

Yet the danger Ellul reacts against is a very real one, a trap Christians have fallen into again and again: being so confident that their project is God's will and part of his kingdom that they will sanction immoral means or go to immoral lengths to promote it. In arguing that Ellul's remedy is unsatisfactory, I have not intended to suggest the danger is not real. Likewise, in showing that Ellul's support for nonviolence is unconvincing, I do not imply that I have refuted all arguments for nonviolence. Is violence *always* an immoral means? That question is still open.

While the position Ellul presents in *Violence* is untraditional, it retains a Christian spirit. Ellul rejects fatalism and determinism; he urges Christians to resist evil and to resist it actively. He waits for the transformation of our sinful culture. But he rejects the traditional direct means for achieving this goal. And in such rejection, he seems to me to have reduced specifically Christian action in the world to a form of paralysis.

NOTES

1. Roland Bainton, *Christian Attitudes toward War and Peace* (Nashville, Tenn.: Abingdon, 1960), p. 14.
2. *Ibid.*, p. 44.
3. *Violence*, p. 17 (italics mine); English ed. 1969.
4. *Ibid.*, pp. 17, 27, and the fact that, of the book's four chapters, chap. 2 is entirely devoted to these "theologians of revolution."
5. *Ibid.*, pp. 2, 4, 5.
6. *Ibid.*, p. 24.
7. *Ibid.*, p. 81.
8. *Ibid.*, p. 130.
9. *Political Illusion*, p. 77; English ed. 1965.
10. *Violence*, p. 92.
11. *Ibid.*, pp. 93–108.
12. *Ibid.*, p. 129.
13. *Ibid.*, p. 128.
14. *Ibid.*
15. *Ibid.*, pp. 127, 129, 133.
16. *Ibid.*, p. 128.
17. E.g. *Ethics of Freedom*, pp. 37–38; French ed. 1970.
18. *Ibid.*, pp. 42–44.
19. *Ibid.*, p. 38.

20. *Violence*, pp. 128–29.
21. *Ibid.*, p. 128.
22. *Ibid.*, pp. 145–46 (Ellul's italics).
23. E.g. *ibid.*, pp. 145, 150.
24. *Ibid.*, pp. 3–4, 97.

CHAPTER 12

The Mythic Meaning of the City

David L. Clark

Jacques Ellul's mastery of mythic communication and his distinctive approach to the sociological significance of biblical myths make *The Meaning of the City* highly important for social scientists analyzing myths as ordering structures for societies. The book's lasting value has been ill served, however, by advertisements and reviews that have characterized it as a polemic against secular-city cultists and urban-renewal planners. Far from being an occasional tract on such matters, the book gains its fullest meaning when understood as part of its author's long-range and multivolume study of theology and society. For these reasons, this essay focuses on Ellul's handling of myths and avoids any extensive commentary on his attitudes toward ecclesiastical involvement in social action and protest.

In the same year that *The Meaning of the City* was first published in English, *The Christian Century* printed an article in which Ellul presented the overall plan for his writing.[1] There he sets forth "composition in counterpoint" as the paramount concept guiding his literary efforts. Just as in music a line of counterpoint adds a related but independent line to the melody, so in Ellul's writing each book adds a related but independent argument to that of one other book. *The Meaning of the City* is a composition in counterpoint to *The Technological Society* first published in 1954. "To my book on technology corresponds my theologically based study of the great city as the supreme achievement of man's technology," writes Ellul when describing how the two books are related. He points out the difference between them by indicating that "every sociological analysis of mine is answered (not in the sense of replying, but in that of noting the other dialectical pole) by a biblical or theological analysis."[2]

When Ellul warns that his biblical and theological analysis is not a "reply" to his sociological analysis, he signals one of his fundamental convictions. Throughout his writings Ellul strongly criticizes the view that Scripture supplies specific answers to social, economic, and political problems. In opposition to such fundamentalist biblicism, Ellul urges that Christians approach the Old and New Testaments as texts that confront us with questions. "God in Jesus Christ," states Ellul, "puts questions to us—questions about ourselves, our politics, our economy—and does not supply the answers; it is the Christian himself who must make the answers."[3] It is such a question-and-answer process that Ellul has in mind when he describes his theological analysis as a dialectical pole in its relationship to his sociology.

"The principle of confrontation" is another phrase which Ellul uses when describing his dialectical mode of analysis. "The only thing that will be of any use," Ellul asserts, "is not synthesis or adaptation, but confrontation; that is, bringing face to face two factors that are contradictory and irreconcilable and at the same time inseparable. For it is only out of the decision he makes when he experiences this contradiction—never out of adherence to an integrated system—that the Christian will arrive at a practical position."[4] By insisting that divine and human realities are inseparable, Ellul makes clear that he is discoursing within a modern scientific and philosophic framework, and that he is not retreating into a pre-scientific "three-decker universe" in which heaven, hell, and earthly life were postulated as three distinct modes of reality. Ellul's preeminent concern is that human beings—individually and collectively—discover a dimension of reality independent of themselves, their societies, and achievements. It is his ability to project a sense of transcendence within the modern cosmology that makes Ellul's writings so important for social scientists, an increasing number of whom recognize the crucial role of transcendental myths in social change.

THE CITY AS SYMBOL IN THE BIBLE

When planning his counterpoint to *The Technological Society*, Ellul searched Scripture for the image most consistently employed to represent man's technological ambitions and achievements. He did not attempt to compose a statement about contemporary urbanism, urban crises, or urban-renewal programs. This should be kept in mind by readers disappointed with the book's failure to discuss timely urban problems. *The Meaning of the City* was not intended as sociological analysis, but rather as the theological pole to be used in dialectical conjunction with *The Technological Society*.

The reader comparing *The Technological Society* and *The Meaning of the City* should focus first on the key image of "the technological process" (or, to use Ellul's term, "technique") in the former book and that of "the city" in the latter. These central images serve more than a literary function, and are more than convenient shorthand abbreviations for their books' theses. Benello, in chapter 5 herein, discusses Ellul's understanding of the technological process or "technique" as an all-pervading principle which dominates modern industrial society. A basic premise of *The Technological Society* is that human values and human beings are given lower priority than the rational, methodical, pragmatic principle of technique. When read by itself, *The Technological Society* adds little to the analysis of industrial society presented by Marx, Weber, Spengler, and Veblen. Ellul depends on the methodology of Marx's *Das Kapital*. Though he shifts from employers' treatment of workers to technique as the preeminent principle, he perpetuates a Marxist analysis of such a principle conditioning men in all sectors of their activities.[5] Ellul is indebted to a Weberian methodology when he elucidates the correlations between motivating factors in economics and those in political, social, and ideological sectors of life.

But when *The Technological Society* is read in conjunction with *The Meaning of the City*, Ellul's thought shows several distinctive touches. Read together, they demonstrate how he has freed himself from the limitations of a Marxist formula, even though Marx's thought continues to shape the way Ellul "sees" social structures. In *The Meaning of the City* he follows Marxist methodology to a degree in isolating "the city" as the foremost principle in the Bible for organizing social institutions. The methodology of Marx and Weber are evident, for example, when Ellul discusses "the city" as a force over which humans have little control. He insists that "the city is a phenomenon absolutely removed from man's power, a phenomenon which he is fundamentally incapable of affecting."[6] On one level such a statement echoes Marx's claim that capitalism is an unnatural force enslaving men through an independent dynamic beyond the understanding and control of even the capitalists who derive their power from that system. But he goes far beyond Marx's insight about the conditioning process of a society's infrastructure. He makes a fundamental break with Marx over the possibility of a revolution releasing men from enslavement to an unnatural social system and initiating a new society conducive to man's natural desires. Ellul condemns such faith in revolutionary ideology as a naive underestimation of man's bondage to "the city" and its conditioning process. From this perspective, Marx is not radical enough; Ellul accuses him of myopic failure to perceive the roots of our society's dehumanizing forces.

The distinctiveness of Ellul's analysis of social evils, then, lies in the depth of his vision. In comparison to Marx, Ellul goes back further in history to seek examples of confrontation between irreconcilable structures of social organization, and deeper into human consciousness to look for the origins of dehumanizing forces. His principle of confrontation is more radical than Marx's; Ellul dares us to enter into a confrontation between human and divine realities.

The fundamental premise in *The Meaning of the City* is that men have been involved in confrontation with divine reality from the beginning of social organization. As a result, biblical records reveal both perceptions about divine reality and human responses to it. Ellul asserts that there is a "harmonious teaching throughout the Scriptures . . . a doctrine of the city, complete, coherent, with an undeniable bearing on man's life, his destiny, his relations with God, and at last his salvation."[7] This "doctrine of the city" or "harmonious teaching" is not a prescriptive code of morality nor a solution to problems which arise in human social organization. "God has given us no commands with regard to the city," states Ellul. "He affords us no law . . . he has never said, 'You shall not live in the city.' "[8] Ellul makes it clear that he is not defending bucolic existence in opposition to the city. Likewise, he insists that we cannot account for the biblical interpretation of the city as the distrust of settled society by the early nomadic tribes who were the ancestors of Semitic people. Ellul rejects this argument because he finds biblical symbolism about the city consistent from the earliest writings through the latest.

Ellul points out the symbolic significance of the Hebrew words *'iyr re 'em* used in the Old Testament to mean "the city." "Now this word has several meanings," he writes, adding:

> It is not only the city, but also the Watching Angel, the Vengeance and Terror. A strange association of ideas; . . . we must admit that the city is not just a collection of houses with ramparts, but also a spiritual power. . . . The city has, then, a spiritual influence. It is capable of directing and changing a man's spiritual life. It brings its power to bear in him and changes his life, all his life, not just his house. And that seems a fearful mystery.[9]

"Spiritual influence" is a key concept in Ellul's communication of "the city" and its impact on humanity. When he refers to spiritual influence, he does not mean religious or divinely ordained influences, but basically a power beyond the control of man. By "spiritual" he means something that affects the spirit of man, the wellspring of human consciousness and motivations. He does not intend to impute a divine origin to such an influence, but he does think that spiritual influences not originating in divine reality have an inner power beyond the control of man. Evil, for Ellul, is more than the absence of good; he thinks within a Pauline and Augustinian framework which defines the demonic as having its own dynamic power. From this perspective Ellul perceives special significance in the fact that the Hebrew word for "city" also connotes "Watching Angel, the Vengeance and Terror." The confrontation between man and the city is for Ellul an *agon* between the merely human and the demonic forces of fallen angels. He communicates his interpretation of "the Fall" in retelling the story of Cain.

Ellul's interest in the symbolic significance of etymology is also demonstrated in his discussion of the first city mentioned in the Old Testament (the city which Cain built and called "Enoch," the name of his first son). He claims that the Hebrew of "Enoch" (*chanakh:* to dedicate, inaugurate, initiate) is a clue to what Cain did east of Eden. Turning his back on the reality created by God for man, Cain prided himself on his ability to procreate a son named Enoch, and to initiate a reality according to his own rebellious devising.

> This first builder of a city thinks of his action as a response to his situation, an effort to satisfy his deepest desires. He will satisfy his desire for eternity by producing children, and he will satisfy his desire for security by creating a place belonging to him, a city. . . . Such is the act by which Cain takes his destiny on his shoulders, refusing the hand of God in his life.[10]

In these words Ellul describes sin as more than rebelliousness against commandments, more than self-indulgence in sexual and other pleasures, more than prideful independence, more than man's irresponsible failure to live in harmony with his environment and capabilities. For Ellul man's profound sinfulness reaches deeply even into his creativity and commitment. In fact, irony is necessary to perceive the depth of human sin. And in order to have a sense of irony, one must have a point of reference, a place to stand outside the situation deemed ironic. *The Meaning of the City* provides this Archimedian locus in relationship to *The Technological Society.* From the dialectical pole of the Bible, Ellul concludes that human victimization by technique is just the latest historical example of man ironically reaping dehumanizing results even from his most creative responses to the human situation. At present we call it technique but in the Bible it is "the city . . . the place where the immense irony of God hides."[11]

ELLUL'S APPROACH TO BIBLICAL MYTH

Ellul depends on the rhetorical mode of irony in communicating his concept of sin, and on the mythic mode in developing his principle of confrontation. Despite the fact that *The Meaning of the City* represents a sophisticated biblical mythology, Ellul eschews extended discussion of myth in the actual text. He tucks away in several footnotes crucial clues about his approach to myth.

In the first of these notes, Ellul explains his reticence about using the term "myth." "I hesitate to use the term 'myth,' for at best it is obscure, appearing in many diverse forms. . . . Barth's criticism of any conception of myth in the Bible is in truth valid only for a relatively minor part of the different possible meanings of this word. He is attacking the mode of interpretation of the Bible used by the historical school, also by form criticism, and finally by Bultmann."[12] After making clear his desire to avoid the "red herring" of demythologizing, Ellul gives his definition of myth:

> When I use the word I mean this: the addition of theological significance to a fact which in itself, as an historical (or supposed to be such), psychological or human fact, has no such obvious significance. Its role is therefore to make a fact "meaningful," to show it up as bearing the revelation of God, whereas in its materiality it is neither meaningful nor of the nature of revelation. This is how myth operates. It does not destroy the historical reality of the event, but on the contrary gives it its full dimensions.[13]

This explanation is a decisive clue that the "meaning" of the city Ellul presents is mythic meaning, and that he holds mythic meaning to be a mode of communication essential to God's revelation in Scripture. Even though wary of involving himself in a lengthy debate about myth and revelation, Ellul forcefully asserts that the mythic form cannot be separated easily or radically from the revelation: "But from the very fact that it is a myth, we cannot be indifferent to its form. We cannot take from it a general idea as its nucleus while neglecting the surrounding material, as one keeps an almond after throwing the shell away. For this very shell, with its words, its literary style, is full of meaning."[14]

This explains why Ellul organized his counterpoint to *The Technological Society* around biblical myths about cities, even though he intended to communicate a theological perspective on the many human activities discussed in his earlier book of sociological analysis. *The Meaning of the City* is not just about urbanism any more than *The Technological Society* is just about technology. Both studies concern the supreme achievements of human creativity which vary in each historical period, but which ironically acquire powers over man and dehumanize him. For Ellul, the Bible deals mainly with this aspect of the human predicament when presenting myths about cities.

Thus, in Ellul's writings, "myth" is not "false story"—as much contemporary usage would have it—but a value-laden story that communicates fundamental aspects of the society producing the myth. Neither does he understand myth in the sense of ideology which rationalizes and veils materialistic motives. Rather, he conceives of myth as a mode of communication different from rational and factual modes of communication, and as a mode that must accompany those others if humans are to express their perceptions fully. Ironic meaning and other modes are often detected by Ellul in biblical myths which set forth the human predicament. In fact, there is a striking affinity between his perception of irony in biblical mythology and the analysis of mythology taught by Claude Lévi-Strauss. For Lévi-Strauss, myths are the means by which a culture simultaneously understands and misunderstands its own structure.

Understanding comes from myths which underscore central cultural structures and resolve disjunctions that threaten the culture's harmony. Misunderstanding results from myths appearing to make coherent and acceptable actual disjunctions that will destroy the culture if not resolved in reality. Although Ellul's writings do not conform to the structuralist school of social science, his approach to myth clearly resembles that of Lévi-Strauss.

Ellul's affinity with Lévi-Strauss's interpretation of myths is clearest in his treatment of the Tower of Babel myth, which Ellul insists revolves around the central "problem of the name, and the city and its tower are the means of obtaining the name."[15] The myth helped Israel understand more deeply her dependence on God. By telling of humans losing in their attempt to name—and thus have power over—the city, the myth deepened the Israelites' recognition that they were objects of God's dominion. They now realized they could not usurp from God their status as subjects by treating nature as reality that humans could name and have dominion over. The Tower of Babel myth provided assurance that man "cannot keep himself, subject in the world, from being an object before God."[16] Ellul interprets the myth as the Israelites' way of dealing with their rebellious defiance of God, and of assuring themselves that God still controlled their destiny, since God won the struggle over naming the city in which men tried to build a tower reaching to heaven. The irony of the myth, according to Ellul, is that this apparent reconciliation misled the people of Israel into thinking that the city was desacralized and demystified by God's triumph over it; through the myth they misunderstood the real significance of God's response to pride in human achievement. "Confusion" is the basic meaning of the word "Babel," according to Ellul, "a name with meaning for the whole story, which is one long confusion—the confusion between man's power and God's, the confusion and obscurity of man's plans, the confusion of man's desire by God."[17]

In his elucidation of these three stages of confusion, Ellul describes the first stage as man's assumption that his technological capacities can make him master over nature. Applying the Tower of Babel myth to contemporary society, Ellul underscores his basic reason for focusing on urbanism in his counterpoint to *The Technological Society:* "The cities of our time are most certainly that place where man can with impunity declare himself master of nature." When he turns to the second stage of confusion, Ellul stresses how humans obscure their real desire to exclude God from his creation by resorting to myths through which they misunderstand their own motivation. The ancient Greeks did so, claims Ellul, by employing the myth of Prometheus as a means of understanding why humans continue to revolt against powers beyond their control, and by deducing from this myth that a fatal flaw could be avoided by accepting human status as that of subjects under divine control. This misunderstanding of human nature is perpetuated by Christian biblical exegetes, claims Ellul, when they pair with the Prometheus myth that of the Tower of Babel and thereby imply that human sin is basically a lack of proportion about man's role and God's role. Following Lévi-Strauss, Ellul stresses the danger of myths appearing to make coherent and acceptable basic conflicts that can rend the structure of a culture if not resolved in reality. This happens, according to Ellul, when society fails to deal with its desire to exclude God from his creation and masks this sin behind the promethean myth through which humans have misunderstood their essential sinfulness for several millennia.

Lévi-Strauss's concept of mythic misunderstanding is especially important to have in mind when considering Ellul's third stage of confusion, "the confusion of man's desire by God." God is the actor in effecting this confusion and "spiritual power" is the means he uses to do so. One reason for man's confusion is that he regularly mistakes God's "spiritual power" for demonic "spiritual power"; both are always at work in human consciousness and in man's environment. But a second reason for man's confusion is that he fallaciously assumes that his actions and his creations can be "neutral," that is, free from "spiritual power" either divine or demonic. This concept of the "neutral" is a refrain throughout *The Meaning of the City*. In the language of modern sociology, a "neutral" action is one free from ideological significance and which therefore can be justifiably required of all citizens without infringing on individual rights. The assessment of taxes, for instance, is frequently cited as an example of a neutral action on the part of governments. However, increasing numbers of citizens in the western world deny this and describe tax collection as a basic way in which governments condition citizens to be obedient and loyal to governmental policies and ideology. When Ellul asserts that human actions in the city cannot be neutral, I believe that he has in mind the kind of example I have just given.

Ellul's main concern is that people understand that technology can never be neutral, but is always conditioning humans to obedient submission to those elites who make the most important policies in technological societies. Humans are misunderstanding their own culture and its dangerous disjunctions when they overlook this conditioning process and believe that technology can be neutral, that is, free from imposing a particular value system on people. Ellul sees this misunderstanding going on when men interpret the Tower of Babel myth as teaching that God desacralizes and demystifies "the city" of human technological creation when he triumphs over arrogant human desires to "build a tower to heaven." "Man wanted to build a city from which God would be absent, but he never managed," states Ellul, who holds that men never can do so because God always remains an actor in his creation and never is a passive object of human actions. Ellul stresses that the inescapable reality of God's expression through spiritual power in the physical world is lost sight of when people fallaciously label as neutral technological programs that actually have a great impact on the values and attitudes of human beings. Such talk, believes Ellul, helps to create a moral vacuum into which rush both demonic spiritual power and divine spiritual power. God acts to nullify man's unacknowledged desire to exclude God from his creation, to "confuse" this human plan, and to defeat the spiritual power of demonic forces man has encouraged through his delusion about human self-sufficiency. "The city is still this spiritual power," proclaims Ellul, adding that "man no longer knows it, and each attempt at establishing a city is met by the failure of his unconscious designs."[18]

Ellul employs the term "city" as a metaphor for human actions aimed at excluding God from his creation, but he also uses "the city" as a metaphor for the point at which divine and human actions meet. "The city" is purposely ambivalent in Ellul's thought, which is always grounded in the principle that reality is unitary and in the conviction that God never deserts human beings no matter how much they rebel from his providential plan. For Ellul "the city" is "both the place where man's conquest is affirmed and the memorial to that conquest. The two phenomena of spiritual conquest and the construction of the city give rise to each other. It is because the city is such a place that man's triumphant march without God can take place, and it is because of this triumphant march that the city is a necessity."[19]

Irony is to be noted in the statement that "it is because of this triumphant march that the city is a necessity." This irony is rooted in Lévi-Strauss's concept that some myths are the result of the human tendency to purposely misunderstand disjunctions in society. Applying this concept, Ellul describes the irony of humans believing that technology can create the perfect city when in fact it creates the dehumanizing condition that makes humans the passive subjects of demonic and divine spiritual powers.

Ellul employs irony about "the city" not for the purpose of cynicism about all human technology, but mainly for the purpose of teaching that human beings should and must be continually involved in improving "the city" through technology. For Ellul, faith is not to be demonstrated by retreat from "the city" but by involvement in it. Ellul does believe that God gives man freedom to decide how he will act and that human ingenuity is a God-given ability. God does not define what will happen in the city or how humans will exercise their freedom and ingenuity in it. Neither does God, according to Ellul's biblical exegesis, proclaim blanket condemnation of all human efforts in "the city." The main biblical message about "the city" is that God "has a decisive role to play in the city's history, decisive but not definitive."[20] This impels us, says Ellul, to judge "the city" when our Scripture-based faith leads us to this stance, but we should also contribute positively, and with daring, to build up "the city" when our faith affirms that to do so is biblically fitting.

There are no easy answers provided by Ellul about when to judge and when to support "the city." Christian faith rests, for him, on God's decisive but secret plan for "the city." Closely related to Ellul's use of irony are his references to mythic "secrets." This statement is characteristic: "Thus a secret thread is woven into the visible side of the city's fabric, and its design is not clearly seen. But on the reverse side of the city's history, on the inside of the cloth, this is the thread which appears as the surest link, and the true design."[21] For Ellul, this "secret thread" is partly revealed and partly hidden. Here is another approach to myth that parallels that of Lévi-Strauss, for whom a myth is a means of communicating both the subconscious and conscious.

But Ellul shows concern for mythic secrets not simply as a theoretician. Just as he uses irony to point to theological truths, so he talks about mythic secrets in order to emphasize the need for faith in what is only dimly perceived. Ellul describes Jonah as wavering in faith when he became angry at God for not destroying Nineveh, as prophesied. "Jonah's attitude is ridiculous," states Ellul, asserting that "we must unceasingly proclaim God's curse and judgment on the city; but we must also pray to God that it will not happen, that he have pity, that he grant life to the city, that he make of it something to his glory."[22] According to Ellul, Jonah misunderstood what God was revealing in myth and in actions and thereby endangered the mission of God's chosen people. Proper understanding of the myth of Jonah recognizes that God's people will suffer if they do not reconcile the need to judge human technology with the equally important need to affirm what it can contribute to the providential purposes of God.

The Myth of the City as Part of the Christian Myth

Ellul often uses the phrase "the Christian myth." This is the clearest indication that he perceives mythology as having a positive and ultimate role in human consciousness. To emphasize this, he contrasts the Christian myth with what he calls common myths: "In the common myths we have a backward movement. The essential point . . . is a refusal of the existing order, a denial of man's 'progress' in the sense of simple evolution, not of improvement."[23] Against the background of such golden-age myths, he underscores the uniqueness of the Hebrew view of linear history as moving from a beginning toward a goal, as affirming the significance of the historical process. The Christian myth, however, adds a new dimension to this linear view of history—an eschatological element that proclaims a radical break with history while affirming its significance. Ellul stresses forcefully the eschatological nature of history's goal. For him this provides the basis of faith in God's plan for the city. Such a faith makes it possible to be fully involved in the city, but at the same time detached enough to judge it.

The ambivalence which Ellul has about the city's role in history carries over to his view of the church's role. He criticizes strongly the tradition which St. Augustine began when he identified the church militant with the inaugurated City of God. At the same time, Ellul condemns movements which hold that Christians must only be a leaven and must abandon institutional structures. He identifies those as perspectives originating early in history within the church's imperialistic mission to control all parts of human culture. "The new Jerusalem is to be established at the end of time, but absolutely not by an human effort," proclaims Ellul.[24] For him the Kingdom of God comes only after a radical break with history and not gradually through attempts to convert everyone and remake all institutional structures according to "Christian" principles.

For Ellul, the only significant transformation of human culture can be nothing short of a "second creation that is just as extraordinary, unbelievable and unexpected as the first."[25] "Instead of being the continuation of history," he adds, "the crowning act of history is a break with history." He repeatedly employs the verb "to transcend" in describing this radical break. He uses this term in a completely different way from Emersonian transcendentalism, Hegelian idealism, or Teilhard de Chardin's theories of man's spiritual evolution. Whereas those approaches stress evolutionary continuity, Ellul emphasizes an abrupt discontinuity between life as we know it and a new creation. At the same time, Ellul speaks of "the new creation" as being "characterized by an acceptance of history, and not by its refusal," and describes the Christian myth as "a kind of adoption, the ennobling of man's work, the very opposite of scorn and rejection."[26]

Ellul does not sidestep the apparent contradiction between the radical discontinuity of history and his claim that the Christian myth accepts history. On the contrary, Ellul recapitulates the argument of his entire book, in order to make clear that his "continuous reading" of the Bible confronts this apparent contradiction. At one point, he reviews his argument in order to demonstrate how the two directions "converge finally in the new Jerusalem" and how "each expresses one form of the saving and kingly act of God in Jesus Christ."[27] Again, this emphasis echoes Lévi-Strauss's teaching about contradictions and their resolution in myths. Ellul begins by assuming that most myths follow that pattern, but he emphasizes how the Christian myth transcends it.

Ellul applies the concept of transcendence in two ways: to the functional aspects of the Christian myth and to his theological understanding of how "the new Jerusalem" relates to the historical process. For Ellul the Christian myth differs from others because most myths reconcile or teach what actions should be avoided, whereas the Christian myth shocks man out of his expectations that he can discover a "center" within himself or within nature. "In all human myths," Ellul states, "the center is a return to the natural state, a recovery of man's situation before civilization, before the Promethean revolt, a return to man's nature."[28]

Mircea Eliade expands on this aspect of mythology when he writes that "every human being tends, even unconsciously, toward the Center, and towards his own center, where he can find integral reality—sacredness. This desire, so deeply rooted in man, to find himself at the very heart of the real—at the Center of the World, the place of communication with Heaven—explains the ubiquitous use of 'Centers of the World.'"[29] Eliade claims that this desire for the center needs to be reawakened in modern men, who have been taught to distrust any force that cannot be accounted for scientifically or through sensual perception. Eliade voices the plea of many for revived interest in myth, symbolism, and the mystical when he calls for man to expand his consciousness beyond the material world and discover a deeper part of reality that can bring greater psychic health. Eliade applies the term "transcendent" to the sacred toward which symbolism, myth, and ritual have pointed in all ages. Eliade warns that man's choice to live only in a sensually perceivable world has cut him off from the transcendent.

Ellul's approach to the "transcendent" differs greatly from Eliade's search for categories of "immanence" and "transcendence" which apply to all myths. In a strongly eschatological approach, Ellul insists that the transcendence witnessed to in the Christian myth is totally different from anything in human life. Foreign to Ellul's way of thinking is any talk about expanding one's consciousness here and now in order to discover the "sacred" or the "transcendent." Fundamentally Ellul adopts the expression "the Christian myth" to stress that it points beyond all of life's categories as we know them and that a radical disjunction will occur when God fulfills the myth.

THE MYTH OF THE NEW JERUSALEM

When Ellul discusses the New Jerusalem myth in the Book of Revelation, he drives home with special forcefulness his radical disjunction between the historical now and the eschatological future. "In the heavenly Jerusalem," he warns, "it is not a primitive equilibrium and happiness that are waiting us. The situation is completely different, and we have no idea, no mental image, no knowledge, no way of measuring what it might be."[30] Why then does he talk about biblical myths, if men should not project into the eschatological future the tangible realities of the present? The question, of course, is a fundamental one about all mythology, but is especially urgent with Ellul since he stresses the great difference between the Christian myth and myths of other religions and cultures.

The main reason why Ellul finds the mythic mode indispensable is his conviction that the Christian gospel can only be comprehended through mythic assertions of God and man interacting as separate wills. He holds a distinctive view of Christ's soteriological work—a view reminiscent of patristic theories of the Godhead emptying itself in order to achieve mankind's redemption.

The most theologically significant, and debatable, statement in *The Meaning of the City* is the assertion that "at the end of history God gave up the plan which he had himself ordained and chosen."[31] Anticipating the response that all transcendence disappears from such a concept of God as changeable, he retorts that "this is no place to get caught up in the ridiculous problems of God's knowledge and omnipotence. . . . If God is truly God, he is outside the reach of our intelligence; if God is truly God, our intelligence can never grasp anything but a falsification of his true nature."[32] Such a passage is reminiscent of those in Calvin's *Institutes* which preface lengthy forays into the nature of God and his omnipotence. However, Ellul differs in that he does not embark on exercises in systematic theology, but returns to the language of myth by speaking in the past tense, the tense of most mythological language: "Man wanted to build a city from which God would be absent, but he never managed. God will make for him the perfect city, where he will be all in all. Thus we might say that it is uniquely man's decision that provoked God to act, which incited him to accept what man was desiring and seeking, and which caused him to transform his creation."[33] Here is the strongest and most noteworthy counterpoint to *The Technological Society*. In fact, Ellul's description of divine grace—of the "emptying out" of God in response to the human predicament—makes him worthy of his self-designation as a "radical optimist."

Although he stresses a fundamental disjunction between the historical and the eschatological, Ellul also insists upon continuity. "Thus the golden age will be characterized by an acceptance of history, and not by its refusal," he insists, but adds: "Instead of being the continuation of history, the crowning act of history is a break with history."[34] Evolution is clearly Ellul's chief concern when he aims to reconcile a "break with history" with the affirmation of history as a significant part of God's dealing with man. To underscore the evolutionary and affirming qualities of the Christian myth, he adds that "Karl Marx was, as many have asserted, directly inspired by Jewish mythology, in which there is nothing to be destroyed from the fantastic adventure of human civilization."[35] Ellul does not call the "crowning act of history" just another evolutionary stage within nature and history, comparable to the classless society as a myth to be fulfilled in history.

He refers instead to Marx's teaching that capitalistic industrialism was a stage of the historical process through which all societies must pass. Marx extols the great achievements of bourgeois culture in overthrowing feudalism and raising men above the level of beasts of burden. Just as Marx accepts all stages of the historical process as contributing to the final one, Ellul argues that mankind's final state would not be "the new Jerusalem" if man had not concentrated his creativity and hopes on this world's cities.

However, for Ellul, the Christian myth resolves life's basic dilemmas only by pointing to an eventual "new creation" beyond and separate from historical and material reality. "It is in the creation of the heavenly Jerusalem that Christ's final victory will take its place in the sphere of reality," he states. The Christian myth does not resolve inner doubts about the worth of current human efforts to reform society, but intensifies our sense of the unresolved dimension of God's plan for mankind. Like an Old Testament prophet, Ellul holds up God's speaking to the patriarchs as a reminder of the gap between God's expectations and man's response. His basic prophetic message is that "man sacrifices man to build his cities, instead of accepting the only sacrifice which would enable him both to found them in truth and purify them of Satan's presence."[36]

THE WORK OF CHRIST AS AGONISTIC MYTH

Whenever Ellul speaks of Christ's work, he assumes that it transforms the world as well as human will. His christology is rooted in patristic views of Redemption as having cosmic significance; it is the context for his statement that "by Christ's triumph over the spiritual powers, he took away every city's spiritual worth."[37] "Spiritual worth" here refers to society's power to condition men so that they serve the interests of the controlling institutional structures; it is man's spirit that thereby suffers loss of freedom.

The turning point of the city's history "from Cain to Jerusalem," according to Ellul, is "that God, by his act in Jesus Christ, made the city into a neutral world where man can be free again, a world where he finds possibilities for action."[38] The mythic past tense is crucial here, for the history involved is mythic history. The key to the Christian myth is that Christ's sacrifice and resurrection have defeated all "spiritual powers" that control man. But Ellul notes that "these conquered powers have not yet been eliminated," so the battle goes on for man, even though the ultimate victory is certain. In developing the mythic story "from Cain to Jerusalem," he employs the paradigmatic myth of agonistic combat.

Ellul follows the agonistic mythic model when he states: "It is in this awful combat on the other side that man's work will find its meaning, because God is destroying the rebellious angel who up till now has animated man's work, and because the Lord himself will take the plan and the role of the rebellious angel."[39] In addition to describing as an *agon* God's combat with the rebellious angel, Ellus also employs the model of an *agon* when discussing man's combat with "angelic powers" in "the city." From Cain's first city down through the present time, Ellul describes the city as "a plaything of the angelic powers which took form in his work and are using it to bring about man's downfall."[40] This interference from "spiritual powers" beyond human control makes it impossible for men to treat the city and human creativity as neutral.

Since man's *agon* with "angelic powers" still goes on in "the city" (even though Scripture reveals that God's *agon* with these powers will ultimately lead to the defeat of the rebellious angel), humans cannot yet assume that technology can be neutral, free from exploitation by these "angelic powers." This mythic perspective on time sequences is crucial for an understanding of how Ellul relates the Incarnation to God's *agon* and to man's *agon*. Ellul asserts that the Incarnation represents God's triumph over evil in a mythic and teleological sense, but that this does not justify the concept now prevalent among Christian social and political activists who justify particular revolutionary programs as ways of continuing, in the contemporary world, Christ's combat with the forces of evil. "Today's incarnation must be that of an already victorious truth into the heart of the city," insists Ellul, thereby emphasizing the transcendent, eschatological, and mythic natures of biblical revelation about God's combat with the forces of evil.[41] These characteristics that give biblical myths their transforming power, Ellul holds, are lost sight of when

Christian activists equate their programs too facilely with scriptural revelation.

MYTHS OF TRANSCENDENCE AND SOCIAL CHANGE

The desire to communicate the transcendence of revelation is a preeminent concern for Ellul when he exegetes biblical mythology. Ellul displays considerable mythopoetic talent and an extraordinary ability for evoking the transcendent in his retelling of biblical myths. These powers make Ellul's writings have great significance to that increasing number of social scientists who acknowledge the importance of transcendence as a force that can mobilize people to effect social change.

Social scientists traditionally have categorized myths of transcendence as ordering structures which legitimize the status quo and any elites who have power in that established system. Increasingly, however, social scientists assert that myths of transcendence have activated some groups at various points in history to change their societies with a radical determination only found in true believers. Certainly one reason for this revisionism about myths of transcendence is the widespread fear that contemporary man has lost a capacity to imagine social structures significantly different from the present. We commonly describe the future as an extension of present technological structures. Abundant documentation illustrates how technological society concentrates power in increasingly small segments. Awareness of this technological determinism leads many social scientists to reexamine with greater openness earlier historical periods in which there was far-reaching reorganization of fundamental institutions and value systems. Behind this revisionism is the pragmatic desire to discover the correlative prerequisites for modern social self-transcendence.

Robert Bellah is one of the best-known contemporary American sociologists who have analyzed myths of transcendence as transforming social forces. He has described this process in words which closely parallel Ellul's statement that Scripture puts questions to us and leaves us to decide on the answers. "The capacity to ask questions of the ultimate is perhaps a consequence of shifting the locus of ultimacy from the natural social order to a transcendent reference point," states Bellah and adds: "From the point of view of the transcendent, everything natural has only relative value and can be questioned."[42] In all of his jeremiads, Ellul holds up institutions and human expectations to a searching scrutiny guided by confrontation with biblical themes. What makes this principle of confrontation distinctive is his refusal to treat Scripture as offering the answers to the inadequacies of human institutions and behavior. He does not exploit myths of the Bible in order to give apparent resolutions to contemporary problems. What Ellul retains from the usual functioning of myth is the "mirror-effect" that allows men to perceive their personal dilemmas as microcosms of those presented in the myths. Most especially, Ellul stresses the agonistic aspects of myths in order to emphasize the decision-making forced upon each Christian.

Throughout most of *The Meaning of the City*, Ellul ridicules and condemns manifestations of human pride in what society can accomplish. At one point, however, he speaks of humor as a way to accept the Christian myth: "Where we are working we absolutely must not take our action seriously, neither ours nor that of our companions."[43] The detachment of being a "fool of Christ," like St. Francis of Assisi, is one aspect of the stance that he seems to have in mind. This detachment drives a Christian to greater concern about cities, not less, just as it drove St. Francis to found a new Christian vocation, that of the friar sent into the cities to preach and succor. "So we must put our heart into the city, but keep it ours by humor," urges Ellul, when he instructs that "our task is to represent Him in the heart of the city."[44]

Ellul's eschatological detachment is similar to that of earlier Calvinists. Michael Walzer has described Puritans strongly opposed to seventeenth-century English monarchy as "strangers and exiles" in their land, willing to risk the loss of familiar sources of security, because their religious training had helped them develop an eschatological detachment.[45] The history of Calvinism includes numerous outstanding examples of social change by an "elect" who opposed status quo systems that they found irreconcilable with Scripture. In fact, a recent study of the Reformation's appeal to urban laymen has employed the label "freedom fighters" to describe sixteenth-century groups who perceived the Reformation as a movement aimed at liberating secular life of burdensome ecclesiastical demands.[46]

Yet these early Calvinists defy twentieth-century labels as does Jacques Ellul. He is scathing in his attacks on liberals who believe in the eventual resolution of social problems through reform movements. Yet Ellul provides no rationale for a conservatism aimed at preserving the status quo. His opposition to ecclesiastical involvement in social and political reform is radical, an opposition springing from his suspicion that such movements only inoculate church members against participation in more fundamental means of transforming society. The effectiveness of Ellul's writing, however, does not depend on his attitudes towards specific programs in church or society. The ambiguity that pervades *The Meaning of the City* is integral to the success of Ellul's presentation of myth. Like a great poem or play, *The Meaning of the City* has a creative power beyond the intent of the author; the book will continue to stimulate the minds of Christian readers when present-day controversies about church policies are forgotten. The main reason for the book's durability is Ellul's handling of myth. Because it evokes a sense of the transcendent so powerfully, *The Meaning of the City* will help Christians of several generations hold up themselves and their values to divine judgment.

NOTES

1. "The Mirror of These Ten Years," *Christian Century*, 87 (18 Feb. 1970), p. 201.
2. *Ibid.*
3. *Ibid.*
4. *Ibid.*
5. This claim is expanded and clarified by David Menninger in chap. 1 herein.
6. *Meaning of the City*, p. 47; English ed. 1970.
7. *Ibid.*, p. 8.
8. *Ibid.*, p. 47.
9. *Ibid.*, p. 9.
10. *Ibid.*, p. 5.
11. *Ibid.*, p. 19.

12. *Ibid.*, p. 18, n. 3.
13. *Ibid.*
14. *Ibid.*, p. 173, n. 3.
15. *Ibid.*, p. 15.
16. *Ibid.*, p. 17.
17. *Ibid.*, p. 18.
18. *Ibid.*, p. 19.
19. *Ibid.*, p. 16.
20. *Ibid.*, p. 77.
21. *Ibid.*, p. 76.
22. *Ibid.*, p. 77.
23. *Ibid.*, pp. 77, 162.
24. *Ibid.*, p. 163.
25. *Ibid.*
26. *Ibid.*, p. 162.
27. *Ibid.*, p. 163; cf. "From Cain to Jerusalem," pp. 163–72; "From Eden to Jerusalem," pp. 173–82.
28. *Ibid.*, p. 162.
29. Mircea Eliade, *Images and Symbols* (London: Sheed and Ward, 1961), p. 54.
30. *Meaning of the City*, p. 163.
31. *Ibid.*, p. 173.
32. *Ibid.*, p. 174.
33. *Ibid.*
34. *Ibid.*, p. 163.
35. *Ibid.*, p. 162.
36. *Ibid.*, p. 171.
37. *Ibid.*
38. *Ibid.*, p. 170.
39. *Ibid.*, p. 172.
40. *Ibid.*, p. 164.
41. *Ibid.*, p. 170.
42. Robert Bellah, *Beyond Belief* (New York: Harper and Row, 1970), p. 96.
43. *Meaning of the City*, p. 181.
44. *Ibid.*
45. Michael Walzer, *The Revolution of the Saints* (Cambridge, Mass.: Harvard University Press, 1965).
46. Steven E. Ozment, *The Reformation in the Cities: The Appeal of Protestantism to Sixteenth Century German and Switzerland* (New Haven, Conn.: Yale University Press, 1975).

On Dialectic

Jacques Ellul
Translated by Geoffrey W. Bromiley

I do not want to make any response here to the remarkable studies which make up this symposium, but simply to express my gratitude to those who have devoted themselves with such seriousness and depth to the long intellectual and spiritual pilgrimage represented by my written work. I have no response to make to the criticisms. I listen to them and try to enter into the point of view or perspective of those who have formulated them in order to advance my own research along the lines indicated.

I am sometimes amazed at all that has been discovered and I ask myself: "Is it possible that I said all that?" I believe in effect there is something important here. In all work such as I have attempted, as in all poetic work, there is an element of inspiration which transcends the author, of which he is unaware, which is not the expression of clear ideas, and which a skilled and attentive reader can bring out, so that in listening to this reader, the author can say: "Yes, this is what I wanted to say and I did not know it. . . ." I have experienced this many times. No matter how willed and planned and structured my research may be, something always escapes it. There is something extra added to my thought, a supplementary gift whose value is seen only when the reader finds it. I am thus grateful to those who have contributed to this work and to those who planned and executed it.

I have just said that I have listened to the remarks, criticisms, and reservations, and have profited by them. This will appear in my future writings if God so wills. In saying this, I do not mean that I will correct my errors. I am not going to go back and list my mistakes as one theologian did. This shows a great deal of humility but is of little practical use. At issue is another process. In dialogue the listener reconsiders his own statements and what he has just heard, and thus moves on to a new stage. This is not a matter of self-criticism, of repeating what was said and modifying what has been found erroneous in it. Nor is it a matter of self-defense, of trying to prove the other speaker wrong. Both these attitudes are sterile. It is a matter of entering a new phase in which the two contradictory statements are adopted and make progress possible.

We are thus set in dialectic. If I have chosen this theme for final reflection (not conclusion or reply), it is because I have the impression it might help to explain some of my "contradictions," and also (if American readers will pardon me) because I have known many American students over the past twenty years and have found that dialectical thinking is strange to them: they do not like entering into it. I am sure that theologians familiar with Barth and Kierkegaard know this form of expression and knowledge, but perhaps not all the readers of this book will be theologians. In virtue of my own twofold intellectual origin in Marx and Barth, dialectic has a central place for me and it might be helpful to explain it more precisely.

A General Sketch of Modern Dialectic

I am not attempting here a general theoretical treatise. Dialectic comes from *dialegein*, to speak in relation, as in dialogue, or with exchange. But *dia* also carries the idea of distance or contradiction. If dialectic can be the art of dialogue, of the development of a thought by questions and answers, it is much more. The greatest difficulty in grasping dialectic is that it has been used and defined in innumerable ways. Thus one might speak of the dialectic of Heraclitus, of Zeno, of Plato, of Aristotle, of Kant, and of Hegel and Marx, who gave birth to the modern understanding of dialectic.

Let us start at the simplest level. We are accustomed to logical reasoning with causes and effects, the sequence of algebraic equations, the linear expression of thought, and the principle of non-contradiction (black cannot be white). We are also accustomed to a binary system of alternatives (naught and one, good and evil). We can accept intermediary nuances but we necessarily arrive at the exclusion of the one by the other. It is true that the clear principle of causality has been seriously challenged by certain sciences and that one normally prefers to speak today of groups of referents, concomitants, or more or less determinative factors. But this does not greatly change the process of thought. One realizes that this principle has also been called in question by McLuhan, who relates it to writing and printing; but the comprehensive mythical thinking which has developed with the new media and electrical transmission does not seem to me to be very convincing. I am in a different world.

The simplest comparison with which to start is as follows: Put a positive charge next to a negative one and you have a powerful flash, but this is a new phenomenon excluding neither the positive nor the negative pole. Can we be sure, then, that positive and negative factors in thought cancel one another, that one cannot maintain a No at the same time as a Yes? But these two ways of putting the question show at once that there are two aspects of dialectic—a dialectic of ideas, but perhaps also a dialectic of facts, of reality.

In the first place, then, is dialectic just a play of ideas functioning according to the well-known classical scheme of thesis, antithesis, and synthesis? Already in Plato we find a larger view than this: "The dialectician is the one who sees the totality" (*Republic,* book VII). Dialectic, then, is not just a way of reasoning by question and answer but an intellectual mode of grasping the real, which itself embraces both the positive and the negative, both white and black. Descartes has an equally interesting observation: "Dialectic teaches us to deal with all things, just as logic gives demonstrations of all things" ("Conversation with Burman," in the *Discourse on Method*). In other words, dialectic is neither demonstrative reasoning nor a system of the formal unfolding of thought. It always claims to have to do with the real, to be a means of taking account of the real. But the real embraces both positive and negative elements, contradictory factors which do not cancel one another but coexist. A vigorous system of thought must, therefore, take into account the Yes and the No without excluding either one or choosing between them, since choice excludes one part of reality.

Hegel did not at first make dialectic a means of comprehending the real, but a means of expressing truth by the dialectic of ideas. On the other hand, how can one perceive the totality without perceiving that it is always changing? This is why reference is often made to the dialectic of Heraclitus, the philosophy of *panta rhei*. Reality includes not only contradictory elements, but a permanent process of change. Now if one relates the two, it is easy to see that the negative element, for example, acts on the positive element and that this entails modification. In other words, the contradictory factors do not just confront one another statically and inertly. They are in interaction. The simple formula of thesis, antithesis, and synthesis already implies this transformation of the first two factors into a third which is neither the suppression of one of the two, nor a confusion, nor an addition. One might also think of a living organism in which forces are constantly at work. Some of these forces tend to keep the organism alive, while others tend to destroy and disaggregate it; and at each instant there is a synthesis of the two groups of forces that produces the state of the live body at a given moment.

At this point, the idea of time or history is introduced into the dialectical relation: here we have a decisive element. Often dialectic is viewed as a type of reasoning, or as the coexistence of contradictory elements. The important thing, however, is that these contradictory factors can subsist (without eliminating one another) only as they are correlative in a flow of time leading to a new situation. On the one side, then, the coexistence is that of the real in history, ruling out any idea of the inert and unchanged absolute and thus finally ruling out metaphysical thinking. On the other side, the way of knowledge has itself to be an evolving one which is adequate to, and coherent with, the contradictory and evolving real (coherent to the extent that during the very time I begin to think about it the real is undergoing change). Thus there is no fixed state of the object that I can impose on it. The flow of time is introduced, then, into knowledge itself. This is why, on the level of Marx for example, reference is made to historical dialectic.

For Marx, all history proceeds in dialectical fashion, that is, by confrontation, by the contradiction of historical factors negating but not excluding one another and, after a certain period of contradiction and conflict, arriving at a historically new situation. In consequence, history can be understood only in terms of conflict. Each existent situation is one of tension. In every social or political context one needs to discern the contradictory forces and interpret their present relation so as to foresee their possible evolution. In a sense one might refer here to the famous interpretation of Toynbee according to which every civilization evolves through the challenges it undergoes, surviving as it finds each time the response to the guantlet thrown down to it. This is true and it is an element in the dialectical interpretation of history, though Toynbee's thinking is not strictly dialectical. If we are to understand the historical process effectively, clearly we must make no mistake regarding the contradictory factors.

In every society there are thousands of mutually contradictory forces. Most of the contradictions are not at all interesting; they have no dialectical value. But some are constitutive of the dialectical process, such as the well-known contradiction maintained by Marx, of the opposition between the forces of production (both technical and economic) and the social relations of production (which organize society).

To understand dialectic as it has influenced me, two points remain to be explained. Hegel in a well-known formula spoke of the positivity of negativity. This is essential, for if the positive remains alone, it remains unchanged: stable and inert. A positive—for example, an uncontested society, a force without counterforce, a man without dialogue, an unchallenged teacher, a church with no heretics, a single party with no rivals—will be shut up in the indefinite repetition of its own image. It will live in satisfaction at what was produced once, and will see no reason to change. Facts, circumstances, and events that might be contrary will be no more than annoying embarrassments for it.

The contrary fact alone, that is to say, is not enough to make us change. The contrary fact will be obliterated or disguised, or the uncontradicted positive will interpret it so as to be able to enter harmlessly into the explicative schema which allows a response to everything. We thus have sclerosis, paralysis, a redundant monologue of self-satisfaction and self-reproduction. This is the situation one encounters in every totalitarian society (I say *society* and not necessarily *power*). But to say this suggests also that there is never any real innovation. Apparent innovations may occur, changes of form, but these do not produce the least mutation. There results, then, an increasing distance between the situation of fact and the organization (or individual) in question. The only thing that can produce change or evolution is contradiction, contestation, the appearance of the negative, negativity. This implies a transformation of the situation.

In the human condition it is not enough that this contradiction be that of facts, events. There usually has to be an express and explicit contradiction put in words by someone who contradicts, who bears the negation. In this way the negativity induces and provokes innovation, and consequently the history, of the group or individual. One can see, then, that negativity has a wholly positive side. If there is transition from one state to another, we can thank negativity alone.

I carefully do not speak of progress here, for I am not certain that transition or innovation necessarily means progress. I thus differ totally from Hegel and Marx, for whom the new state has to be progress in relation to the previous one, since for them the fact of the synthesis (though Marx does not use this term) of the two preceding factors (the positive and the negative) implies that the new state is superior. I have no guarantee of this, and in Hegel and Marx its affirmation simply rests on a belief and an ideology of progress. What I am sure of is that life simply presupposes the innovation, that man is a history which includes negativity, and that to rest in an achieved state is in reality to deny both the life and the history or specificity of man, to claim to stop history, which is (perhaps . . .) to enter the Kingdom of God!

For me, then, negativity always has a positive value even though I am not sure that the product of this dialectical step is necessarily superior to the preceding state. There are always favorable and unfavorable elements. The new state or synthesis —or, if one will, equilibrium—always brings inevitably another negativity which reproduces the contradiction and the ineluctable movement. But why should this be better than definitive order and repetitive organization? I will not enter into a discussion of entropy, of the total disorder that is ultimate stability, but simply emphasize that human life has no meaning if there is no chance of changing anything, no part of one's own to play, that is, if there is no history begun but not yet finished. And this is the precise moment that negativity comes to the fore. In one of my books, I adopted the famous statement of Guehenno: "The first duty of man is to say No."

To make these general considerations more precise we must look at the question of crisis. When we talk of thesis, antithesis, and synthesis, we cannot help dreaming of a tranquil intellectual activity in the peaceful study of a philosopher. We know, however, that a chemical synthesis, for example, consumes a good deal of energy and can mean the dissolution of the basic structure of the bodies entering into the synthesis. We must have no illusions, then, about intellectual synthesis. When we go on to the minute demonstration or "unpeeling" of the operations of intellectual analysis, the synthesis escapes our comprehension. When synthesis takes place in a poet in the creative act, or in a philosopher suddenly achieving the intuition of a new understanding, it is inexplicable. Creative synthesis is reached only with explosions and acts of destruction. This applies in every dialectical movement. There is no peaceful and self-evident historical and temporal transition from a (positive-negative) preceding state to a succeeding state. To reach the latter, one has to go through crisis, a period of intense trouble, of fire and explosion, in which the former elements are dissolved and destroyed. In the historical and social field this crisis is called revolution; in the spiritual field, conversion. And if dialectic is dealing with the real, it will be understood that neither conversion nor revolution is ever entirely for good, but both are constantly summoned to begin again. Thus, crisis in a society, church, or human being is always a sign of confrontation by a negativity that has to be overcome in the creating of a radically new state. But surely what we again find here is the theory of challenge. Has this living organism adequate resources to survive the crisis and reach a new equilibrium, or will it fall into neurosis, disorder, and incoherence—always a possibility? Dialectic is not a machine producing automatic results. It implies the certitude of human responsibility and therefore a freedom of choice and decision.

BIBLICAL DIALECTIC

There is a tradition among philosophers that dialectic begins with the Greeks. Some suggest that Heraclitus (end of the sixth century, B.C.) created it with his theory of becoming on the basis of contrariety, conflict being at the origin of all things but contrariety giving birth to concord. Others, following Aristotle, think that Zeno of Elea (fifth century, B.C.) invented dialectic, although even if he uses the word he does not seem to go much beyond the idea of argumentation and the technique of discussion. Others derive dialectic from Plato. My own claim, however, is that well before these intellectual formulations from the eighth century, B.C., dialectic appeared in Hebrew thought, and that the whole of the Old Testament expresses a dialectic.

I am not saying that there is an explicit theory of dialectic, or that the word is used, but that we are in the presence of an original process of thought which bears the marks of what later came to be called dialectic (in the ontological sense and not just the technical one of discussion). I am completely opposed to the idea that if the word does not exist neither does the thing. I believe, on the contrary, that the reality is there first, and that the term arises only in understanding it, in taking cognizance of an experienced reality. In other words, the Hebrews formulated God's revelation dialectically without examining what they were doing intellectually, without working out the noetic aspect. I will take five examples of this dialectical process, giving just brief sketches and making reference to well-known questions.

First, we have the global affirmation that God enters history and accompanies man in his history. This is no less astonishing than the incarnation in Jesus Christ. We have the affirmation that the unique God, the Creator, comes to be with his people; that his glory is carried by a people (chosen because it is the least numerous of all peoples); that this God, who is so different from all the divinities of Egypt and Greece (which all either symbolize nature or have a kind of intrinsic temporality), that this God as a referent, as a partner in dialogue, enters into relation with a people in such a way that all one can know about the one comes from the other, and all that the second lives out is not determined but defined by the first. This is dialectic precisely because the God in question is the contradictory pole of all that was lived out by the people indissolubly associated with him.

The process of command—disobedience—judgment—reconciliation is precisely one of total dialectic. Now this is no chance process. It is not the process of a little story (as among the Greek gods) which might have been different. It is a schema repeated strictly at every historical stage of this people. And each time there is a synthesis of the preceding factors (including disobedience) by way of crisis. This historical process does not allow the revealed God to be metaphysical or to be constructed and known according to a metaphysical process. To define God as omniscient, omnipotent, impassible, imperturable, eternal, etc. is not to have understood the biblical revelation at all. One might say all this on the one side, but on the other the God of the biblical revelation enters time and history, suffers man's misery and sin, tolerates initiatives, limits his power, repents, revokes his condemnations, etc. Nor can we have one side without the other. A contradiction? Precisely. Logically insoluble, but it creates the biblical dialectic which makes man's relation to God not a repetition, a fixity, a ritual, a scrupulous submission, but a permanent invention, a new creation of the one with the other, a challenge, a love affair, an adventure whose outcome can never be known in advance. It is all the incredible revelation of man's freedom established within God's freedom,[1] the one not excluding the other but expressing the dialectical development of the relation in revelation. One can only understand this revelation if one thinks dialectially, instead of formulating "either-or's" as one is tempted to do (either God is omnipotent and man a slave, or man is free and God does not exist, etc.). It is no mere question of philosophical formulation, then, but of the new understanding of a revelation which never took place anywhere else, but which implies that if we are to give an intellectual account of it we must proceed dialectically.

A second aspect of this fundamental biblical dialectic, which underlines the fact that there can be many others, is the one that has been brought to light by Moltmann, for example, in his *Theology of Hope:* the process of development, which, throughout the Old Testament, moves from the promise to its fulfillment, the fulfillment containing a new promise moving toward a new fulfillment. We must not simplify the movement as many Christians have done, by saying that all the promises of the Old Testament are fulfilled in one single point, Jesus Christ. This is true, to be sure, but in saying it we must not leap over the road which leads to Jesus Christ and which also leads from him, for we, too, live by a promise (God's Parousia and kingdom), but a promise which is not theoretical and global. On the contrary, this promise multiplies itself in the course of the church's life, and our own, in the form of promises and partial fulfillments which for us, as for the Jews, always contain new promises and show us a new path on which to go. This is how it is in the relations of grace, sin, and repentance. Is grace given before repentance? Does repentance have priority over the gratuitousness of salvation? To this insoluble biblical question Luther replies with his famous "Always and at the same time sinner and righteous and penitent" (we should not forget the third term). "At the same time" means at each moment afresh.

It would be possible to quote several biblical passages that express this contradiction. Let us just give one example, Psalm 130, where we find the astonishing statement: "But there is forgiveness with thee, that thou mayest be feared" (v. 4). Forgiveness ought to bring love or gratitude. Fear ought to be inspired by justice or wrath. But no, the biblical text relates fear to love and forgiveness. God is feared because He is the one who forgives; He manifests His final greatness not by refusing forgiveness but by being the only one who can forgive. The dialectic of forgiveness and fear is essential.

Thus the entire unfolding of the existence of God's people, the church, and the individual Christian is dialectical in this constant renewal of promise and fulfillment (or, in other words, of the Already and the Not Yet). The Kingdom of Heaven is *already* among you or in the midst of you or in you, but it will still come at the end of the ages. The God of Abraham is *already* fully revealed but *not yet*, since he will not be revealed except in Jesus Christ. Jesus Christ is *already* the Lord of the world but *not yet*, since he will be so only at his Parousia. Nor should we add words which attempt a logical reconciliation. We should not say that Jesus is virtually or secretly the Lord, nor even that his lordship will be revealed in the last days. To do this is to take away the tension. It is to accept a supposed explanation instead of living with the contradiction of what is totally fulfilled but is clearly seen to be unfulfilled. It is in this contradiction that the Christian life is set.

If it is correct—as we have shown dialecticians to believe—
that life historically lived develops and evolves only by the fact of
dialectical contradiction, the same applies to the Christian life. If
everything is fulfilled and we stop at that, there is no *useful* life
or life worth living; everything is in vain. If everything is fulfilled, no life is *possible*. Yet we do not have a mixture of one
thing and the other. It is not our duty to fulfill what is not yet fulfilled (a regress to moralism). An actual plenitude of fulfillment
goes hand in hand with an actual experience to total fulfillment.
It is this indissoluble relation which makes the Christian life possible and significant in its movement from crisis to crisis (as demonstrated in the historical life of the church!).

The third aspect of biblical revelation that I like to recall is
that of the relation between the whole and the remnant. It is obvious that one part of this evolution moves toward an apparent
reduction of election, from the race to a people, from a people to
a remnant in Israel, from the remnant to a man (Jesus). Yet, on
the other hand, the proclamation is on each occasion more uni-
versalistic, until we come to the recapitulation of all history and
nature and all human works in the last days. The more the historically elect remnant narrows down, the more universal election really is, and therefore the more representative the remnant
is of the whole. At the same time, though it is not the same phenomenon, the process is dialectical to the extent that with each
break or fracture there results a reintegration of the excluded
whole with the manifested remnant. The election of the chosen
people implies the reintegration of the human race. The election
of the remnant implies the reintegration of all Israel. The election of Jesus implies the reintegration of the remnant. From the
biblical standpoint, then, the development of judgment is never
a mechanism to separate the good and the bad (as though these
were *simply* rejected, eliminated, excluded, etc.). It is an election of the bad mediated by that of the good. Jesus is not just the
mediator between God and men. He signifies the universal salvation of all Israel, and hence of the race, and hence of all creation.
But obviously this is not a fixed schema which can be reduced to
a formula. It presupposes a historical development, a constant
tension between contradictory factors.

Having given these three examples, I want to emphasize the

error of a whole theological trend influenced by one type of Greek philosophy, namely, the error of regarding the good as unitary, of identifying all division, fracture, and separation as the bad, and of seeing it as a duty to seek metaphysical unity (for example, mystical fusion in a great totality). This obsession with "the one," which has led some to rejection of the Trinity, others to theism, and still others to pantheism, entails a complete misunderstanding of revelation and its replacement by an explicative system (for example, the pyramidal one of gnosticism).[2] The temptation to take this course constantly recurs, structuralism being one of the most recent examples.

The first three instances which we have just sketched have principal reference to the Old Testament. I now want to take two more specifically from the New Testament. We undoubtedly find here, too, the dialectic of Already and Not Yet (with the Kingdom as already indicated), but at another level, especially in Paul, whose thinking is essentially dialectical. As one example, at the center of his thought we find, "You are saved by grace through faith." This is clear and simple. We know the tremendous developments of this statement. But then the same Paul adds: "*Therefore* . . . work out your salvation with fear and trembling"–an obvious contradiction. If we are saved by grace there is no need to work out our salvation and vice versa. Then the contradiction doubles itself in Philippians: "Work out your salvation with fear and trembling—for it is God who works in you to will and to do according to his good pleasure." Nor should we try to reduce this contradiction by establishing continuity. On the contrary, the very contradiction constitutes life in Christ. When God works in us to will and to do, we have to take up our responsibility as if [3] we were without God and everything depended on us. For this God is both the unknown God and love. Thus, there can be no "pietistic" attitude which tries to find out in every situation what is, here and now, the "response" and the "will" of God. As we work out our salvation with fear and trembling and do the impossible, in the last resort we can only give glory to this God who has already saved us. But to believe that this attitude frees us from working is to have misunderstood the Incarnation, to scorn salvation, and not really to believe at all in salvation by grace.

The dialectical process here, in the individual Christian life, consists of the renewing of the discovery of what can manifest salvation by grace (and the glory of the God who shows me grace), but only by way of the crisis which arises when, in the measure that grace is shown, we move on from the judgment that we are called upon to suffer for what we have already done. That judgment thrusts us toward the new situation of the reception of salvation by grace, and this can only make us live out the search for the salvation granted. Thus all Christian ethics, the whole conduct of the Christian life, can be thought of only in the dialectical relation of the two contraries of salvation by grace and the works of life.

I will take, as my last example, history and the Parousia. Linear and logical thinking tends to say: History is a co-creation with God. It leads naturally to God's Kingdom. There is continuity between the two. History is a kind of beginning with progressive evolution toward the Kingdom. Millenarians hold this ideology: We are now establishing the Kingdom of God on earth by social reforms and when we have done it the Messiah will come again. Roman Catholic theology says something similar, as when Péguy calls carnal cities "the image and commencement, and the body and sample of the house of God." This is also the conviction of the proponents of the theology of liberation or revolution. On the other hand, the same linear and logical thinking will say: Everything is destroyed in the judgment. The Kingdom of God is something absolutely new, God's gracious gift. There will be new heavens and a new earth where righteousness will dwell. Everything old is abolished. Thus human history, politics, etc. has no meaning, value, or interest.

As I see it, both views are biblically incorrect precisely because what the Bible shows us is a dialectical process. On one hand, history moves toward judgment and catastrophe, so that no continuity is possible, but on the other hand, and at the same time, history is extraordinarily important. And the thing which already shows history's importance is, shall we say, God's decision to write himself on the pages of human history. The note in Luke 2: 1–2 about the decree of Caesar Augustus and Cyrenius as governor of Syria is enough to remind us that human history is not without value and importance before God.

What does all this imply? First, there is always *one* history (not two, a secular and a sacred), made up of the conjunction, opposition, and contradiction of the independent work of man and the "relational" work of God. All history in every real and concrete event is an expression of this double force. There is the product of man's work. This is no ascent or progress but a multiplication of the results and capacities or potentialities of man. I am tempted to say that history will not end until all possible combinations between man's initiative and God's are exhausted, that is, until all man's initiatives are exhausted and can produce nothing new (God's initiatives being eternal). I might adopt a musical illustration, that of a theme and variations. The composition will end, history as a piece of music will stop, when no more variations are possible. I believe that this takes into account the relation between human invention and the basic theme of the alliance or covenant. And it all leads not to the Kingdom of God, but to the crisis provoked by the absolute contradiction between the vacuum achieved by man and the exclusive new thing of God. But this crisis (judgment) does not mean the annulment or insignificance of history. As in the dialectical crisis, no one factor is *suppressed*, but both are integrated into a synthesis. Thus all human history will enter into the heavenly Jerusalem.[4] On the one side is the theme of reconciliation, on the other that of the creation of the last city which is the perfect fulfillment (not the result) of all that man has attempted in the course of his history. Nothing of this history (collective or individual) is lost, but all of it is qualitatively transformed. There is a natural body and there is a spiritual body, but undoubtedly, if there had not been a natural body there would not be a spiritual body either. We can thus understand the revelation of the kingdom only in dialectical fashion.

These very summary examples are perhaps enough to show that, for me, only dialectical thinking can give a proper account of scriptural revelation, such revelation itself being fundamentally and intrinsically dialectical.

Dialectic in My Own Books

To speak of "my work" would be pretentious, and yet the sum of my books constitutes a whole consciously conceived as such. At root—to the extent that I became convinced on one side that it was impossible to make a unity of the study of modern society, and on the other that it was equally impossible to do a theological study without reference to the world in which one is—it became indispensable for me to find the link, and this could only be the dialectical process.

I found it impossible to join Christianity and the world into a single whole. From my very first writings I showed that there is no Christian politics, whether pursued by a Christian party or union, or Christian economics, or, epistemologically, Christian history, science, etc. In the first case, there can be only a kind of ideological covering, in the second, only a deformation of methods and results. Naturally, an ethics written by a Christian can be a Christian ethics, but acceptable only to Christians. Similarly a Christian can study history or biology, recognizing (like any scientist) what his presuppositions are and how they might very well affect his conclusions. Similarly a Christian can be a member of a union or a political party, playing a singular role and not pretending to be a Christian politician, which I have found from experience to be impossible and untenable.[5]

On the other hand it seemed no less certain to me that it is unacceptable to think of Christianity apart from the working reality of society, that it is unacceptable for the Christian to live a life by eternal principles without reference to this actual world. It would be idealistic and worthless to pretend either that Christianity can penetrate and modify the structures of society (and here I came across the analysis of the function of ideology according to Marx) or, conversely, that Christianity should be adapted to and modeled upon the needs, exigencies, and orientations of the world. This has always been done, even to the point that, politically, French Christianity became successively monarchist under Louis XIV, revolutionary in 1792, Napoleonic in 1800, republican in 1875, and was on the point of becoming socialist in 1950. The theologies of liberation and revolution seem to me to be simple proponents of a pure and simple adaptation of Christianity to circumstances. At the same time, it seemed impossible to me to proclaim that the world is lost and, conversely, that the church has no significance.

Thus I found myself forced to affirm both the independence of the analysis of contemporary society, and the specificity of theology, both the coherence and importance of the world in which we live and also the truth without common measure of the revelation in Christ—two factors both alien and yet also indissolubly bound to one another. The relation, then, could only be dialectical and critical. At the noetic level, we can only state the two contradictions, pushing the contradiction to the limit, and at the active level we can only introduce the dimension of mutual criticism, the world being critical of the church, and science being critical of theology, and conversely, as we should not forget, the church being critical of the world, and theology being critical of science. And to the extent that the synthesis, or the negation of the negation, or, in whatever form, the appearance of a new state can only be the product of history, there can be no question of presenting this synthesis in an arbitrary intellectual way in a single work which would correspond only to an appearance of response. I was thus led to work in two separate spheres, one historical and sociological, the other theological. This was in no sense a dispersion, nor the expression of diverse curiosities, but the fruit of essentially rigorous reflection. Each work would have to be exactly equal and as immune as possible from contamination by the other. As a sociologist I had to be realistic and specific, using exact methods, although here I had methodological quarrels and proceeded to contest certain methods. As a theologian I had to be equally intransigent, presenting as strict an interpretation of revelation as possible without concession to the spirit of the age.

If, however, dialectic is at issue, the whole must not be made up of two unrelated parts: there has to be correlation. The negative exists only in relation to a positive; the positive exists only in relation to a negative. The two play their parts reciprocally as in musical counterpoint. Hence it is perfectly possible to think of a correspondence between apparently unrelated books. There is counterpoint, for example, between *The Political Illusion* and *The Politics of God and the Politics of Man*, or *The Ethics of Freedom* and the exact dialectical counterpart of the two books on technology (*The Technological Society* and *The Technical System*). I have at once provided both an instrument of knowledge and the possibility of progression through a crisis. This crisis may actually be seen in our society, in the political and economic sphere as well as in the Christian and ecclesiastical. But it cannot have a positive outcome, and avoid sinking into incoherence and nonsense, unless there is a clear recognition of the two factors present. This is what I have tried to offer. In truth, however, my attempt seems to have failed: no one is using my studies in correlation with one another, so as to get at the heart of our crisis in a conscious manner, based on a Christian understanding of it; instead, they continue reacting unconsciously, using reflex not reflection, and adopting Christian positions on which no reflections has been done.

Having said this, I must note finally that dialectic does not merely operate between the two sections of my writing, but also functions as a double element: on one side, as that which comprehends or embraces some of my positions, and, on the other, as my most profound conviction regarding the actual situation.

In illustration of the first element, I might say that it is a dialectical attitude which leads us either to consider that man seems impotent in relation to structures and necessities but he should attempt all that can be attempted; or to affirm constantly that society, as an expression of determinisms and as the exclusion of freedom, must be unceasingly attacked but our efforts must all be toward maintaining this society, so that we must not give way to destructive anger but simply prevent society from ossifying; or to claim that all human enterprises are eminently relative and do not represent any supreme value but they should all be taken with absolute seriousness as if they did have supreme value; or to say that the values and morality produced by a human group are not really values or morality, whether natural, or absolute, or expressive of God, but we should defend, uphold, and practice them (whatever they are) because the group in question (and therefore man) cannot live without these values and this morality. Thus we are not to establish any rivalry between them and either the Christian truth, which is supposed to drive off the errors in other beliefs, or the exclusively good Christian morality, which ought to be substituted for other moralities. If it is a matter of setting up a dialectical contradiction, this is sound. If it is a matter of a judgmental attitude and a desire to eliminate, this is untenable.

In conclusion, let us look at the second element, my basic conviction regarding the actual situation. I will briefly sum up the issue.[6] If the technological system is, as I think I have shown, a total system which embraces all activities, which has its own logic, and which progressively assimilates all cultures, then there is no longer any dialectical factor in relation to it. It tends to become a totality, a unity. If, however, we believe that the dialectical process is indispensable to life and history, it is absolutely necessary that this dialectical factor exist. If the technological system is total, then this factor has to exist *outside* it. But only the transcendent can be outside it. For me, then, the transcendent is, in the concrete situation in which technology has put us, the necessary condition for the continuation of life, the unfolding of history, simply the existence of man as man. This transcendent, however, cannot be a self-existing and unknown one. It has to be a *revealed* transcendent if man is to have reason and opportunity to launch upon a dialectical course in spite of the autonomy and universality of technology. In saying that, I am in no sense engaging in apologetics, but simply pointing to the unavoidable result of the twofold flow of my research, sociological and theological.

NOTES

1. I tried to explain this in my commentary on Kings, *The Politics of God and the Politics of Man.*
2. A. Dumas, in *Théologies politique et vie de l'église* (1977), has clearly shown, e.g. the inadequacy of monism and dualism. "Dualism separates man from God and God from man. It is a structure of distance, whereas the Bible is a history of alliance. . . ." It is evident, however, that alliance occurs only between two that are at the same time distinct, different, and separated, and yet also united.
3. I have often insisted on the "as if . . ." in the life of Jesus. Jesus was no Harlequin, but the divine splendor was *veiled* in his lowly appearance and he constantly accepted suffering and then death *as if* he were not God.
4. Cf. *The Meaning of the City;* English ed. 1970.
5. I wrote all this as early as 1937 and repeated it in 1944: *Foi et vie et associations professionnelles protestantes.*
6. For an elaboration see my article "Dieu," *Revue des Études Théologiques et Religieuses de Montpellier* (1977).

Bibliography

David W. Gill

Preparation of a truly comprehensive bibliography of the writings of Jacques Ellul has been a challenging task, not only because of the sheer volume of Ellul's literary output, but also because his writings have appeared in so many different books and periodicals, and because many citations of his materials in previous bibliographies have proven to be unreliable. For this bibliography I have, in fact, collected 90 percent of the materials listed; the remaining citations are those I am virtually certain are correct.

Part I of the bibliography is divided into two sections. The first lists Ellul's books, in order of date of first publication. In the second section are Ellul's essays, articles, and reviews, listed alphabetically by title within each year; I have omitted from this section those items (about sixty citations) which I could not verify and examine, due to erroneous or incomplete information. I have also not listed Ellul's many brief "Liminaires" to issues of *Foi et Vie* (Paris), the bimonthly theological journal which he has edited since 1969.

Part II, the listing of secondary sources (primarily North American), is divided into three sections. Owing to the absence of published book-length discussions of Ellul's thought, serious students will want to consult the doctoral theses in the first section. The next section contains what I feel are the most substantial or interesting reviews of Ellul's books in their English-language editions; many other brief reviews and notices have been omitted. The third section lists books containing explicit reference to Ellul and articles dealing with Ellul's thought.

PART ONE: THE WORKS OF JACQUES ELLUL
Books

1936   *Étude sur l'évolution et la nature juridique du mancipium.* Thése pour le doctorat. Bordeaux: Imprimerie-Librairie Delmas, 1936.

1941   *Essai sur le recrutement de l'armée française aux XVIe et XVIIe siècles.* N.p.: Mémoires académie sciences morales, 1941.

1943   *Introduction à l'histoire de la discipline des Eglises Réformées de France.* Bordeaux: the author, 1943.

1946   *Le fondement théologique du droit.* Neuchâtel & Paris: Delachaux et Niestlé, 1946. *The Theological Foundation of Law.* Garden City, N.Y.: Doubleday, 1960; New York: Seabury, 1969. Translation Marguerite Wieser.

1948   *Présence au monde moderne.* Geneva: Roulet, 1948. *The Presence of the Kingdom.* Philadelphia: Westminster, 1951; New York: Seabury, 1967. Translation Olive Wyon. Introduction (Seabury ed.) William Stringfellow.

1951   *Histoire des institutions.* Paris: Presses Universitaires de France. Vol. I/II: *L'antiquité.* 1951–52. rev. ed., 1972. Vol. III: *Le moyen age.* 1953–56. Vol. IV: *XVIe–XVIIIe siècles.* 1956. Vol. V: *Le XIXe siècle (1789–1914).* 1956.

1952   *Le livre de Jonas.* Paris: Cahiers Bibliques de Foi et Vie, 1952. *The Judgment of Jonah.* Grand Rapids, Mich.: Eerdmans, 1971. Translation and preface G. W. Bromiley.

1953   *L'homme et l'argent.* Neuchâtel and Paris: Delachaux et Niestlé, 1953.

1954   *La technique ou l'enjeu du siècle.* Paris: Armand Colin, 1954. *The Technological Society.* New York: Knopf, rev. Amer. ed., 1964. Translation and introduction John Wilkinson. Foreword Robert K. Merton.

1962   *Propagandes.* Paris: Armand Colin, 1962. *Propaganda: The Formation of Men's Attitudes.* New York: Knopf, 1965. Translation Konrad Kellen and Jean Lerner. Introduction Konrad Kellen.

1964   *Fausse présence au monde moderne.* Paris: Les Bergers et les Mages, 1964. *False Presence of the Kingdom.* New York: Seabury, 1972. Translation C. Edward Hopkin.

Le vouloir et le faire: recherches éthiques pour les chrétiens. Introduction (première partie). Geneva: Labor et Fides, 1964. *To Will and To Do: An Ethical Research for Christians.* Philadelphia: Pilgrim, 1969. Translation C. Edward Hopkin. Foreword Waldo Beach.

1965   *L'illusion politique.* Paris: Robert Laffont, 1965; 2nd ed. with new postscript, 1977. *The Political Illusion.* New York: Knopf, 1967. Translation Konrad Kellen.

1966   *Exégèse des nouveaux lieux communs.* Paris: Calmann-Lévy, 1966. *A Critique of the New Commonplaces.* New York: Knopf, 1968. Translation Helen Weaver.

      Politique de Dieu, politiques de l'homme. Paris: Presses Universitaires de France, 1966. *The Politics of God and the Politics of Man.* Grand Rapids, Mich.: Eerdmans, 1972. Edited, translation, and preface G. W. Bromiley.

1967   *Histoire de la propagande.* Paris: Presses Universitaires de France, 1967; 2nd ed., 1976.

      Métamorphose du bourgeois. Paris: Calmann-Lévy, 1967.

1969   *Autopsie de la révolution.* Paris: Calmann-Lévy, 1969. *Autopsy of Revolution.* New York: Knopf, 1971. Translation Patricia Wolf.

      Violence: Reflections from a Christian Perspective. New York: Seabury, 1969. Translation Cecelia Gaul Kings. *Contre les violents.* Paris: Le Centurion, 1972.

1970   *The Meaning of the City.* Grand Rapids, Mich.: Eerdmans, 1970. Translation Dennis Pardee. Introduction John Wilkinson. *Sans feu ni lieu.* Paris: Gallimard, 1975.

      Prayer and Modern Man. New York: Seabury, 1970. Translation C. Edward Hopkin. *L'impossible prière.* Paris: Le Centurion, 1971.

1971   avec Charrier, Yves, *Jeunesse délinquante: une expérience en province.* Paris: Mercure de France, 1971.

1972   *De la révolution aux révoltes.* Paris: Calmann-Lévy, 1972.

      L'espérance oubliée. Paris: Gallimard, 1972. *Hope In Time of Abandonment.* New York: Seabury, 1973. Translation C. Edward Hopkin.

1973   *Éthique de la liberté.* Geneva: Labor et Fides, vol. I, 1973, vol.

II, 1975. *The Ethics of Freedom*. Grand Rapids, Mich.: Eerdmans, 1976. Edited and translation G. W. Bromiley.

Les nouveaux possédés. Paris: Arthème Fayard, 1973. *The New Demons*. New York: Seabury, 1975. Translation C. Edward Hopkin.

1975   *L'Apocalypse: architecture en mouvement*. Paris: Desclée, 1975. *Apocalypse: The Book of Revelation*. New York: Seabury, 1977. Translation George W. Schreiner.

Trahison de l'occident. Paris: Calmann-Lévy, 1975. *The Betrayal of the West*. New York: Seabury, 1978. Translation Matthew J. O'Connell.

1977   *Le système technicien*. Paris: Calmann-Lévy, 1977. *The Technological System*. New York: Seabury, 1980.

1979   *L'ideologie marxiste-chretienne*. Paris: Le Centurion, 1979.

1980   *L'empire du non sens (L'art dans la societe technicienne)*. Paris: Presses Universitaires de France, 1980.

Essays, Articles, and Reviews

1937   "Le fascisme, fils du libéralisme." *Esprit*, 1 Feb. 1937, pp. 761–97.

1938   "Note sur les impôts municipaux à Montpellier aux XIIIe et XIVe siècles," *Revue historique de droit français et étranger*. Ser. 4, year 17 (1938), 365–403.

1939   "Droit." *Foi et Vie*, 40 (Mar.–June 1939), 262–80.

1942   "Les communauté naturelles." In J. Ellul, L. Joubert, *et al.*, *Communauté*. Paris: Editions "Je sers," 1942, pp. 57–79.

1945   "Signification actuelle de la réforme." In M. Boegner and A. Siegfried, ed., *Protestantisme français*. Paris: Libraire Plon, 1945, pp. 137–65.

1946   "Chroniques des problèmes de civilisation." *Foi et Vie*, 45.6 (Sept.–Oct. 1946), 678–98.

"Problèmes de notre société." *Le Semeur*, 1946, pp. 407–26.

1947   "L'économie, maîtresse ou servante de l'homme." In J. Ellul, A. Bieler, *et al.*, *Pour une économie à la taille de l'homme*. Geneva: Roulet, 1947, pp. 43–58.

"Indications sur les taches actuelles des juristes chrétiens." *Le Semeur*, 1947, pp. 485–93.

"Note sur le procès Nuremberg." *Verbum Caro*, 1947.

"On demande un nouveau Karl Marx!" *Foi et Vie*, 46 (May 1947), 360–74.

"Le réalisme politique et réalisme chrétien: problèmes de civilisation, III." *Foi et Vie*, 46 (Nov.–Dec. 1947), 698–734.

"Vers un nouvel humanisme politique." In J. Ellul, P. Tournier, and R. Gillouin, *L'homme, mesure de toute chose*. Geneva: Centre d'études protestant, 1947, pp. 5–21.

1948 "The Situation in Europe." In W. A. Visser 'T. Hooft, ed., *Man's Disorder and God's Design*, vol. III: *The Church and the Disorder of Society*. The First Assembly of the World Council of Churches. London: SCM, 1948; New York: Harper & Bros., 1949, pp. 50–60.

1949 "Note problématique sur l'histoire de l'Église." *Foi et Vie*, 48 (July–Aug. 1949), 297–324.

1950 "Aspects de piété et de théologie médiévale." *Foi et Vie*, 49 (Nov.-Dec. 1950), 572–75.

"La Bible et la ville." *Foi et Vie*, 49 (Jan.–Feb. 1950), 4–19.

"L'humilité précède la gloire." In J. Ellul, E. Jeanneret, *et al.*, *Appel aux laics*. Geneva: Roulet (Les cahiers du renouveau III), 1950, pp. 29–42.

"Le mystère de l'histoire de l'Église." *Foi et Vie*, 49 (Sept.–Oct. 1950), 466–70.

"Notes sur les problèmes éthiques du rapport Kinsey." In *Das Menschenbild im Lichte des Evangeliums*. Festschrift für Emil Brunner. Zürich: Zwingli-Verlag, 1950, pp. 139–52; also in *Universitas* (1950), p. 1465ff.

"Protestantisme en Cultuur in het Frankrijk van nu." *Wending*, vol. 5, no. 10 (Dec. 1950), 552–62.

"Réflexion sur le monde de la nécessité." *Vie, Art, Cité* (Revue "suisse romande"), ser. 14, no. 1 (1950), 37–9.

"Urbanisme et théologie biblique." *Dieu vivant*, 16 (1950), 109–23.

1951 "Les fondements bibliques de notre responsibilité." *Foi et Vie*, 50 (1951). Repr. in *Actes et travaux du troisième congrès médico-social protestant*. Bordeaux: Cahors, Impr. Coneslant, 1952.

"Le pauvre." *Foi et Vie*, 50 (Mar.–Apr. 1951), 105–27.

1952   "L'argent." *Etudes théologiques et religieuses*, vol. 37, no. 4 (1952), 25–66.

"Les causes sociales et culturelles des divisions des églises." *Foi et Vie*, 51 (Sept.–Oct. 1952), 393–430. Partially repr. as "The Cultural and Social Factors Influencing Church Division," in *Ecumenical Review*, 4 (Apr. 1952), 269–75, and in C. H. Dodd, G. R. Cragg, and J. Ellul, *Social and Cultural Factors in Church Divisions*. New York: World Council of Churches, 1952, pp. 19–25.

"Propagande et démocratie." *Revue française de science politique*, 2 (July–Sept. 1952), 474–504.

"Strategie der Kirche und Soziologe." *Reformatio* (Zeitschrift für evangelische Kultur und Politik), 1 (1952), 263–76.

1953   "Thèse sur la notion de souveraineté nationale." *Foi et Vie*, 52 (1953), 306–10.

1954   "Position des Eglises protestantes a l'égard de la famille." In R. Prigent, ed., *Renouveau des idées sur la famille*. Paris: Universitaires de France, Cahiers de "Travaux et Documents," no. 18, 1954, pp. 269–74.

"Sur le pessimisme chrétien." *Foi et Vie*, 53 (Mar.–Apr. 1954), 164–80.

1956   "La publicité: sa signification et ses dangers." *Coopération*, 26 (Mar. 1956), 11–14.

1957   "Information and Propaganda." *Diogenes: International Review of Philosophy and Humanistic Studies*, no. 18 (Summer 1957), 61–77.

"Über die soziologischen Voraussetzungen des modernen Menschen." *Evangelische Theologie*, 1957, pp. 516–28.

1958   "La crise de l'opinion et la propagande." *Foi et Vie*, 57 (Jan.–Feb. 1958), 4–23.

"En plaine morale (l'homme et les techniques)." *Le Semeur*, 56 (1958), 2–5.

"Modern Myths." *Diogenes*, no. 23 (Fall 1958), 23–40.

1959   "Actualité de la Réforme." *Foi et Vie*, 58 (Mar.–Apr. 1959), 39–64.

"The Obstacles to Communication Arising from Propaganda Habits." *The Student World*, no. 52 (1959), 401–10.

"Propositions concernant l'attitude chrétienne envers le droit."
Foi et Vie, 58 (Jan.–Feb. 1959), 32–43.

1960 "Christianisme et droit. Recherches américaines." *Les archives de philosophie du droit*, no. 5 (1960), 27–35.

"Notes en vue d'une éthique du temps et du lieu pour les chrétiens." *Foi et Vie*, 59 (Sept.–Oct. 1960), 354–74.

"Les relations de l'éthique et de la coopération internationale dans les groupes de culture en France." In Bart Landeer, ed., *Ethical Values in International Decision-Making*. The Hague: Nijhoff, 1960, pp. 84–93.

"La technique et les premiers chapitres de la Genèse." *Foi et Vie*, 59 (Mar.–Apr. 1960), 97–113.

1961 "Essai sur la signification philosophique des Réformes actuelles de l'enseignement du droit." *Les archives de philosophie du droit*, no. 6 (1961), 1–18.

"L'homme occidental en 1970." *Bulletin Sédéis*, 1961. Repr. in Bertrand de Jouvenal, ed., *Futuribles: Studies in Conjecture*. Geneva: Droz, vol. I, 1963, pp. 27–64.

1962 "Evangelisation und Propaganda." *Wort: Das missionarische Organ der Arbeitsgemeinschaft für Volkmission*, 1962, pp. 47–50.

"Realité sociale et théologie du droit." In Thomas Würtenberger, ed., *Existenz und Ordnung*. Festscrift für Erik Wolf. Frankfurt am Main: V. Klostermann, 1962, pp. 36–61.

"La sens de la liberté chez Saint Paul." *Foi et Vie*, 61 (May–June 1962), 3–20.

"The Technological Order." *Technology and Culture*, 3 (Fall 1962), 394–421. Papers from the Encyclopaedia Britannica Conference on the Technological Order, Mar. 11–16, 1962, Santa Barbara, Calif. Repr. as Carl F. Stover, ed., *The Technological Order*. Detroit: Wayne State University Press, 1962. Ellul's essay repr. in part as "Ideas of Technology." In Fred H. Knelman, ed., *1984 and All That*. Belmont, Calif.: Wadsworth, 1971, pp. 11–20.

1963 "De la signification des relations publiques dans la société technicienne." *L'Année sociologique*, 1963, pp. 69–152.

"Désacralisation et resacralisation dans le monde moderne." *Le Semeur*, no. 2 (1963), 24–36. "Über das Heilige in der modernen Welt." *Monatschrift für Pastoraltheologie*, 53 (1964), 11–25.

"La propagande et la démocratie." *Res Publica*, 5 (1963–64), 323–33.

"Sur l'artificialité du droit et le droit d'exception (Part 1)." *Les archives de philosophie du droit*, 8 (1963), 21–33.

1964   "Max Weber: *L'éthique protestante et l'esprit du capitalisme.*" *Bulletin Sédéis*, vol. 905, supp. 1 (20 Dec. 1964), 4–17.

"Propagande et personnalisation du pouvoir." In *La personnalisation du pouvoir*. Paris: Presses Universitaires de France, 1964, pp. 331–45.

1965   "Le grand inquisiteur. L'amour et l'ordre." *Cahiers du Sud*, 40 (Aug.–Oct. 1965), 44–52. "Love and Order." *Katallagete*, 9 (Summer 1976), 28–33.

"Is It A Dream or A Nightmare?" *Saturday Review*, 48 (6 Feb. 1965), 58–9. Excerpt from *Technological Society*.

"Law as Representation of Value." *Natural Law Forum*, 10 (1965), 54–66. "Reflexions sur le droit cours representation." In *Philosophy and Christianity: Essays Dedicated to Prof. Herman Dooyeweerd*. Kampen: J. H. Kok, 1965, pp. 262–76.

"Réflexions sur l'ambivalence du progrès technique." *La revue administrative*, year 18 (July–Aug. 1965), 380–91.

"Sur l'artificialité du droit et le droit d'exception (Part 2)." *Les archives de philosophie du droit*, no. 10 (1965), 191–207.

1966   Preface. P. Fouchier, *De l'Église du Christ á la place publique*. Paris: Les Bergers et les Mages, 1966.

"Réponse à M. Marle au sujet de l'illusion politique." *Revue française de science politique*, 16 (1966), 87–100.

1967   "Le facteur déterminant des problèmes et de l'évolution de la société contemporaine: la technique." *Sciences*, Mar.–Apr. 1967, pp. 28–44.

"Information et vie privée: perspectives." *Foi et Vie*, 66 (Nov.–Dec. 1967), 52–66.

"Jeunesse inadaptée." *Le Monde*, 2 Sept. 1967, p. 10.

"Rappels et réflexions sur une théologie de l'état." In J. Jullien, P. l'Hullier, and J. Ellul, *Les chrétiens et l'état*. Paris: Maison Mame, 1967, pp. 129–81.

"Reflections on Leisure." *Interplay*, 1 (Dec. 1967), 51–56.

"La responsabilité de la société dans la guérison du malade." In J. Ellul, P. Tournier, *et al.*, *Dynamique de la guérison*. 8ᵉ Congrès medico-social protestant de langue française, Cannes, 1967. Neuchâtel and Paris: Delachaux et Niestlé, 1967, pp. 60–78.

"Technique et civilisation." *Terre entière* 1967; "Technik und Zivilisation," *Dokumente*, 1968, pp. 119–28.

"The Technological Revolution and its Moral and Political Consequences." In Johannes B. Metz, ed., *Concilium. The Evolving World and Theology*. New York: Paulist, 1967, pp. 97–107.

"The Technological Society." In Bernard Rosenberg, ed., *Analyses of Contemporary Society*, vol. II. New York: Thos. Crowell, 1967, pp. 1–45; chap. 5 from *Technological Society*.

1968   "Absolutisme." In *Encyclopaedia Universalis*, vol. I (1968), pp. 39–41.

"Between Chaos and Paralysis." *The Christian Century*, 85 (5 June 1968), 747–50.

"Cain, the Theologian of 1969." *Katallagete*, 2 (Winter 1968–69), 4–7.

"Jesus Christ." *La Table Ronde*, 1968, 19–20.

"Monarchie." In *Encyclopaedia Universalis*, vol. XI (1968), pp. 213–17.

"Notes innocentes sur la 'question herméneutique.'" In *L'Evangile hier et aujourd'hui*. Melanges offerts au Prof. Franz J. Leenhardt. Geneva: Labor et Fides, 1968, pp. 181–90.

"The Psychology of a Rebellion, May–June 1968." *Interplay*, 2 (Dec. 1968), 23–27. Repr. in G. A. Kelly and C. W. Brown, ed., *Struggles in the State*. New York: J. Wiley, 1970, pp. 496–506.

"Rapports présentés par M. Ellul." In *Églises Réformées de France: évangelisation information*, no. 1 (Jan.–Feb. 1968), 74–92.

"Technique, Institutions, and Awareness." *The American Behavioral Scientist*, 11 (July–Aug. 1968), 38–42.

"You Can't Act Without Getting Your Hands Dirty." *The At-*

lantic Monthly, 221 (May 1968), 56–9. Repr. from *A Critique of the New Commonplaces.*

1969 "Can French University Reform Succeed?" *Interplay*, 3 (1969), 16–18.

"Comment nommer la société actuelle?" *Recherche sociale*, 1969, pp. 49–70.

"L'Inadaptation des jeunes, signe d'une société?" *Economie et humanisme* no. 185 (1969), 26–34.

"L'Information dans la société technicienne." *Revue générale Belge*, Jan. 1969, pp. 45–62.

"La jeunesse, force révolutionnaire?" *La Table Ronde* 1969, pp. 150–68.

Preface. A Chouraqui, *Psaumes.* Paris: Presses Universitaires de France, 1969.

1970 "Ellul Replies on Violence." *Christianity and Crisis*, 30 (19 Oct. 1970), 221.

"From Jacques Ellul." *Katallagete* 2 (Winter–Spring 1970), 5–6. Also in James Holloway, ed., *Introducing Jacques Ellul.* Grand Rapids, Mich.: Eerdmans, 1970, pp. 5–6.

"L'Information aliénante." *Économie et humanisme*, no. 192 (Mar.–Apr. 1970), 43–52.

"Mirror of These Ten Years." *The Christian Century*, 87 (18 Feb. 1970), 200–204. Repr. in *Theological Crossings*, D. Peerman and A. Geyer, ed. Grand Rapids, Mich.: Eerdmans, 1971, pp. 41–50.

"Les religions séculières." *Foi et Vie*, 69 (Sept.–Dec. 1970), 62–78.

1971 "Letter to the Editor." *Playboy*, Mar. 1971, pp. 55–56.

"L'Irréductibilité du droit à une théololgie de l'histoire." In E. Castelli, ed., *Révélation et Histoire.* Paris: Montaigne, 1971, pp. 51–69.

"Le néo-romantisme moderne." *Contrepoint*, no. 4 (Summer 1971), 45–60.

"Théologique dogmatique et spécificité du christianisme." *Foi et Vie*, 70 (Mar.–Aug. 1971), 139–54.

"Watch and Pray." *Eternity*, 22 (Oct. 1971), 26–27, 43–44. Repr. from *Prayer and Modern Man.*

1972 "Conformism and the Rationale of Technology." Jacques Ellul interviewed by G. R. Urban; originally broadcast over Radio Free Europe, 1970–71. In George R. Urban and Michael Glenny, *Can We Survive Our Future?* New York: St. Martin's, 1972, pp. 89–102.

"Diritto E. Storia." *Revista Internazionale di Filosofía del Diritto*, 50 (Oct.–Dec. 1972), 675–84.

"L'Interférence du politique dans le christianisme protestant d'aujourd'hui." *Contrepoint*, no. 6 (Spring 1972), 25–37.

"Notes préliminaires sur l'Église et pouvoirs." *Foi et Vie*, 71 (Mar.–June 1972), 2–24.

"Témoignage et société technicienne." *La Testimonianza. Archivo di Filosofía* (Padua), 1972, pp. 441–55.

"Work and Calling." *Katallagete* 4 (Fall–Winter 1972), 8–16. Repr. in J. Y. Holloway and W. D. Campbell, ed., *Callings*. New York: Paulist, 1974, pp. 18–44.

1973 "A Little Debate about Technology: Replying to Thomas G. Donnelly." *The Christian Century*, 90 (27 June 1973), 706–7.

"Les antinomies de la foi chrétienne et du progrès." *Lumiére et Vie*, 22 (Jan.–Mar. 1973), 69–80.

Reviews of Jürgen Moltmann, *L'Espérance en action*; Heinz-Dietrich Wendland, *Éthique du Nouveau Testament*; and Peter Brown, *La vie de St. Augustin. Foi et Vie*, 72 (Sept.–Dec. 1973), 98–103.

"Search for an Image." *The Humanist*, Nov.–Dec. 1973, pp. 22–25.

"Social Change." In Carl F. H. Henry, ed., *Baker's Dictionary of Christian Ethics*. Grand Rapids, Mich.: Baker, 1973, pp. 629–32.

"Du texte au sermon: les talents, Matthieu 25:13–30." *Études théologiques et religieuses*, vol. 48, no. 2 (1973), 125–38.

"With a View toward Assessing the Facts." *New York Times*, 1 July 1973.

1974 "Anarchie et christianisme." *Contrepoint*, no. 15 (1974), 157–73.

"De la mort." *Foi et Vie*, 73 (Mar. 1974), 1–14.

"Loi et sacré, droit et divin: de la loi sacrée au droit divin." In *Le Sacré*. Paris: Aubier, 1974, pp. 179–99.

"Le rapport de l'homme à la création selon la Bible." *Foi et Vie*, 73 (Sept.–Dec. 1974), 137–55.

"Réflexions sur le changement des études de théologie." *Études théologiques et religieuses*, vol. 49, no. 4 (1974), 489–97.

Review of Jacques Sarano, *Le défi et l'espérance*. *Foi et Vie*, 73 (Mar. 1974), 73–4.

" 'The World' in the Gospels." *Katallagete*, 6 (Spring 1974), 16–23.

1975   "Coda for Christians." *Katallagete*, 6 (Fall 1975), 33–44. Repr. from *The New Demons*.

Review of Marie-Joseph le Guillou, O.P., *Le Mystère du père*. *Contrepoint*, no. 16 (1975), 170–75.

Review of Jürgen Moltmann, *Traduction historique et politique de Évangile*. *Foi et Vie*, 74 (Dec. 1975), 112–14.

1976   "Érôs et agapé." *Foi et Vie*, 75 (Mar.–Apr. 1976), 62–81.

"Et le reste." *Foi et Vie*, 75 (Mar.–Apr. 1976), 93–100.

"Problems of Sociological Method." *Social Research*, 43 (Spring 1976), 6–24.

Review of Pierre Daix, *Le Socialisme du silence*. *Foi et Vie*, 75 (Dec. 1976), 131–34.

"Sur une lecture matérialiste des évangiles." *Foi et Vie*, 75 (Dec. 1976), 20–47.

1977   with E. Kressmann and J. Baubérot. "Bibliographie sur les problèmes liés à l'écologie." *Foi et Vie*, 76 (Apr. 1977), 156–66.

"Dieu." *Études théologiques et religieuses*, vol. 52, no. 4 (1977), 471–87.

"Impressions d'Israël." *Foi et Vie*, 76 (Aug. 1977), 1–72.

"Réflexions sur *Foi et Vie*." *Foi et Vie*, 76 (Dec. 1977), 3–6.

1978   "Les chrétiens et la socialisme." *Contrepoint*, 25 (1978), 37–50.

"Karl Barth and Us." *Sojourners*, 7 (Dec. 1978), 22–24.

"Notre Père. . . ." *Foi et Vie*, 77 (June 1978), 24–29.

1979   "Ideas: Jacques Ellul." Jacques Ellul interviewed (Oct.–Nov. 1979) in five-part radio program "Ideas" over Canadian Broadcasting Corporation by Bill Vanderberg and others. Information on tapes or transcripts from "Ideas," Box 500, Terminal A, Toronto, Ontario, Canada M5W 1E6.

Part Two: Secondary Sources

Dissertations and Theses (Unpublished)

Christians, Clifford G. *Jacques Ellul's "La Technique" in a Communications Context.* Ph.D. diss., University of Illinois, 1974.

Gill, David. W. *The Word of God in the Ethics of Jacques Ellul.* Ph.D. diss., University of Southern California, 1979.

Ihara, Randall H. *Redeeming the Time: Theology, Technology, and Politics in the Thought of Jacques Ellul.* Ph.D. diss., University of Tennessee, 1975–76.

Matheke, David G. *To Will and To Do God's Word: An Examination of the Christian Meaning of the Works of Jacques Ellul.* D. Div. diss., Vanderbilt Divinity School, 1972–73.

Menninger, David C. *Technique and Politics: The Political Thought of Jacques Ellul.* Ph.D. diss., University of California, Riverside, 1974.

Miller, Duane R. *The Effect of Technology upon Humanization in the Thought of Lewis Mumford and Jacques Ellul.* Ph.D. diss., Boston University, 1970–71.

Mulkey, Robert C. *The Theology of Politics in the Writings of Jacques Ellul.* Th.D. diss., Southern Baptist Theological Seminary, 1973.

Ray, Ronald R. *A Critical Examination of Jacques Ellul's Christian Ethic.* Ph.D. diss., University of St. Andrews (Scotland), 1973.

Temple, Katherine C. *The Task of Jacques Ellul: A Proclamation of Biblical Faith as Requisite for Understanding the Modern Project.* Ph.D. diss., McMaster University, Hamilton, Ont., Canada, 1976.

Book Reviews

Apocalypse: The Book of Revelation
   Études théologiques et religieuses, vol. 52, no. 4 (1977), 577–79, Michel Bouttier.
   Princeton Seminary Bulletin, n.s., 1 (1977), 155–57, Rodney L. Peterson.
Autopsy of Revolution
   Christian Advocate, 16 (9 Nov. 1972), 11–12, George Schreiner.
   Harper's, 244 (Apr. 1972), 96–101, Richard Shickel.
   National Review, 24 (4 Feb. 1972), 104–5; Gerhart Niemeyer.

The Betrayal of the West
> *Canadian Forum*, Oct.-Nov. 1978, pp. 42–44, Edgar Z. Friedenberg.
>
> *Christianity Today*, 24 (4 Jan. 1980), 38–39, Harold O.J. Brown. *New Oxford Review*, Apr. 1979, pp. 15–17, Stephen J. Tonsor. *Sojourners*, 8 (Oct. 1979), 26–29, Dale W. Brown.

A Critique of the New Commonplaces
> *The Christian Century*, 85 (13 Nov. 1968), 1436, Ernest L. Snodgrass.
>
> *Newsweek*, 71 (13 May 1968), 104, Saul Maloff.

The Ethics of Freedom
> *Christianity Today*, 20 (10 Sept. 1976), 1220–22, David W. Gill.
>
> *Études théologiques et religieuses*, vol. 51, no. 3 (1976), 417–20; vol. 51, no. 4 (1976), 542–44, Phippe Rochette.
>
> *Journal of Religion*, Jan. 1978, p. 77, James M. Gustafson.
>
> *Reformed Journal*, 27 (Feb. 1977), 26–27, Jay Van Hook.

False Presence of the Kingdom
> *The Christian Century*, 89 (4 Oct. 1972), 989–90, Donald W. Dayton.
>
> *Religion In Life*, 42 (Summer 1973), 283–84, Duane R. Miller.

Hope In Time of Abandonment
> *The Christian Century*, 90 (12 Sept. 1973), 891–92, James A. Moran.
>
> *Christianity Today*, 17 (28 Sept. 1973), 31–34, Harold O. J. Brown.
>
> *Christian Scholar's Review*, vol. 4, no. 2 (1974), 154–55, Jay M. Van Hook.
>
> *Religion In Life*, 43 (Autumn 1974), 379–81, James Y. Holloway.
>
> *Religious Studies*, 10 (Sept. 1974), 362–63, David A. Pailin.
>
> *Review and Expositor*, 70 (Fall 1973), 534–35, Robert C. Mulkey.

The Judgment of Jonah
> *Duke Divinity Review*, 37 (Fall 1974), 172–74, L. R. Bailey.
>
> *Interpretation*, 26 (Jan. 1972), 98–99, George M. Landes.
>
> *Lutheran Quarterly*, 24 (Aug. 1972), 328–29, E. M. Carlson.

The Meaning of the City
> *The Banner*, 16 July 1971, pp. 24–25, Lester De Koster.
>
> *The Christian Century*, 88 (3 Mar. 1971), 299, Walter G. Muelder.
>
> *Christian Scholar's Review*, 1 (Winter 1971), 155–56, Lon D. Randall.

Christianity Today, 15 (4 Dec. 1970), 18–20, David L. McKenna.
Commonweal, 94 (9 July 1971), 351–57, Harvey Cox.
Dialog, 10 (Winter 1971), 74–76, Philip A. Quanbeck.
Journal of the American Academy of Religion, 40 (Mar. 1972), 118–22, Gibson Winter.
Journal for the Scientific Study of Religion, 12 (Mar. 1973), 120–21, Jeffrey Hadden.

The New Demons
American Scholar, 45 (Spring 1976), 310–12, Robert Nisbet.
The Banner, 27 (Aug. 1976), 24, Jay Van Hook.
Christianity Today, 20 (7 May 1976), 32–33, David W. Gill.
Études théologiques et religieuses, vol. 48, no. 4 (1973), 554–56, A. Gounelle.
Foi et Vie, 73 (Mar. 1974), 86–89, E. Cruse.
Psychology Today, 9 (Nov. 1975), 18–19, Richard L. Rubenstein.
Reformed Journal, 26 (Mar. 1976), 28–30, Robert K. Johnston.
Sojourners, 5 (Nov. 1976), 36–37, Dale W. Brown.

The Political Illusion
Atlantic Monthly, May 1967, p. 133, Oscar Handlin.
Commonweal, 87 (13 Oct. 1967), 56–57, Joseph L. Walsh.
New York Times Book Review, 14 May 1967, p. 28, Gerald Sykes.
Saturday Review, 50 (29 Apr. 1967), 27–28, Saul K. Padover.

The Politics of God and the Politics of Man
Christian Scholar's Review, vol. 3, no. 2 (1973), 172–73, David A. Hubbard.
Interpretation, 27 (Apr. 1973), 238–40, Richard S. Hanson.
Journal of Biblical Literature, 92 (Sept. 1973), 470–71, Walter Brueggemann.
Lutheran Quarterly, 24 (Nov. 1972), 420–21, George O. Evenson.

Prayer and Modern Man
Christian Scholar's Review, vol. 2, no. 4 (1973), 378–79, Nigel Kerr.
Études théologiques et religieuses, vol. 47, no. 4 (1972), 516–17, Daniel Lys.
Foi et Vie, 71 (Jan. 1972), 76–79, Alain Georges Martin.
Interpretation, 26 (Jan. 1972), 117–18, Richard Ray.
Journal of the American Academy of Religion, 40 (Mar. 1972), 118–22, Gibson Winter.

Presence of the Kingdom
Scottish Journal of Theology, vol. 5, no. 3 (1952), 321–24, J. K. S. Reid.

Theology Today, 10 (Jan. 1954), 568–69, Fred Denbeaux.
Propaganda: The Formation of Men's Attitudes
    America, 114 (8 Jan. 1966), 48, J. J. Karch.
    American Sociological Review, 29 (Oct. 1964), 793–94, Daniel Lerner.
    Book Week, 28 Nov. 1965, pp. 5, 25, 27, Marshall McLuhan.
    The Nation, 202 (4 Apr. 1966), 397–98, Christopher Lasch.
    New York Times Book Review, 6 Mar. 1966, p. 47, Seymour M. Lipset.
    Saturday Review, 48 (25 Dec. 1965), 37, John Hohenberg.
The Technological Society
    The Christian Century, 90 (17 Jan. 1973), 65–68, Thomas G. Donnelly.
    Commonweal, 81 (2 Oct. 1964), 49, John P. Sisk.
    Harper's 229 (Oct. 1964), 124, Paul Pickerel.
    The Nation, 199 (19 Oct. 1964), 249–52, Robert Theobald.
    New Statesman, 69 (23 Apr. 1965), 654, W. G. Runciman.
    New York Times Book Review, 18 Oct. 1964, pp. 32–34, Raymond Williams.
    Our Generation, Mar. 1967, pp. 105–13, George C. Benello.
    Saturday Review, 47 (26 Sept. 1964), 48, Harry H. Ransom.
    Scientific American, 212 (Feb. 1965), 125–28, A. Rupert Hall.
Theological Foundation of Law
    Christianity Today, 5 (5 Dec. 1960),40–41, C. Gregg Singer.
    Concordia Theological Monthly, 32 (Mar. 1961), 186–87, A. C. Piepkorn.
    Encounter, 31 (Summer 1970), 286–87, Daniel Cobb.
    Journal of Bible and Religion, 29 (July 1961), 257–58, L. H. DeWolf.
    Lutheran Quarterly, 13 (Aug. 1961), 274–75, Paul L. Holmer.
    Scottish Journal of Theology, 15 (Sept. 1962), 305–10, Arnold T. Ehrhardt.
To Will and To Do
    Saturday Review, 52 (13 Dec. 1969), 40, T. F. Driver.
Violence
    The Center Magazine, 2 (July 1969), 21–25, Hallock Hoffman.
    The Christian Century, 86 (24 Sept. 1969), 1223, Martin Marty.
    Commonweal, 91 (23 Jan. 1970), 459, Anne Fremantle.
    Dialog, 8 (Autumn 1969), 308, William H. Jennings.
    Ecumenical Review, 23 (Apr. 1971), 188–90, M. M. Thomas.
    Journal for the Scientific Study of Religion, 10 (Spring 1971), 57–58, Henry Carsch.

Books and Articles on Ellul

Christians, Clifford G. "Jacques Ellul and Democracy's 'Vital Information' Premise." *Journalism Monographs*, 45 (Aug. 1976), 1–42.

_____. "Jacques Ellul's Concern with the Amorality of Contemporary Communications." *Communications: Internationale Zeitschrift für Kommunikationsforschung*, 3 (Jan. 1977), 62–80.

_____, and Michael Real. "Jacques Ellul's Contributions to Critical Media Theory." *Journal of Communication*, 29 (Winter 1979), 83–93.

Cox, Harvey. *The Seduction of the Spirit*. New York: Touchstone, 1973, pp. 69–77.

_____. "The Ungodly City: A Theological Response to Jacques Ellul." *Commonweal* 94 (9 July 1971), 351–57.

De Rubertis, Kim. "In Defense of Dubos and Ellul." *Civil Engineering*, 42 (Dec. 1972), 51–53.

Despland, Michel. "Le christianisme en tant que religion." *Studies in Religion/Sciences Religieuses*, vol. 4, no. 3 (1974–75), 248–59.

Donnelly, Thomas G. "In Defense of Technology." *The Christian Century*, 90 (17 Jan. 1973), 65–69.

Eddy, William O. "Of Techné and Humanitas." *Phi Kappa Phi Journal*, 55 (Fall 1975), 17–25.

Eller, Vernard. "A Voice on Vocation: The Contribution of Jacques Ellul." *The Reformed Journal*, 29 (May 1979), 16–21.

_____. "Four Who Remember: Kierkegaard, the Blumhardts, Ellul, and Muggeridge." *Katallagete*, 3 (Spring 1971), 6–12.

_____. "How Jacques Ellul Reads the Bible." *The Christian Century*, 89 (29 Nov. 1972), 1212-15.

_____. "The Polymath Who Knows Only One Thing." *Brethren Life and Thought*, 18 (Spring 1973), 77–84; also in *The Lutheran Forum*, Aug. 1973, pp. 16–21. Repr. in *The Wittenburg Door*, no. 22 (Dec. 1974-Jan. 1975), 8–12; and in *Journal MPL (Minister's Personal Library)*, vol. 1, no. 2 (1979), 3–9.

Fager, Charles. "Jacques Ellul: An Introductory Review." *New Age*, Dec. 1976, pp. 50–55.

_____. "Marching in Selma While Reading Ellul." *Sojourners*, 6 (June 1977), 9–11.

_____. "Searching: Dan Berrigan Revisits Scripture." *National Catholic Reporter*, 9 (22 Dec. 1972), 5–6.

Ferkiss, Victor C. *Technological Man: The Myth and the Reality*. New York: New American Library, Mentor Books, 1969.

Florman, Samuel C. "Anti-Technology: The New Myth." *Civil Engineering*, 42 (Jan. 1972), 68–70.

———. *The Existential Pleasures of Engineering*. New York: St. Martin's, 1976.

———. "In Praise of Technology." *Harper's*, 251 (Nov. 1975), 53–72.

Gill, David W. "Activist and Ethicist: Meet Jacques Ellul." *Christianity Today*, 20 (10 Sept. 1976), 1220–22.

———. "A Study in Contrasts: Bennett and Ellul." *Radix*, 8 (July-Aug. 1976), 6.

———. "Prophet in the Technological Wilderness." *Catholic Agitator*, Oct. 1976, pp. 3–4.

Gorman, William. "Jacques Ellul: A Prophetic Voice." *The Center Magazine*, 1 (1968), 34–37.

Grounds, Vernon C. *Revolution and the Christian Faith*. Philadelphia: Lippincott, 1971.

Guinness, Os. "The Critical Voice of the Seventies." In his *The Dust of Death* (Downers Grove, Ill.: InterVarsity Press, 1973), pp. 131–37.

Gustafson, James M. *Christ and the Moral Life*. New York: Harper & Row, 1968, pp.17–29.

Heddendorf, Russell. "The Christian World of Jacques Ellul." *Christian Scholar's Review*, vol. 2, no. 4 (1973), 291–307.

Hillerdal, Gunnar. *Gehorsam Gegen Gott und Menschen*. Göttingen; Vandenhoeck and Ruprecht, 1955.

Holloway, James Y., ed. *Introducing Jacques Ellul*. Grand Rapids, Mich.: Eerdmans, 1970. Orig. pub. in *Katallagete*, 2 (Winter-Spring 1970). Essays by James Y. Holloway, Will D. Campbell, Gabriel Vahanian, Christopher Lasch, Julius Lester, Stephen Rose, William Stringfellow, James W. Douglass, James Branscome, and John Wilkinson, with a brief note "From Jacques Ellul."

Holmes, Arthur. "Human Variables and Natural Law." In Clifton Orlebeke and Lewis Smedes, ed., *God and the Good*. Grand Rapids, Mich.: Eerdmans, 1975, pp. 63–79.

Hunter, Robert. *The Enemies of Anarchy*. Toronto: McClelland & Stewart, 1970, pp. 134–54.

Kuhns, William. *The Post-Industrial Prophets*. New York: Weybright and Talley, 1971, pp. 82–115.

Logan, James. "An Ethics for Modern Noah." *Sojourners*, 6 (June 1977), 13–15.

Maddox, John. *The Doomsday Syndrome*. New York: McGraw-Hill, 1972.

Marty, Martin E. "The Protestant for this Summer." *National Catholic Reporter*, 6 (3 July 1970), 17–18.

McFerran, Douglass D. "The Cult of Jacques Ellul." *America*, 124 (6 Feb. 1971), 122–24.

Menninger, David C. "Jacques Ellul: A Tempered Profile." *The Review of Politics*, 37 (Apr. 1975), 235–46.

Middelmann, Udo. *Pro-Existence*. Downers Grove, Ill.: InterVarsity Press, 1974.

Miller, Duane R. "Watergate and the Thought of Jacques Ellul." *The Christian Century*, 90 (26 Sept. 1973), 943–46.

Minnema, Theodore. "Evil in the Thought of Jacques Ellul." *Reformed Journal*, 23 (May-June 1973), 17–20.

Mitcham, Carl, and Robert Mackey. "Jacques Ellul and the Technological Society." *Philosophy Today*, 15 (Summer 1971), 102–22.

Nisbet, Robert A. "The Grand Illusion: An Appreciation of Jacques Ellul." *Commentary*, 50 (Aug. 1970), 40–44.

Pickerel, Paul. "Heading toward Postcivilization: Boulding, Ellul, Snow, Murdoch, Bellow." *Harper's*, 229 (Oct. 1964), 122–26.

Ray, Ronald R. "Jacques Ellul's Innocent Notes on Hermeneutics." *Interpretation*, 33 (July 1979), 268–82.

Ritterbush, Philip C., ed. *Technology as Institutionally Related to Human Values*. Washington, D.C.: Acropolis Books, 1974.

Rose, Stephen. "Bethge's Monument." *Christianity and Crisis*, 30 (20 July 1970), 154–55.

Shorter, Edward. "Industrial Society in Trouble: Some Recent Views." *The American Scholar*, 40 (Spring 1971), 334–36.

Shriver, Donald W. "Man and His Machines: Four Angles of Vision." *Technology and Culture*, 13 (Oct. 1972), 531–55.

Sklair, Leslie. "Opposition to Science and Technology." *Comparative Studies in Society and History*, 13 (Apr. 1971), 217–35.

Stover, Carl F., ed. *The Technological Order*. Detroit: Wayne State University Press, 1963.

Stringfellow, William. "Jacques Ellul: Layman as Moral Theologian." *The Messenger*, 3 Dec. 1970, pp. 25–28.

Van Hook, Jay. "The Burden of Jacques Ellul." *The Reformed Journal* 26 (Dec. 1976), 13–17.

Walters-Bugbee, Christopher. "The Politics of Revelation." *Sojourners*, 6 (June 1977), 5–8.

Wheeler, Harvey. "Means, Ends, and Human Institutions." *The Nation* 202 (2 Jan. 1967), 9–16.

Wilkinson, John. "The Divine Persuasion." *The Center Magazine*, 3 (May 1970), 11–17.

———. "The Quantitative Society." *The Center Magazine*, 2 (July 1969), 64–71.

———, ed. *Technology and Human Values*. Santa Barbara, Calif.: The Center for the Study of Democratic Institutions, 1966.

Winner, Langdon. *Autonomous Technology: Technics-out-of-Control as a Theme in Political Thought*. Cambridge, Mass.: MIT Press, 1977.

Wogaman, J. Philip. *A Christian Method of Moral Judgment*. Philadelphia: Westminster, 1976.

Wolterstorff, Nicholas. "More on Vocation." *The Reformed Journal*, 29 (May 1979), 20–23.

Woodruff, Michael. "Who Is Jacques Ellul?" *His*, 31 (Nov. 1971), 8–9, 14.

Notes on Contributors

C. GEORGE BENELLO first wrote on Ellul in 1966 as editor of *Our Generation*. He is now Coordinator of the Five College Project on Economic Participation and Self-Management based at Hampshire College in Amherst, Mass. He is an editor of *Social Anarchism*, co-editor of *The Case for Participatory Democracy*, and contributor to several books and journals in organization theory and self-management.

GEOFFREY W. BROMILEY is Professor of Church History and Historical Theology at Fuller Theological Seminary, Pasadena, Calif. He co-edited and translated Barth's *Church Dogmatics* and several of Ellul's books.

CLIFFORD G. CHRISTIANS teaches the social and moral philosophy of comunications at the University of Illinois at Urbana-Champaign. He wrote his doctoral dissertation on Ellul's *la technique* and several articles applying Ellul's ideas to communication theory.

DAVID L. CLARK is Professor of History at Hope College, Holland, Mich. He has held several research grants related to the Reformation and Renaissance, and recently was a fellow of the National Humanities Institute at the University of Chicago.

VERNARD ELLER is Professor of Religion at the University of La Verne, Calif. An authority on Kierkegaard, his many books and articles also have given considerable attention to Ellul—with whom he has maintained a long-standing correspondence.

JACQUES ELLUL is Professor of the History and Sociology of Institutions in the faculty of law and economic science of the University of Bordeaux. Social activist and former mayor of Bordeaux, he has written thirty-five books and more than a hundred essays on politics, sociology, communications, and theology.

DAVID W. GILL teaches Christian Ethics at New College for Advanced Christian Studies, Berkeley. He wrote his doctoral dissertation on Ellul's theological ethics at the University of Southern California. He has published several articles and reviews on Ellul and regularly teaches courses on Ellul's thought.

ARTHUR F. HOLMES is Chairman of the Philosophy Department of Wheaton College, Ill. Among his numerous writings is a recent essay on Ellul's concept of natural law.

KENNETH J. KONYNDYK is Chairman of the Philosophy Department at Calvin College, Grand Rapids, Mich. He has authored several essays and recently studied at Brown University under a National Endowment for the Humanities Fellowship.

MARTIN E. MARTY is Fairfax M. Cone Distinguished Service Professor of the History of Modern Christianity at the University of Chicago. He is Associate Editor of *Christian Century* and co-editor of *Church History*, author of *A Nation of Behavers* and *Righteous Empire*, and winner of the 1972 National Book Award.

DAVID C. MENNINGER wrote his doctoral dissertation on Ellul's political thought at the University of California, Riverside. He is now Assistant Professor of Politics at Fordham University's Lincoln Center campus in New York City.

ROBERT A. NISBET is Albert Schweitzer Professor in the Humanities Emeritus, Columbia University. He has written frequently for *Commentary, The Public Interest, Yale Review,* and the *New York Times Book Review.* Among his books are *Community and Power, Emile Durkheim, The Sociological Tradition,* and *Sociology as an Art Form.*

GENE OUTKA has been a Cross-Disciplinary Fellow at Oxford, a Visiting Scholar at the Kennedy Institute of Ethics, and Associate

Professor at Princeton University. He now teaches in the Department of Religious Studies and in the Divinity School at Yale University. Two recent volumes are *Agape: An Ethical Analysis* and *Religion and Morality* (ed. with John Reeder).

MICHAEL R. REAL is Associate Professor of Telecommunications at San Diego State University. He teaches Ellul, has presented his ideas at academic conferences, and has interpreted his work in a recent volume, *Mass-Mediated Culture.*

JOHN L. STANLEY is Professor of Political Science at the University of California, Riverside. He has published extensively on social and political philosophy, the latest a book entitled *The Sociology of Virtue: The Social and Political Thought of Georges Sorel.*

JAY M. VAN HOOK is Professor of Philosophy at Northwestern College, Orange City, Iowa. His research for this chapter was done in connection with a National Endowment for the Humanities Summer Seminar at Duke University.

Index